AF263606

Petra Rephotographed:

A Century of Change in the Rose Red City

By Kaelin Groom

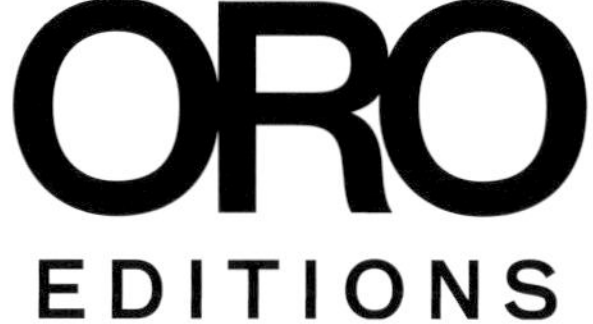

ORO EDITIONS

ORO Editions
Publishers of Architecture, Art, and Design
Gordon Goff: Publisher

www.oroeditions.com
info@oroeditions.com

Published by ORO Editions

Author: Kaelin Groom
Project Manager: Jake Anderson

Book Design: Pablo Mandel, Gustavo Ibarra / CircularStudio
Typeset in TT Norms and Lyon Text.

10 9 8 7 6 5 4 3 2 1 First Edition

ISBN: 978-1-961856-70-7

Prepress and Print work by ORO Editions Inc.
Printed in China

This book is dedicated to the incredible people
of Jordan, Wadi Musa, and Umm Sayhoun
—the greatest treasures
of Petra.

Shukran Jazeelan

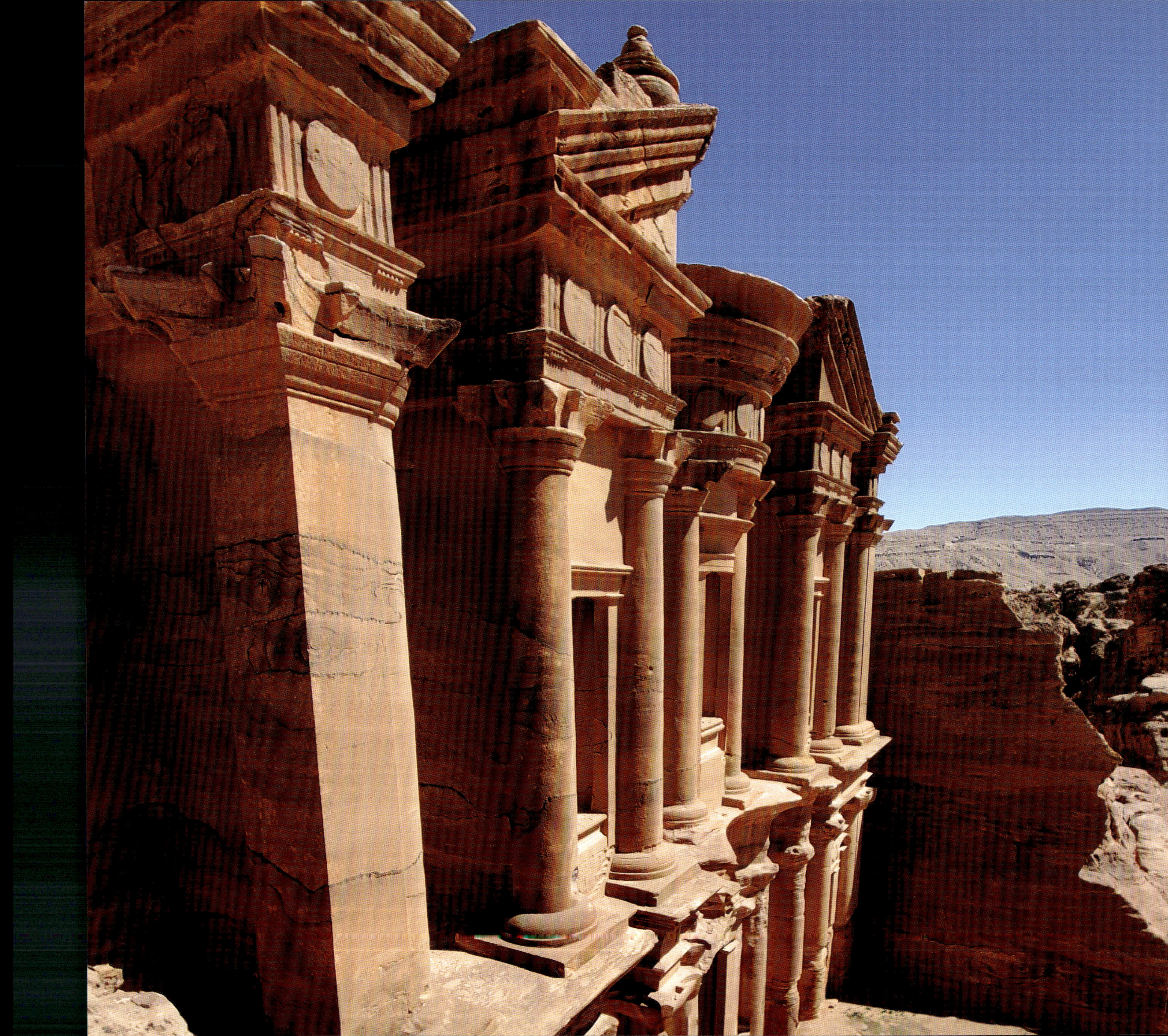

Table of Contents

11   FOREWORD

15   INTRODUCTION

17   TWO SCHOLARS A CENTURY APART

26   OVERVIEW OF THE ROSE RED CITY

     33   The Grand Entrance: Al-Khazneh and the Greater Siq Region

     57   Eastern Highlands: Royal Tombs, Nasara Ridge, and Jabal Khubtha

     81   Center of It All: Qasr al-Bint, al-Habis, and Wadi Turkmaniya

     101   Top of the World: Deir Plateau and the Northwest Ridges

     121   Trail to the Heavens: Wadi Farasa, Obelisk Ridge, and the High Place of Sacrifice

     141   Outer Fringes: Jabal Harun, Bayda, Wadi Mousa, and the Southern Tombs

160   PETRA'S ENDURING LEGACY

170   ACKNOWLEDGMENTS

172   ABOUT KAELIN GROOM

174   SELECT BIBLIOGRAPHY AND FURTHER READINGS

Side view of the impressive
Deir Monument.

Foreword

By His Royal Highness Prince El Hassan Bin Talal of the Hashemite Kingdom of Jordan

Through photography, we create images of our world and reality just as we do with language. Whether moving or still, the images we create open a window into the world despite the difference between the object as it appears, the image, and the world. After the author, Dr. Kaelin Groom, asked me to write a foreword for this book, I was captivated by the images within for far longer than I expected. The book displays dozens of photographs that expand our understanding of the artistic creativity of the Nabataean architectural style. In addition to the author's deep passion, the book's success, in my view, can be ascribed to the masterful use of the techniques of modern digital photography, which lie behind much of the transformation of our cultural experiences and artistic expression. Photography has earned its place as fine art, helping us deepen our understanding of reality. The images in this volume, through the creative use of light, shadow, angle, and tasteful composition, testify to this transformative power.

Dr. Groom masterfully overcame the technical limitations of the camera that distort the relationship between image and reality, portraying Petra's beauty with bravura. With her images, she raises questions about the nature of reality and subjectivity that go beyond perception, revealing to us the wonder of viewing these Nabataean monuments with the naked eye. Dr. Groom has presented this wonder to anyone interested in Petra, whether tourists, amateurs, researchers or otherwise. This book is a reference that enables us to compare photographs taken of Petra almost a hundred years ago with those of today, where we can see the extent of the damage Petra has suffered over the course of a century and the ability of this city to withstand the challenges posed by nature and human activity. The book does not only take us on a journey through images but also presents us with a fun, attractive, and enticing place for people to visit, confidently conveying the magnificence and strength of the city hidden behind the rose-red mountains.

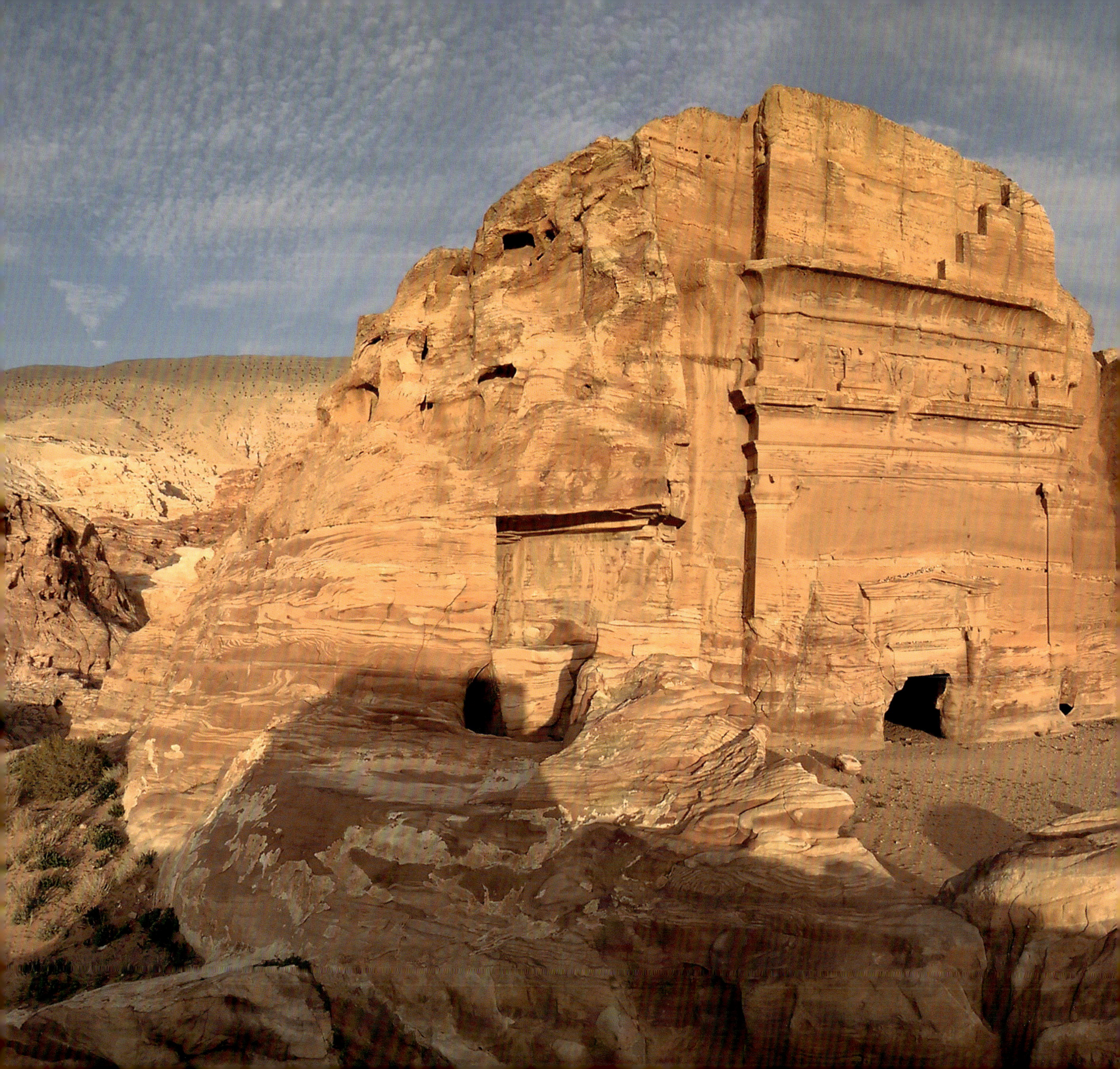

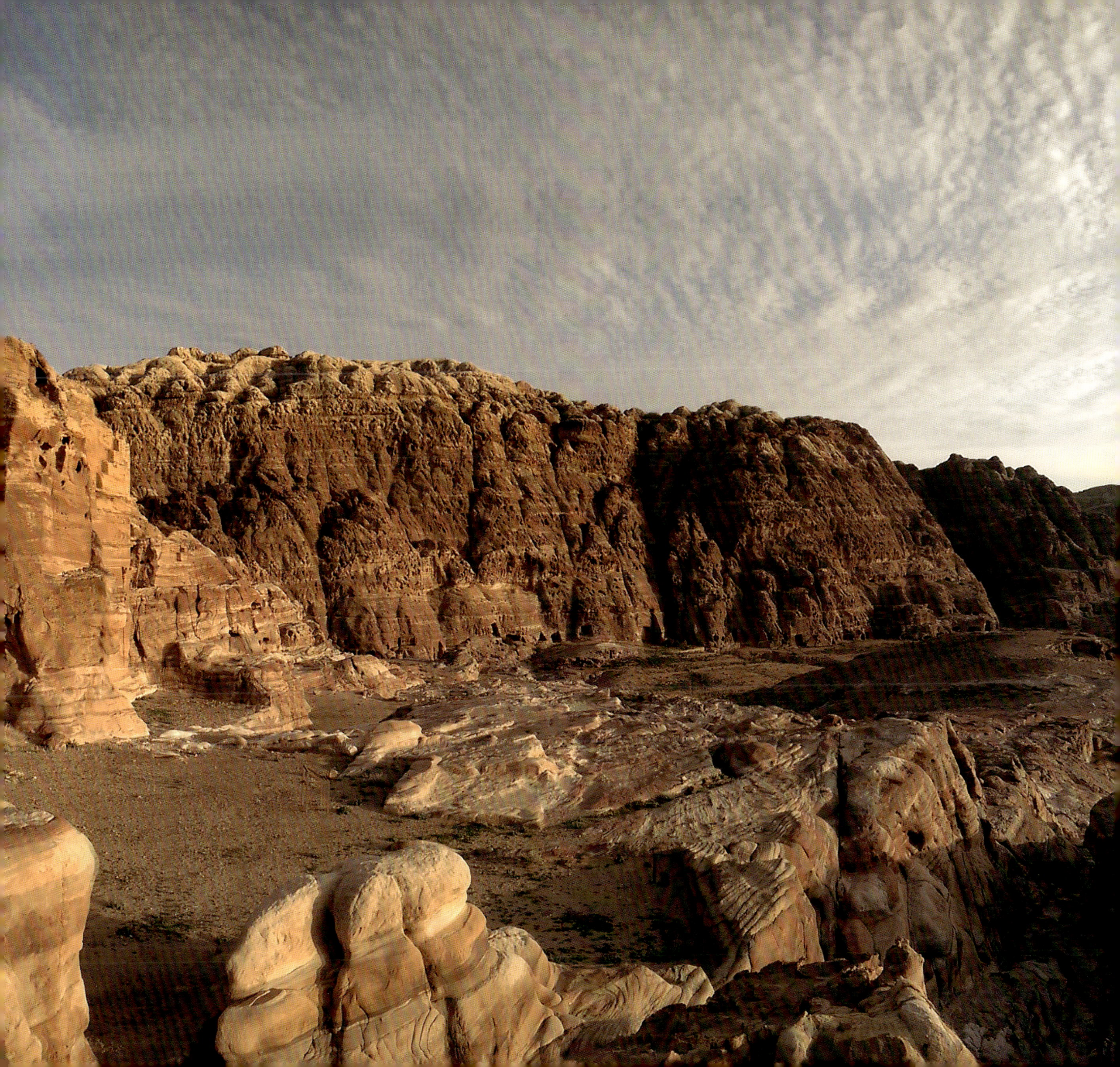

"Petra, O Leeds, is the most wonderful place in the world,
not for the sake of its ruins, which are quite a secondary affair,
but for the colour of its rocks, all red and black and gray
with streaks of green and blue, in little wriggly lines... and for
the shape of its cliffs and crags and pinnacles, and for the
wonderful gorge it has, always running deep in spring-water,
full of oleanders, and ivy and ferns, and only just wide enough
for a camel at a time, and a couple of miles long. But I have
read hosts of the most beautifully written accounts of it,
and they give one no idea of it at all . . . so you will never know
what Petra is like, unless you come out here. . . . Only be assured
that till you have seen it you have not had the glimmering
of an idea how beautiful a place can be." —A LETTER FROM
T. E. LAWRENCE ("LAWRENCE OF ARABIA") TO HIS CHILDHOOD
FRIEND E. T. LEEDS, FEBRUARY 1914[1]

PREVIOUS SPREAD: The
Mughur Al-Nasara tombs in
the soft light of the setting sun.

1 J. M. Wilson, ed., *Letters to E.T. Leeds* (Andoversford, UK: Whittington Press, 1988).

Introduction

I first gazed up in awe at Petra's impressive Treasury in 2013—a fledgling graduate student at the time, set to study the *how* and *why* behind deterioration on a small stone monument in the Middle Eastern country of Jordan. Well, to be more accurate, the first time I saw the Treasury was in the movie *Indiana Jones and the Last Crusade* (1989). This popular film ignited the world's interest in the archaeological wonder, and the final scene became synonymous with Petra to the worldwide audience. Few people knew, however, that the Treasury was only one tiny piece of a much larger landscape. In fact, the ruined city of Petra comprises hundreds of massive carved and hewn buildings and façades across a vast valley encompassing nearly 260 square kilometers beyond its dramatic main entrance (slightly larger than Sacramento, California; Seattle, Washington; Las Vegas, Nevada; or roughly the size of Malta at 300 km²).

After completing my research on a remote outcrop, my advisor joined me for a enlightening tour of Petra proper, accentuated by stories of past civilizations intermixed with enthralling tales of his own experiences living and working in Petra for more than thirty years. He introduced me to the works of Sir Alexander B. W. Kennedy, a British scholar and photographer who had traveled to Petra in the early 1920s and published a book containing hundreds of photographs he had taken throughout the valley. While perusing Kennedy's photographs and comparing them to the Petra of today, it was fascinating to visualize changes that had occurred in the region over the past century. However, since Sir Kennedy's works were not the focus of my graduate work, these curiosities were set aside for the moment. But Petra has a certain magic: it beckons your return.

Years later, after completing my graduate programs, I returned to Jordan as a Fulbright Scholar (not once, but twice) to pursue the photographic comparison of Petra that had so

piqued my curiosity as a student. I spent the
next half-decade studying, photographing, and
immersing myself in various aspects of Jordanian
culture. To capture the precise rephotographs,
I traveled to Petra several times throughout the
changing seasons of the year, ensuring exact
matches to Sir Kennedy's original images.
Through the years, I made lifelong friends with
Bedouins, government officials, and colleagues
—all with a similar mission as mine: to continue
to learn about and promote Jordan's iconic
treasure. This book invites you to join us.

As you explore a century of change in the "Rose
Red City" through the lens of repeat photography,
I hope you become inspired to explore the magical
city that so captivated Sir Kennedy, myself,
and millions of annual visitors, explorers, artists,
and scholars. The myriad mysteries of Petra are
celebrated in the pages to come, complemented
by a brief history of Petra along with the story
of Sir Kennedy's keen observations and my own

contemporary perspectives. If you have already
witnessed Petra's wonder, then I genuinely hope
this book reignites fond memories that allow you
to experience its majesty in a new way. If you've
yet to visit this mesmerizing place, perhaps
this book will inspire you to respond to Petra's call
and lose yourself in its sincere beauty.

Two Scholars a Century Apart

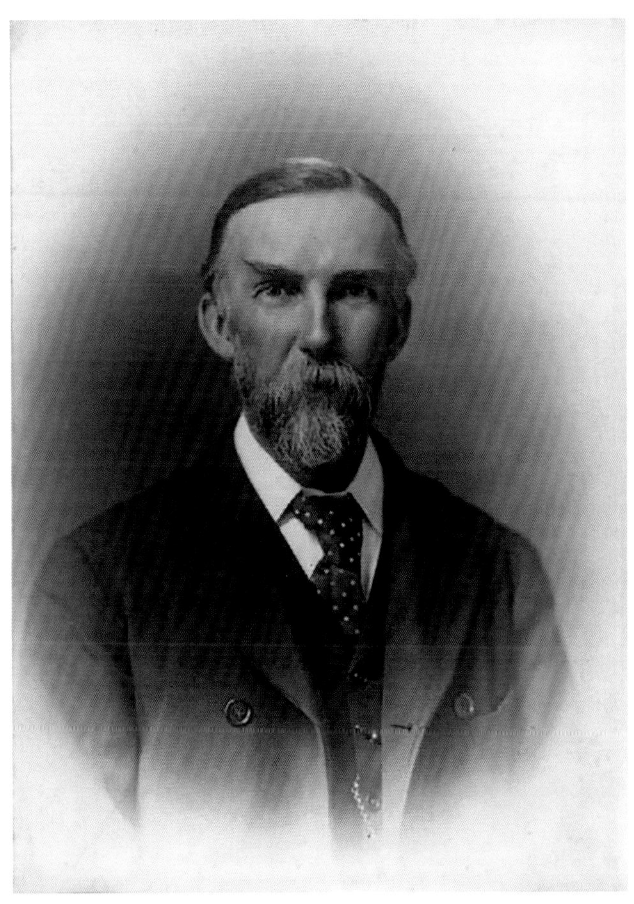

Portrait of Sir Alexander B.W. Kennedy (1847–1928).

In 1923, retired civil engineer and avid photographer Sir Alexander Blackie William Kennedy received a rare invitation to visit a Bedouin camp in Jordan. The Great War was finally over, making it possible for foreign travelers to once again safely explore the enigmatic Middle East. For centuries the region's reclusive beauty had remained mostly off-limits to the Western world. With the end of the war, however, the once-powerful Ottoman Empire was in pieces, each allocated among various European powers as spoils of war; Great Britain claimed the Levantine region of The Trans-Jordan. From his London home, Sir Kennedy had been keenly following sporadic reports from his countrymen abroad regarding the curious ruins of an ancient city hidden in the crags of the Jordanian highlands: a mysterious place called Petra. The few Western explorers who dared venture into the newly opened region returned with extraordinary tales of the area's unique geological and archaeological marvels. Their stories entranced Sir Kennedy:

"To me this fascination was so great that I accepted with enthusiasm an invitation to a prolonged visit to the Amir Abdullah's camp there."[2]

At the golden age of seventy-five years old and armed only with the field camera of his day, Sir Kennedy embarked on his Middle Eastern adventure with a singular plan to photograph the entirety of Petra. With what must have been continual and overwhelming wonder, he spent weeks exploring Petra's expansive ruins and its massive rock carvings. Even so, the site was so grand, and yet so wild and raw, that not all of Sir Kennedy's contemporaries saw its natural beauty:

> Strange and horrible as a pit of inhuman deadness of nature is this site of the Nabataeans' metropolis. The eye recoils from the mountainous close of iron cliffs, in which the ghastly waste monuments of a sumptuous barbaric art are from the first glance an eyesore. —ENGLISH POET AND TRAVELER CHARLES MONTAGU DOUGHTY[3]

Yet, Sir Kennedy's personal experience in witnessing the naked splendor of Petra far surpassed the reports that had originally sparked his interest. The previous accounts did not adequately reveal the wonder, uniqueness, nor breathtaking beauty of this place. Not an archaeologist himself, the British scholar expressed frustration regarding the limited access and breadth of materials being published on the ruins. In his mind, the information sent back to Europe arrived with incomplete descriptions, was published in journals inaccessible to the general public, and/or lacked the fitting appreciation for the profound and holistic nature of Petra. After reading the published writings of his time, Sir Kennedy lamented the narrowminded content and disrespectful attitude of his fellow scholars regarding Petra's fate:

> The large number of visitors who published their recollections or experiences during the remainder of the century have, with very few exceptions, confined themselves to looking at, and admiring—or criticising, as they felt inclined—the half-dozen most notable classical monuments, and when this duty was performed, to spend the rest of their time and pen and ink in a most unchristian rejoicing —one may, in fact, say, a pious chortling— over the fact that Edom was cursed in the Old

2 A. B. W. Kennedy, *Petra: Its History and Monuments* (London, UK: Country life, 1925).
3 C. M. Doughty, *Travels in Arabia Deserta* (New York: Boni & Liveright Inc., 1923).

Testament, that Petra was part of Edom,
and that the curses have come home to roost.[4]

Since words could not truly represent the
magnificence of Petra, Sir Kennedy turned to
photography—a relatively new technology at the
time—as a medium for sharing the city's profound
beauty with the world. His final volume, *Petra:
Its History and Monuments*, published in 1925,
contains hundreds of photographs displaying
Petra's multitude of façades, sweeping views, and
stone carvings—all taken at a time when tourism
was practically nonexistent in the region. His
intentions were not to conduct archaeological
research nor determine the significance of Petra
itself, but to bring the wonder of the city to a
larger audience. He wanted to share the majesty
of Petra with the world, reflecting the dignity and
respect it so deserved.

Now, a century later, Sir Kennedy's photographs
lay the foundation for yet another ambitious
photographic journey through Petra: my own.
I first discovered Sir Kennedy's works while I was
in graduate school, brand new to the world of
Petra, Jordan, and the complexities of landscape
change. Much like Sir Kennedy, my first visit to
Petra was by invitation: from my graduate advisor,
Dr. Thomas Paradise, a renowned scholar who
had conducted research in the southern Jordanian
region for more than thirty years. When I took
those first steps through the famous sandstone
narrows of the Siq, wandering the cobbled Avenue
of Façades, and getting lost in the massive scale
of the Colonnade in absolute awe, little could
I have known I would spend the next decade of
my life falling in love with this magical place.
Following the completion of my doctorate and
securing funding from the Jordanian-American
Commission on Educational Exchange (JACEE)
and Council on International Exchange (CIE)
through the US State Department's Fulbright
program, I was able to return to Petra specifically
to replicate Sir Kennedy's photographic journey.

Like Sir Kennedy, my time in Petra has
been enriched by the warm hospitality of local
Bedouins—perhaps even more so as a female
scholar in the predominantly Muslim country.
The desert is a harsh place, but the people who
thrive there are quite the opposite. Embraced by
the community almost immediately, I spent many
afternoons sipping sweetened hot tea from well-
worn glasses and swapping stories inside woven
goat-hair tents. As a woman, I was welcomed
into a private world rarely seen by outsiders and

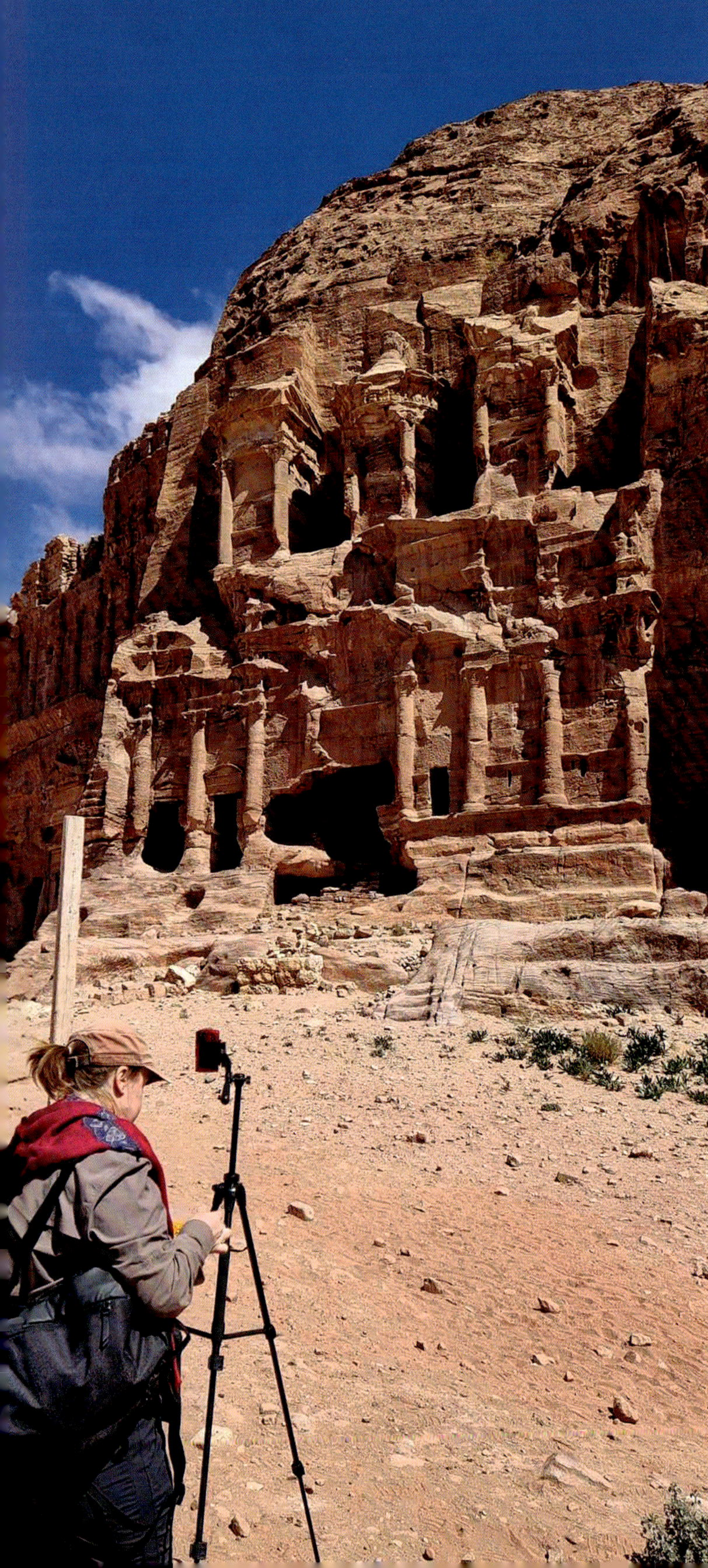

enjoyed the security and safety offered by the Bedouin community. The locals featured in many of Sir Kennedy's photographs served as his guides and interpreters. To me, they are so much more. Guides, yes, but also friends and protectors, among the greatest treasures of Petra.

The paths of Sir Kennedy's and my own journeys in Jordan overlapped in many ways, a century apart, with one specific focus tying us together forever—our desire to celebrate the marvel of Petra through the lens of a camera. Sir Kennedy took many of the earliest photographs from a region the Western world had never seen and certainly created the most comprehensive collection of images in his time. Continuing with Sir Kennedy's adventurous spirit and tenacious curiosity, and armed with the field camera of *my* day, I have retraced his steps one hundred years later to replicate his original photos as accurately as possible. In doing so, a great purpose is served by us both, each in our own way. Sir Kennedy's purpose in photographing Petra lay in the mystery of it all: Who lived here? When? What did they do? How did they survive? What historical treasures remain buried under centuries of sand?

My purpose in rephotographing the original scenes was not only to promote history, but also to discover changes that occurred over the past century. For instance, what impact have travelers

Setting up my tripod and camera
at the base of the Corinthian Tomb,
part of the Royal Tombs complex.

had on the site—the very visitors Kennedy enticed to the region 100 years ago? How have the natural forces of this harsh environment altered the landscape? What secrets have been revealed, obscured, or buried in the name of archaeology? How have those charged with Petra's protection stabilized and safe-guarded the fragile façades? And most importantly, how can we as a global community of world travelers help maintain the integrity of this landscape for posterity? With meticulous eye to detail, I have attempted to recapture Sir Kennedy's original images from the exact location, angle, and even time of day and year. Adhering strictly to the principles of rephotography, we can see where, how, or if, Petra's complex geography has changed since Sir Kennedy first traversed the landscape in the early 1920s.

When in Petra, life often seems to revert to olden times, but with a twist of modernity. The sound of goat bells clanging from their necks as they traverse the cliffs echo throughout the valley, complemented by traditional Bedouin music playing from Bluetooth speakers dangling from a shepherd boy's saddlebag. It's not uncommon to jump out of the way to accommodate a group of brilliantly decorated saddled camels sauntering past along the often-narrow trails. Ever present campfires heat copious pots of tea, while colorful stalls filled with handcrafted jewelry and woven camel hair rugs dot the landscape of present-day Petra. I can imagine Sir Kennedy may have possibly encountered many of these sights and sounds one hundred years before me, although seeing nomads on cell phones and shopkeepers exchanging credit card readers would have seemed like science fiction in Sir Kennedy's days. What I do appreciate is that the retired civil engineer and I saw the same hand-carved monuments and breathtaking landscapes. Petra has never been dead, as some might believe, but has remained a dynamic, timeless place of adaptation for a vibrant people. Through photography, this book not only honors Petra's history, but also celebrates its life.

MODERN REPEAT PHOTOGRAPHY
AND CHALLENGES

To duplicate the photographs of Sir Kennedy, I utilized a process called repeat photography, also known as rephotography, which entails replicating a previous photograph from the exact perspective to compare and analyze changes, similarities, or differences that occurred over the time between the two sets of images—not always an easy feat over short time span, let alone a century later.

It must be acknowledged that there is a significant technological gap between Sir Kennedy's photography and my own. In his preface, Sir Kennedy wrote that he was quite proud of his procurement of a brand-new travel camera: the *1923 Dallmeyer "Speed" Camera.* The slightly less-bulky camera captured negatives on 4.5 × 6 cm glass plates that had to be transported back to London with him to be developed—an admittedly risky situation since it would have been rare for all plates to arrive unbroken or cracked. I didn't share that same risk, although one time I did temporarily misplace one of my memory cards (not a fun evening). My camera setup included a tripod-mounted *Olympus Tough TG6* that, when paired via Bluetooth with a Samsung Galaxy S7 tablet, allowed me to check the accuracy of my new images by digitally overlaying them on Sir Kennedy's original photographs while still vin the field.

I made every effort to repeat Sir Kennedy's photographed scenes as precisely as possible. Identifying the photographed landmarks and their locations was only the first step. The more tedious task was determining the exact vantage point to correctly align all elements in the foreground, midground, and background of the historic images. This included capturing images, field checking their accuracy, and adjusting the camera position accordingly—a process repeated as many times as necessary to best match the height, angle, and location of the historic photograph. I was determined to perfectly match each image with its historic counterpart, even if that meant I needed to scale a steep hillside or

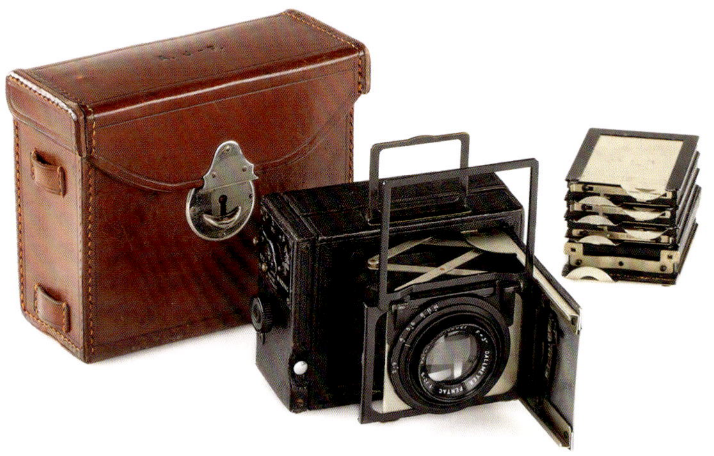

Dallmeyer Speed Camera with 4.5 x 6 cm plates ca. 1925.

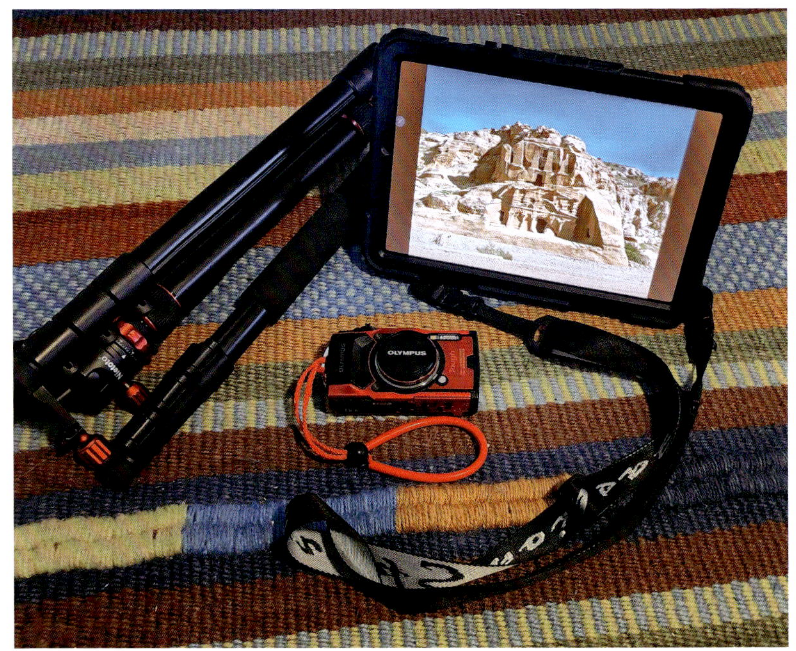

My camera set up: Olympus Tough TG 5, Samsung Galaxy tablet, and field tripod.

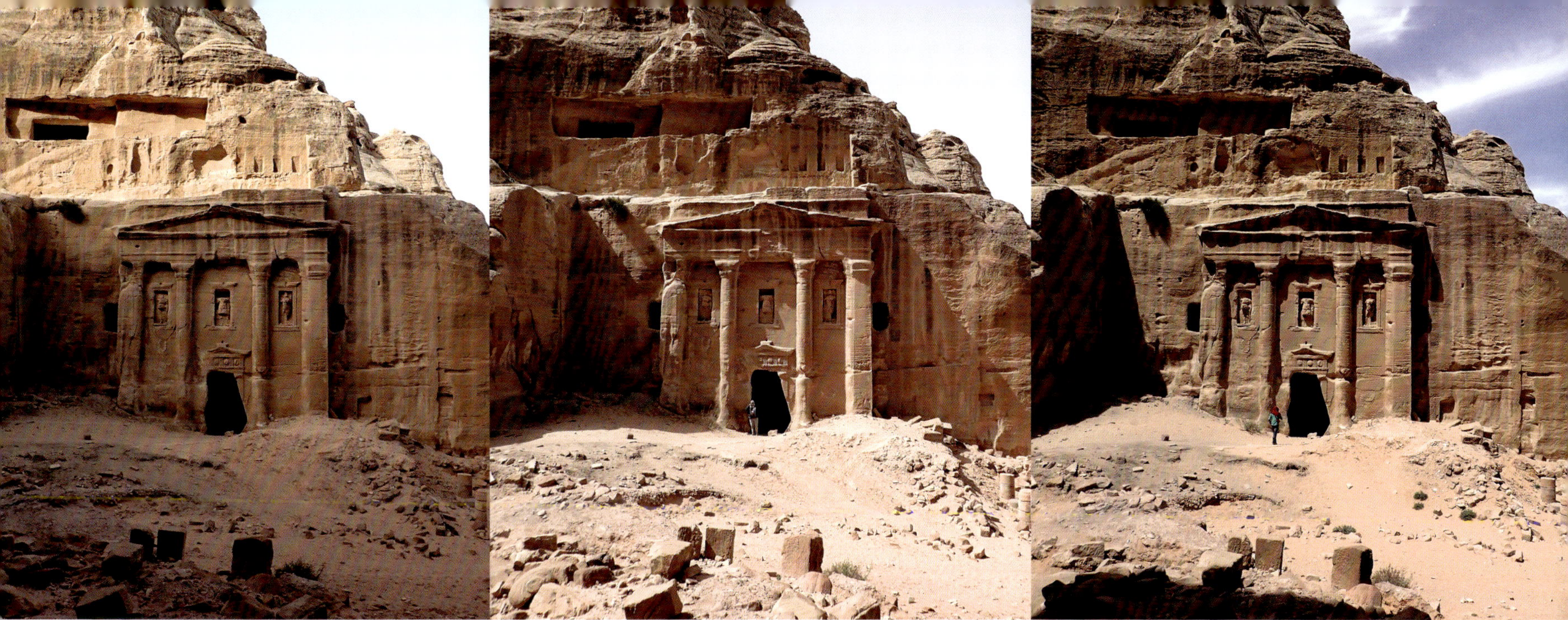

Three photographs of the famed Soldier Tomb in the Wadi Farasa taken at different times to demonstrate the visual influence of the sun's angle. From left the right: 8 am in March, 10 am in March, 10 am in May.

crawl under a bush that wasn't present when Sir Kennedy took his photograph a century earlier. One image required me to dig a small trench in a riverbed that had been buried since Sir Kennedy's visit and lie flat on the ground to capture the image, much to my field assistant's amusement. It was also imperative that I duplicated Sir Kennedy's approximate time of day so that the harsh desert sunlight and distinctive shadows were comparatively displayed in both images. This required a good deal of trial and error, planning, and unrelenting patience. Through the seasons, it quickly became apparent that

I also needed to give additional attention to determining—and matching—the estimated time of *year* in which the original photographs were taken, to account for the north-south seasonal migration of the sun's path, which influences the angle of shadows cast on Petra's steep cliffs and detailed façades.

Ultimately, repeat photography provides a powerful visual tool for understanding and communicating the ever-changing visual nature of the Rose Red City and beyond. It helps bridge the gap between past and present, offering insights into the complexities of environmental, cultural, and geological changes over time. By capturing images at different points in time, researchers can gain insights into the rate and extent of changes. This technique of repeated and duplicated photography is used commonly in several scientific disciplines, including archaeology, biology, ecology, environmental science, geography, geology, and history—or in this case, a little bit of each.

For practicality and brevity, I have curated Sir Kennedy's original 200-plus photographs into a representative collection for this book. In the following pages, you will see the century-old differences in Petra's most iconic landscapes, monuments, buildings, tombs, and façades exemplifying the Rose Red City's various regions. May these photos continue to inspire the magic of Petra for generations to come.

AUTHOR'S NOTE:

In Arabic language, there are several letters not present in English, resulting in a variety of different possible spellings for the same word, and, as seen in many of the historic quotes, they are not always consistent. For example, both "Bab al-Siq" and "Bab as-Siq" are considered grammatically correct but "Bab as-Siq" is more linguistically accurate and used in my modern transliterations. Out of respect for my Jordanian friends, all place names and transliterations in the new text are based solely on input from Jordanian regional experts and local preferences. When quoting Sir Kennedy and his contemporaries, all British spelling is reprinted as originally written, and place names are listed as they were known at the time. Also, unless otherwise specified, all historic photographs and their descriptions presented in the following pages were taken directly from Sir Kennedy's 1923 and 1924 expeditions as published in his seminal book *Petra: Its History and Monuments* (1925).

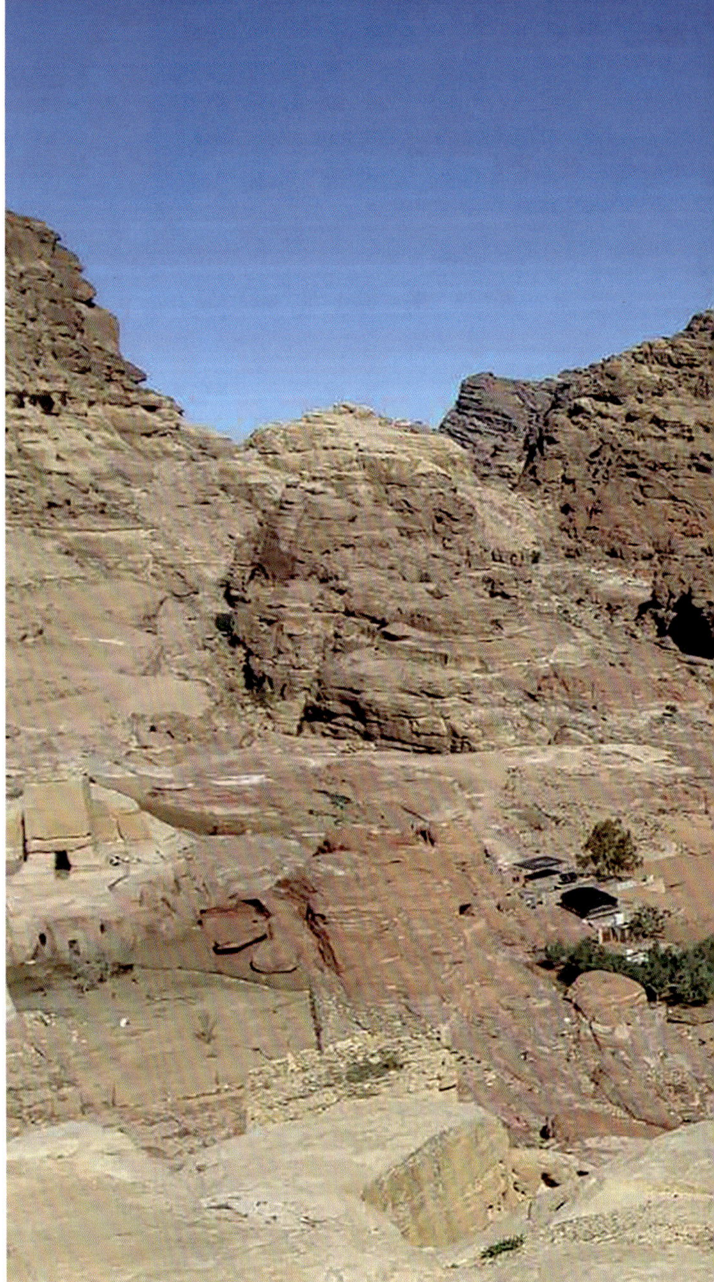

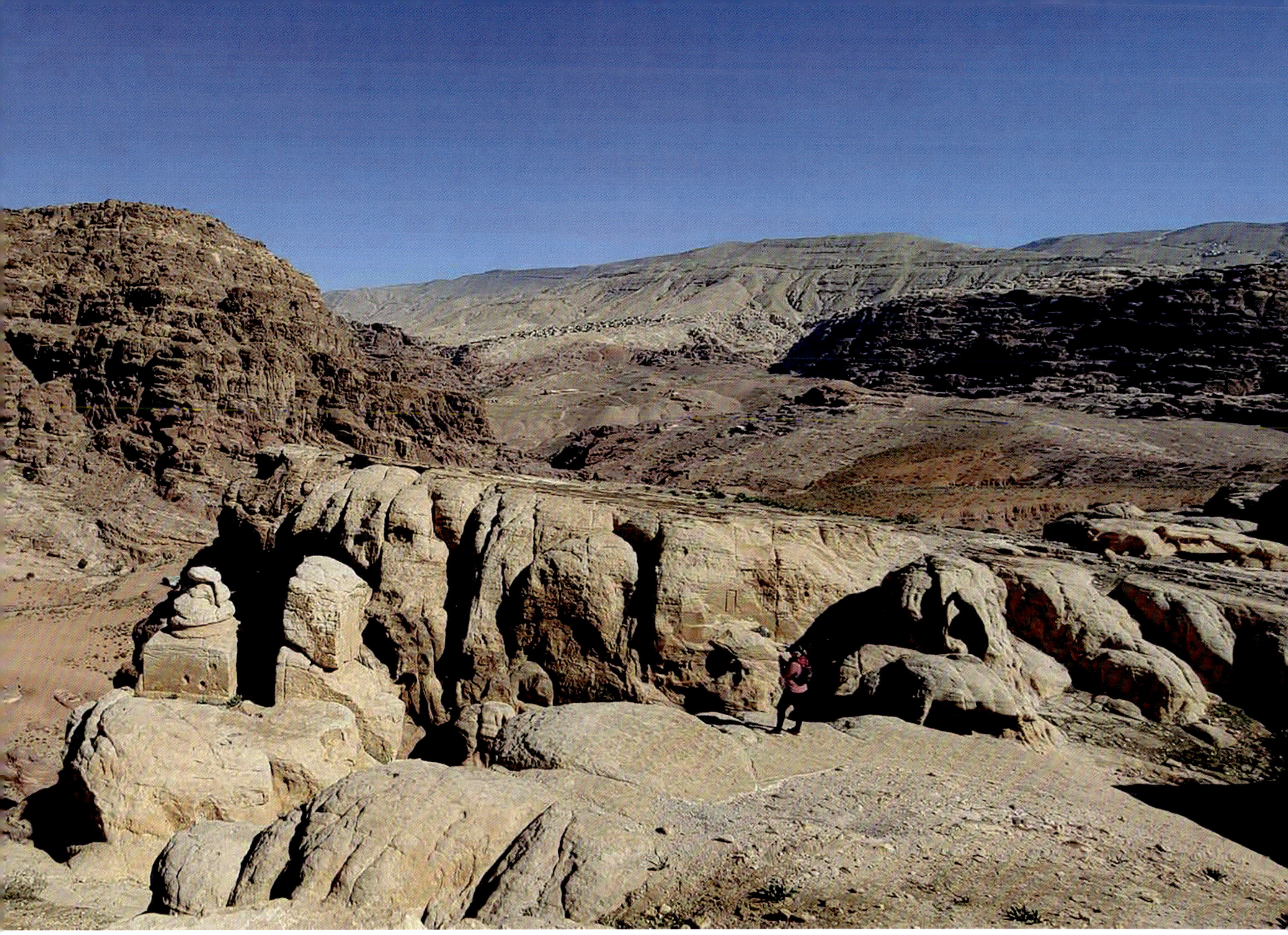

View of Petra from the Southern Tombs. Notice the difference
between the rounded creamy Disi stone outcrops in
the foreground and the ragged red Umm Ishrin cliffs
in the distance. Author Kaelin Groom is seen standing
on the lower edge for scale.

Overview of the Rose Red City

Petra, Jordan, one of the New Seven Wonders of the World, stands on the fringes of the Arabian Desert as a living testament to the brilliance of past civilizations and the enduring spirit of human innovation. The city's haunting array of vacant monuments and tombs represents a long occupational history fostered by protective cliffs and unique environmental conditions. Today, as visitors explore the curious remnants of Nabataean temples, Roman amphitheaters, and Byzantine churches within Petra's breathtaking landscape, they bear witness to the echoes of empires responsible for shaping this extraordinary city over the centuries. The story of Petra is not just an account of civilizations long gone, but a living, thriving narrative of enduring spirit of place, weathering countless natural and political storms. It still stands at the ready, defiantly, to tell its tale and inspire future generations.

Accommodating the city's classical architecture and embedded monuments, the valley's vividly colored sandstone offers a dynamic show of color and texture. The contrasting red and beige sandstones, interweaving iron veins and nodules, and rich desert rock coatings have inspired countless artistic monikers for Petra, such as the "Rose-Red City half as old as time" first coined by the poet John William Burgon in 1845. Yet this vibrancy goes deeper, woven into the very rocks themselves.

As a lifelong student of geography and the Earth sciences, I would be remiss if I did not include at least a brief celebration of Petra's unique geologic characteristics that decorate its delicate carvings and sweeping vistas. Petra's rock formations exhibit two distinctive layers: the older reddish Umm Ishrin Sandstone along the city's base, and the younger lightly colored Disi Sandstone above. As food analogies always seem to be the most effective, at least to me, think of Petra as a cake: the Umm Ishrin is the base with vibrant swirls of rich spices punctuated with nuts and chocolate chips, and the Disi is the smooth, buttery frosting spread across the top in rounded whipped peaks. The Umm Ishrin is the source of the famous "rose red" color found throughout the city, although its iridescence also exhibits other colors such as smokey salmon, burnt umber, chocolate brown, rich indigos, and deep mustard yellow. The distinctively creamy-white Disi Formation is much coarser in texture and composes much of the city's higher elevations and cap rock. Together, these geologic layers of Petra create its beautiful spectrum of hues and tones in a spectacular whirlpool of color in an otherwise beige and barren landscape.

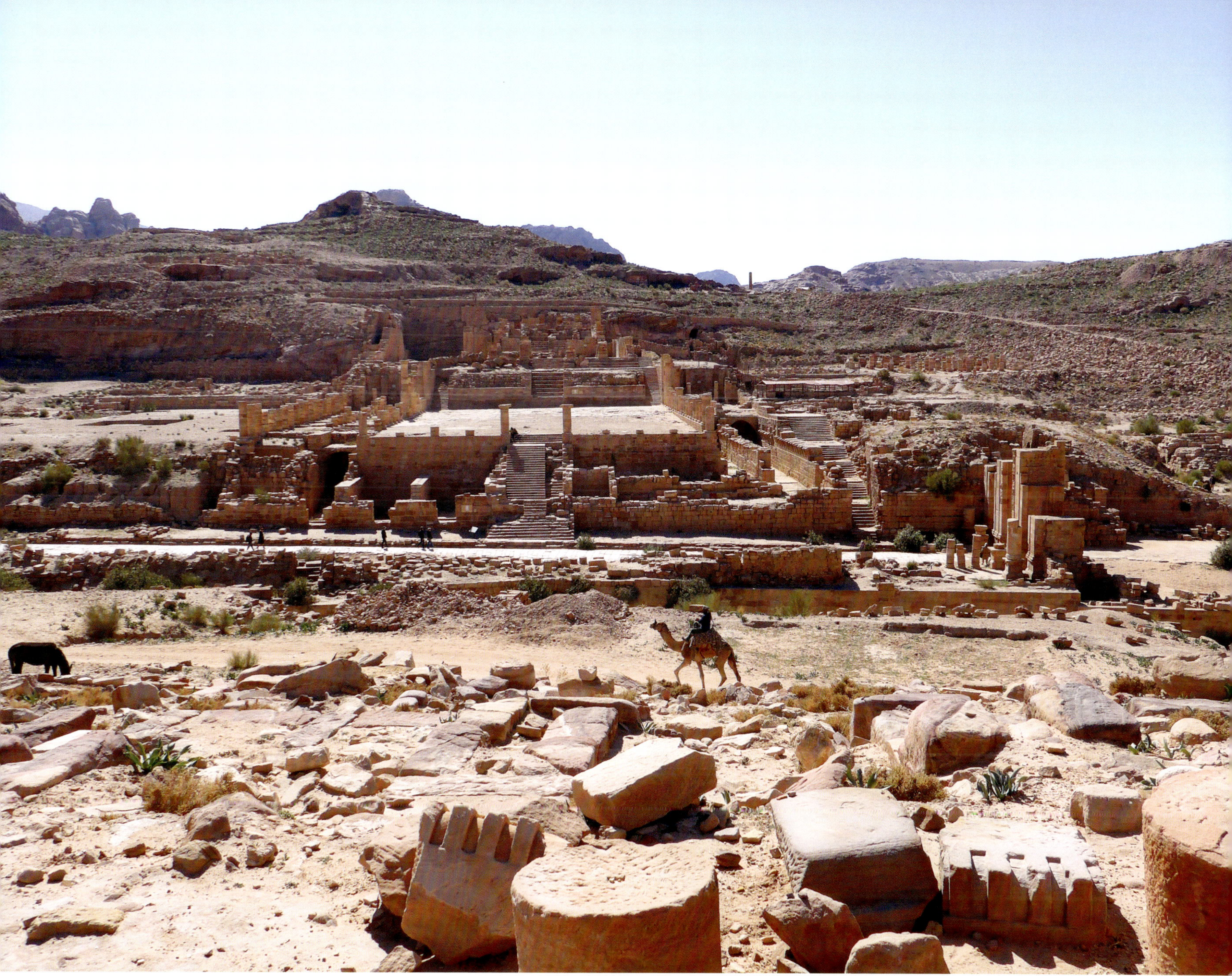

View of the Great Temple presiding over the city center with
a Bedouin camel driver sauntering along the main trail and
the remains of the Temple of Winged Lions' toppled columns
in the foreground.

Often called the "Lost Kingdom of the Nabataeans," the history of Petra actually spans over millennia and weaves together the stories of multiple different civilizations that once called this metropolis home. Each occupational era left its own indelible mark on the city, including the current tourist-focused economy. Most popularly associated with Petra, the Nabataeans inhabited the city from the third century BC to the second century AD. As visionary builders, many of the city's trademark hewn monuments—such as the monolithic tombs of al-Khazneh (the Treasury) and ad-Deir (the Monastery)—were created during this era. Their elaborate stonework, innovative urban planning, ingenious water management systems, and success in trade and diplomacy created a legacy that transcends time.

The official Roman annexation of Petra occurred in 106 AD, opening a new chapter in the city's history. The legendary Theatre of Petra, with its capacity to hold thousands of spectators, exemplifies Roman engineering and their commitment to fostering cultural expression. These architectural interventions transformed Petra from a primarily Nabataean city into a multicultural cosmopolitan center that embraced Roman administrative ideals while retaining its unique cultural identity. Despite tremendous Roman investment turning Petra into an opulent trade oasis, the long-term viability of the city began to show signs of decline as early as the late third century AD.

Records mentioning Petra begin to diminish until 363 AD when an earthquake leveled much of the city, providing a convenient marker for the end of the Roman period in Petra. After the earthquake Petra was slow to recover, but the construction of a few key structures, such as the intricately mosaiced Petra Church, indicate conditions in the city eventually improved. Petra was later designated the capital of the Byzantine Palestina Tritia province during much of the fifth and sixth centuries. Reports of Byzantine Petra end after the foundation of Islam and the subsequent Arab expansion throughout the region. Strategically located, Petra's Crusader occupation in the early twelfth century was limited to a few military outposts, such as the small mountain fort of al-Habis in the main valley and the larger fortress of al-Wu'aira on the opposite side of al-Khubtha Mountain. After the Crusader Kingdom dissolved in 1191 AD, Petra quietly fell into obscurity.

Forgotten by the Western world, Petra lay in waiting for several centuries until 1812 when it was rediscovered by Swiss explorer Johann Ludwig Burckhardt (1784–1817), who famously disguised himself as an Arab to travel freely throughout the region. Word of his discovery spread quickly, and by the 1820s other explorers and artists began traveling to the grand city. Notable among these early twentieth-century artists was Scottish painter David Roberts. Though he traveled throughout all of the Holy Lands, Robert's paintings of Petra, characterized by a delicate interplay of light and shadow mixed with the local people and a little artistic license, especially convey the timeless splendor of the Nabataean city—so much so, his lithographs were chosen to herald each subregion of Petra within this volume. Even so, visitors to Petra remained minimal for decades, limited by access, funds, and social and political instability in the region. It was at this time that Sir Kennedy made his grand tour of the mysterious city. The landscapes shown in his images reflect the general wildness of the ruinous valley and unpaved trails. Looking at Sir Kennedy's photographs, readers can get a sense of what it must have been like exploring the relatively untouched scenery.

A major turning point for modern Petra came in December 1985: Inscription into the United Nations Educational, Scientific, and Cultural Organization's (UNESCO) World Heritage Conservation program. Nominated by the International Council on Monuments and Sites (ICOMOS) as an irreplaceable archaeological site of global significance, Petra gained the esteemed distinction "Cultural World Heritage Site," bringing the value of the protected cultural resource to the world's attention. Within less than a century of Western rediscovery, Petra went from a forgotten desert refuge to a booming tourist destination witnessing millions of visitors every year. Consequently, the Jordanian government founded the Petra Development and Tourism Regional Authority (PDTRA) in 2009 specifically to facilitate and manage the growing tourism in the region.

THE BEDOUIN AND INDIGENOUS LEGACY OF PETRA

It is important to remember that while it is often called a "lost" city, Petra was never completely deserted. Generations of semi-nomadic, indigenous Bedouins have lived among the ruins, making use of the numerous caves and water retention systems. A few tribes in particular, the Bani Layth, Badul, Amarin, Masha'alah, Nafilah, and Tawaisa, have an intimate relationship with Petra, inhabiting the valley and its surrounding regions long before Burckhardt arrived in the early 1800s. For centuries, these tribes have called the rugged terrain home, utilizing the city's hewn monuments and caves as homes, shelters, mangers, and storage spaces. This organic integration of archaeological architecture and contemporary usage creates a fascinating juxtaposition of historic stone masonry and Bedouin ingenuity. Following UNESCO regulations prohibiting permanent residency in archaeological sites, the Bedouin village of Umm Sayhoun was built by King Hussein and the Jordanian government in 1985 as compensation to the families living in the Petra Valley, an often-uncomfortable situation tempered by the amiability of Bedouin culture. Many of the changes seen in the following pages reflect modern Bedouin adaptations of Petra's landscape through the generations.

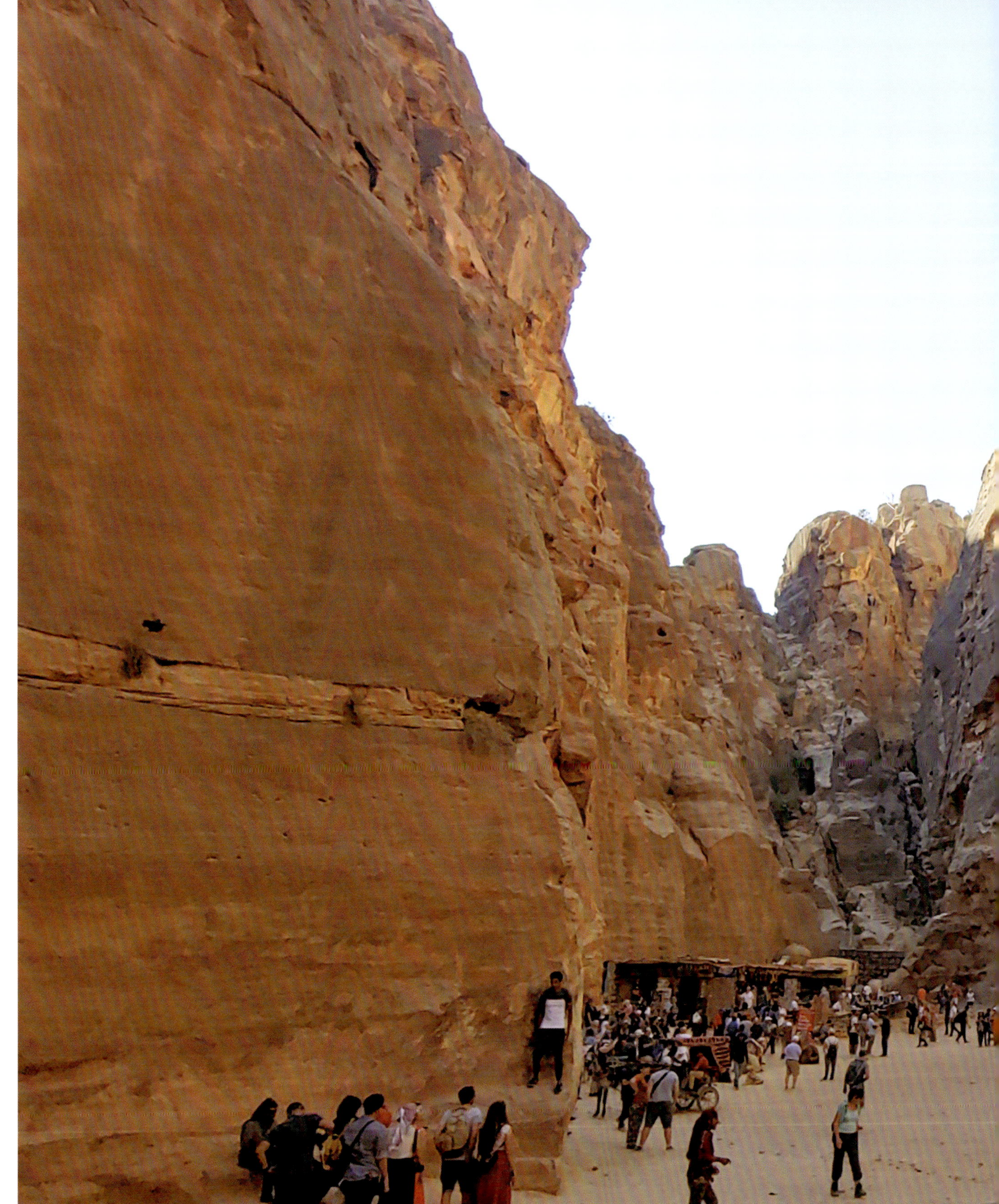

Typical crowd of tourists coalescing at the base of the iconic Khazneh Monument.

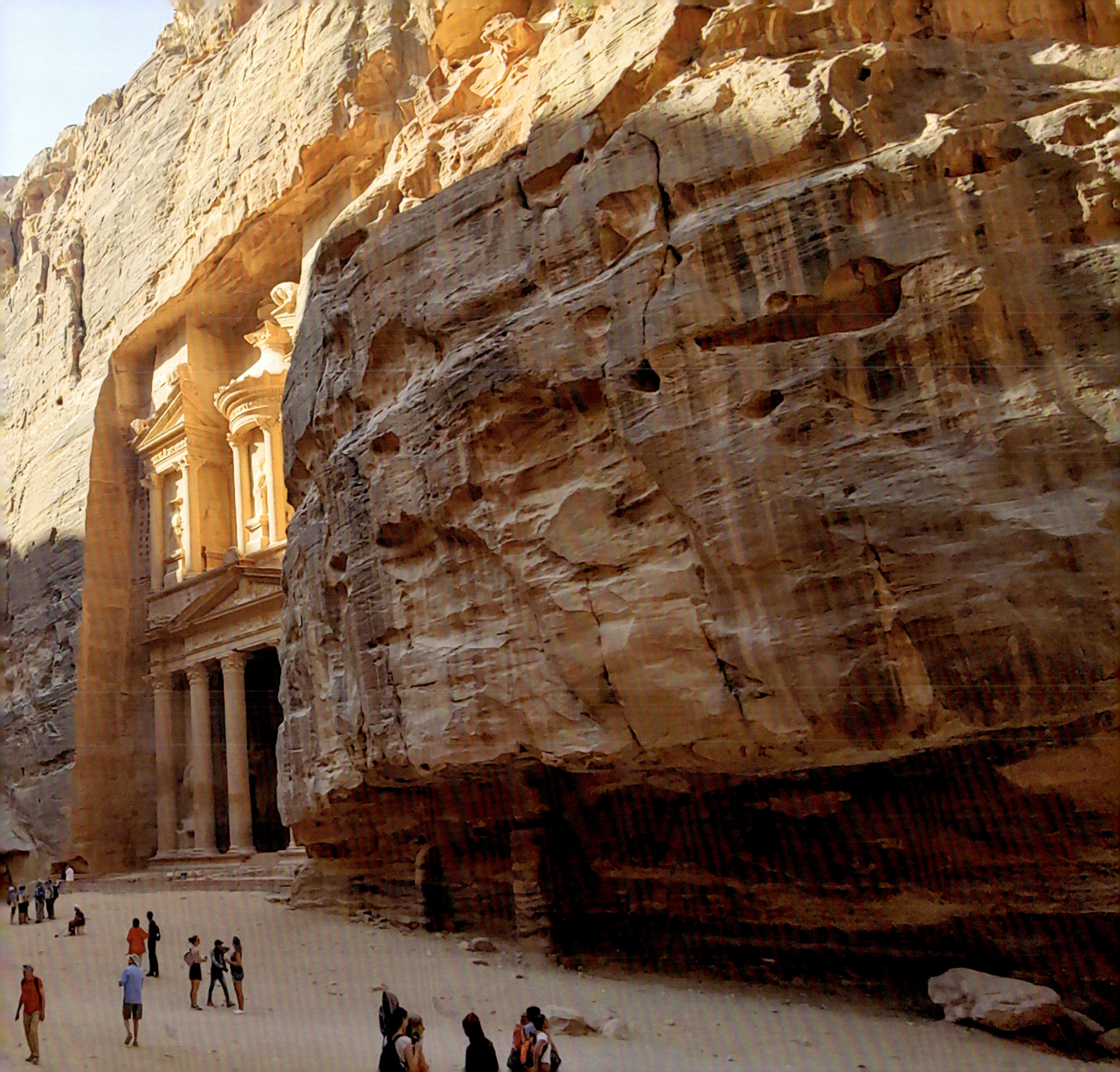

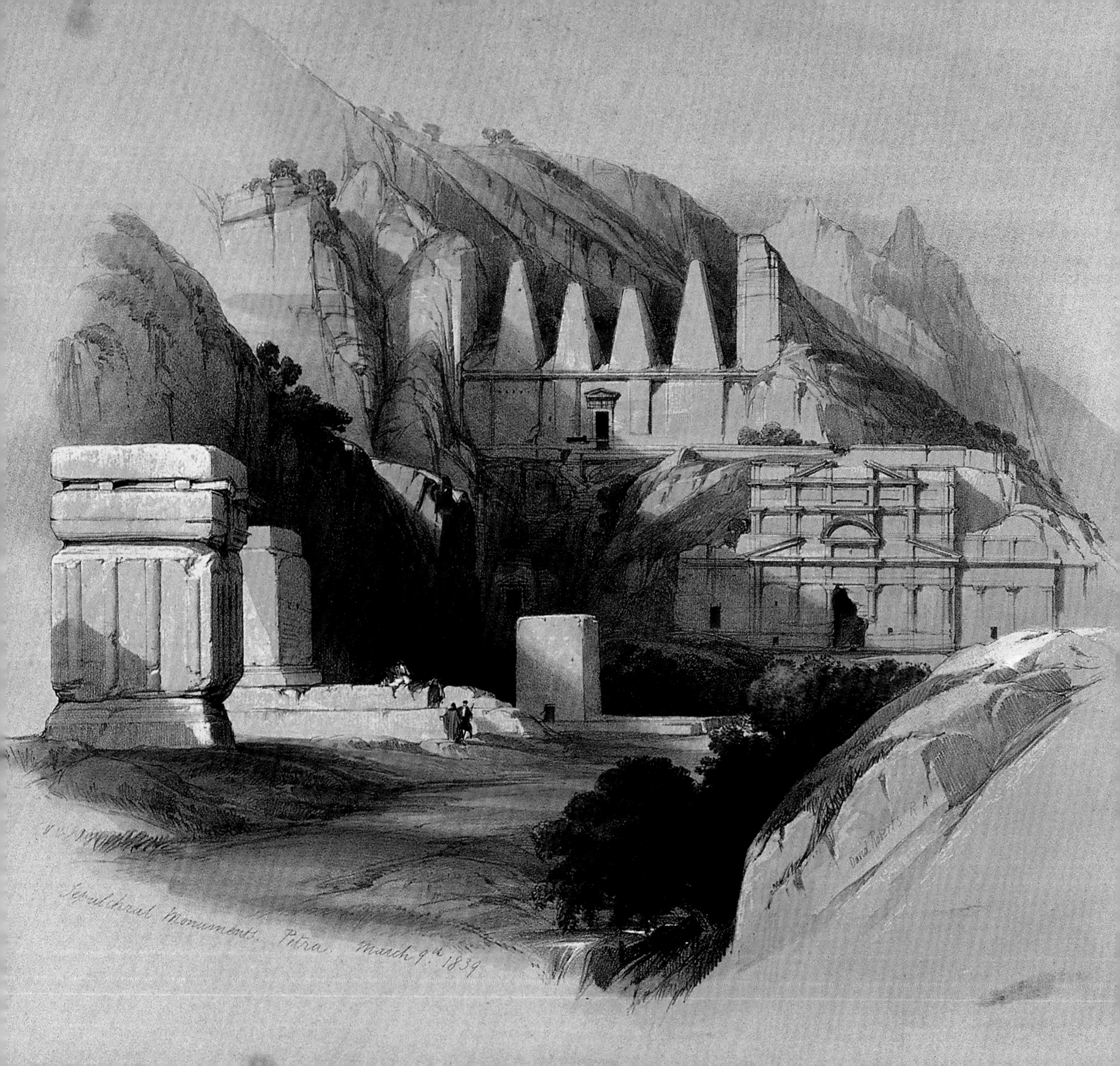
Sepulchral Monuments. Petra. March 9th 1839
David Roberts R.A.

The Grand Entrance:
Al-Khazneh and the Greater Siq Region

Easily the most famous views of Petra, this region introduces readers to the enigmatic Djinn Blocks guarding Petra's entrance, the twists and turns of the imposing Siq slot canyon, and the awe-inspiring emergence of the iconic Khazneh (the Treasury) monument which opens the way to the vast city beyond.

> "That most perfect of the monuments, Khasna Faraoun, whose sculpted columns and cornices are pure lines of a crystalline beauty without blemish, where upon the golden sun looks from above, and Nature has painted that sand ruck ruddy with iron rust." — MR. CHARLES MONTAGU DOUGHTY [5]

Lithograph by nineteenth-century artist David Roberts of the Djinn Blocks and monuments at the entrance to Petra.

5 Doughty, *Travels in Arabia Deserta*, 41.

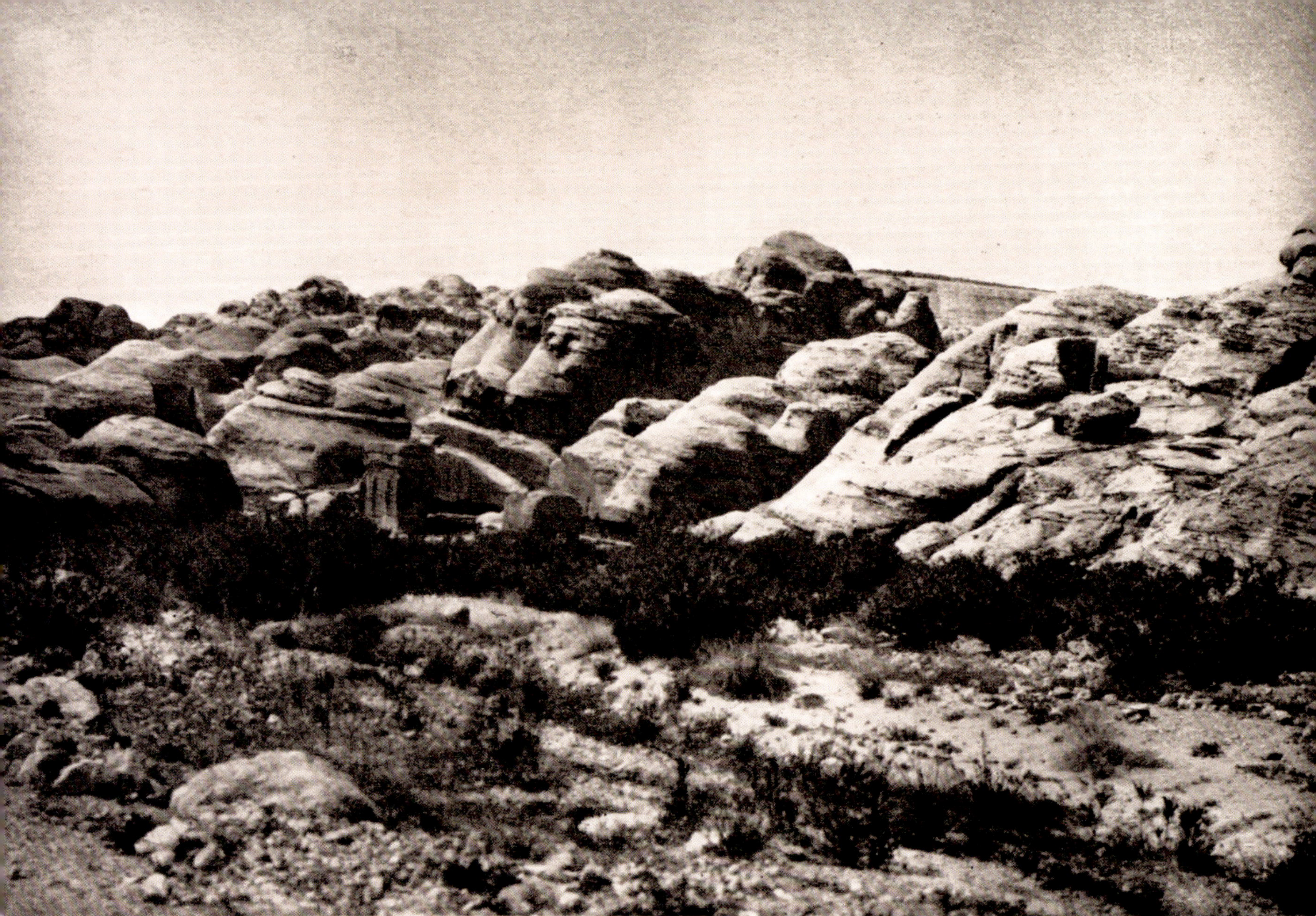

TRAIL FROM ENTRANCE

"The best-known approach to Petra, and certainly the line of approach most likely to be used in the future, enters the city from the east, through or near [Wadi Musa], and thence by the open valley now called the Bab al-Siq, which leads directly into the Siq itself." — SIR KENNEDY (1925, pg. 72)

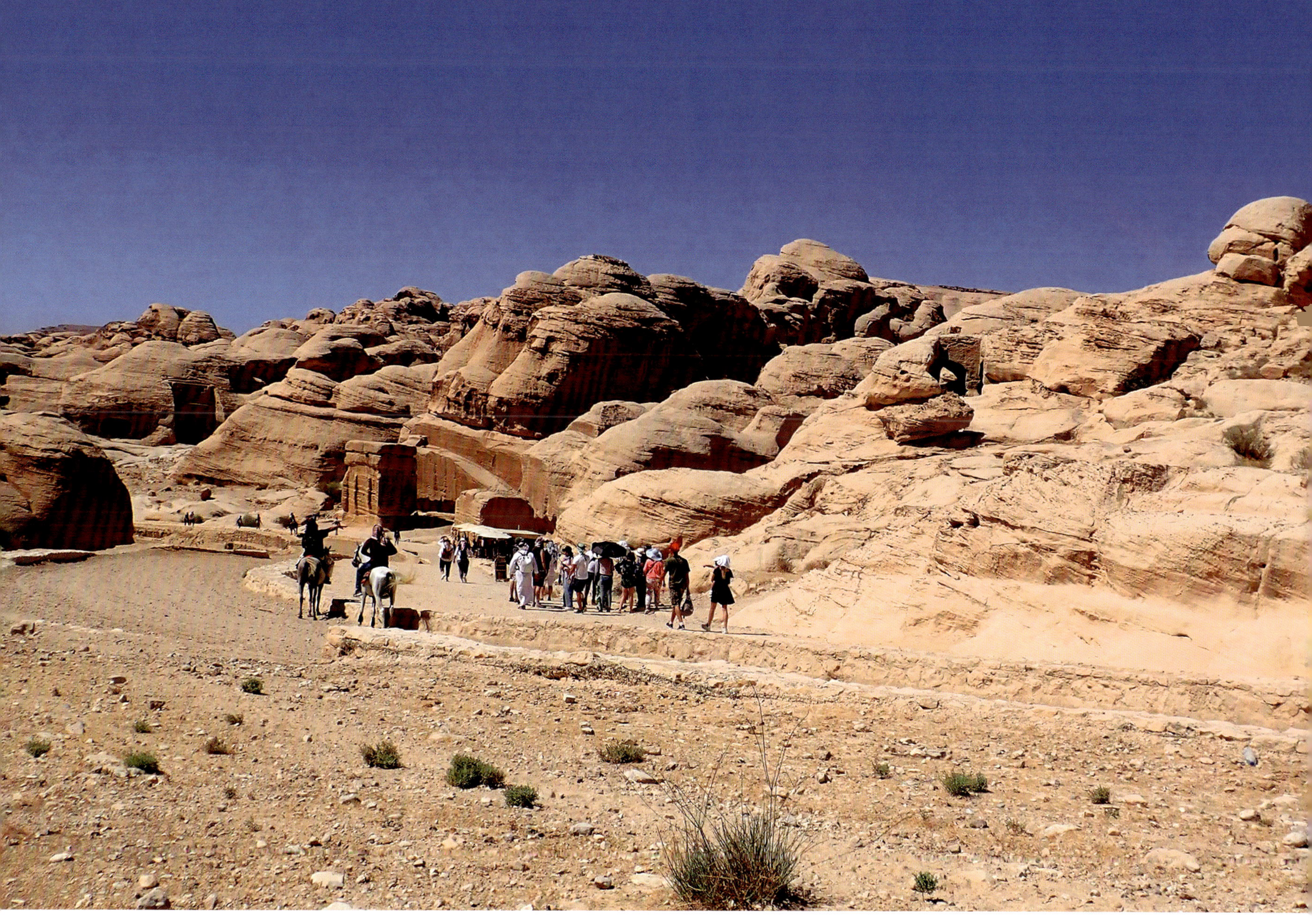

Sir Kennedy was right about the future significance of the Bab as-Siq: it is now the primary entrance to Petra. Where once there was only a rough footpath navigating the usually dry riverbed dotted with bushes, there now run two adjacent avenues: the main walking trail and a small road for horses and electric carts escorting visitors to and from Petra's city center. The famous Djinn Blocks are now prominently highlighted in the center of the image.

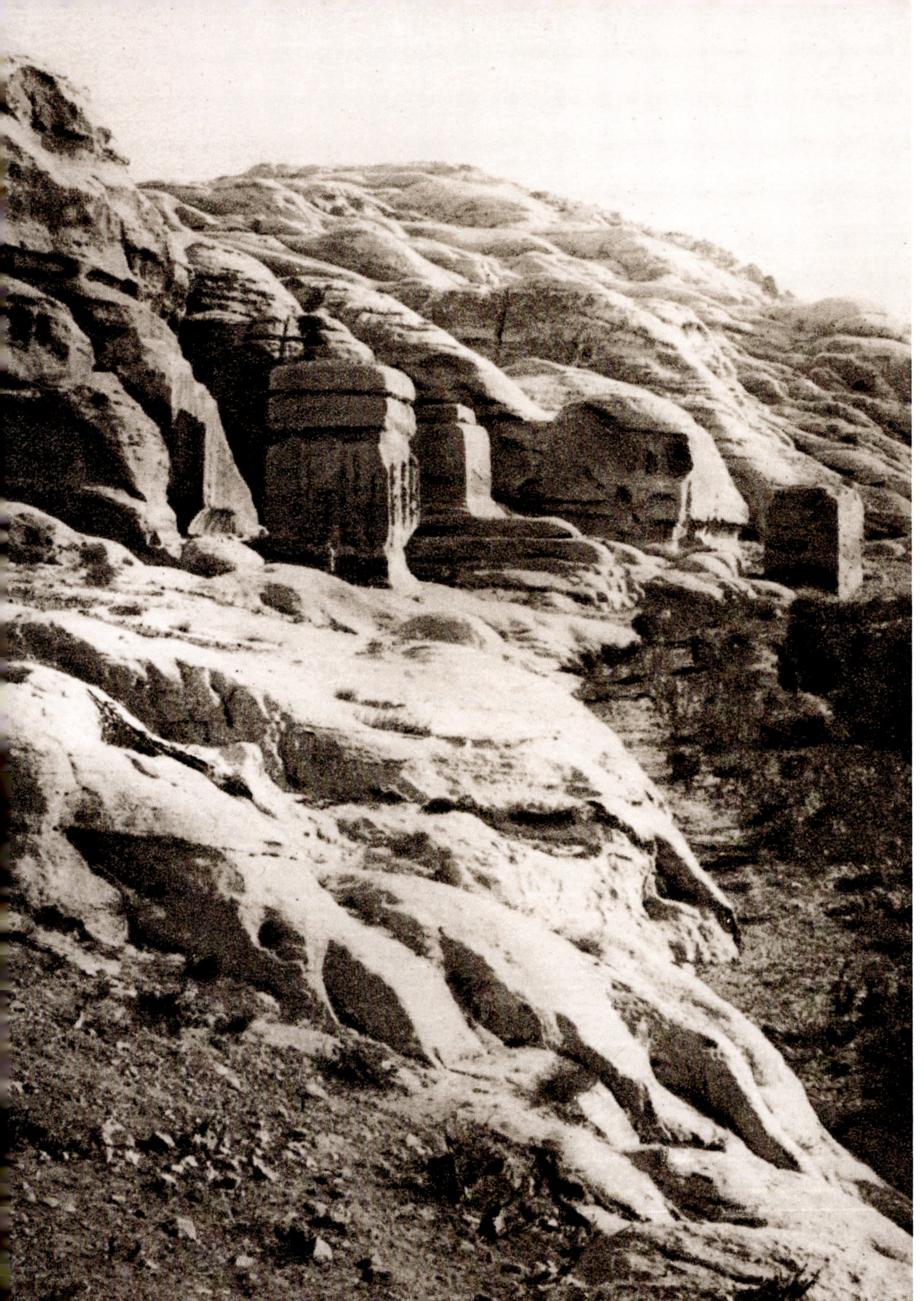

DJINN BLOCKS AT BAB AS-SIQ

"A view of the bed of the Wadi Musa and the Bab al-Siq with three Sahrij monuments looking back towards the east. It may have been that the towers were looked at simply as glorified versions of the block symbol of Dusares, used by their constructors to represent the deity they worshipped, or of the altar used in his worship." — SIR KENNEDY (1925, pg. 41)

A closer look at the distinctive stone towers—
what Sir Kennedy calls "Sahrij," an Arabic
word for "cistern" or "basin," reflecting their
similar shape to water storage tanks found
throughout the region, despite no evidence
they were ever used for such purposes. Local
lore interprets the name more figuratively.
Instead of storing water, the towers are
fabled to hold something else entirely:
mischievous spirits called jinn (Arabic for
"genie")—thus their modern name: Djinn
Blocks. Regardless, these monuments
highlight the profound resilience of Petra's
landmarks. Despite the development of the
entrance trail directly at their feet, the blocks
themselves stand resolute and unchanged,
with the most significant changes being
shifts in soil levels and vegetation cover.

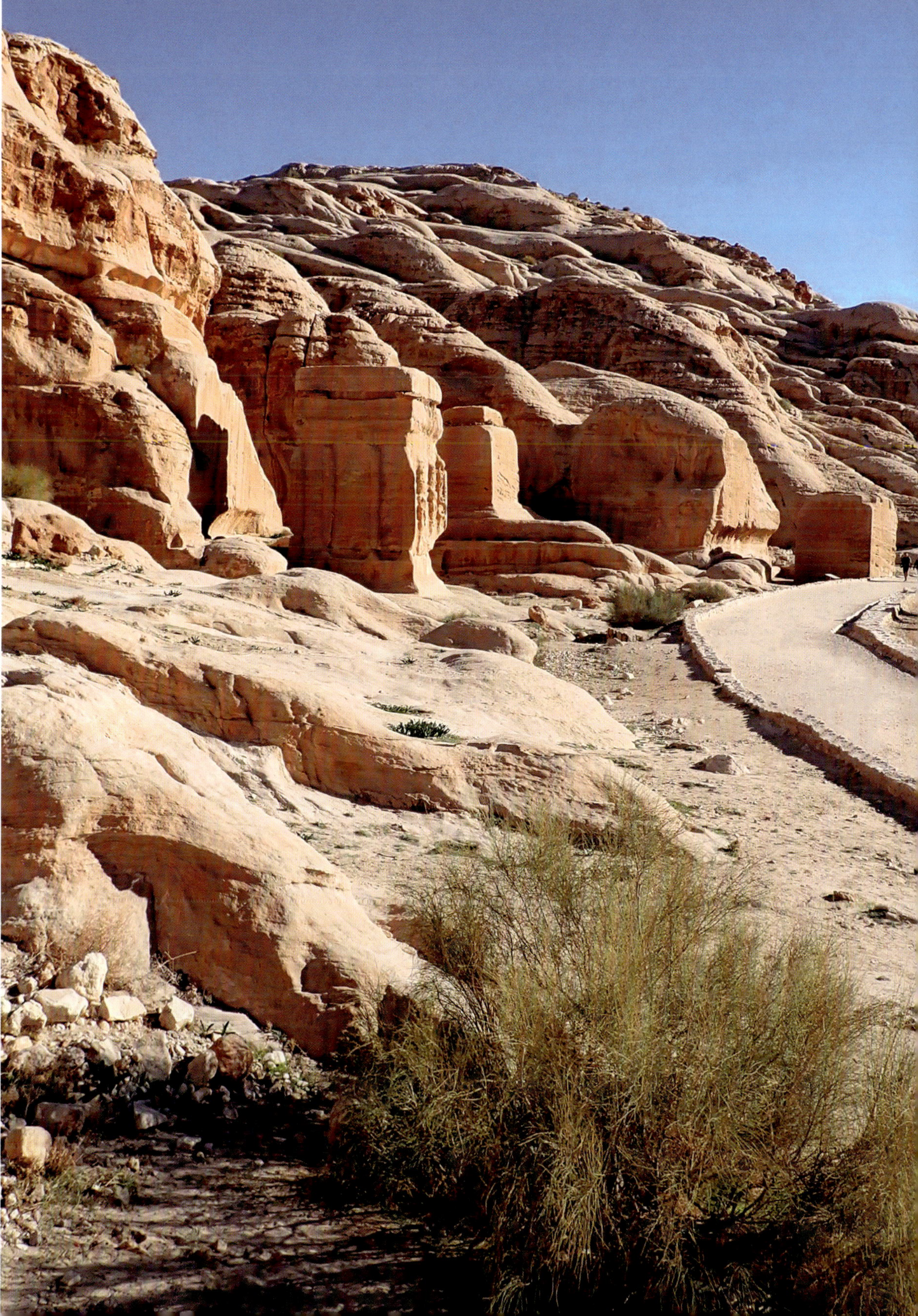

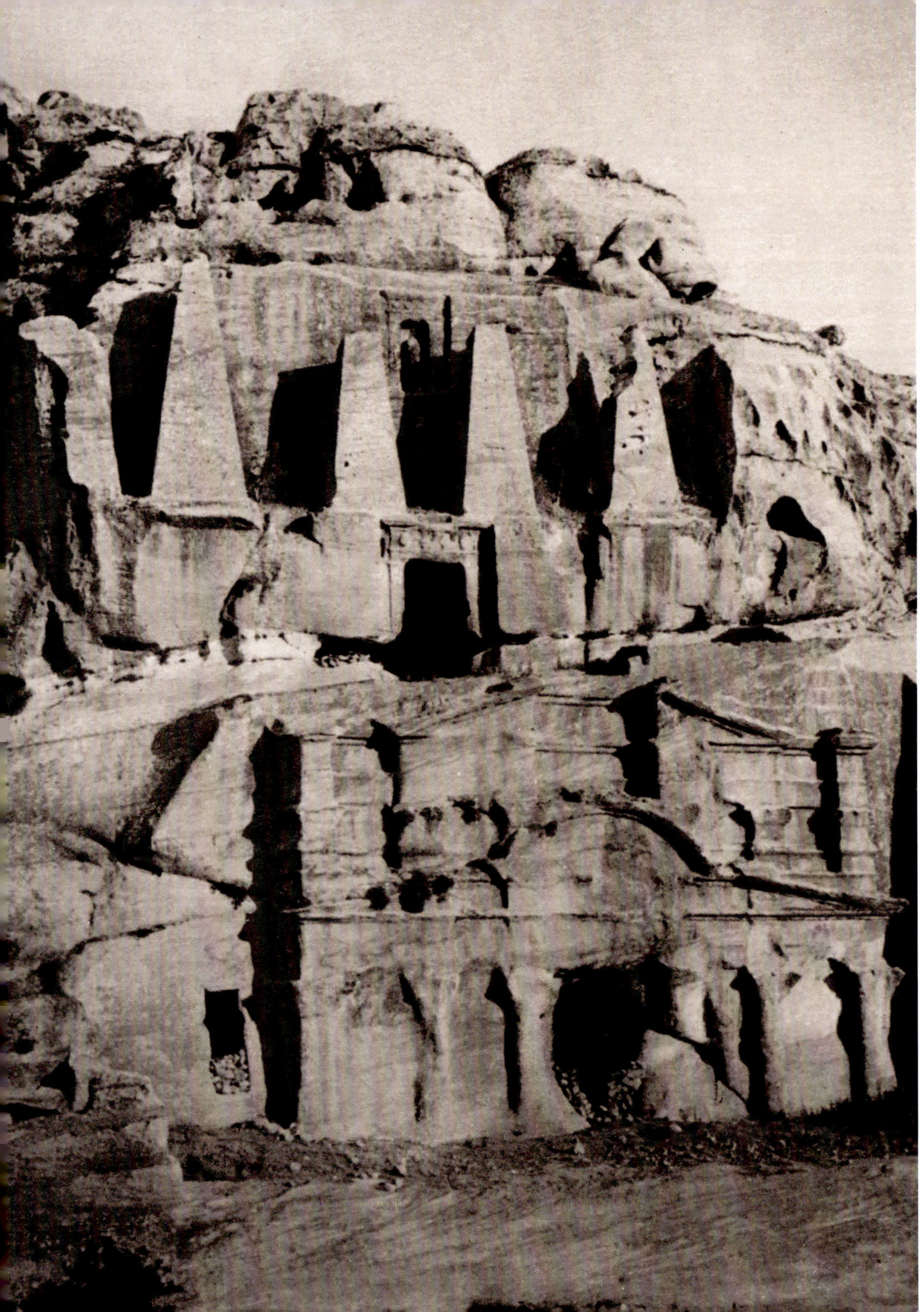

OBELISK TOMB

"The place of the usual carved façade [on the upper monument] is taken by four large obelisks, quite detached from the front wall of the chamber, each standing on a square base, and devoid of any ornament. The monument below it is purely classical—and not Nabataean—in its architecture, and from its florid design would naturally be placed somewhat late in the classical period." — SIR KENNEDY (1925, pg. 44)

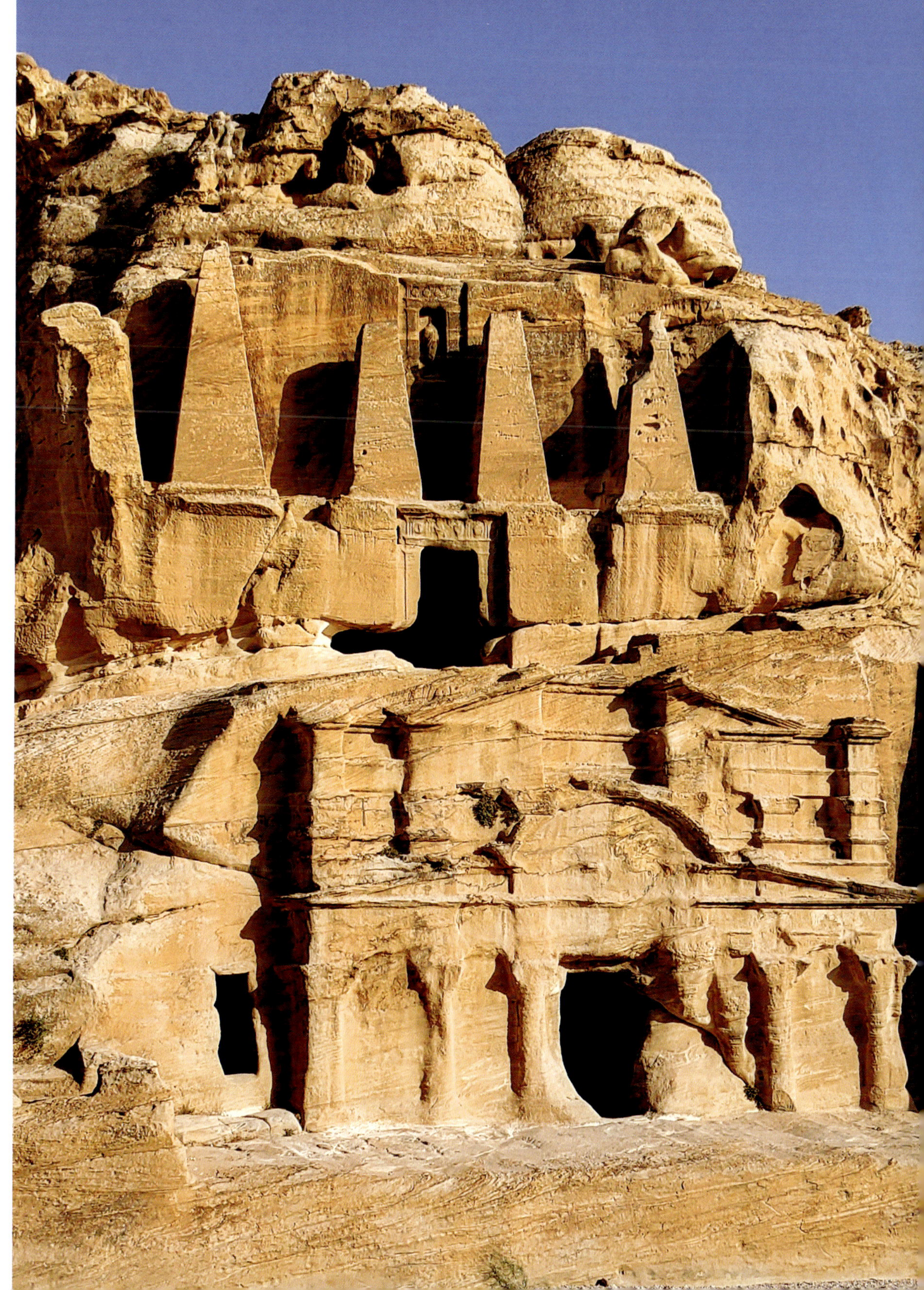

The dramatic view of the obelisk tomb remains a highlight along the Bab as-Siq trail, its stark windows and doors cleared of debris offering an even more pristine appearance. The most significant difference between the photographs can be seen just beyond their view: the gentle wadi described by early travelers flowing below this monument is now a deeply entrenched river basin steeply separating this monument from the entrance trail on the opposite bank.

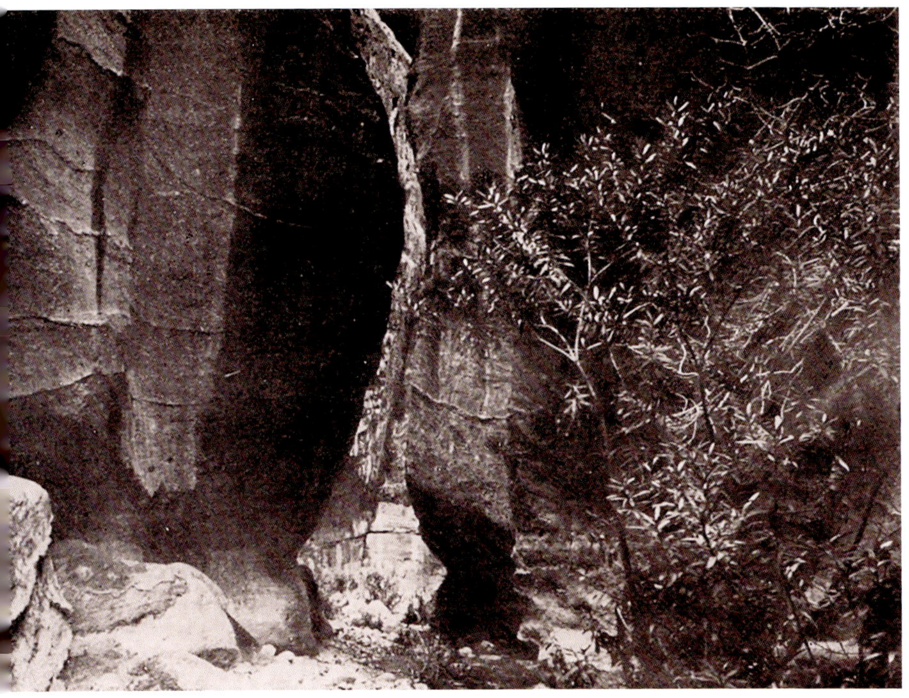 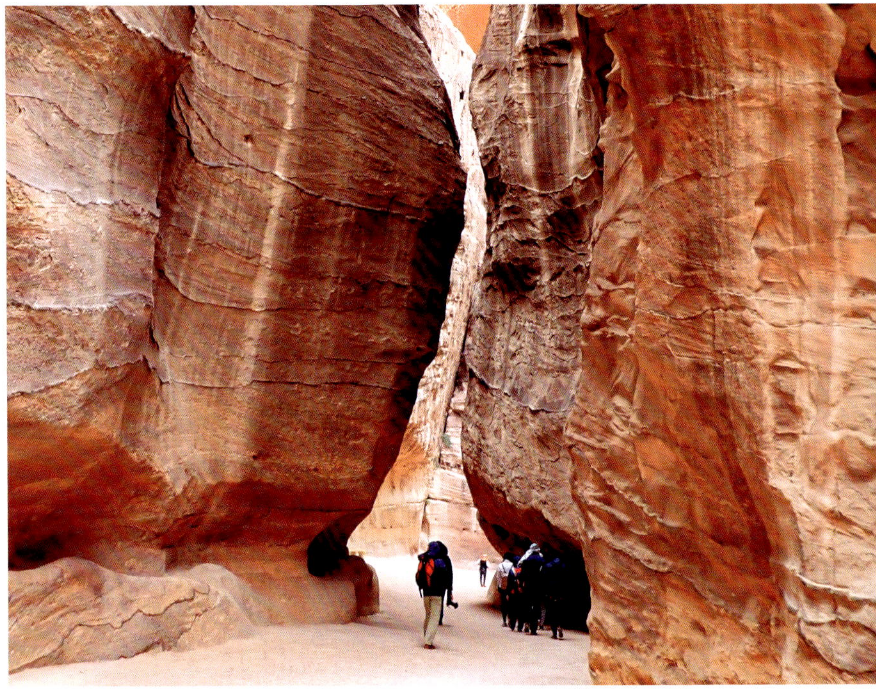

THE SIQ

Despite Sir Kennedy's mission to capture the entirety of Petra's marvels, his tome is surprisingly lacking images of one of the city's most breathtaking features: the Siq. Curiously, he presents several close-up photographs of generic niches carved within the narrow canyon's walls, but none of the imposing gorge itself—perhaps the result of photographic plates lost in transit. Unlike Sir Kennedy's collection, I would not consider this book complete if it did not include at least one photographic comparison of the site's premier geologic wonder. In that spirit, the two repeated images here are from professors William Libbey's and Franklin E. Hoskins's expedition report titled The Jordan Valley and Petra published in 1905.

"Such is the Siq: the famous gorge which in ancient times was the chief, if not only, approach to the strangest city in the region. It was the great glory and the strength of Petra, and is still unique among the sights of the Earth." — LIBBEY AND HOSKINS [6]

[6] W. Libby and F. E. Hoskins, *The Jordan Valley and Petra*, vol. 2. (New York: G. P. Putman's Sons, 1905), 88.

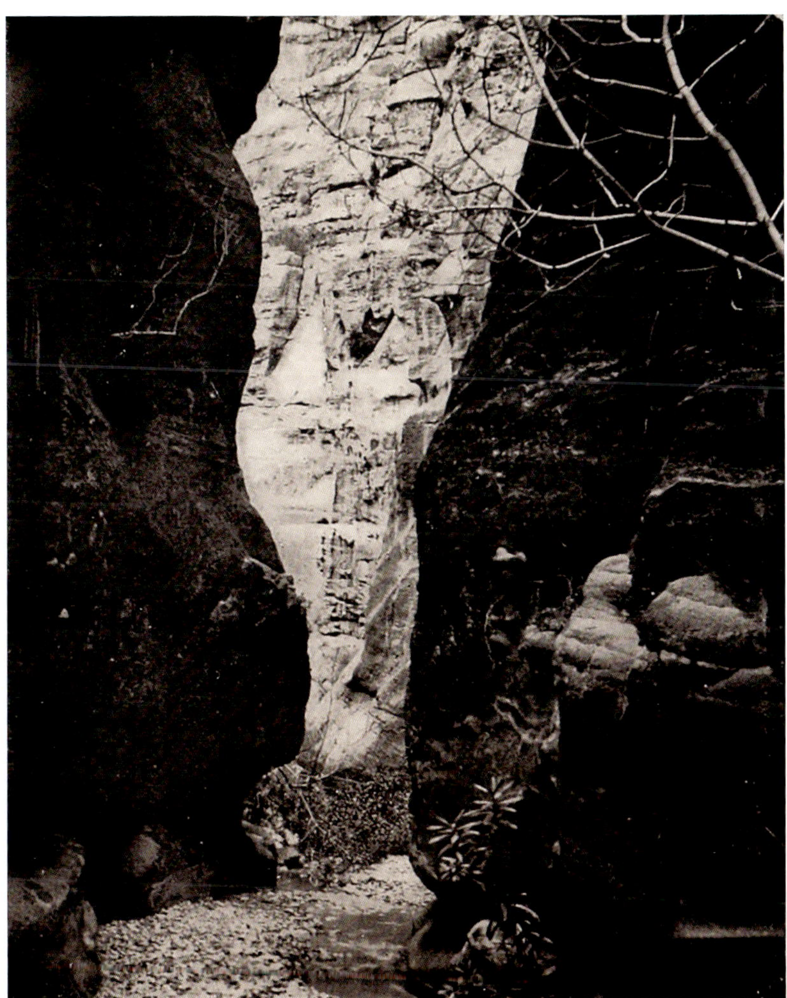 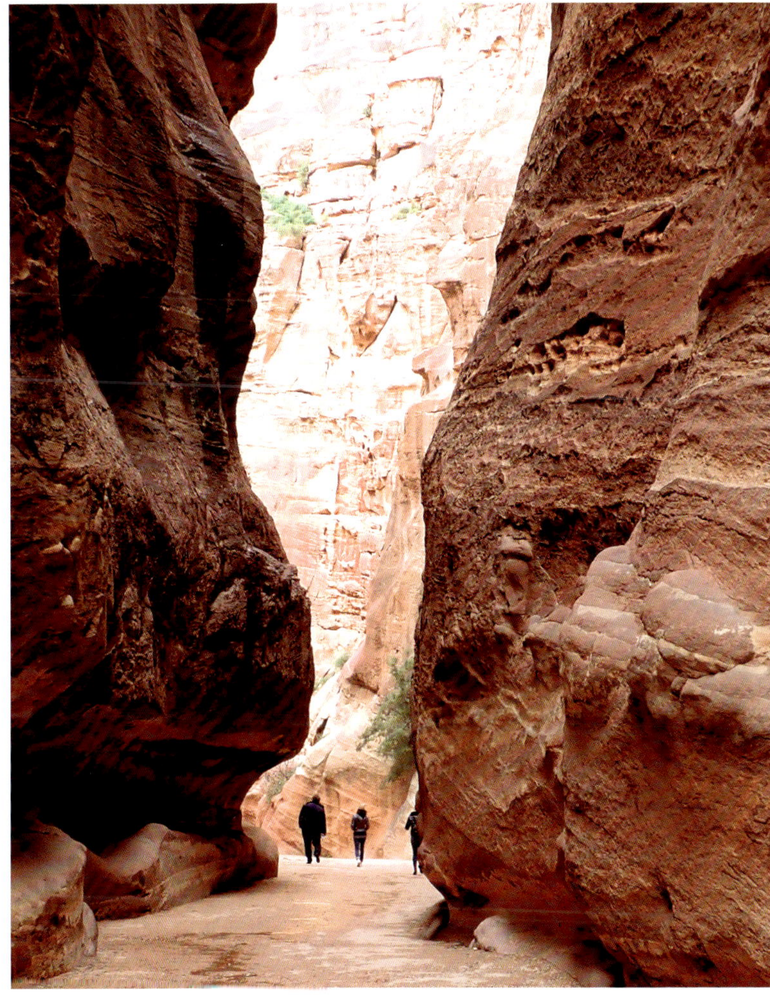

Depicting two different sections of the Siq canyon, both repeat image pairs showcase the extraordinary beauty of the sandstone ravine and how it has changed over time. Trees and oleander bushes have been replaced with eager visitors weaving their way through the twists and turns of the rocky embrace. The once cobbled riverbed has been cleared and paved—further exposing the ingenious Nabataean water channels running along the cliff face. It is strangely encouraging, however, that despite the undeniable influence of development and tourism, there is still no denying the humbling awe and amazement invoked by the seemingly endless serpentine passageway.

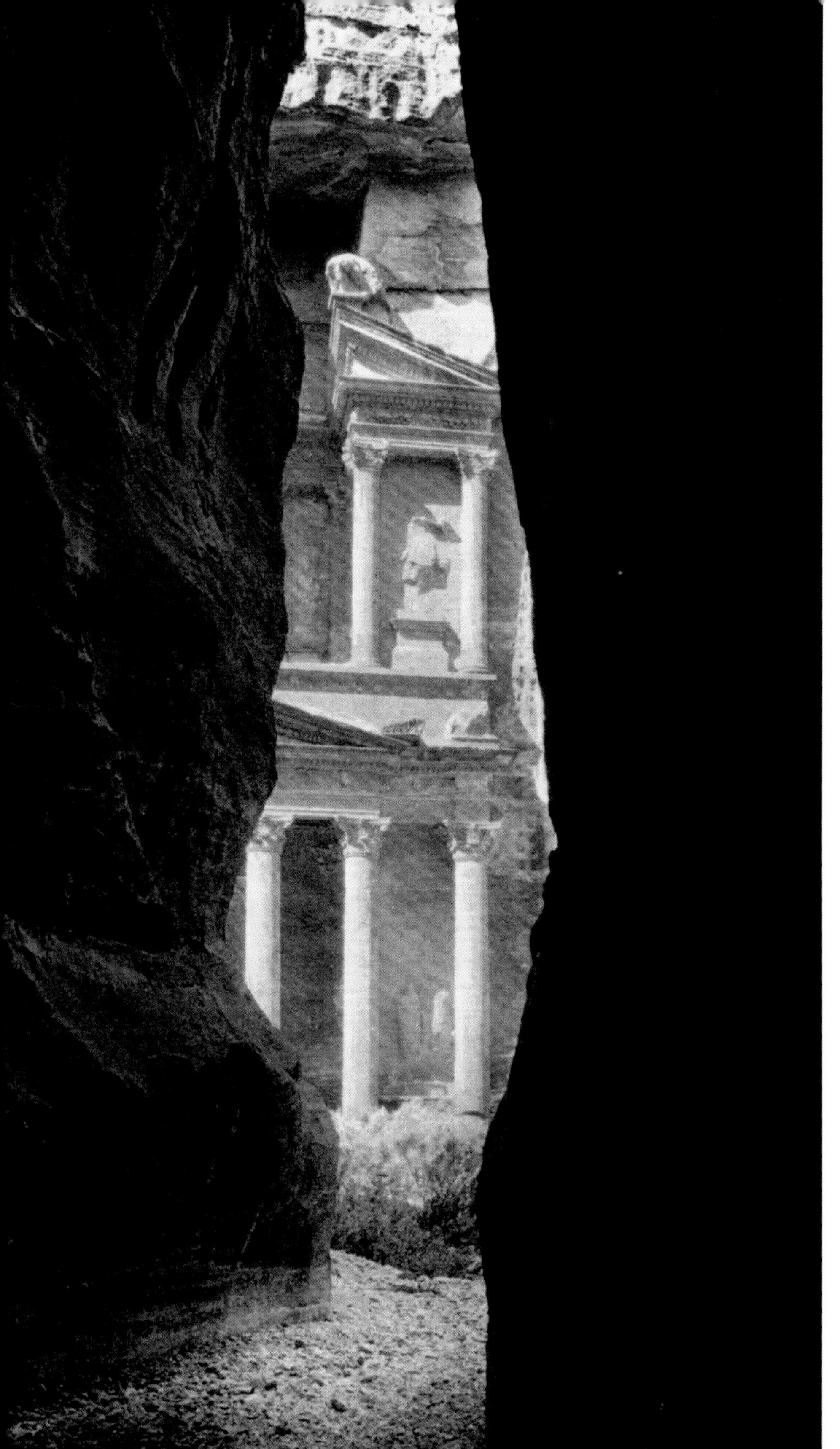

AL-KHAZNEH THROUGH THE SIQ

"Within the Siq itself, in a cross opening near its western end, stands the Khazna Fir'un, which from its picturesque and unexpected appearance in the ravine, as well as from its striking form, has become the best known and most discussed of all the Petraean monuments." — SIR KENNEDY (1925, pg. 51)

This now-famous view of the Khazneh emerging from the Siq has become an iconic image of Petra, and quite justifiably so. It is stunning. And unexpected. Ironically, this was also one of the most difficult images to recapture without throngs of delighted visitors completely obscuring the narrow entrance. This challenge was exacerbated by requiring the photograph be taken during a particularly busy time of day to match the sharply angled shadows seen in the original photograph. Those wishing for a more private audience with the striking monument should arrive in those early hours when the ethereal tranquility of Petra breathes magic.

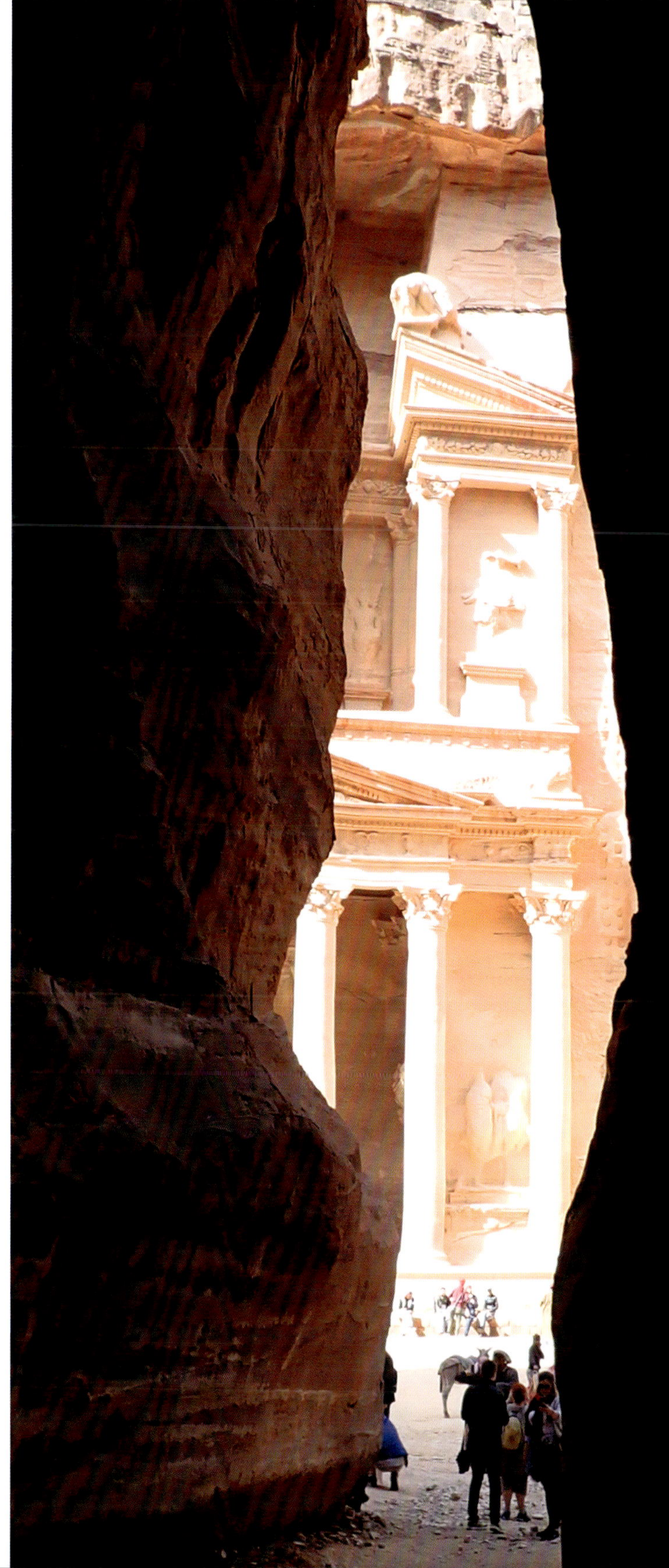

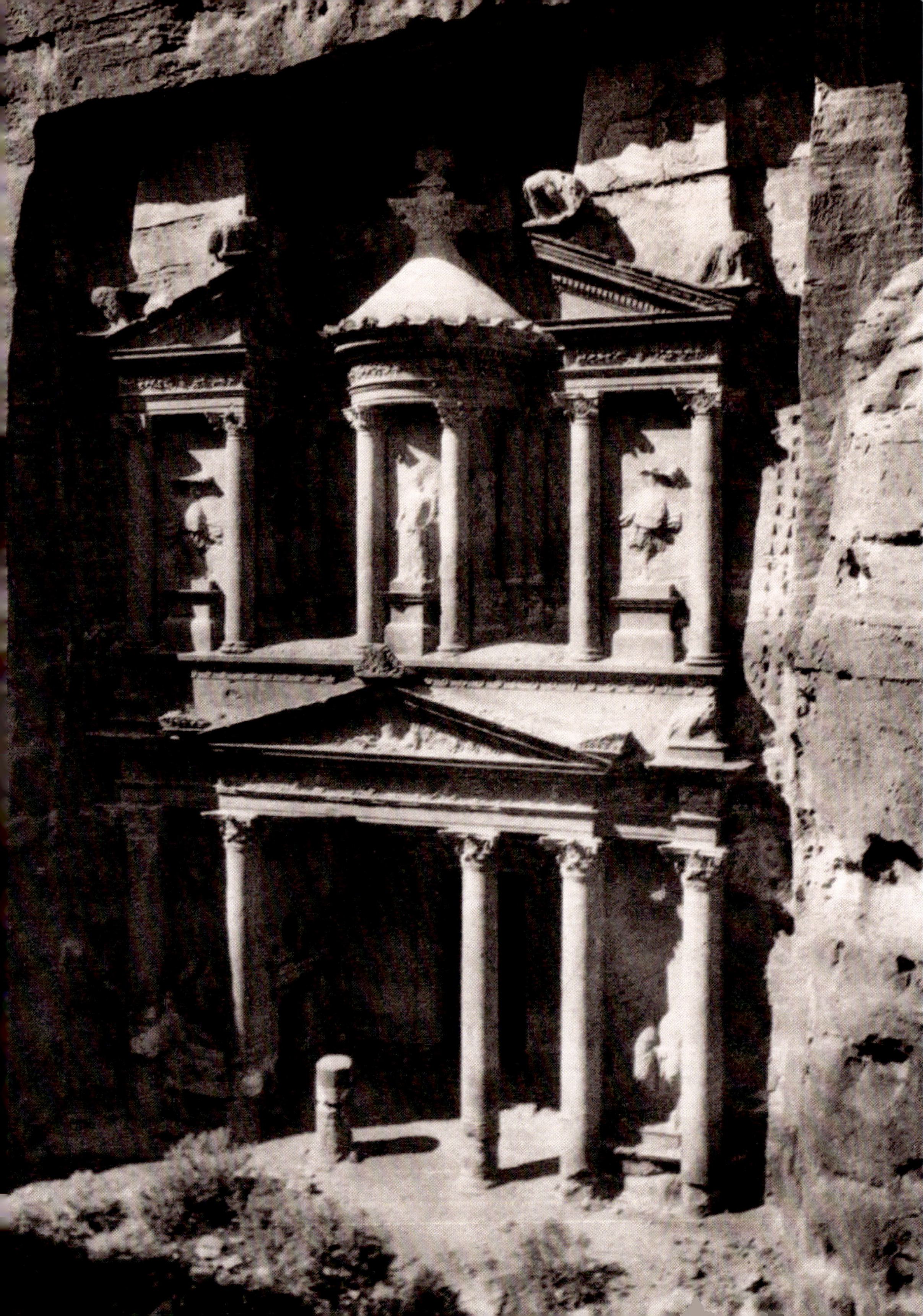

"Al-Khazna, the so-called 'Treasure-House of Pharaoh', known also as al-Jarra (the Urn) on account of the urn which surmounts it, and which has been traditionally supposed to contain the 'treasure' and has in consequence been the target of many bullets in the vain hope that it could be broken open."
— SIR KENNEDY (1925, pgs. 53, 54)

Easily the most recognizable monument in Petra, the famed Khazneh—also known as the Treasury—continues to triumphantly welcome visitors to Petra as they finally emerge from the sinuous constraints of the Siq. While the central urn and some of the more delicate façades still bear the bullet scars of eager marksmen mentioned in Sir Kennedy's notes, much love and attention have since been given to the iconic monument. The broken column seen in Sir Kennedy's photograph was reconstructed by the Jordanian Department of Antiquities in the early 1960s, and continued excavations have since revealed steps leading up to the main platform as well as the discovery of another level below the current ground level that can be viewed through grates in front of the columns.

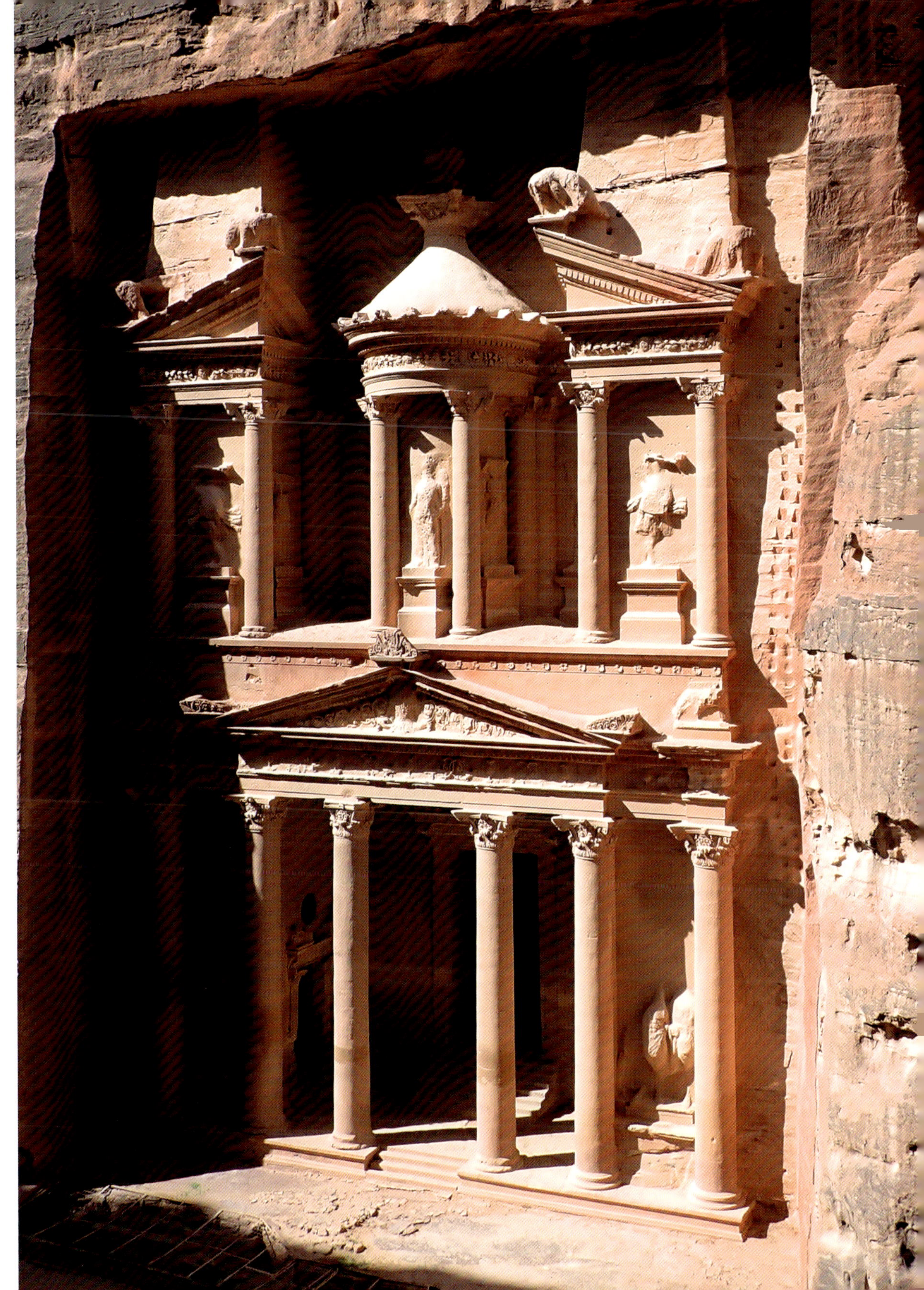

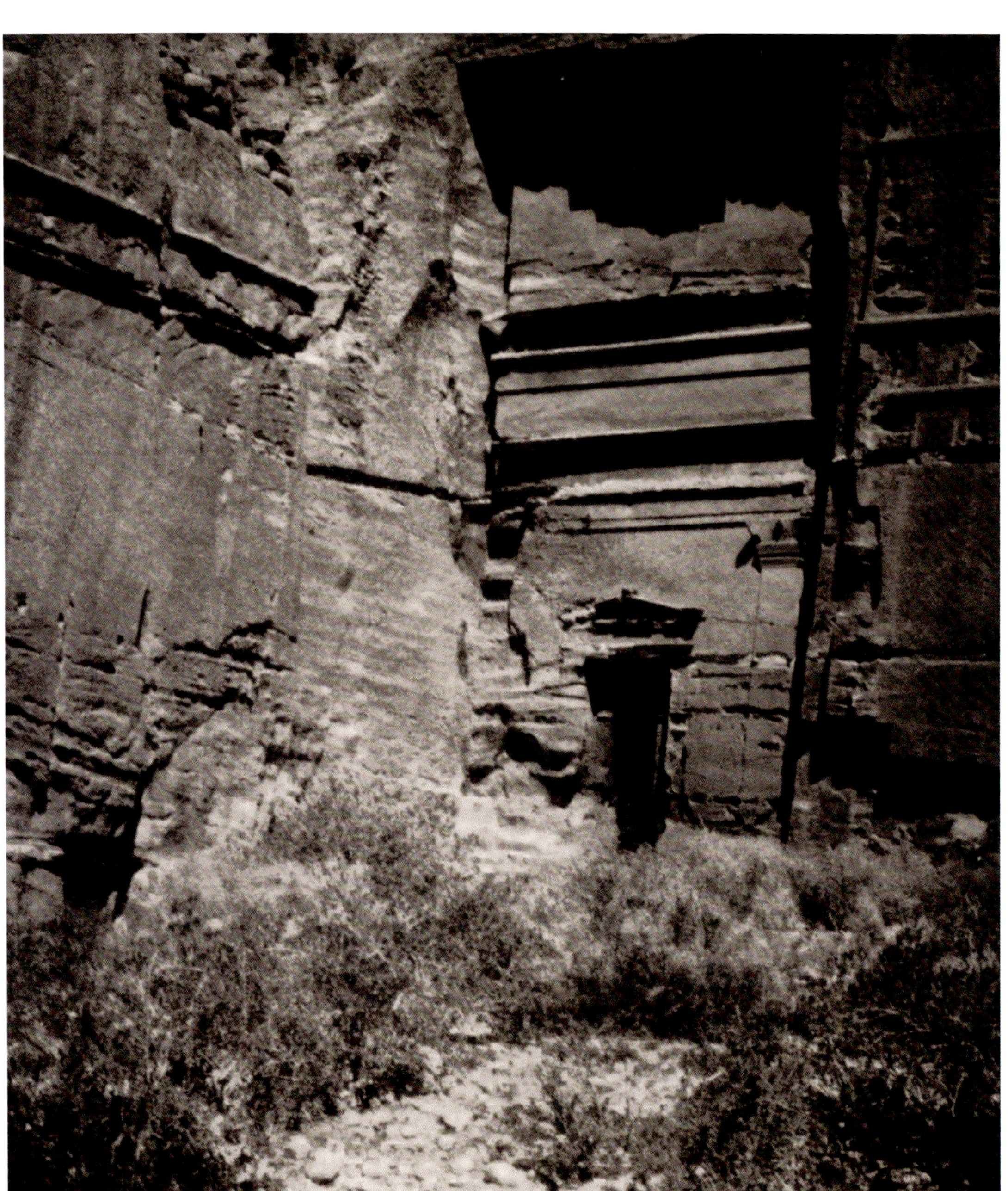

"[This monument] is quite unique in its internal arrangement. It contains a large chamber, on the floor of which are fourteen graves, very irregularly disposed... On one side-wall a group of five obelisks has been scratched, and a single obelisk on the other wall... On the bases of two of the obelisks are scratched short inscriptions naming a son and a grandson of one Iakum, but no indication as to their date." — SIR KENNEDY (1925, pgs. 48, 49)

The once rocky streambed in the foreground has been cleared and smoothed, creating the primary walking path leading visitors towards Petra' sprawling city center. The striking monument on the far wall carries the designation BD Tomb 825, in reference to the extensive archeological taxonomy developed by early archaeologists Rudolf Brünnow and Afred von Domaszewski, the first survey of its kind in Petra. The interior of the tomb is equally impressive, as noted by Sir Kennedy, but is now gated to protect the intricate carvings and alcoves within from human-related deterioration. The uniquely shaped entrance on the monument next door has since been exposed—either by excavation or by the periodic floods that surge through the outer Siq. An interpretive sign was erected to provide more information about the monument, but it has since been cut off by the entrenched ravine (seen running through the center of the image) engineered to capture and contain the seasonal flood waters.

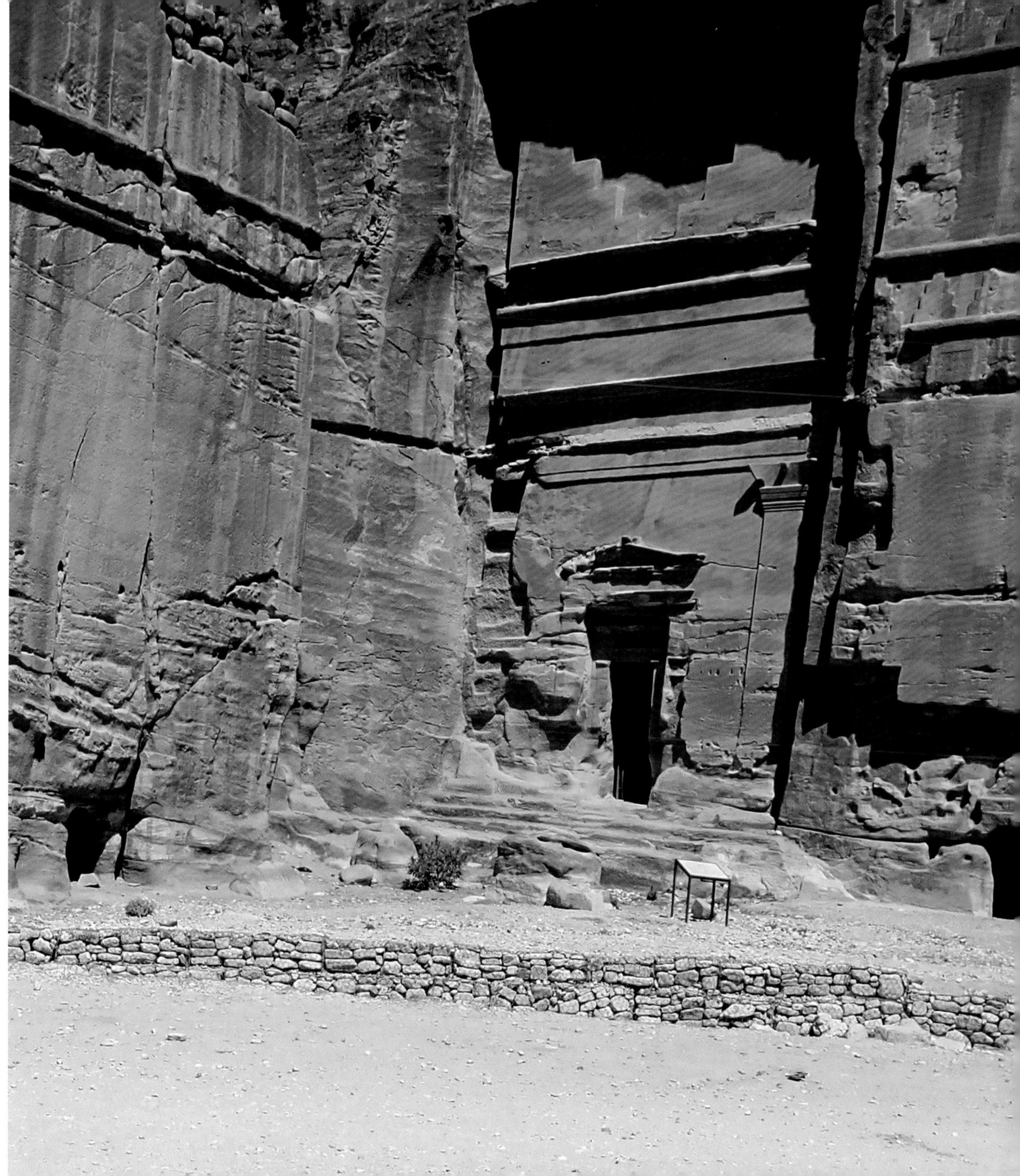

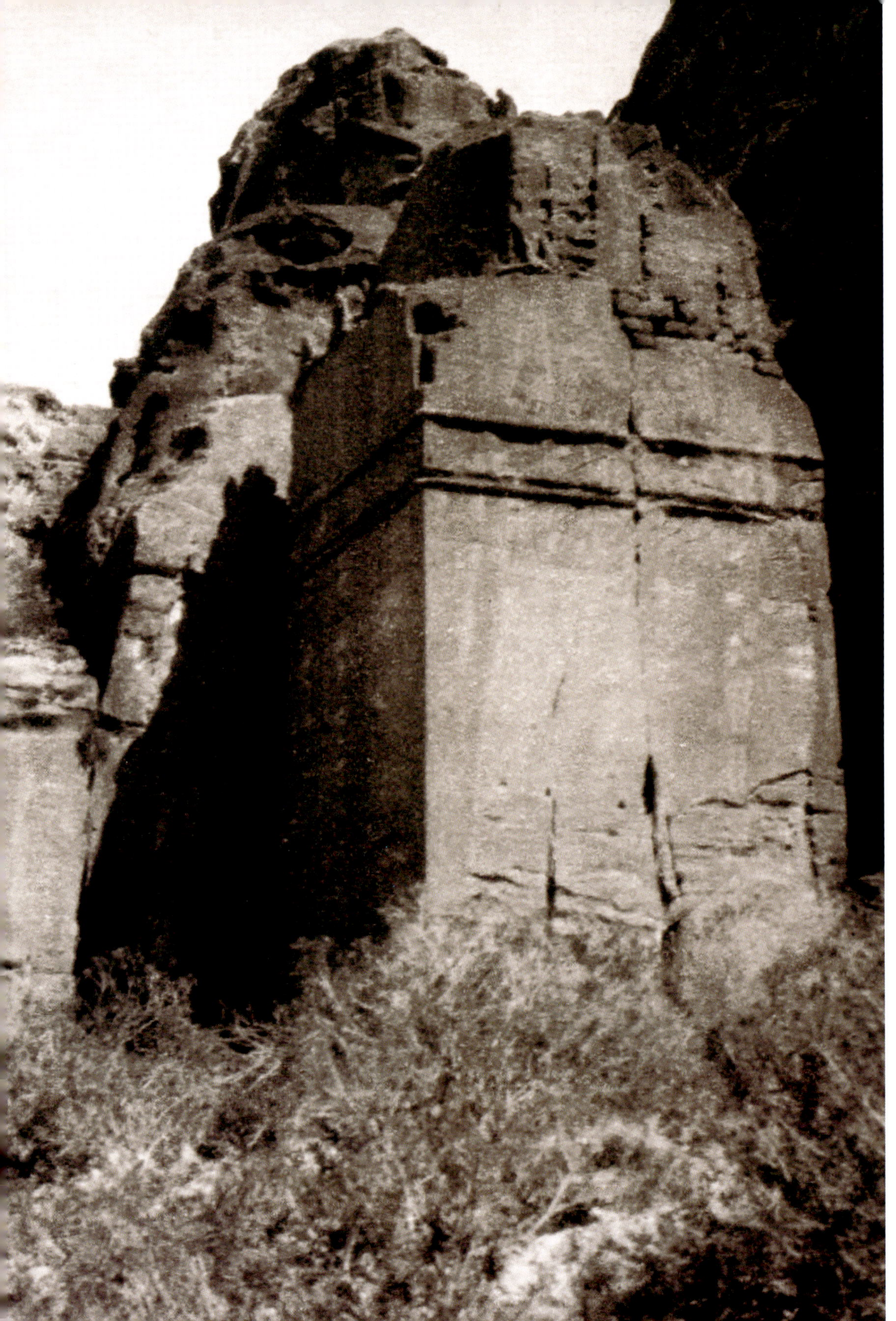

DJINN BLOCK IN OUTER SIQ

"An isolated block on the opposite side of the valley [from the theatre] and shows one of the instances in which the block is surmounted by crowstepped ramparts in addition to having a normal Nabataean frieze." — SIR KENNEDY (1925, pg. 41)

While much of Sir Kennedy's attention was given to the decorated Djinn Block in his photograph, the changes in the foreground are perhaps more amusing. Where once the view of this admittedly impressive Nabataean tower was obscured by desert brush and oleander, it is now equally blocked by various Petra-themed trinkets, souvenirs, and keepsakes. Once again, the landscape may change and the purpose of the place has evolved, but the core structures and stone wonders that occupy the valley remain as stalwart and majestic as ever. The owner of this particular shop was especially gracious when rephotographing the scene, as it required my burrowing quite deep within his handicrafts display in order to capture the same vantage point as Sir Kennedy's original photo. *Shukran* (thank you), Abu Omar.

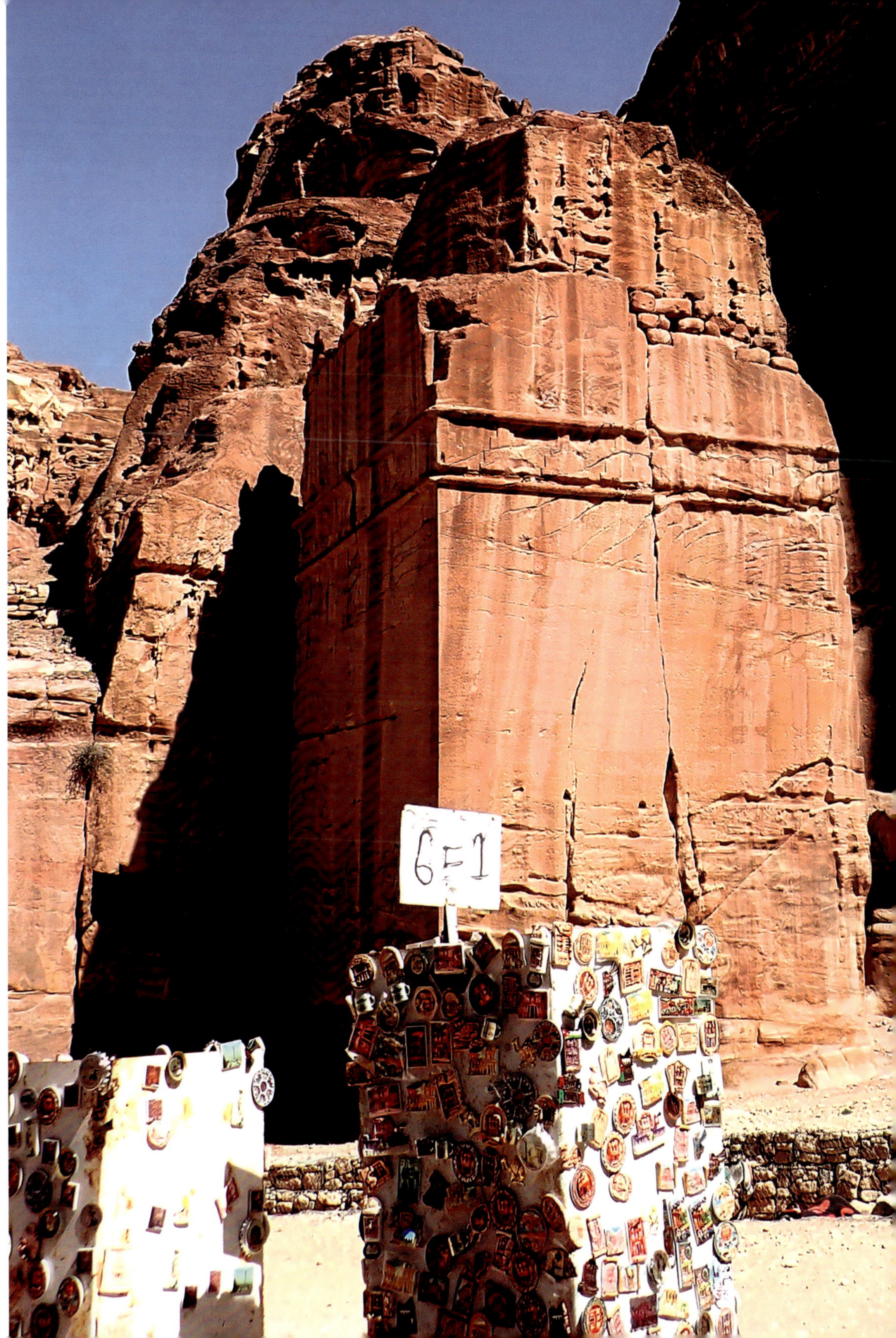

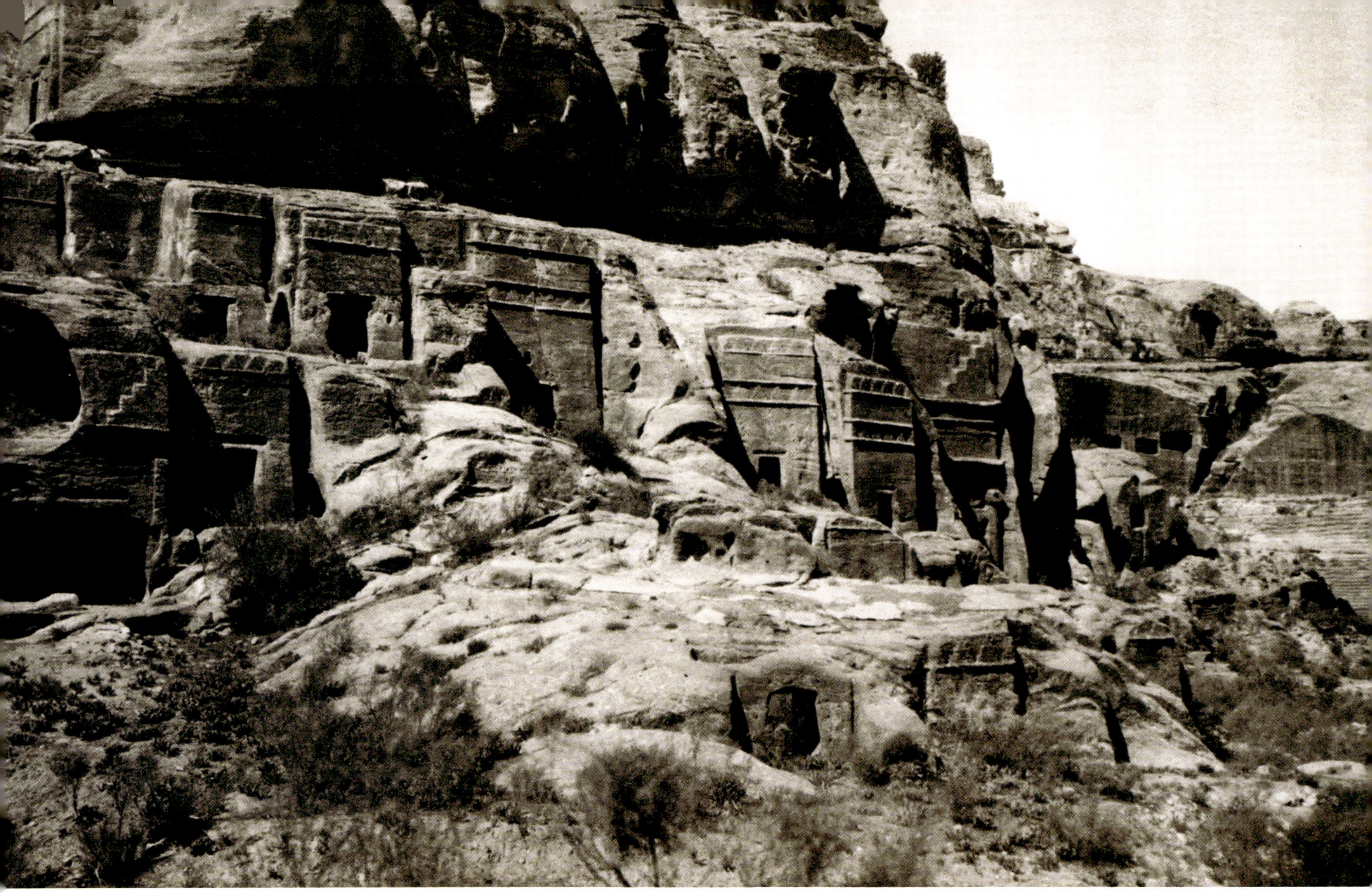

THE STREET OF FAÇADES

"A part of the immense group of monuments on the west side of the outer Siq and adjoining theatre, a portion of the latter being visible on the right of the photograph. A great fall of rock and debris has at some time overwhelmed many of these monuments, of which there have been apparently three, if not four, rows, one above the other."
—SIR KENNEDY (1925, pg. 46)

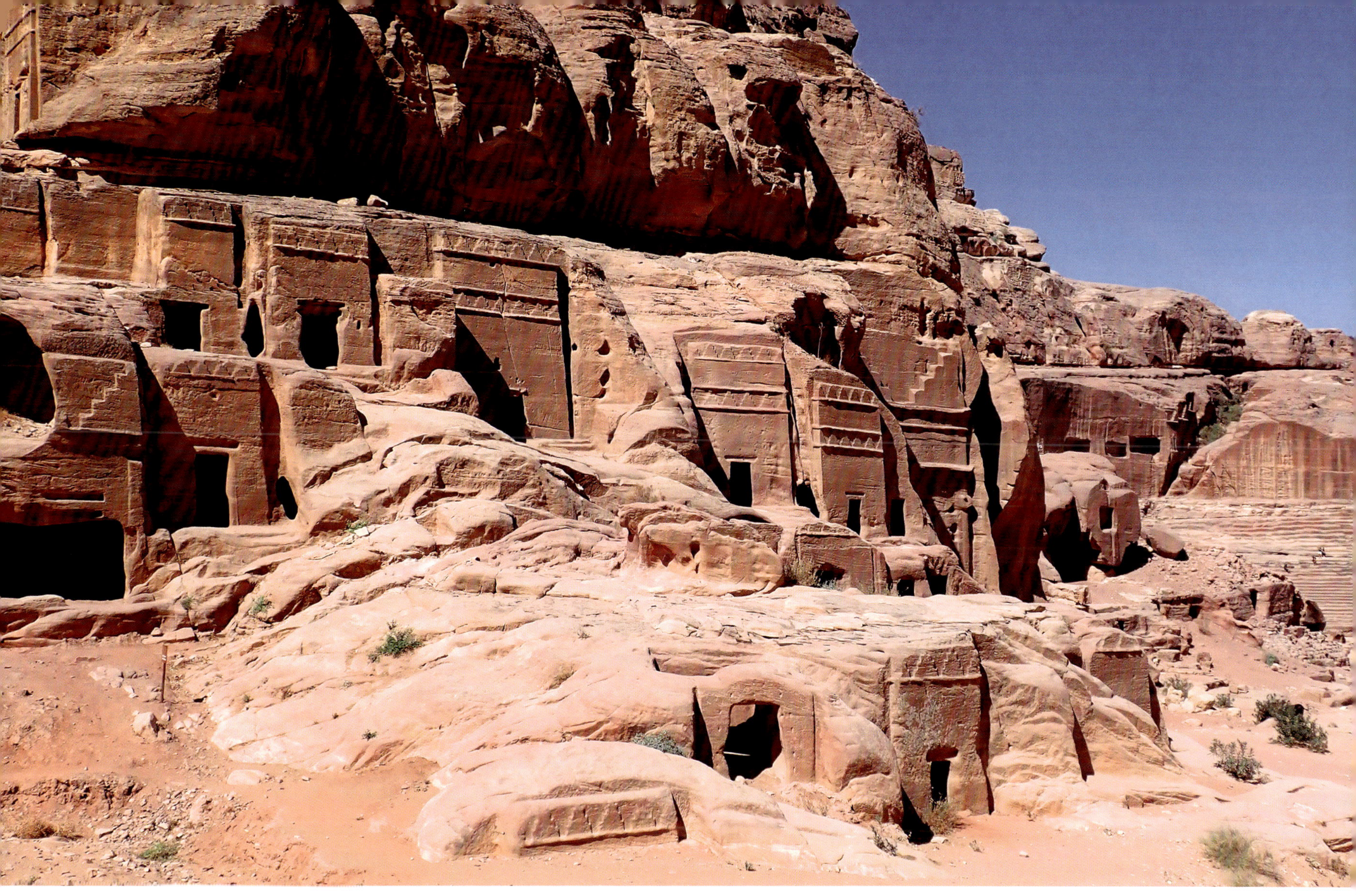

Once visitors navigate the inner Siq, marvel at the Khazneh, and proceed into the outer Siq region, or *Sharia' al-Wajahat* (Street of Façades), they are almost accosted by the sheer number of tombs and monuments scattered across the opening walls—such as those represented here. The incredible plethora of façades are made even more notable by their humbling resilience, as evidenced by the relative lack of change between Sir Kennedy's photograph and the modern image. The only obvious changes include the excavated buried crowsteps in the extreme foreground, cleared rubble from some of the doorways, and loss of vegetation along the now well-worn paths. For the most part, however, these enduring stone wonders emulate the uncanny timelessness of Petra: perpetually frozen in a state of indomitable ruin.

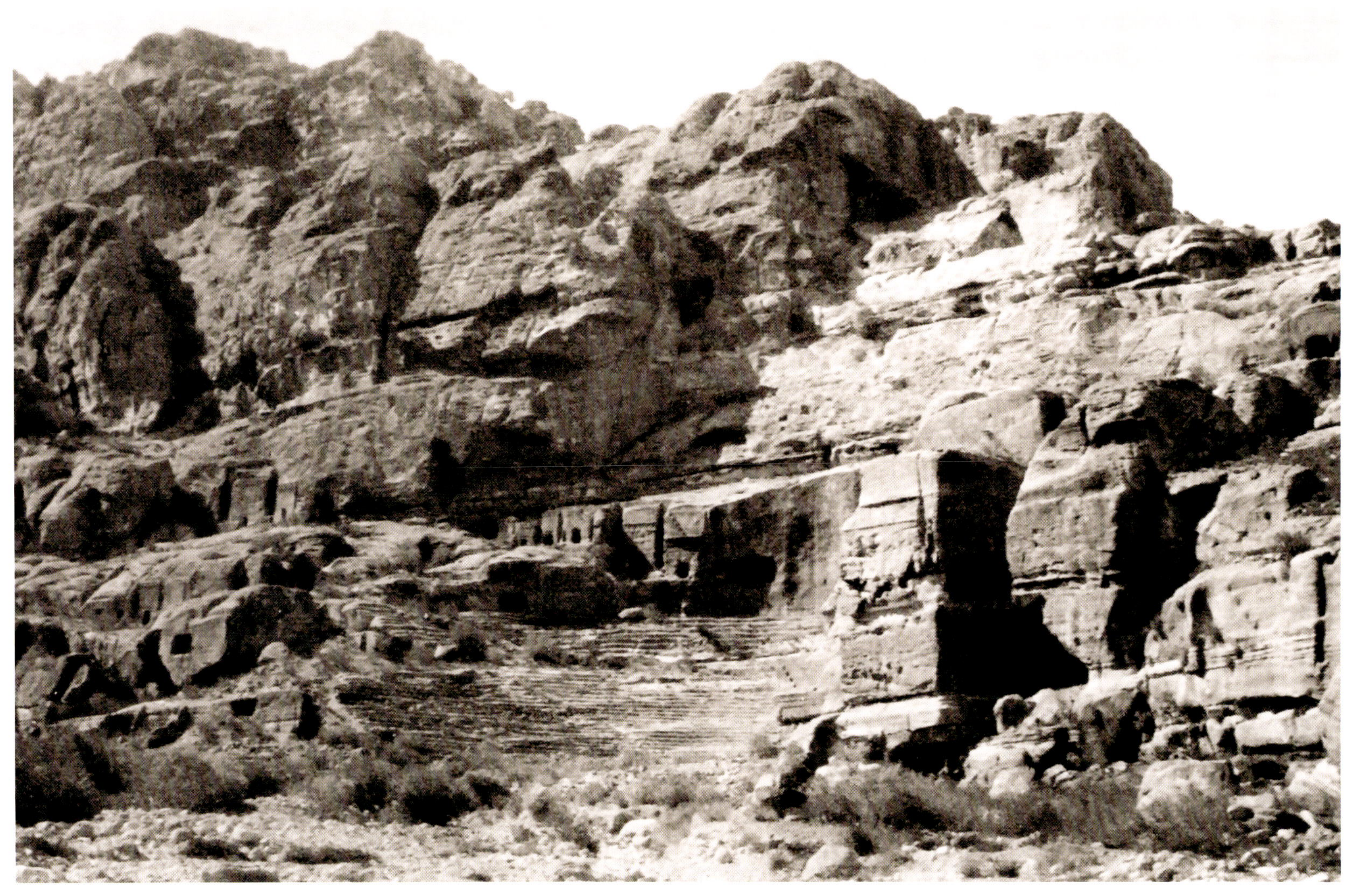

THE ROMAN THEATRE

"As regards physical magnitude the greatest
relic of Roman work is naturally the theatre...
If the dimensions are correct the seating
capacity has not been exaggerated as
between 3,000 and 4,000... The proscenium
has disappeared, a few fragments of columns
only remain on the ground, and what is
apparently an entrance to a blind corridor."
—SIR KENNEDY (1925, pg. 60)

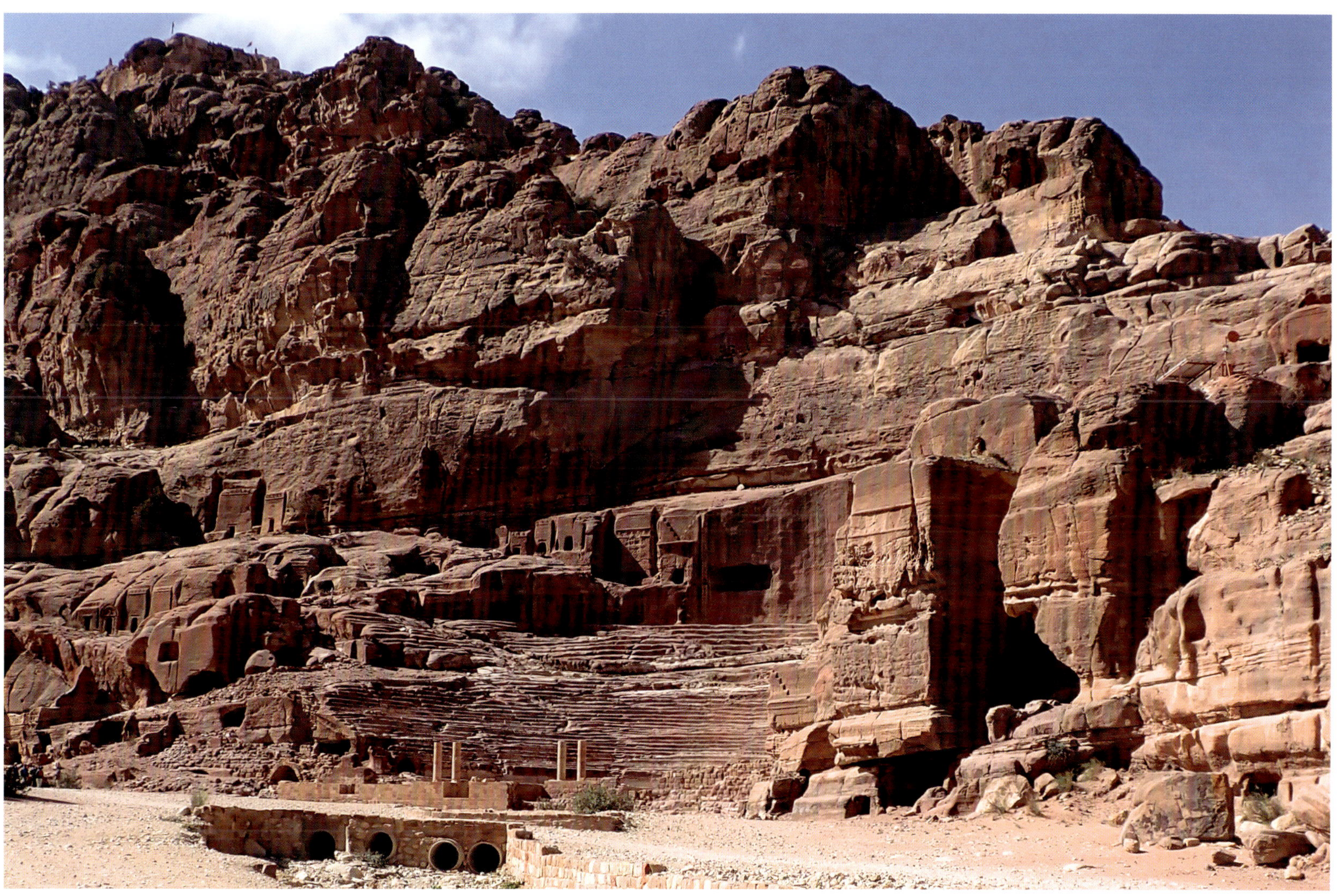

Taken from farther down the trail and looking back towards the outer Siq, this image pairing highlights some of the changes necessary to accommodate the site's contemporary tourism industry, namely the construction of robust water channels and drainage systems to protect visitors and monuments from the occasional flashfloods that have ravaged the city in the past. Above the new bridge, the collapsed stage—what Sir Kennedy called the "proscenium"—is visible but has been reconstructed for a better comparison to showcase the sheer size of Petra's colossal amphitheater sculpted into the cliffside.

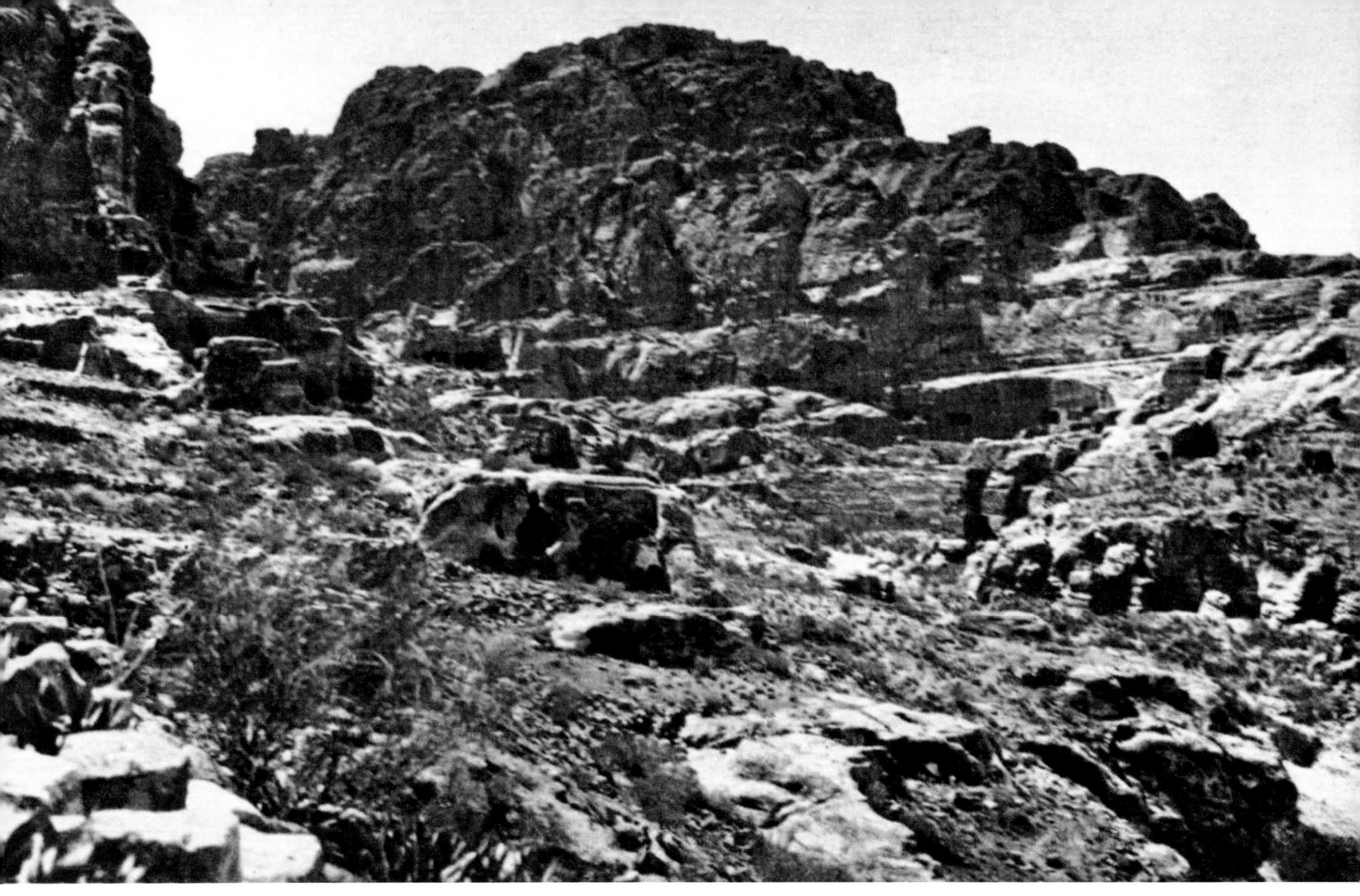

"The Obelisk Ridge, as forming both the south-western boundary of the outer Siq and the eastern wall of the city area itself is one of the most conspicuous features of Petraean scenery, as well as one of the most important regions in reference to its richness in monuments. The wall... carries the theatre, beyond which it is covered by at least three tiers of monuments, mostly tombs. From the point of view of [this photograph], one of the obelisks [at the High Place of Sacrifice] can just be seen on the skyline across the square niche close to the left-hand edge of the ridge." — SIR KENNEDY (1925, pg. 74)

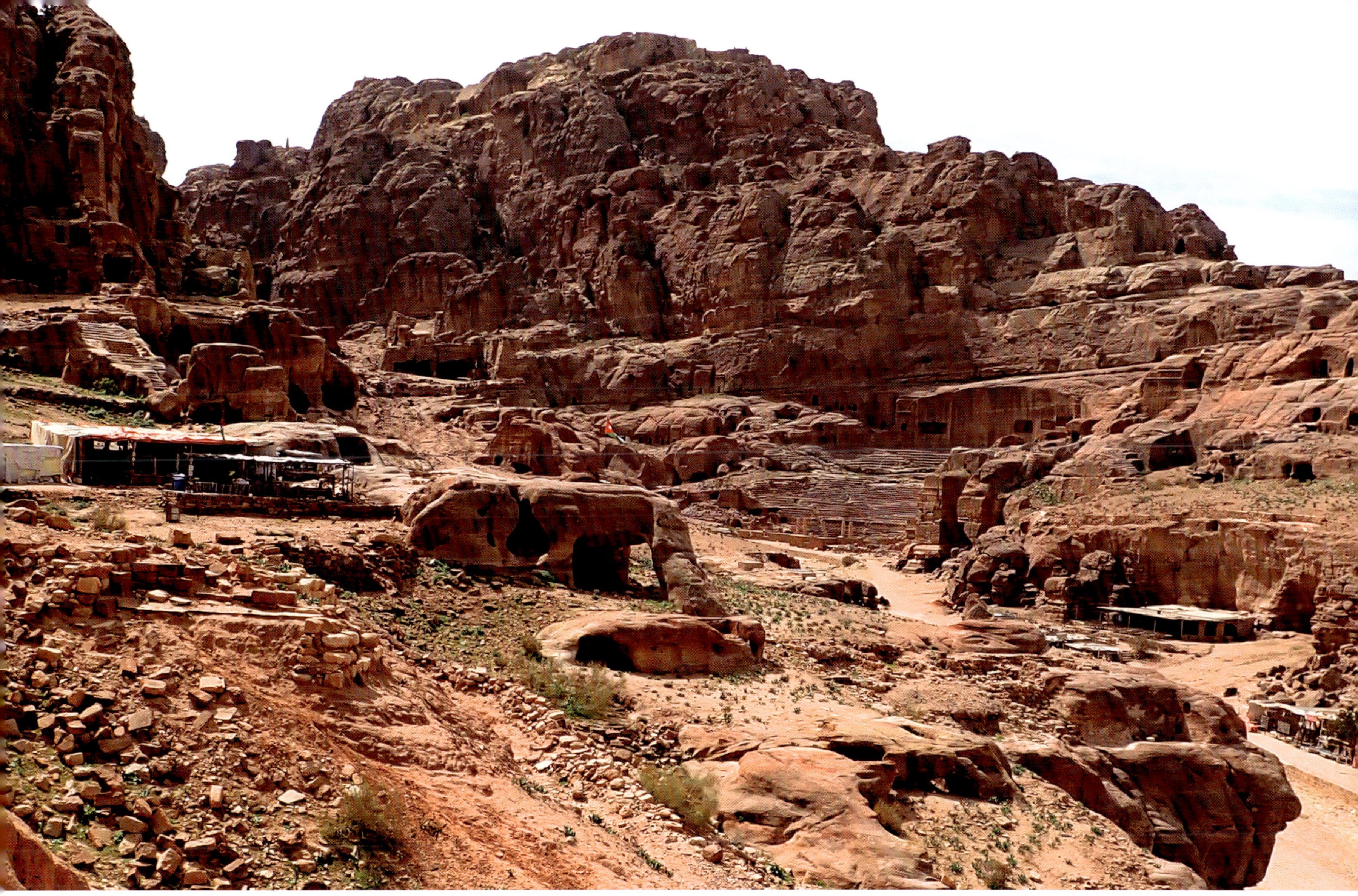

The final view of the greater Siq region is from a collapsing cliff face just below the so-called Royal Tombs looking back at the theatre, the outer Siq, and mighty Obelisk Ridge looming over it. The main roadway leading into central Petra can clearly be seen in the bottom right, as well as several new shops and structures erected by entrepreneurial Bedouins in the valley below and along the elevated trail. Amazingly, the distant obelisk described in Sir Kennedy's caption is still visible in the upper left corner of the photograph. The large shop along the upper trail (left) is a lovely stopping point for some traditional Bedouin tea and conversation with the ever-hospitable locals—which can be further enjoyed from the nearby protruding ledge (center) now housing a picturesque Jordanian flag and multiple benches overlooking the theatre and central valley.

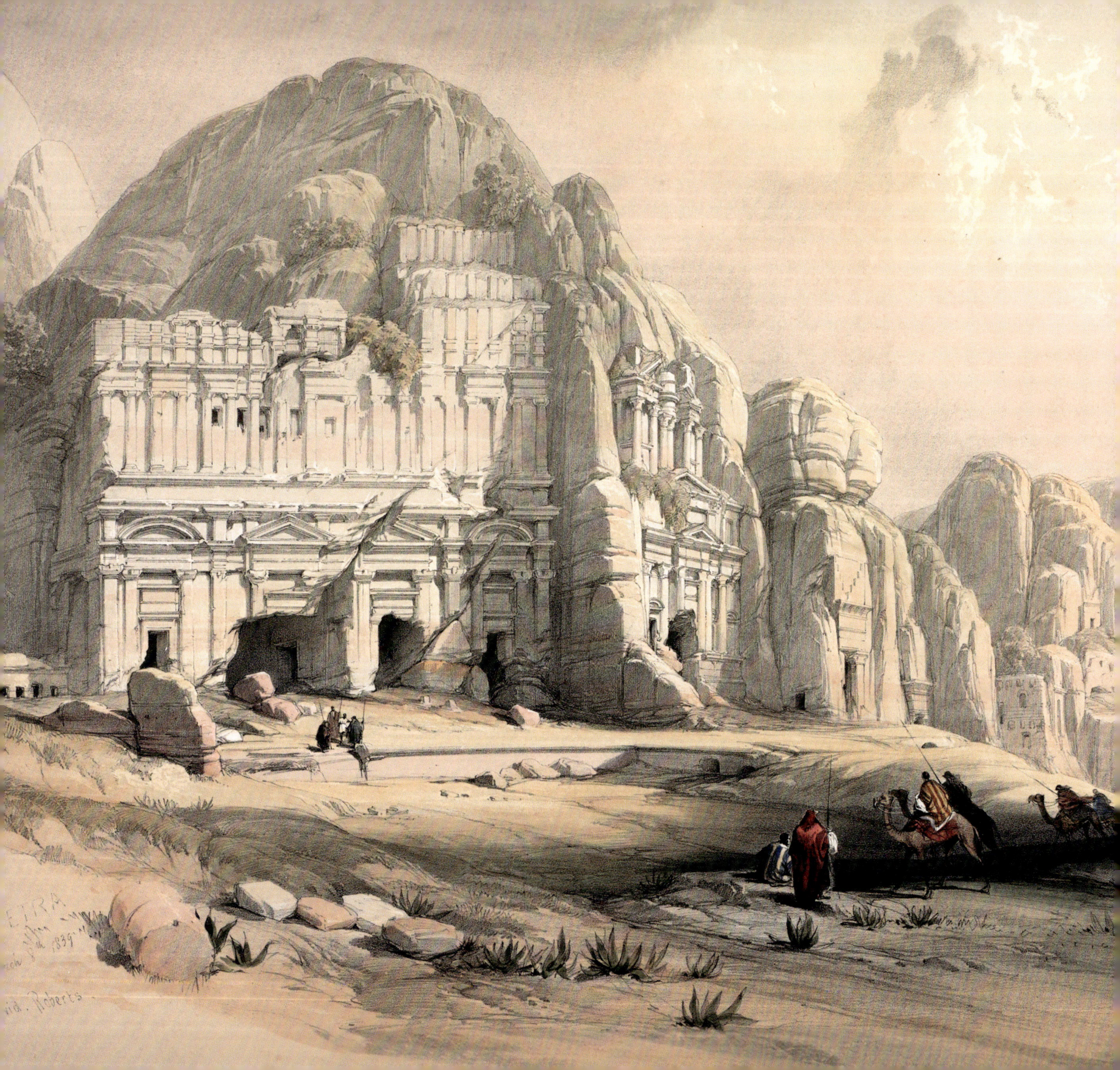
PETRA
1839
David Roberts

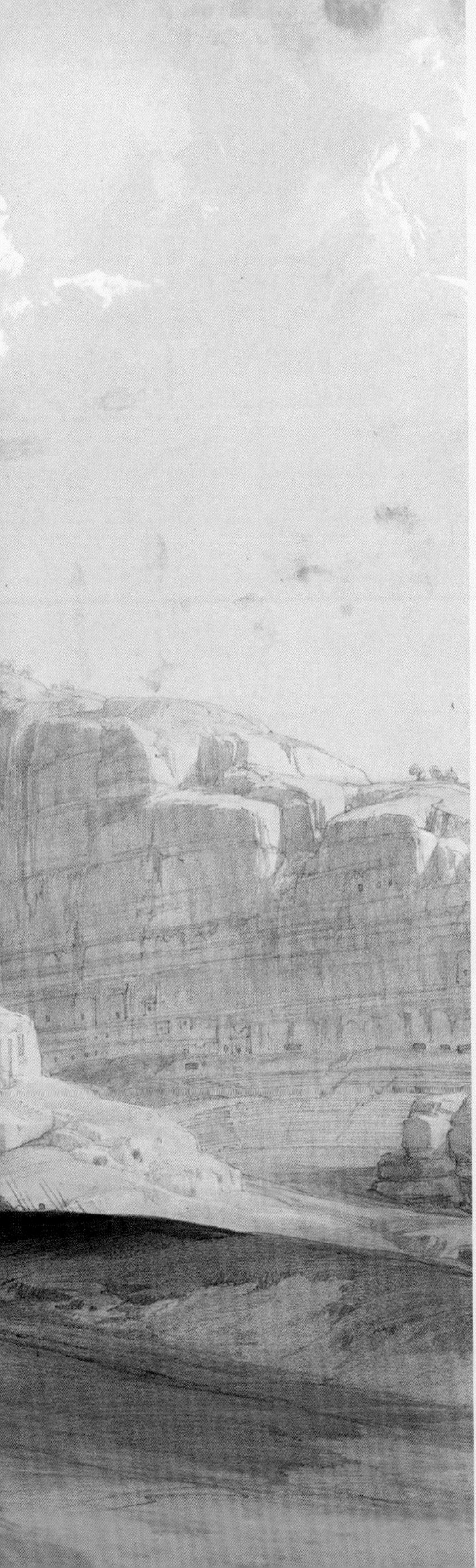

Eastern Highlands:
Royal Tombs, Nasara Ridge, and Jabal Khubtha

Looming over the main city center, the Royal Tombs are named for their intricate designs, unique attributes, and panoramic vistas. This region examines these regal tombs in greater detail, as well as exploring the upper trail leading to the peak of Jabal Khubtha and the city's eastern edge.

> "On all sides the gaunt red cliffs stand, honeycombed by rock dwellings and tombs, with here and there a pseudo classic facade or one that reminds you of Assyria or Egypt; immense headlands stand up against a sapphire sky. It is all new, strange and indescribably old; which may sound paradoxical, but which is strictly true." — MRS. STEUART ERSKINE[7]

7 S. Erskine, *The Vanished Cites of Arabia* (New York: E.P. Dutton & Co., 1925), 27.

Lithograph by nineteenth-century artist David Roberts of the Royal Tombs overlooking the Petra Valley.

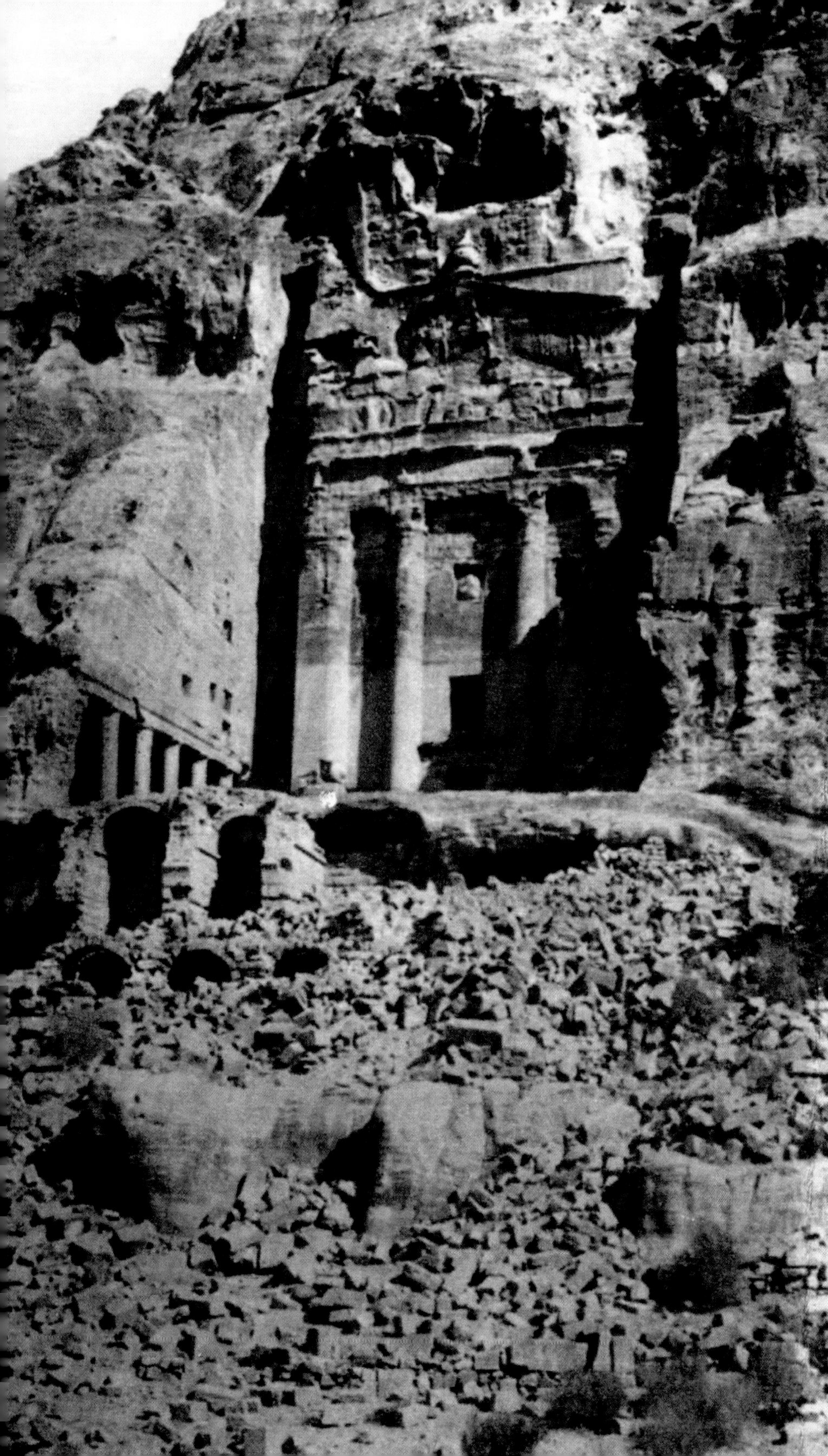

THE URN TOMB

"On the east side of the outer Siq, immediately facing the theatre, is a notable temple surmounted by a large urn, which has given it the name of the 'Urn Tomb,' although it does not appear to be in any way connected with sepulture." — SIR KENNEDY (1925, pg. 51)

Where Sir Kennedy had to rely on his imagination to see a grandiose stairway through the tumbled mound of debris and rubble before him, modern visitors to Petra can marvel at the proud Roman arches carrying them skyward to the Royal tombs. The arches and alcoves were reconstructed by the Jordanian Department of Antiquities during revitalization of the Royal Tombs in the 1970s and 1980s. A row of Bedouin shops that line the upper trail can be seen at the very bottom of the modern image. Additionally, the minuscule visitors seen at the edge of the upper court perfectly illustrate the impressive scale of this elevated tomb and its elaborate arcade.

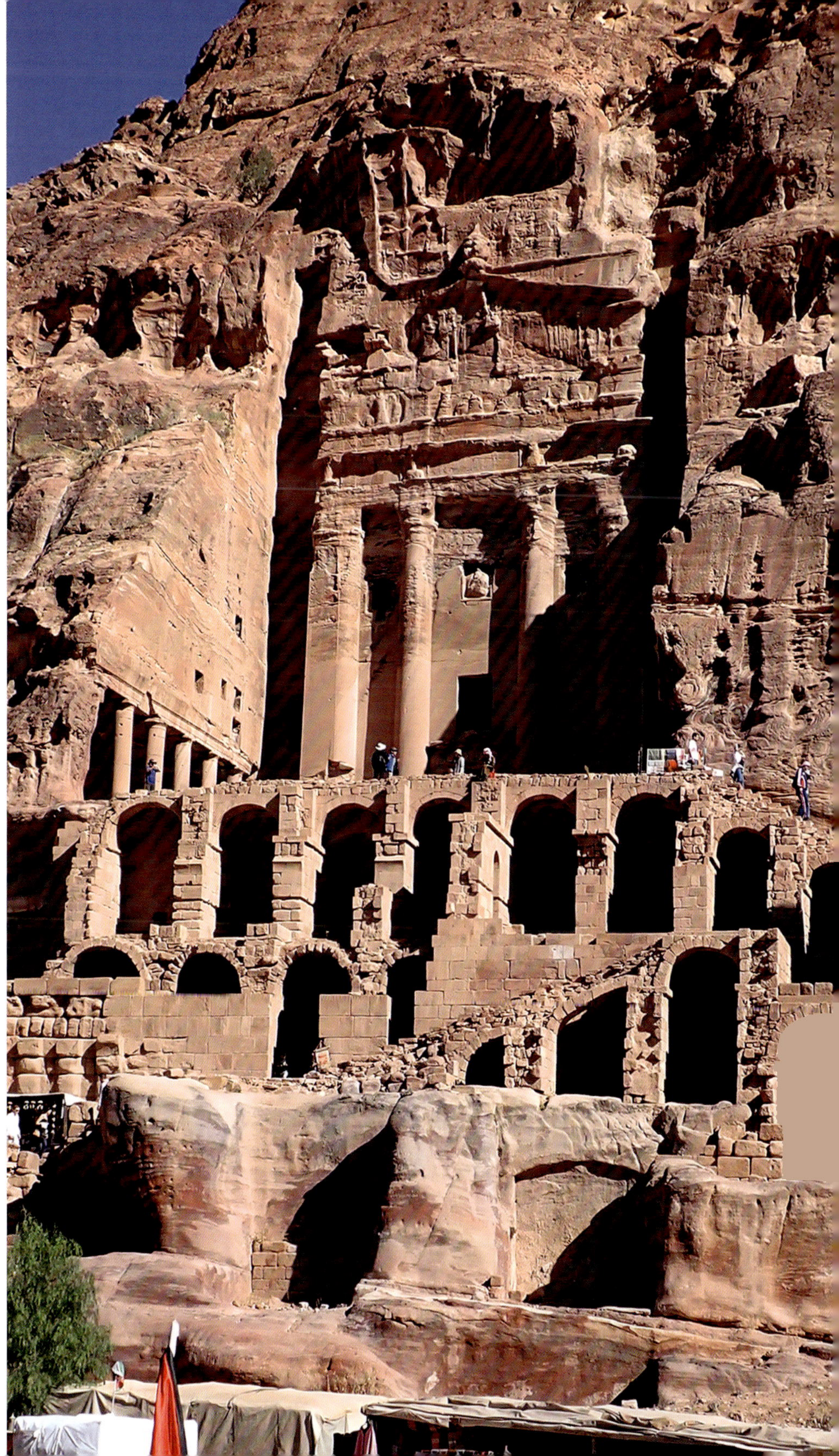

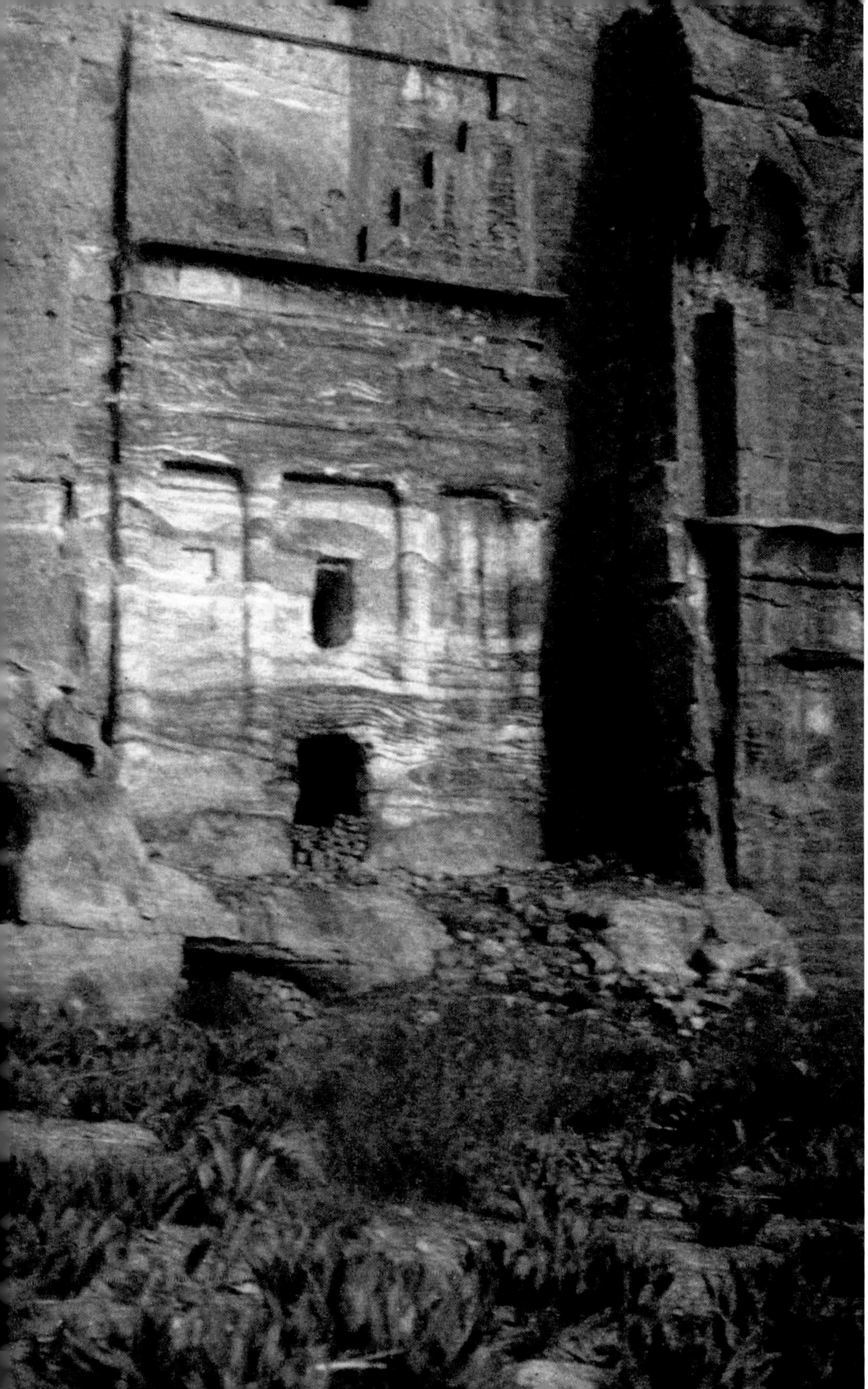

THE SILK TOMB

"One of the most beautiful of the Petraean decorated monuments is under the east wall of al-Khubtha, close to the Palace and Corinthian monuments. Its beauty, however, depends chiefly on its colours and not on its form, and these cannot, of course, appear in the photograph." — SIR KENNEDY (1925, pg. 49)

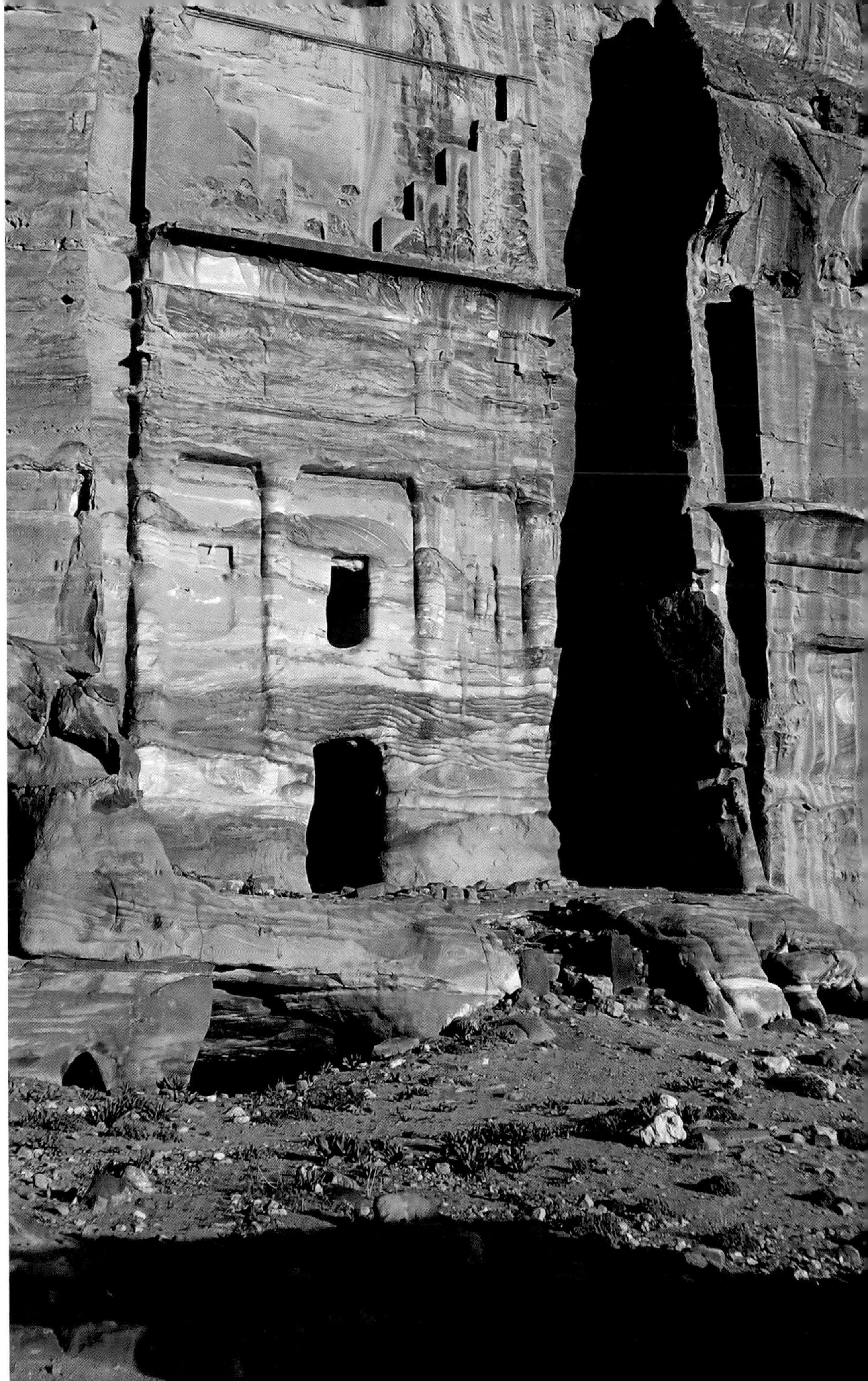

Later named the "Silk Tomb" because of its smooth-looking surface, this monument is truly breathtaking in its natural vibrancy and kaleidoscopic coloring. In some ways, the intricate play of undulating colors is made even more dramatic by the relatively simple design. Nestled among some of the most complicated and detailed monuments in the valley, the humble Silk Tomb instead favors nature's artistry and the exquisite beauty of Petra's technicolor sandstone cliffs. In terms of change, aside from the cleared doorway, there is significant subsidence in the soil level that has exposed new natural caverns at the base of the platform. The shadow of a Bedouin stall now occupies the foreground of the modern photograph.

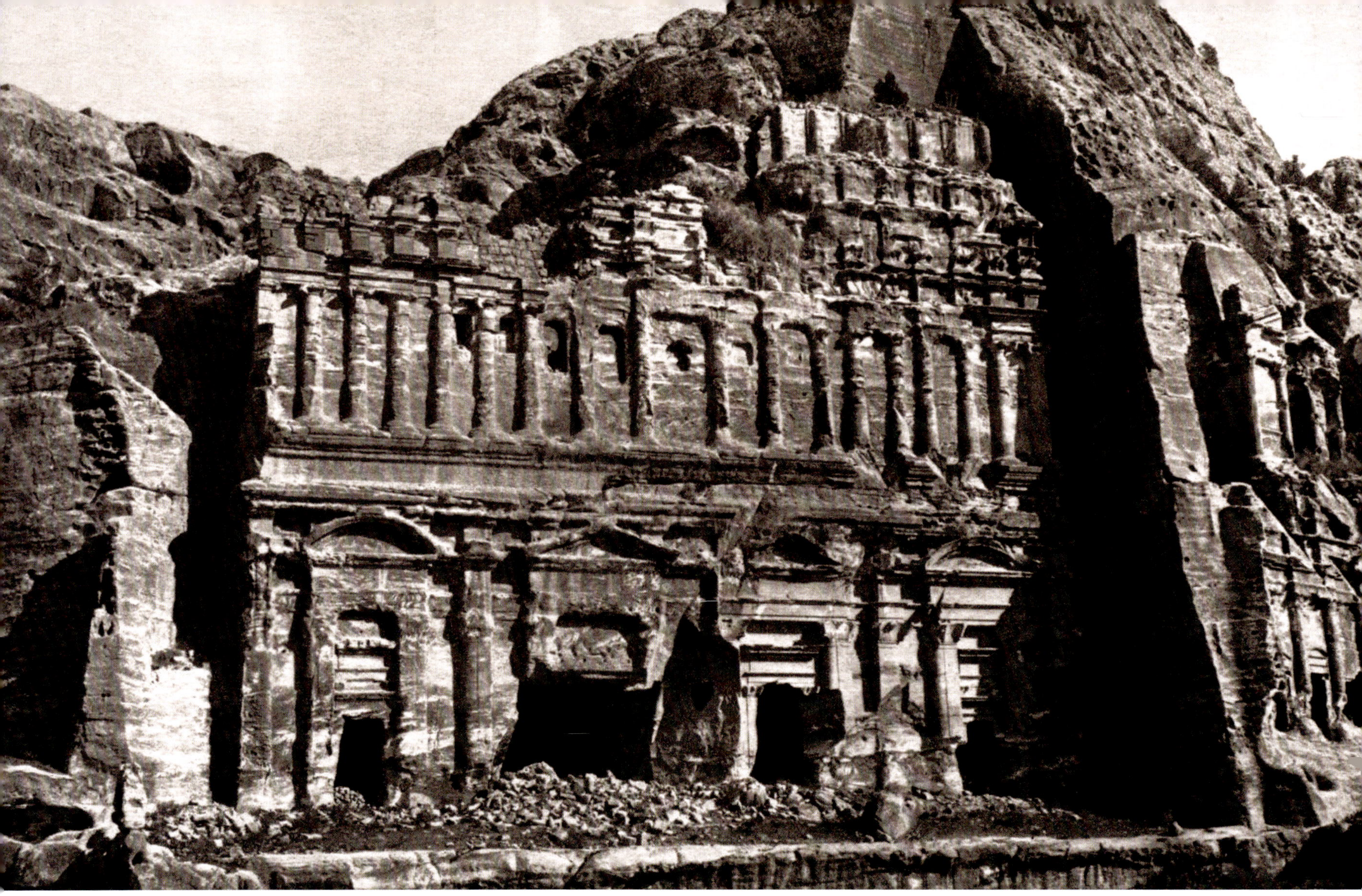

THE ROYAL TOMBS

"In the wall of al-Khubdha [al-Khubtha], stands a very badly weathered monument, generally called the 'Corinthian' tomb from the fact that the capitals of its columns are—or supposed to have been— of the Corinthian order. Next to this, northwards, stands an immense façade, unique in its design as regards Petra, which is a copy, in arrangement, of the front of a Roman palace, and which it will be convenient to refer to simply as 'the Palace'."

—SIR KENNEDY (1925, pg. 51)

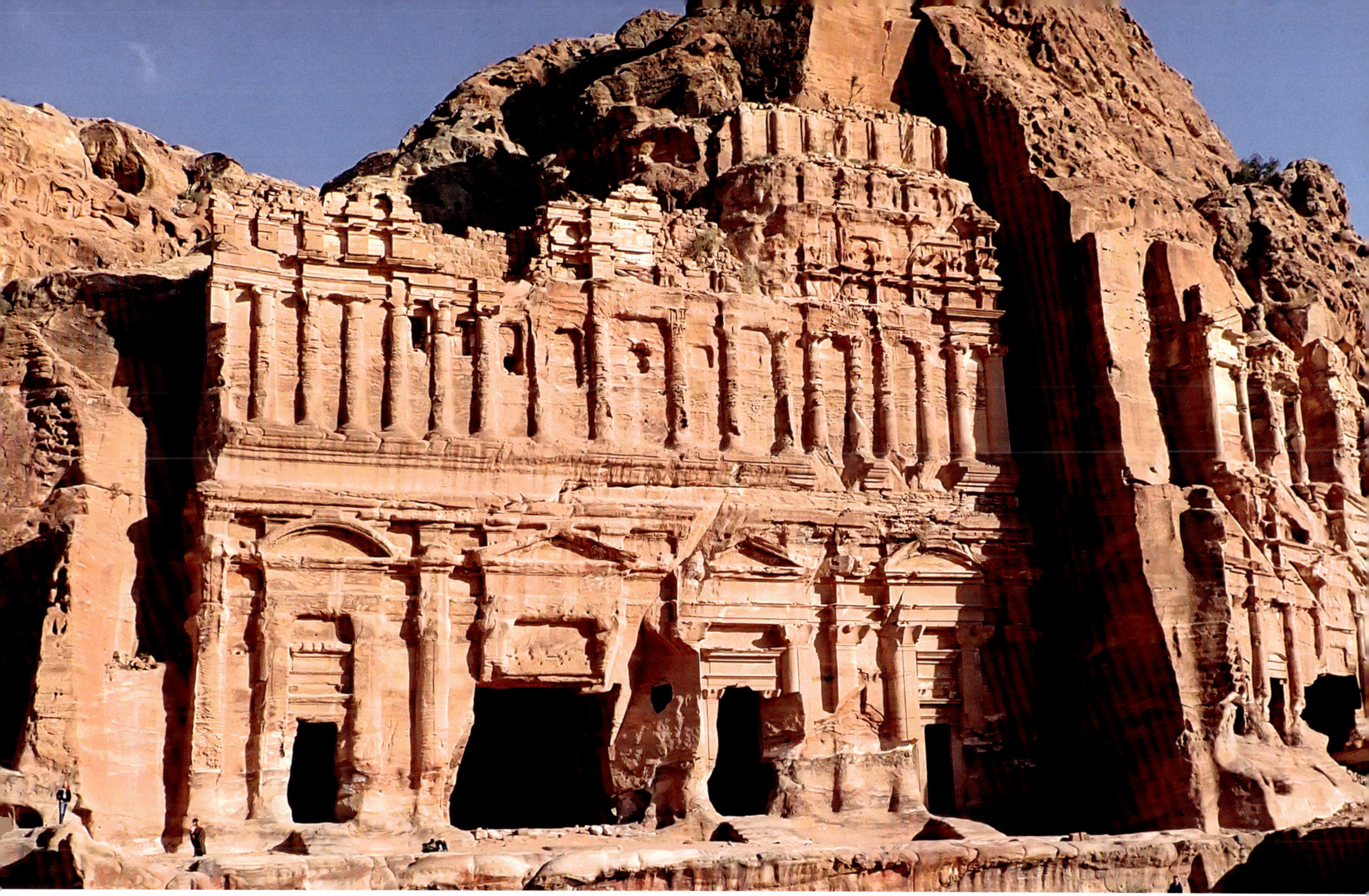

While both the Corinthian (right) and Palace (center) Tombs can be seen in this photo, the Palace Tomb's towering mass of columns, cornices, and friezes dominates the image. Even with the cleared debris, the scale of the photograph makes it difficult to convey the sheer size of this monumental façade. It is truly enormous, and it is crumbling. Many of the upper decorations have required modern stabilization and reconstruction—some as recent as 2022. Sir Kennedy did include in his tome another image focused on the Corinthian Tomb, but its inferior quality and awkward lighting negated its viability for replication. Capturing the entire façade of the monolithic Palace for this repeat image required placing the camera in the middle of a large, unshaded boulder field, a situation made far more delightful with the company of a young Bedouin child bringing tea from her mother's nearby stall and helping to "stabilize" the camera tripod by stacking loose pebbles around its feet.

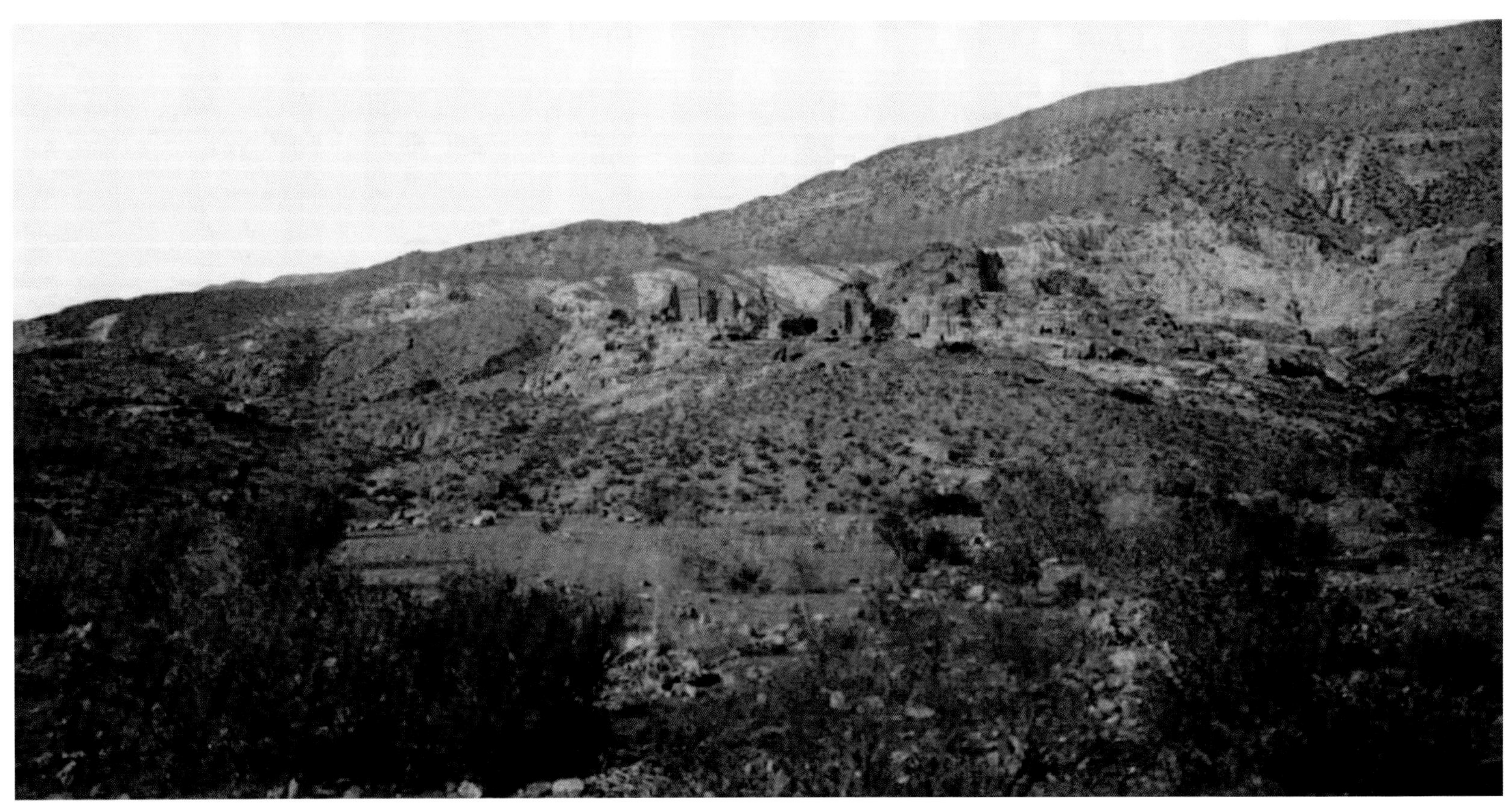

NASARA RIDGE
FROM THE ROYAL TOMBS

"The dome-like configuration of the white sandstone area contrasts markedly with the flattened summits of the red sandstone, which forms a narrow elongated plateau. The ruddy sandstone, which occupies its western face and southern portions, is also of a more varied colouring than that of the western range, being here and there 'shot' with all the colours of the rainbow, of which the ancient settlers of Petra took advantage in the excavation of their tombs and other monuments." — SIR KENNEDY (1925, pg. 12)

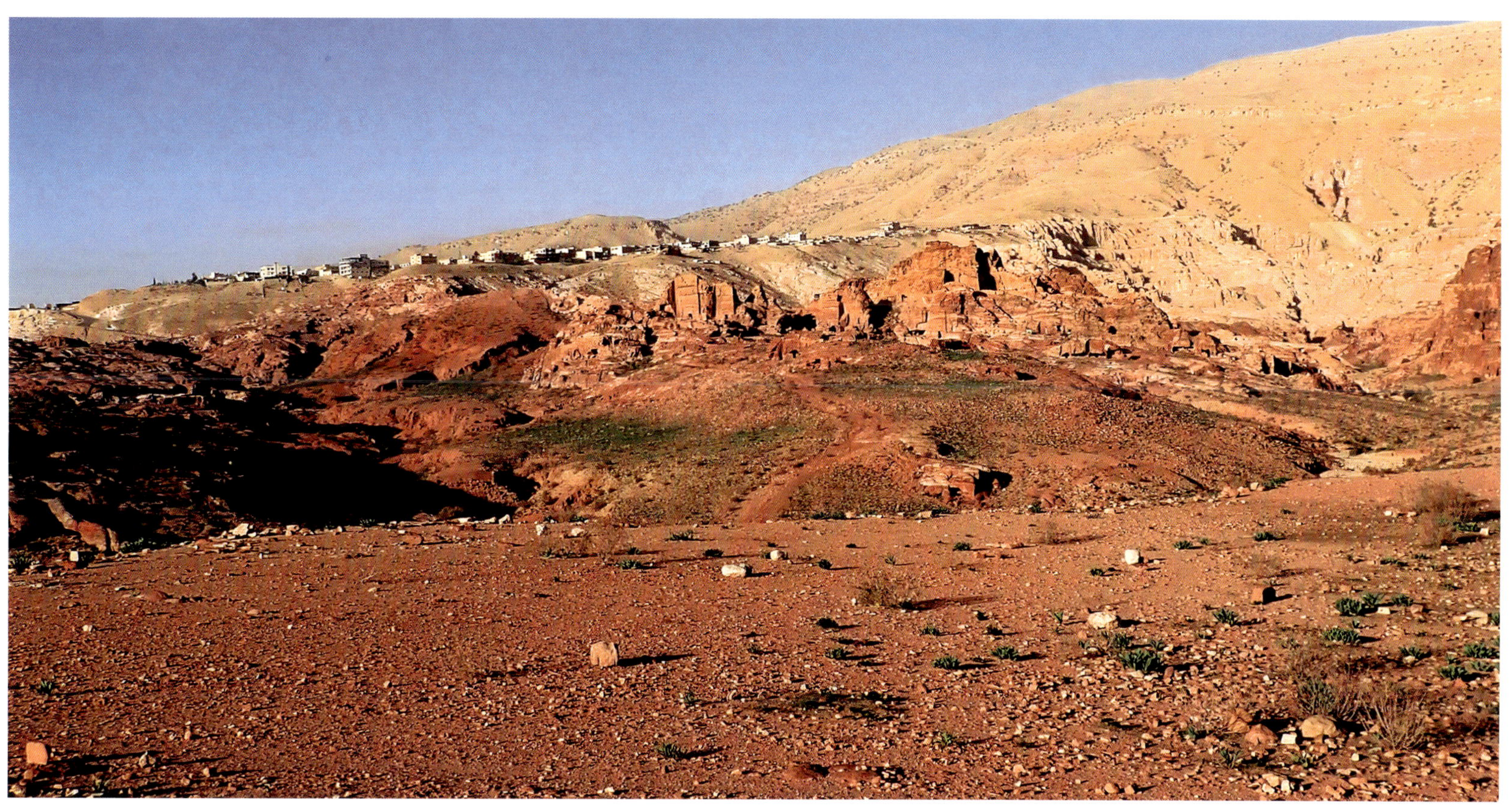

As seen from the northern edge of the Royal Tombs, this vantage of the Nasara Ridge displays several noteworthy features of modern Petra. Beyond the dramatic depletion of vegetation in the foreground, the most prominent change is the construction of Umm Sayhoun village along the plateau in the background. The time-worn footpath leading to and from the village transects the hillside, expertly navigating steep slopes, rock fall debris, and the looming Nasara Tombs above them.

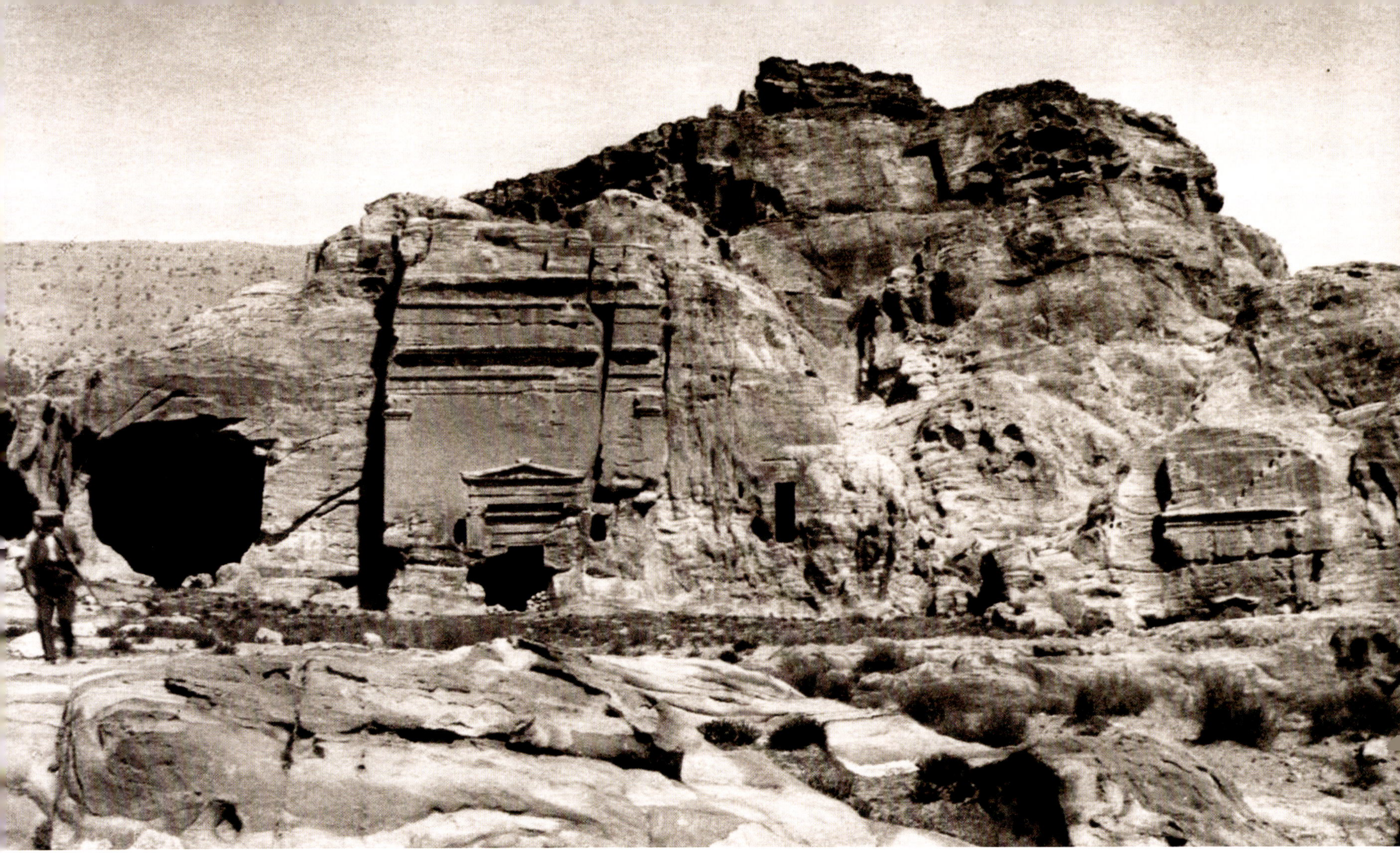

AL-NASARA MONUMENTS

"It is singular, and very notable, that in the Petraean monuments the large double crowsteps are always accompanied by the heavy cornice, and the cornice by the double crowsteps. A monument in al-Nasara, shows a very elaborate doorway and a perfectly plain attic, half the crowsteps being broken off. The occurrence of such grouped graves is no doubt an indication ... that as a place of worship, the Nasara district had some special sanctity." — SIR KENNEDY (1925, pg. 49, 50)

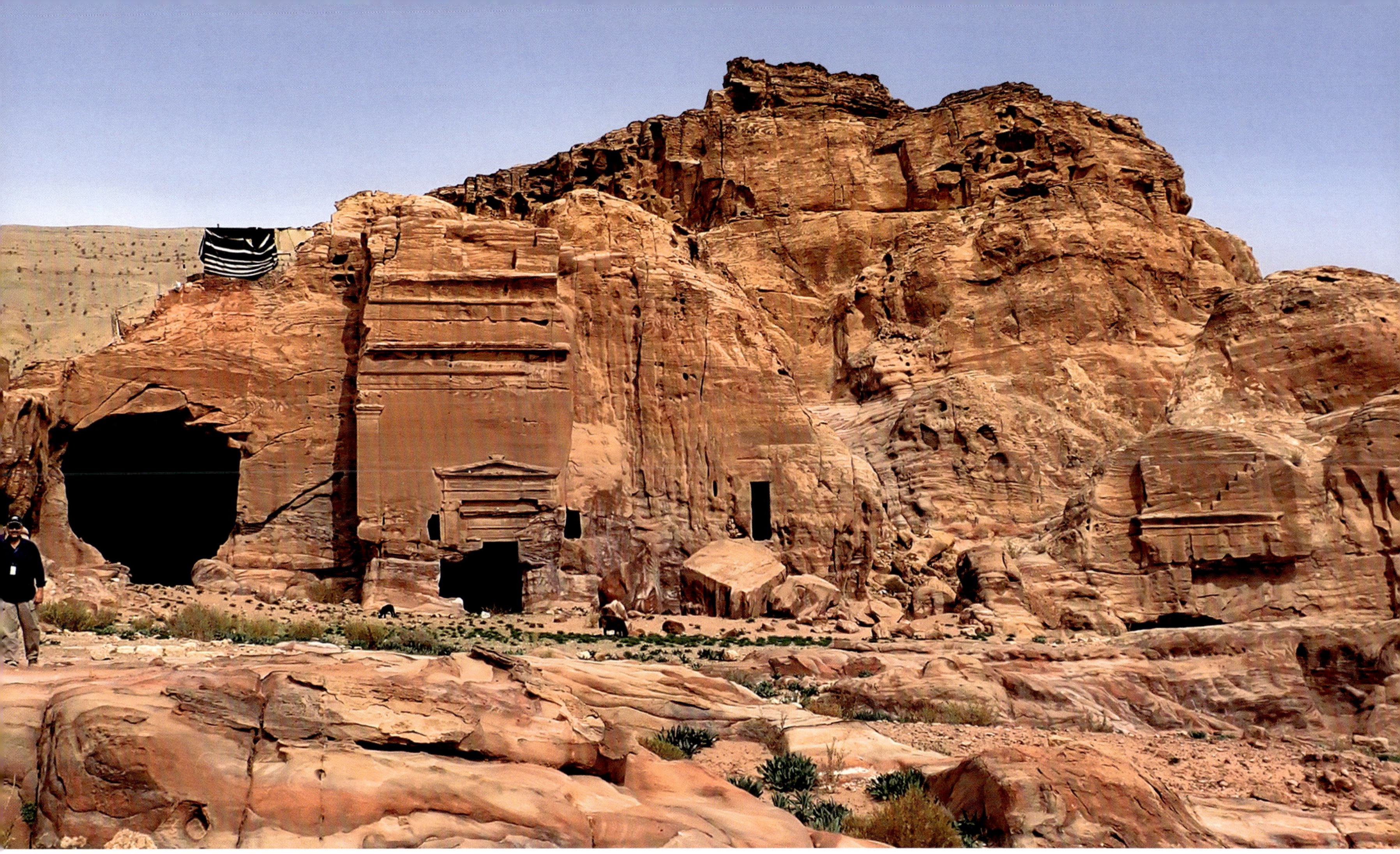

Since Sir Kennedy's visit, the central monument has lost a good deal more than just some crowsteps—an entire section has completely collapsed, its derelict remains now resting crumbled at the foot of the adjacent doorway. The smaller monument to the right has also lost substantial portions of its lower half. These types of large rock fall events have plagued several façades in Petra, mostly those carved in the softer, white Disi Sandstone, indicating localized areas of internal structural weaknesses within the stone itself. Even so, a small traditional Bedouin tent has been erected on the upper left ledge. Ever-vigilant field assistant, Dr. Casey Allen can be seen taking the place of the nameless gentleman in Sir Kennedy's photograph on the far left.

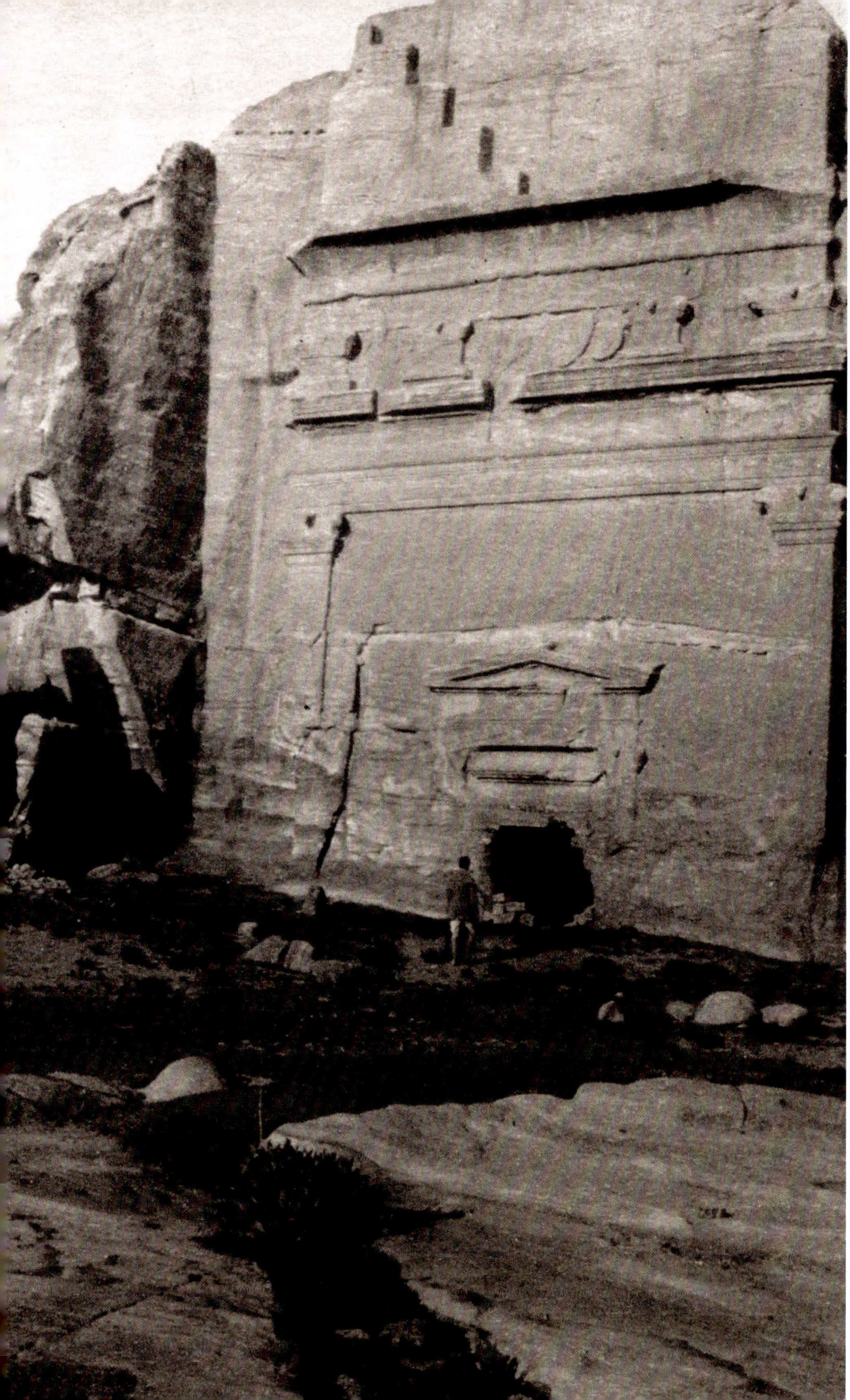

THE ARMOR TOMB

"[The photograph] appears to be a large triclinium... standing immediately above a hollow way which forms part of an ancient route from Petra northwards. The attic is so shallow as to allow just depth only for the copied capitals. Between them is placed a group of four shields and two medusa heads." — SIR KENNEDY (1925, pg. 50)

The four shield decorations of this façade
have earned this monument the moniker
of "Armor Tomb," but it takes a rather
determined imagination to identify Sir
Kennedy's medusa heads in the outer
recesses. There is evidence of more rock
fall to the left of the façade and a notable
change in ground covering vegetation.
Once again, Dr. Casey Allen reenacts the
steps of Sir Kennedy's unnamed companion
in the photograph.

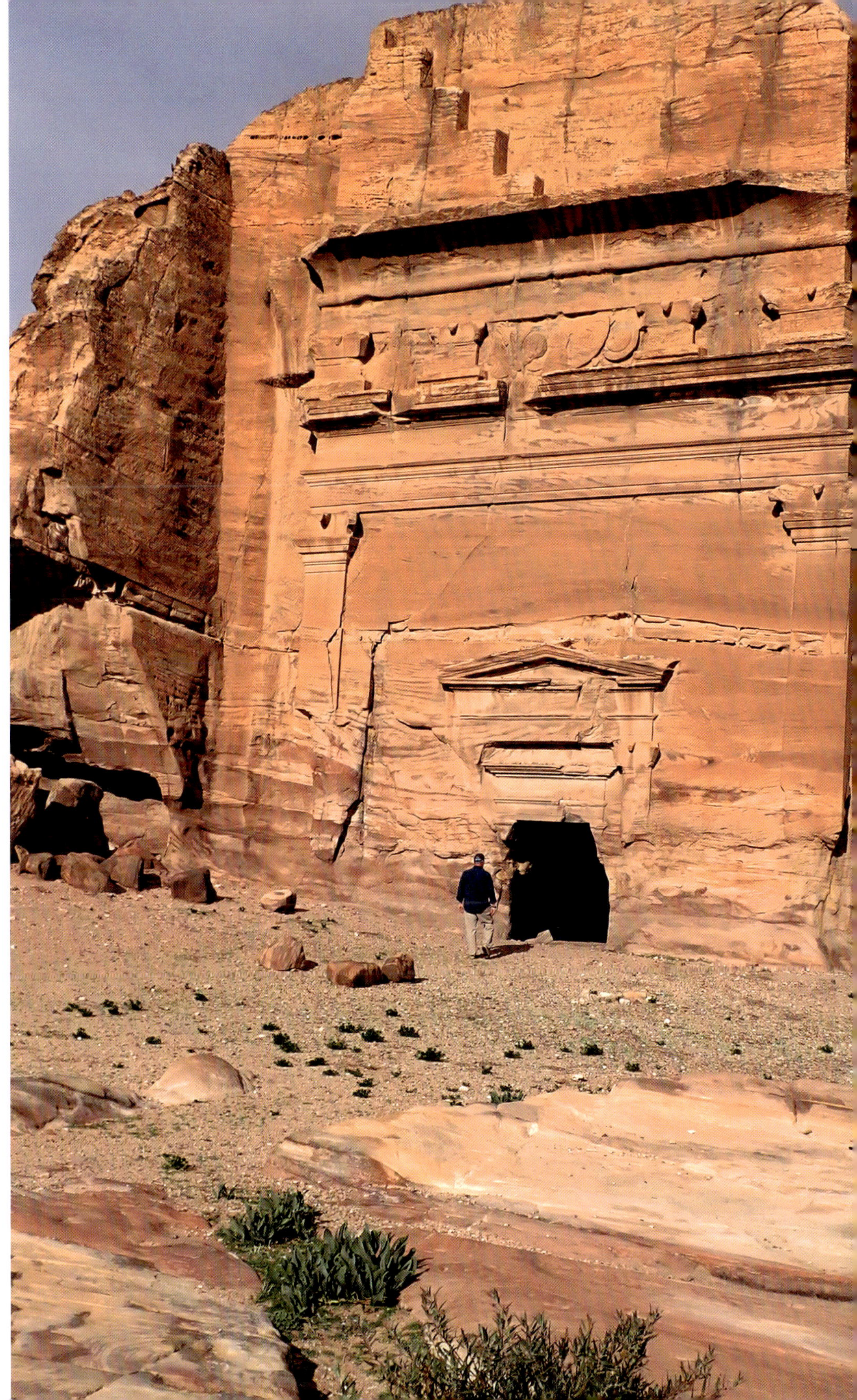

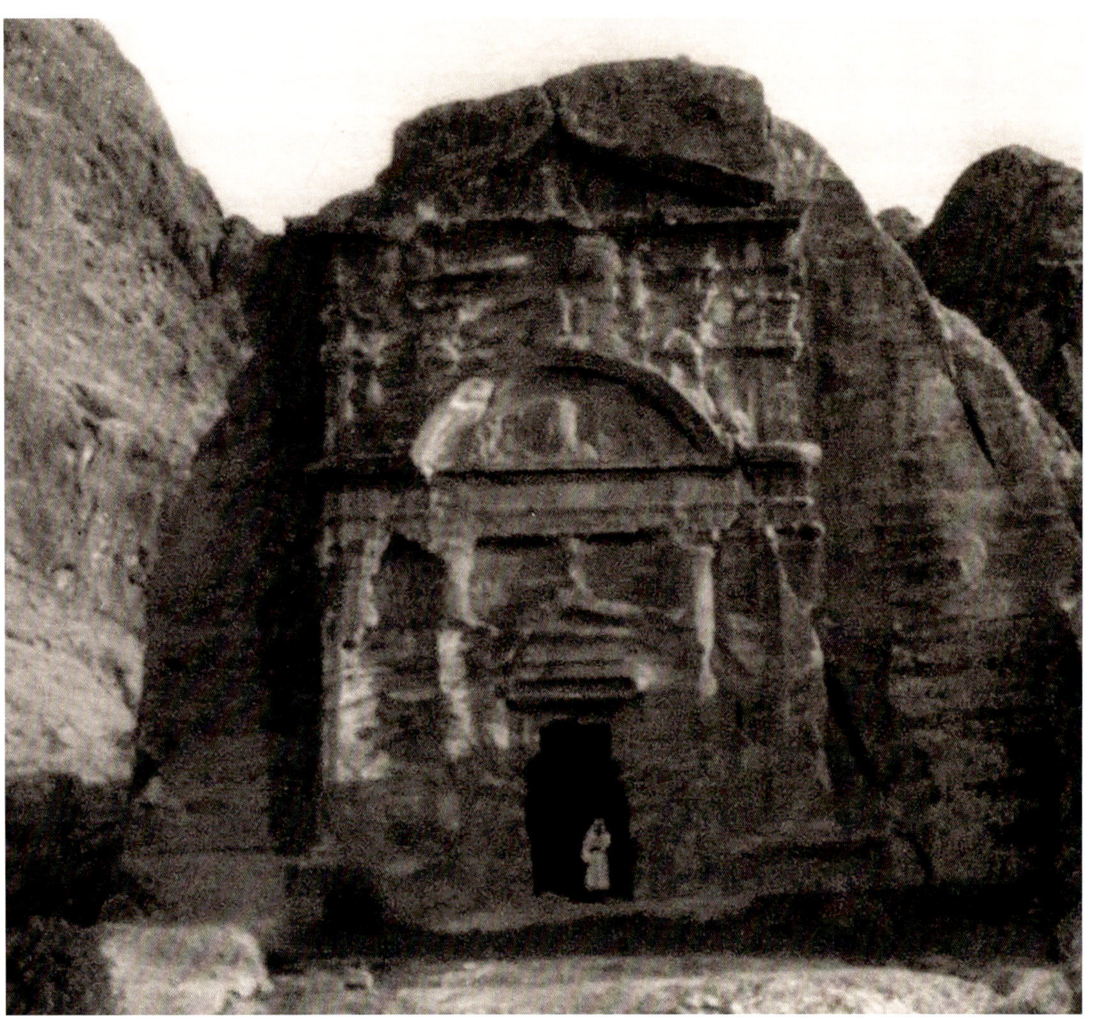

"The tomb of Florentinus has been made at the end of a somewhat narrow promontory projecting from the west face of al-Khubdha. The photograph shows the ornate nature of the façade as well as its ruined condition allows." — SIR KENNEDY (1925, pg. 56)

Returning to the Royals from the Nasara Ridge brings visitors past this remarkable hidden gem. The large Latin inscription across its upper cornice makes it one of the few tombs in Petra containing a written record of its original patron: in this case a second century Roman officer by the name of Sextius Florentinus. Providing a sense of scale and occupying the place of Sir Kennedy's Arab guide in the tomb's doorway is field assistant Casey Allen. Initially, this position was attempted by an older Bedouin woman who came by with her goat herd while we were waiting for the correct shadows to appear on the tomb's façade. She reminisced on how her grandfather used to live in this monument and pointed out the caves on a nearby cliff where her family has housed their goats for generations, reaffirmed by their bleating calls echoing through the canyon. Unfortunately, her traditional black *abaya* (dress) and *hijab* (head scarf) were too dark within the shaded doorway to clearly show in the repeat photograph, and Dr. Allen graciously replaced her.

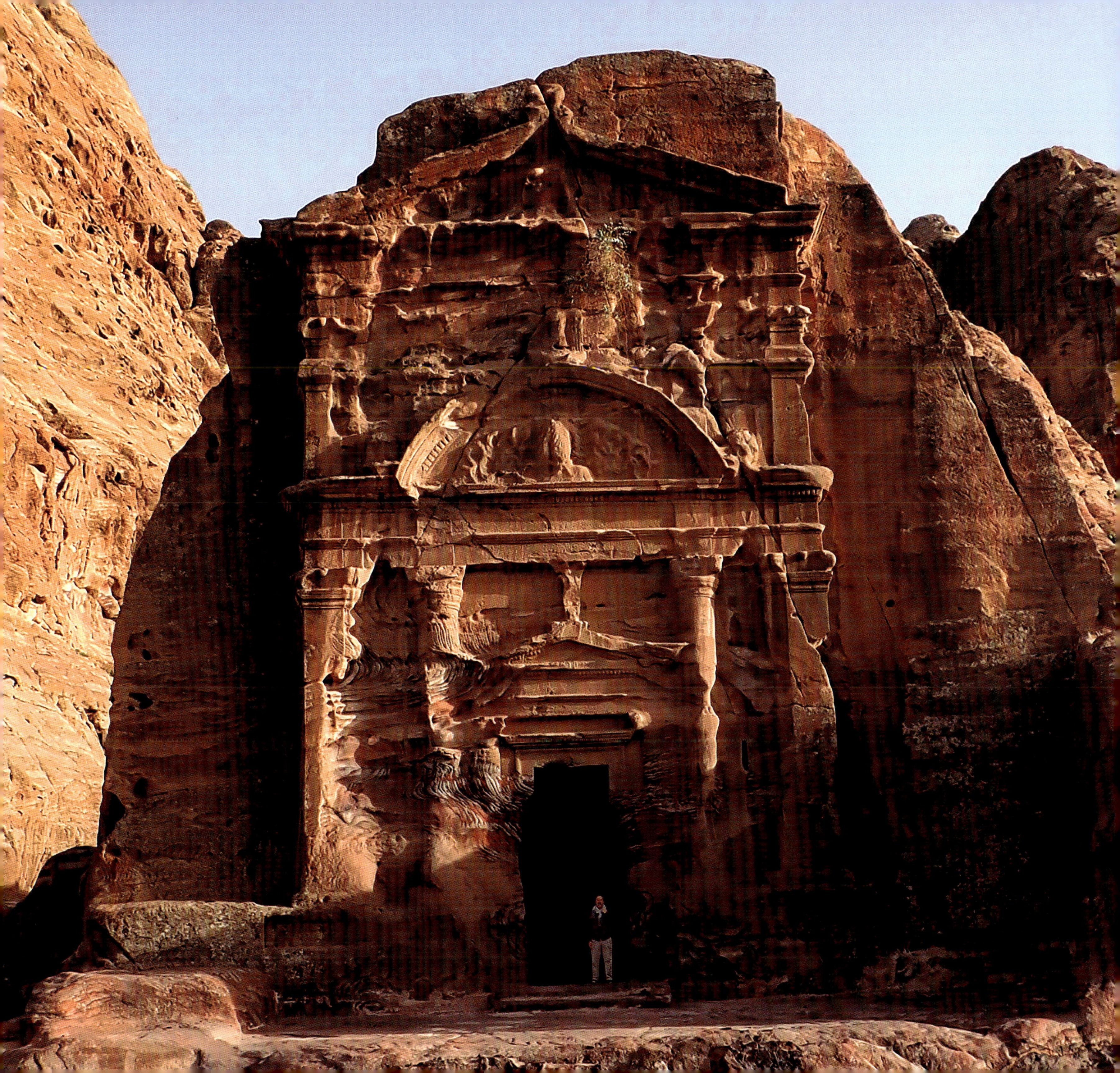

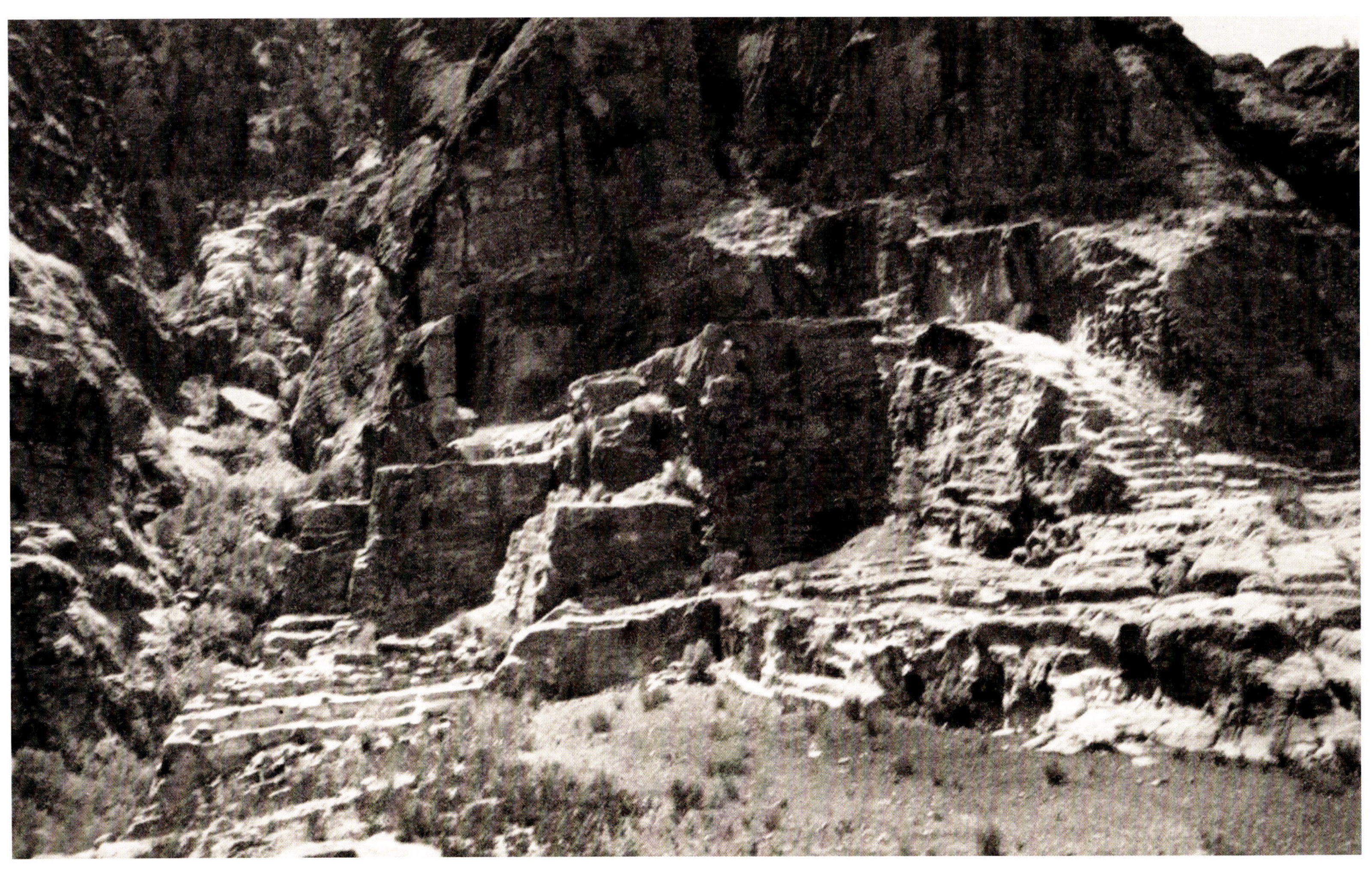

JABAL AL-KHUBTHA TRAILHEAD

"The route [of al-Khubtha Trail] which has probably been the most important starts by the gully beyond the Florentinus tomb, which can either be ascended directly from the ground or by the flight of steps beside it."
—SIR KENNEDY (1925, pg. 71)

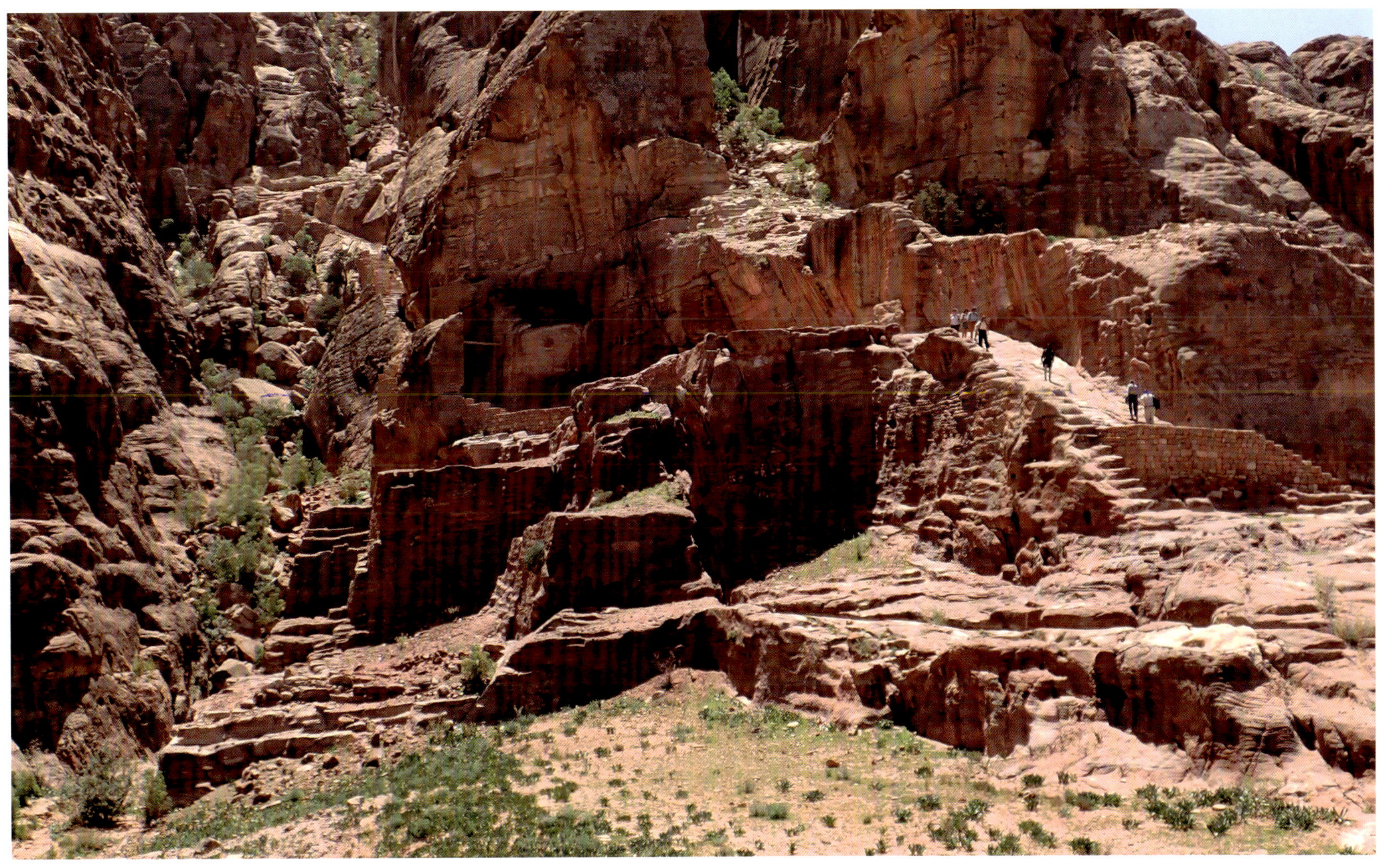

Taken from atop the protruding outcrop housing the Florentinus Tomb, the trailhead of the strenuous al-Khubtha trail seems to have only experienced relatively minor changes. The stairway mentioned by Sir Kennedy has been reinforced with modern steps, seen to the right with visitors for scale, and the colossal stone pillar adorning the narrow trail has been secured with a large beam attaching it to the adjacent mountainside. It is also heartening to see vegetation in this area is still thriving with new trees in the upper valleys and verdant grasses blanketing the stone platform at the base of the trail.

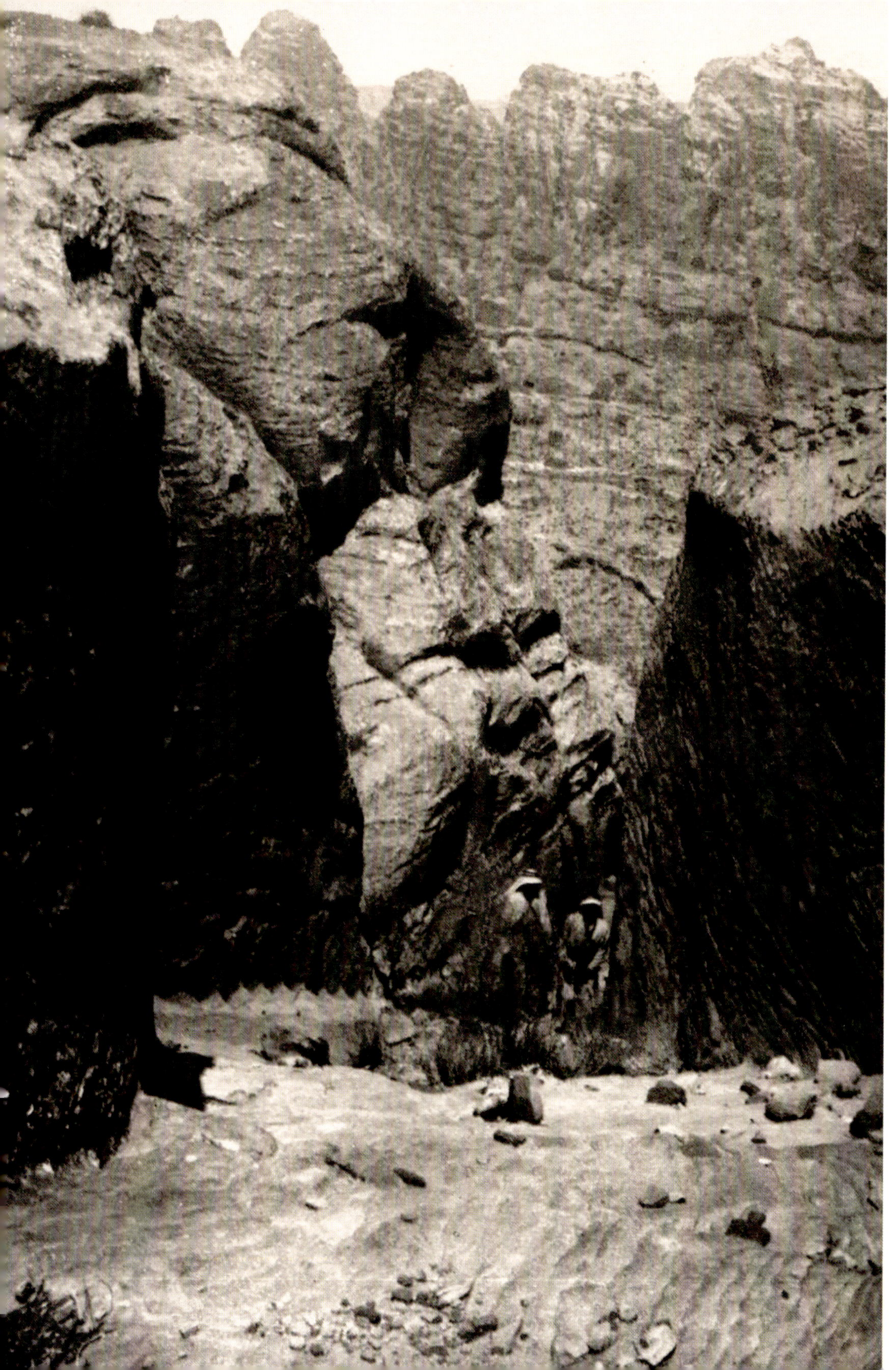

AL-KHUBTHA TRAIL STEPS

"The trouble which must have been taken to cut out this gangway is some indication of the great importance of the places of worship to which it led." — SIR KENNEDY (1925, pg. 71)

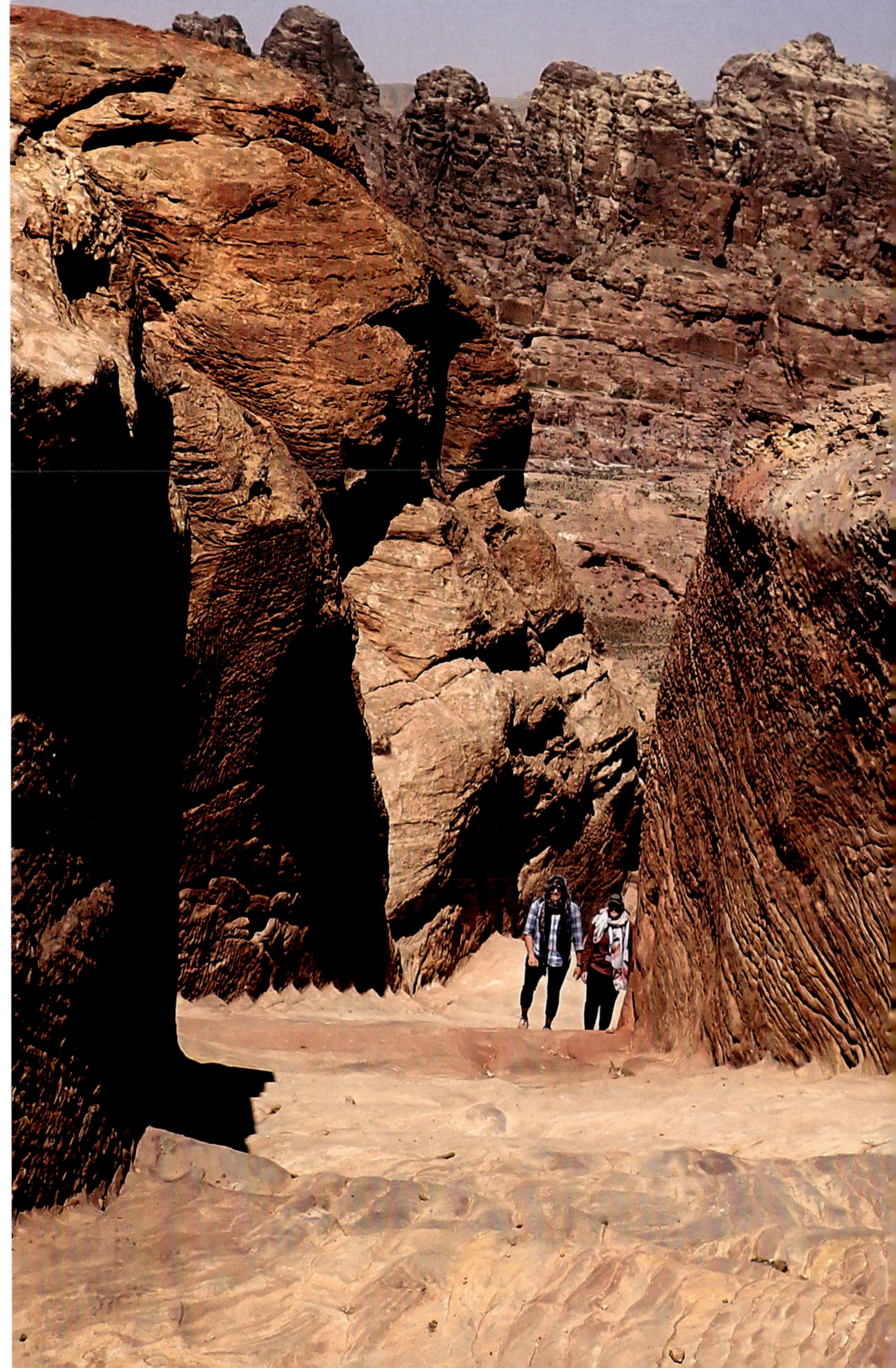

Since Sir Kennedy's visit, the vibrant sandstone steps of the al-Khubtha trail have been cleared of loose debris and rebellious vegetation growing through the cracks, making the stark channeled stairway even more dramatic. The "trouble" now is simply making the arduous climb, shown here with field assistants McKay Barker (left) and Molly Groom (right).

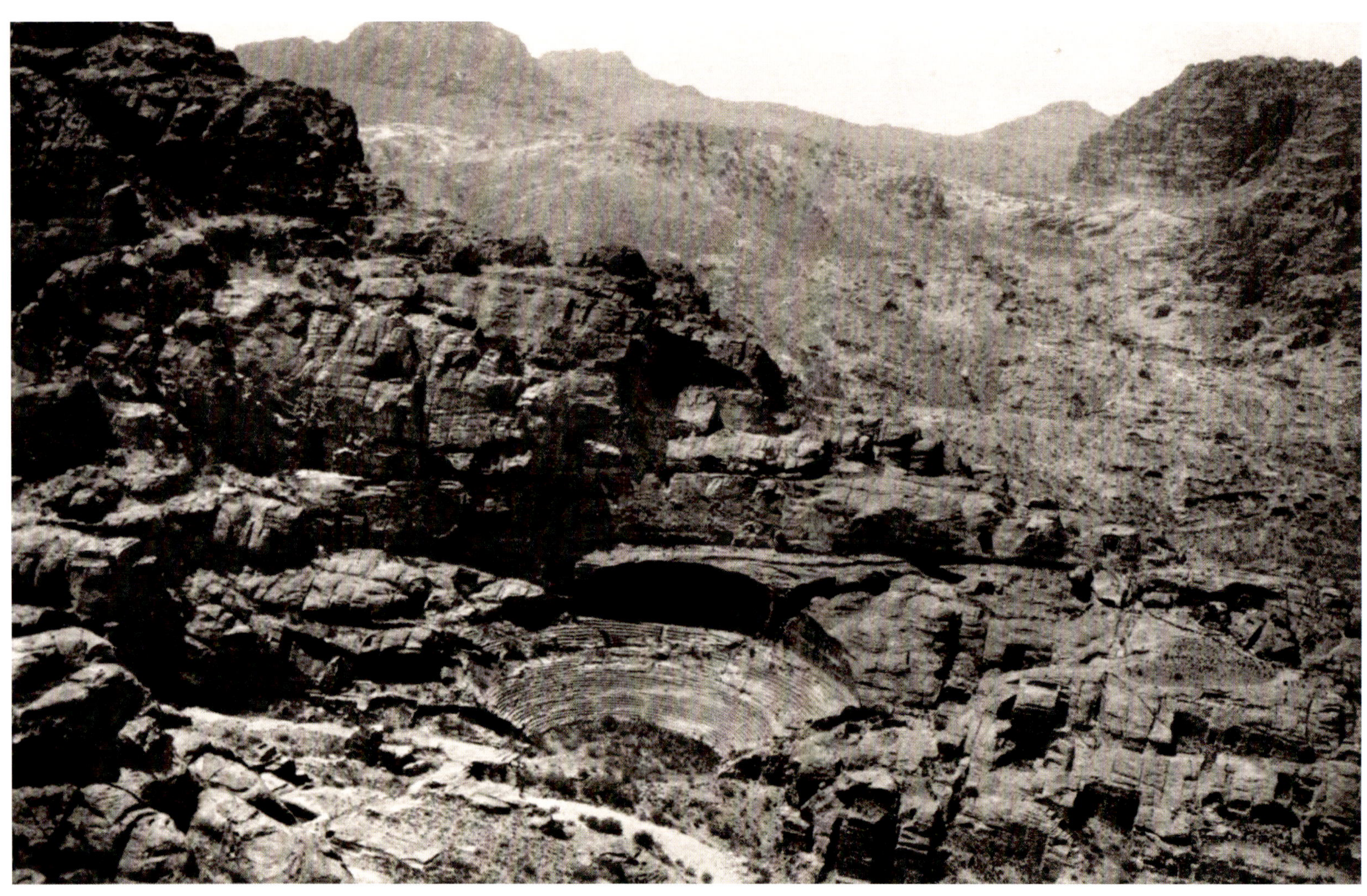

**ROMAN THEATRE
FROM ABOVE**

"All photographs of the theatre taken from near ground-level give it, inevitably, [a] flat appearance... Seen from a height, as from al-Khubdha, its proportions are much better seen, and it is shown to cover more nearly a half-circle." — SIR KENNEDY (1925, pg. 60)

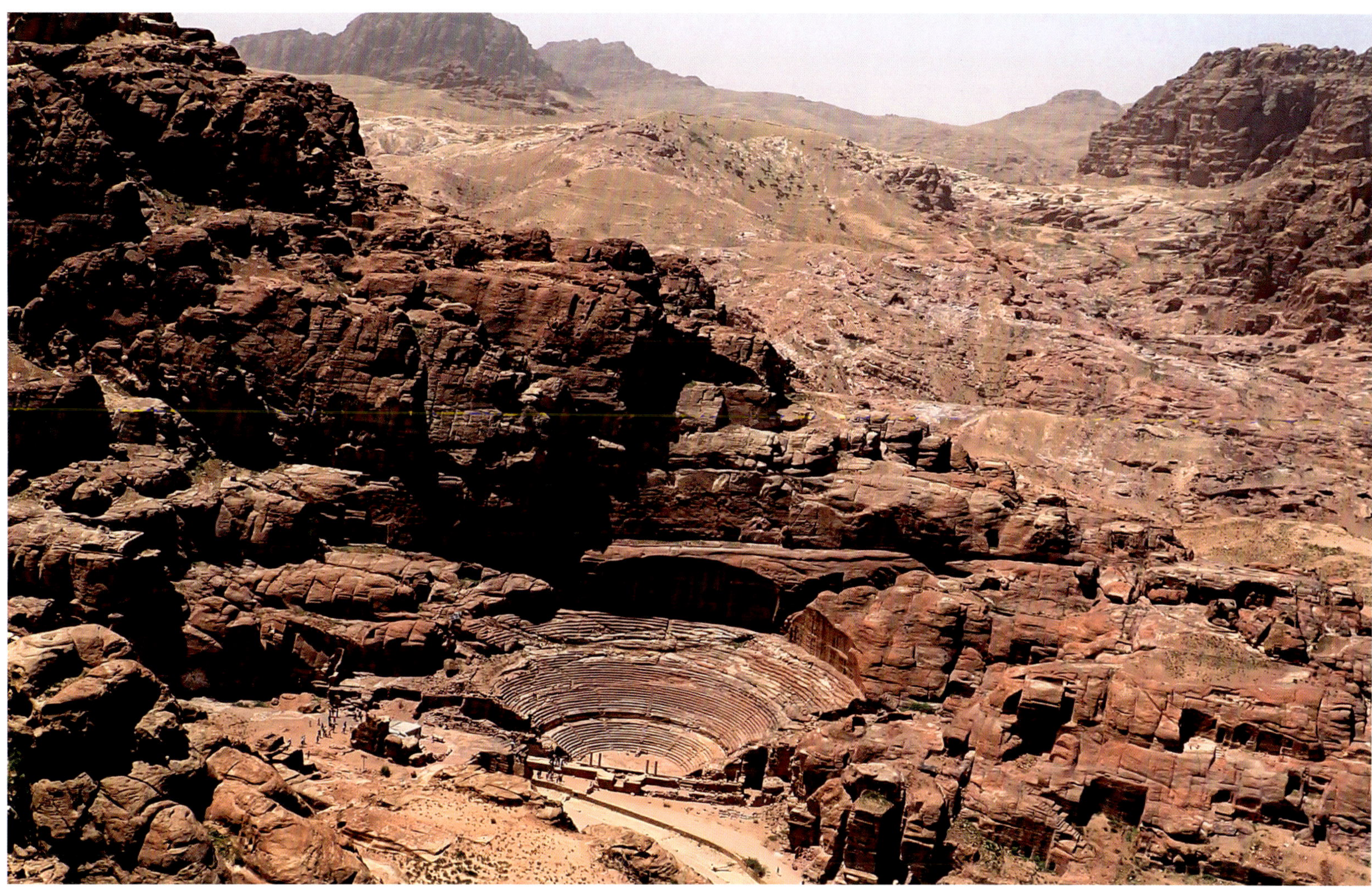

Visitors tenacious enough to make the grueling climb up the eastern mountain are rewarded by this panoramic view of the theatre and valley beyond. As stated in Sir Kennedy's caption, the concave shape and goliath size of the theatre can be better appreciated from above—as well as its restorations and the development of roads and cleared walking trails in front of it. Next to the viewpoint of this photo is a traditional Bedouin hospitality tent offering a place of respite for visitors still catching their breath from the ascent. These tents, woven from goat hair, provide shelter from the scorching sun, chilling desert nights, and occasional seasonal downpour. I have enjoyed many cups of tea with Bedouin friends at this particular outlook before heading farther up the trail to the peak of Jabal al-Khubtha and a stunning view from above al-Khazneh.

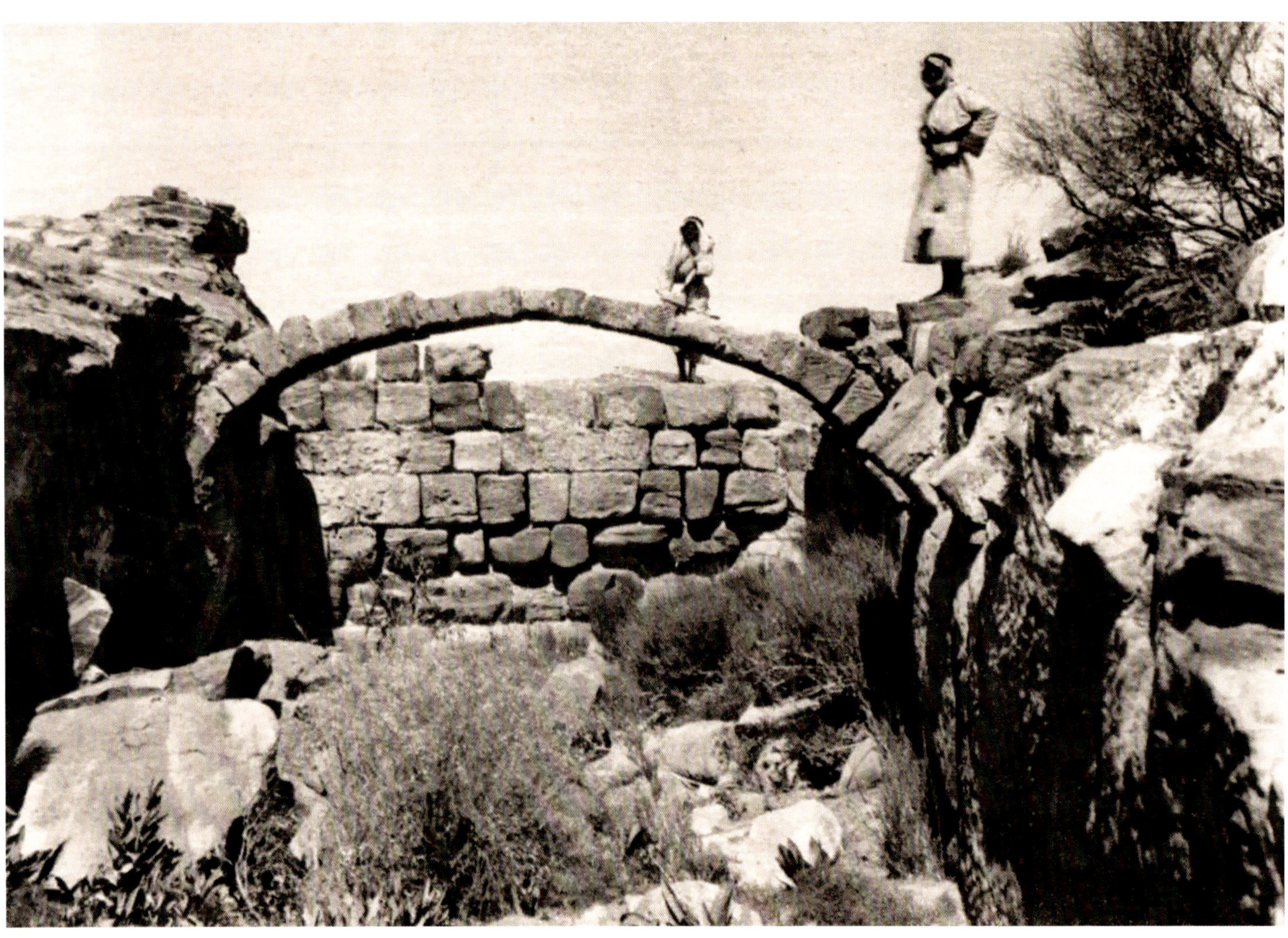

"A continuation of the original gully [above he 'Palace'] shows on the right-hand the remains of a large water-channel. At its upper end the gully is closed by the wall of a large reservoir, which has obviously once been arched over. (The photograph shows the springing blocks of the arch, or arches, on the right.)"
— SIR KENNEDY (1925, pg. 71, 72)

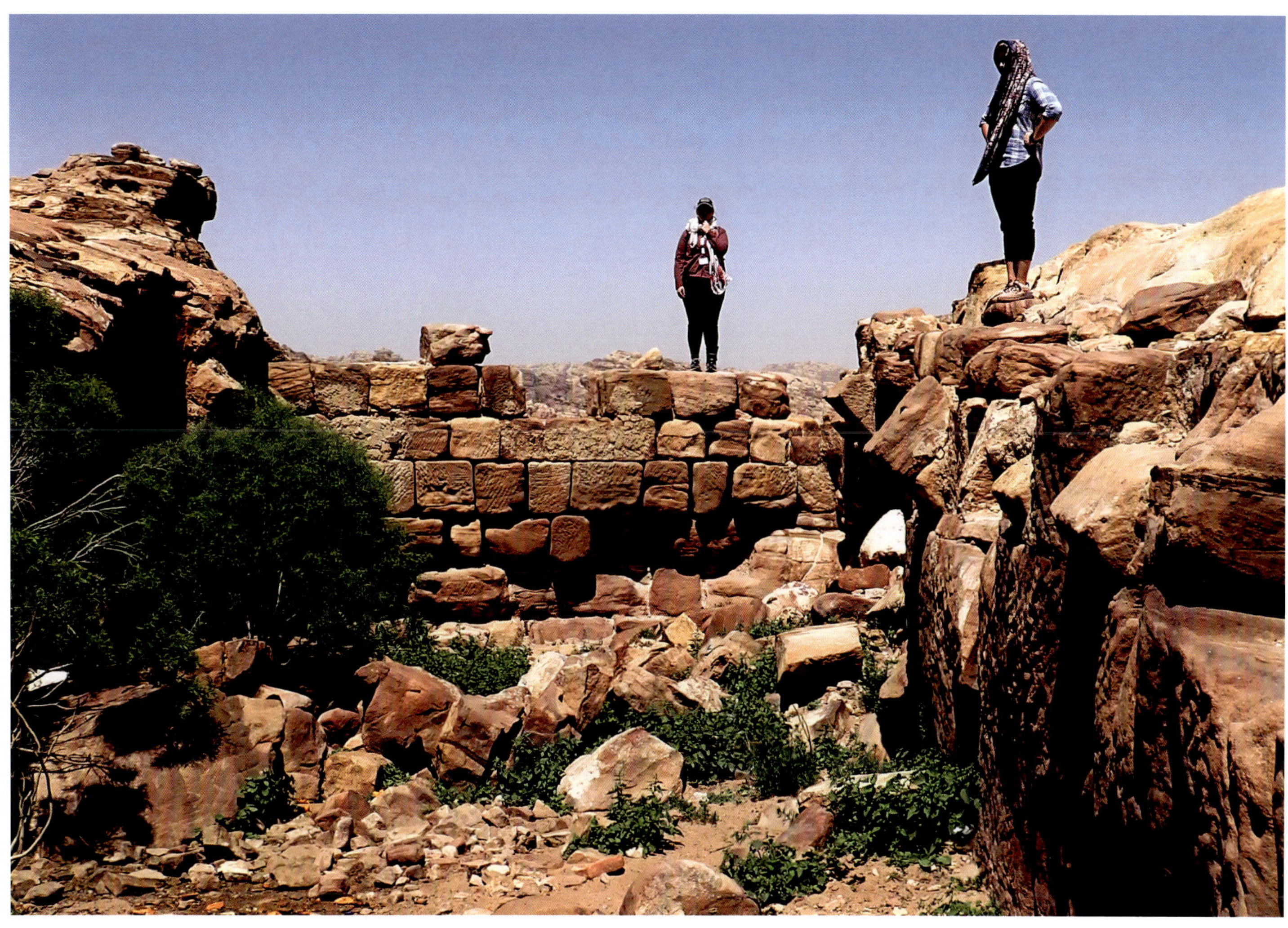

Nestled on the rugged apex of Jabal al-Khubtha, this large rectangular cistern has succumbed to the unremitting toll of nature and time—its lonely arch collapsing to join the other broken arches as rubble in the cistern's basin. Imagine how magnificent this cistern would have been with multiple stone arches, each sprouting from the empty footers mounted along its upper rim. Many early explorers to Petra mention a grand arch spanning the narrow width of the Bab as-Siq (the entrance to the Siq ravine) but it had fallen even before Sir Kennedy's expedition—much to his disappointment. Similarly, my climb up Jabal al-Khubtha was hopeful, excited to see the reservoir's impressive arch, only to be equally dismayed finding it in pieces. However, the hearty vegetation within its walls speak to the cistern's lasting ability to retain water, a testament to the Nabataean's water management prowess. In place of Sir Kennedy's companions are field assistants Molly Groom (center) and McKay Barker (right).

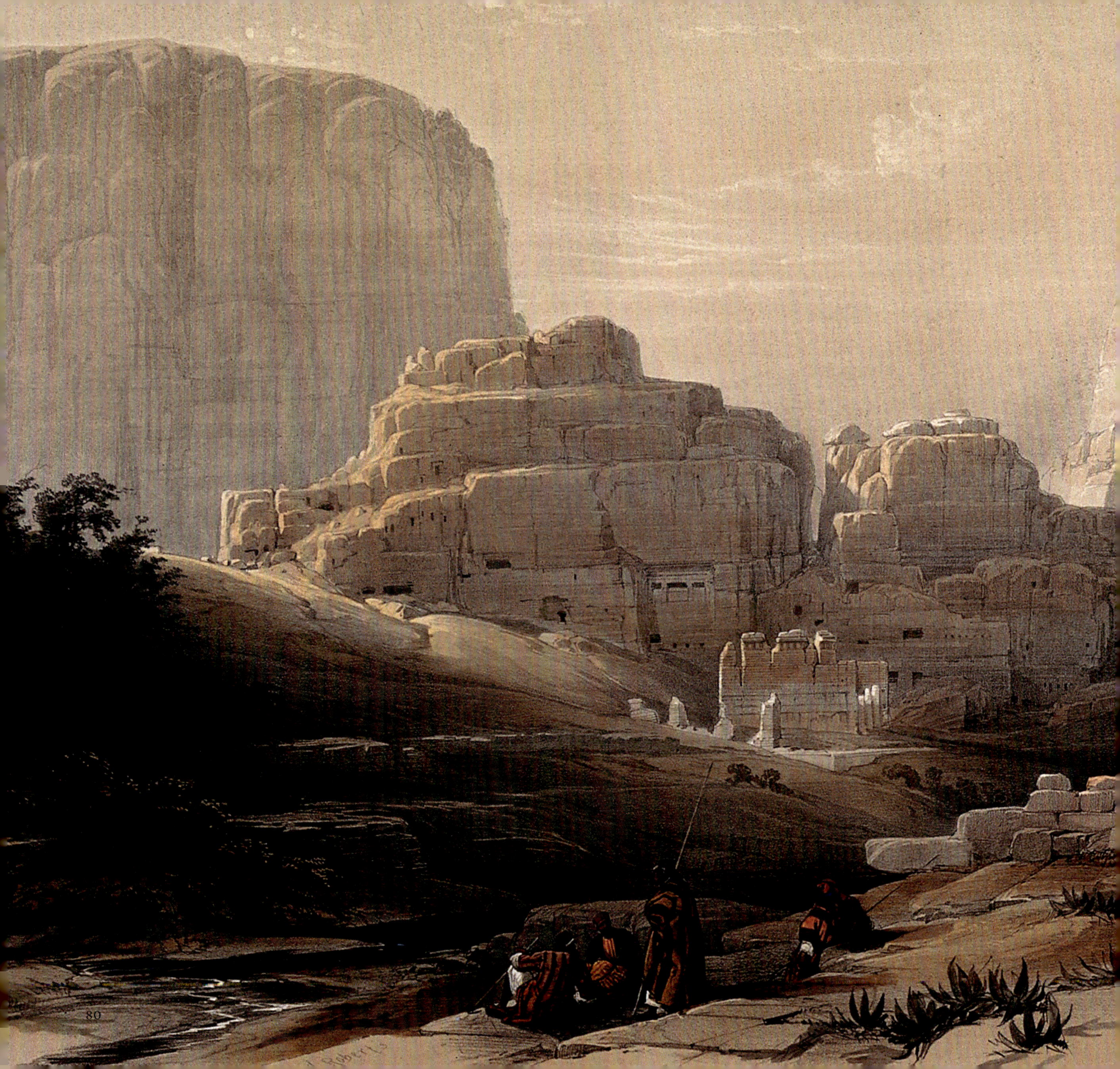

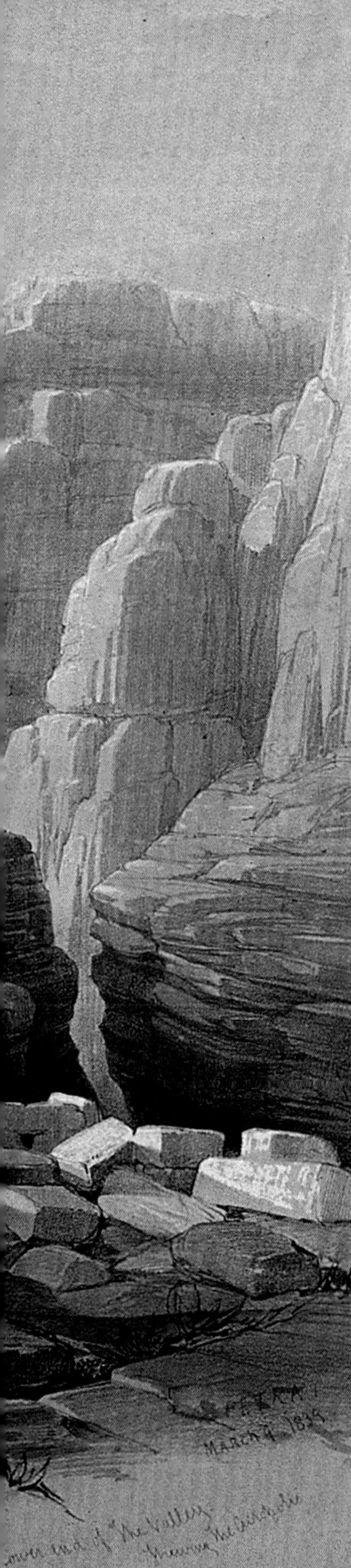

Lithograph by nineteenth-century artist David Roberts of the looming Al Habis outcrop with the resolute Qasr Al Bint at its base.

Center of It All:
Qasr al-Bint, al-Habis, and Wadi Turkmaniya

Housing most of Petra's Roman-Era structures, the city center is unique for its built monuments, as opposed to being carved directly into the mountains. The central corridor also exhibits significant modern development as well as decades-long excavations and reconstruction, further highlighting various tourism adaptations seen throughout the city.

"Here the ground is covered with heaps of hewn stone, foundations of buildings, fragments of columns, and vestiges of paved streets; all clearly indicated that a large city once existed here. In the valley near the river, the buildings have probably been swept away by the impetuosity of the winter torrent; but even here are still seen the foundations of a temple and heaps of broken columns; close to which is a large *birket*, or reservoir of water, still serving for the supply of the inhabitants during the summer." — MR. JOHANN LUDWIG BURCKHARDT [8]

"What a busy scene Petra must have presented when a caravan arrived! The clerks and the customs officers hurried out to meet the long string of heavily loaded camels outside the town, to take stock of their merchandise. To the merchants and drivers it must have seemed like arriving at a gay metropolis after their toilsome march across the desert waste from one oasis to another. How different from these streets that were crowded with the living are the empty tombs where the footfall is noiseless on the fine, heaped-up red sand." — MRS. STEUART ERSKINE [9]

8 J. L. Burckhardt, *Travels in Syria and the Holy Lands* (London: John Murray Publishing, 1822), 427.
9 Erskine, The Vanished Cites of Arabia, 34-35

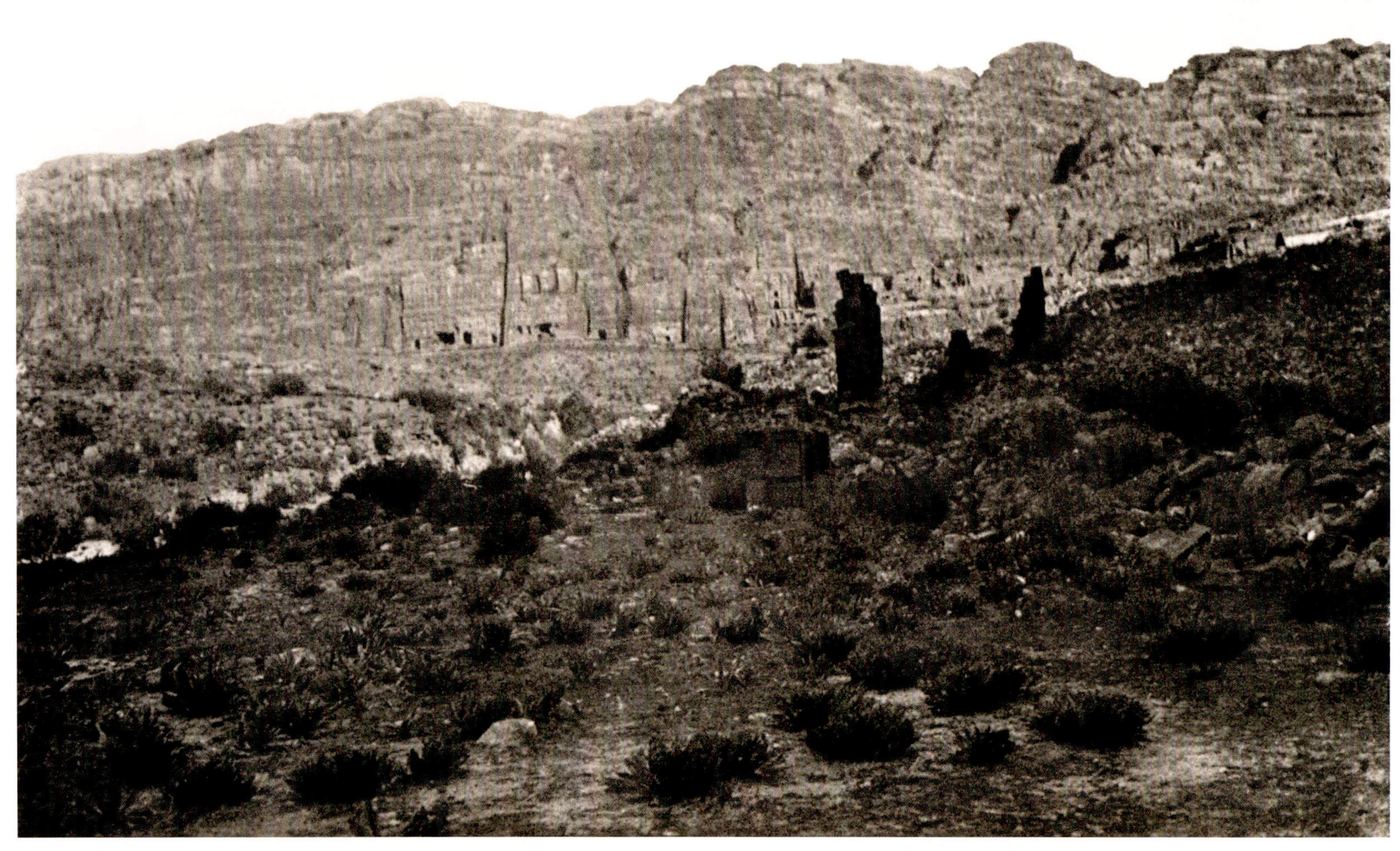

CITY CENTER AT SUNSET

"The Roman city which flourished for several centuries, and once covered both banks of the wadi Musa, is now represented practically only by ruins. The sites of at least two temples are indicated by their fallen columns, and also the probable site of baths." — SIR KENNEDY (1925, pg. 59)

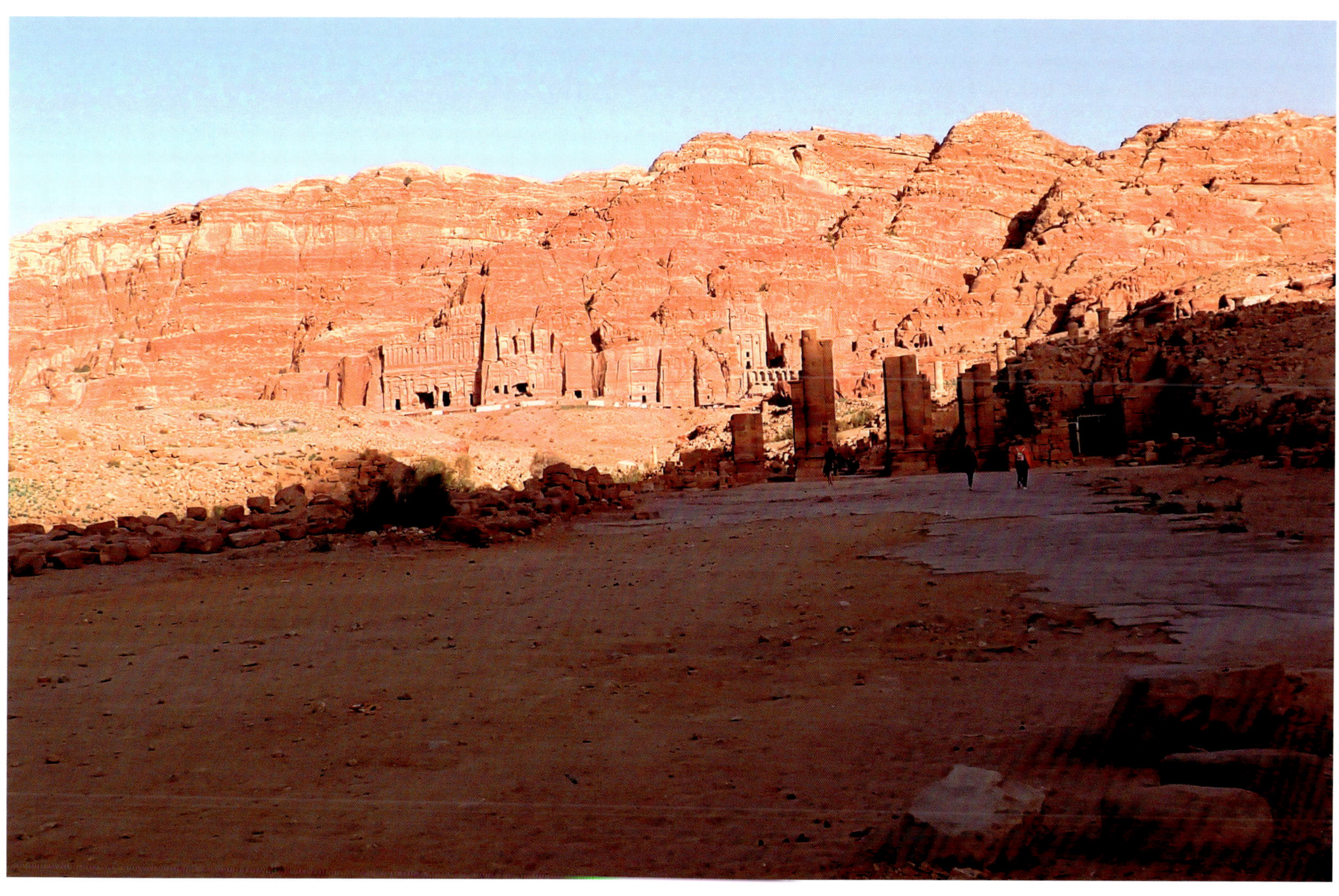

Taken at that golden hour when the setting sun casts its warm glow across the eastern highlands, this photograph captures the prestige of the aptly named Royal Tombs as they overlook the entire city center —which has experienced notable change over the years. As mentioned in Sir Kennedy's musings, the city center is indeed the location of substantial Roman architecture, including Sir Kennedy's predicted bath complex. From 1993 to 2000 Brown University (USA) excavated and conserved the Great Temple, whose reconstructed pillar-lined court is seen peaking above the rubble wall just beyond the Roman Gate (center). Perhaps the most dramatic change, however, is the exposure and expansion of the original Roman street itself, complete with large rectangular paving stones scarred with long grooves and indentations from centuries of carts and carriages traversing the path. The walkway has also been broadened to accommodate modern flood control measures in the central wadi, highlighted by the loose paving stones lining the dry riverbed's edge (left).

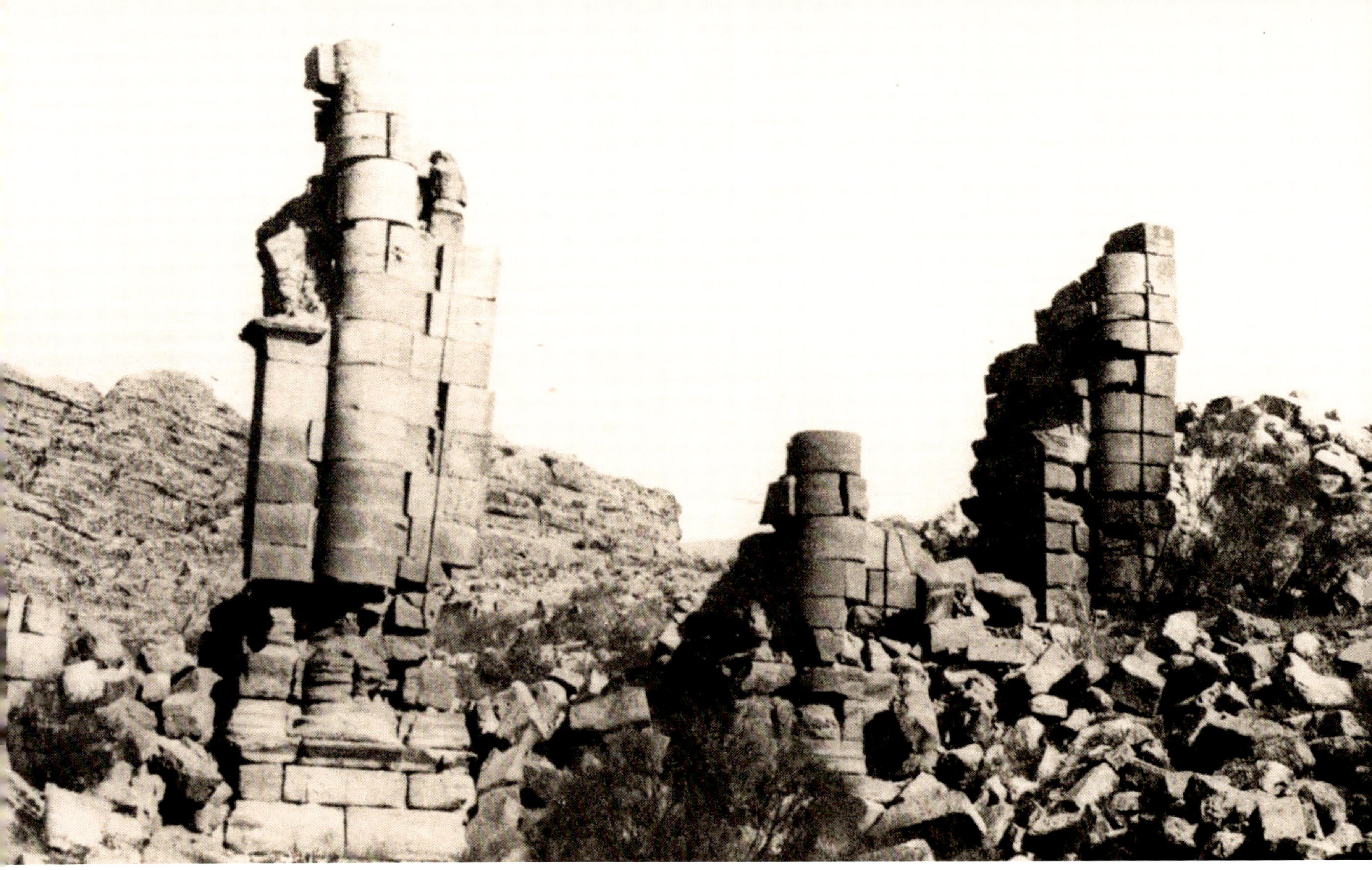

THE ROMAN TEMENOS GATE

"The piers of the archway were once decorated with applied plaques like the Temple, and the stones now lying all round them show moulded carvings. From the archway the line of road was bordered on the north by columns, of which the bases only are left, as far at least as a great square clearing which may have been the forum." — SIR KENNEDY (1925, pg. 60)

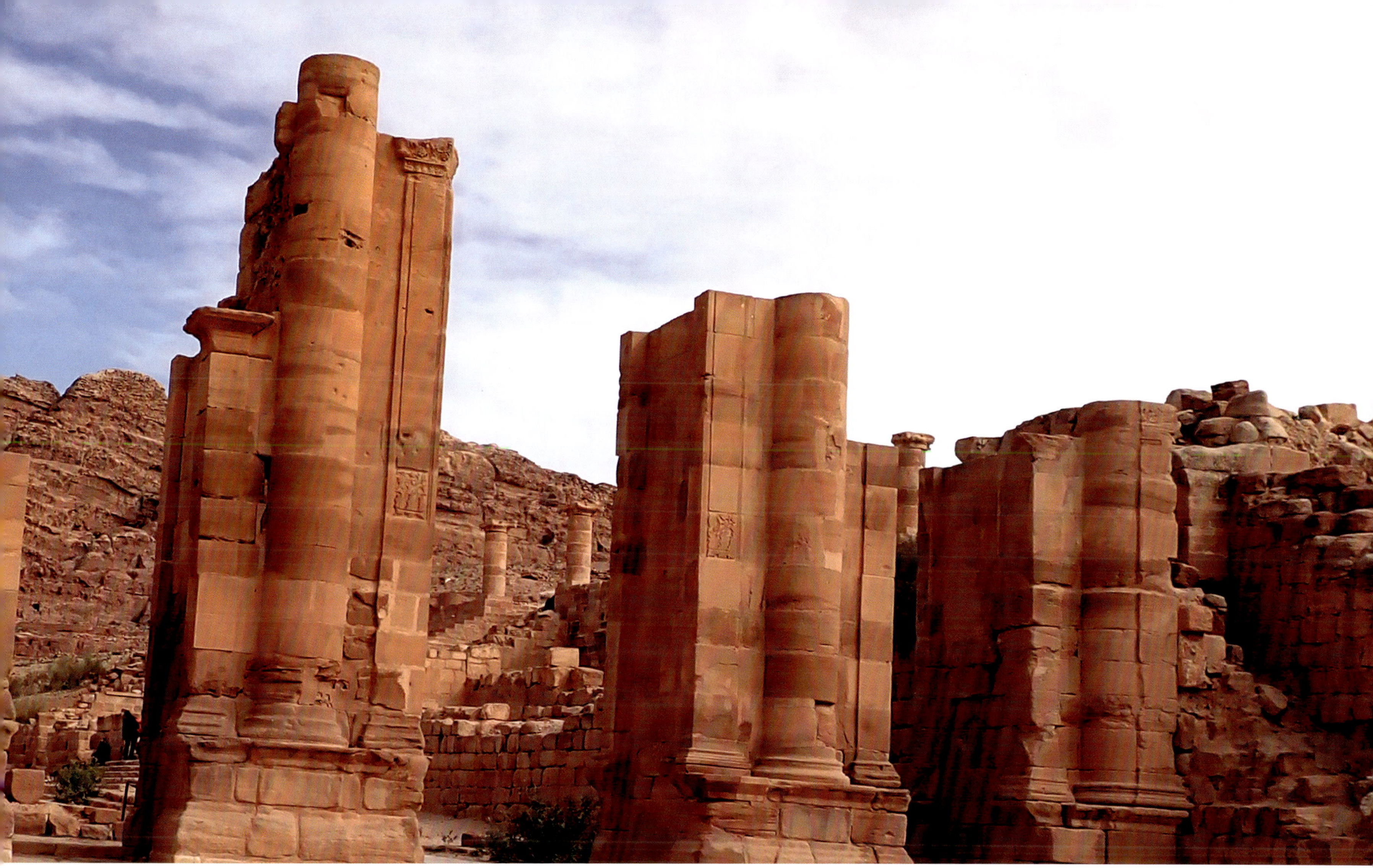

Here is a closer look at the fragmented Roman Temenos Gate that still beckons visitors to what was once the bustling colonnaded street of Roman-Era Petra. Many of the loose stones mentioned by Sir Kennedy were reintegrated into the large pillars during the restoration of the colonnaded street by the Jordanian Department of Antiquities in the late 1960s and early 1970s.

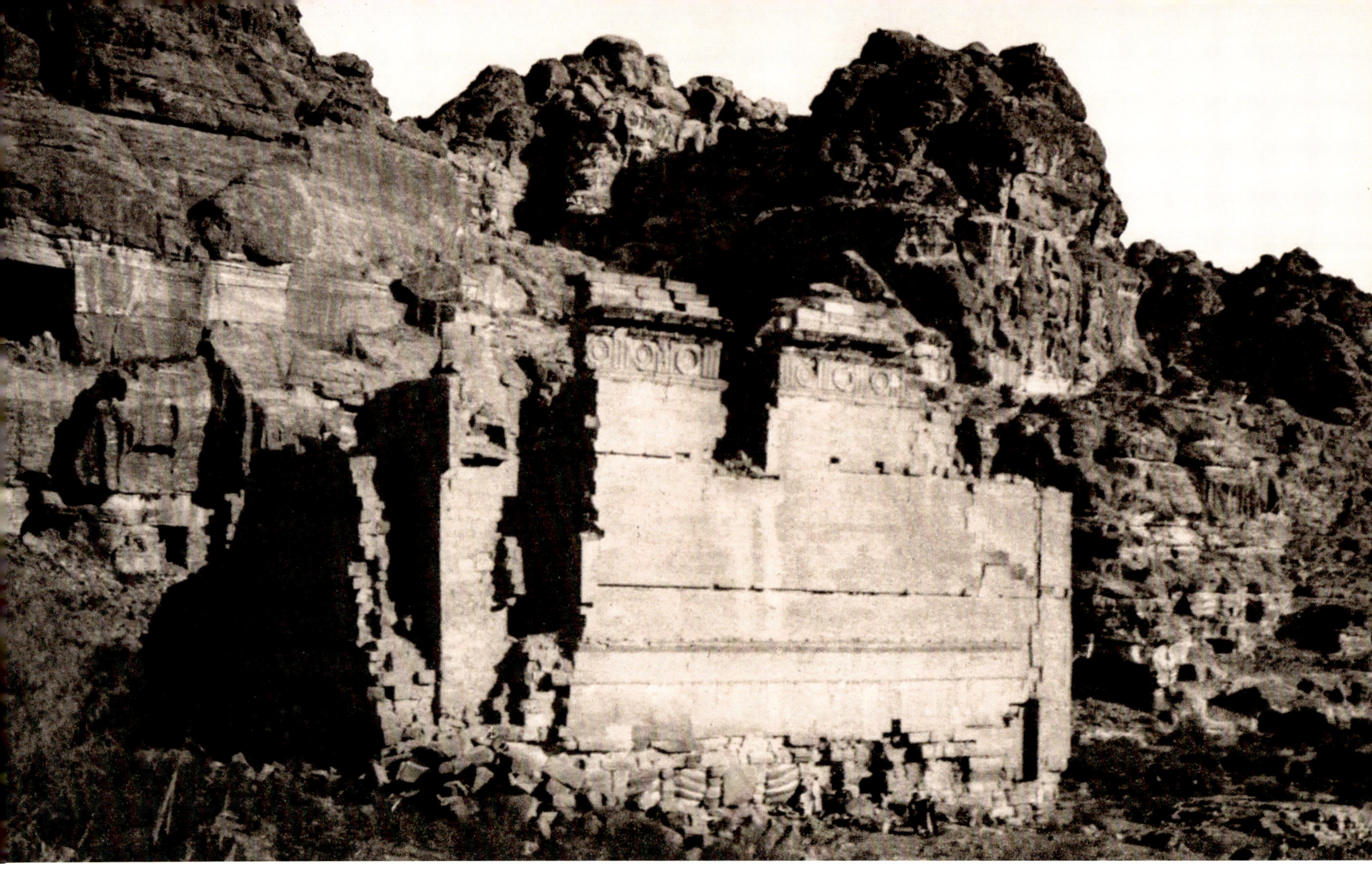

QASR AL-BINT

"The only building left standing, or partially standing, is that known as the Qasr al-Bint, or Qasr Bint Fir'un (the palace of the daughter of Pharaoh). It stands near the entrance to the Siyagh, and under the rock of al-Habis, the so-called 'Acropolis.' It has been frequently suggested that the existence of the upper storeys favours the idea that the building was rather a dwelling-place than a temple, but the reasoning seems inconclusive." — SIR KENNEDY (1925, pg. 60)

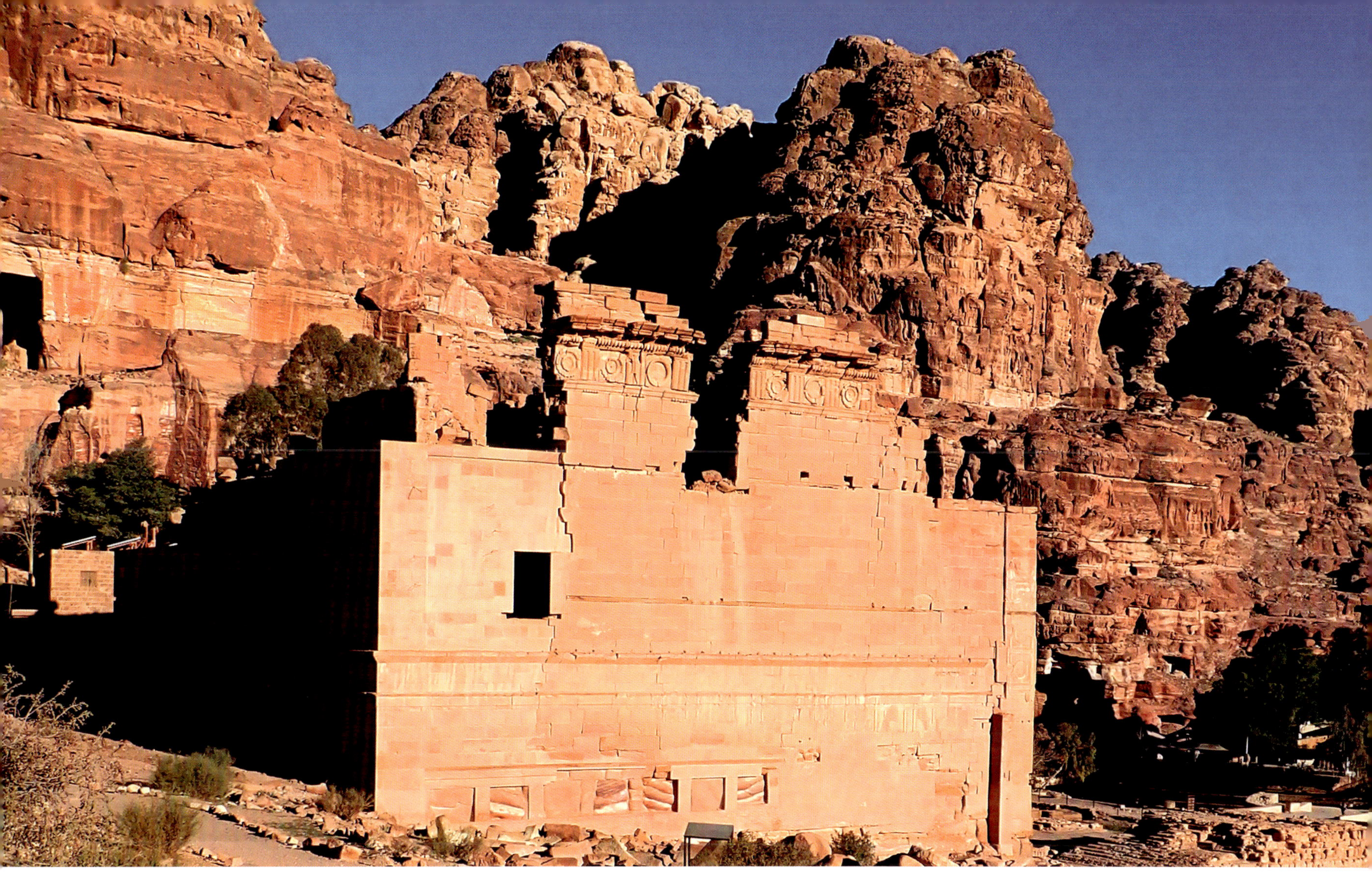

The lonely figure of the Qasr al-Bint still punctuates the western end of the Roman street, seen here from a trail leading above the Great Temple to the Wadi Farasa. The most obvious change between the photographs is the southwestern corner's significant restoration, completed by the Jordanian Department of Antiquities in 1985, highlighted in the repeated image by the bright early morning sun. Less obvious in the images are the changes surrounding the solitary building. Directly to the west (left), the historic Nazal Camp dig house and its shade trees peek out from behind the solitary monument. This building was renovated in 1995 and still hosts visiting archaeology teams conducting research in Petra. Across the valley (bottom right), the Basin Restaurant offers visitors traditional Jordanian meals or respite on their large veranda, whose copious voluminous trees provide an unexpected, but much appreciated, oasis from the harsh desert sun.

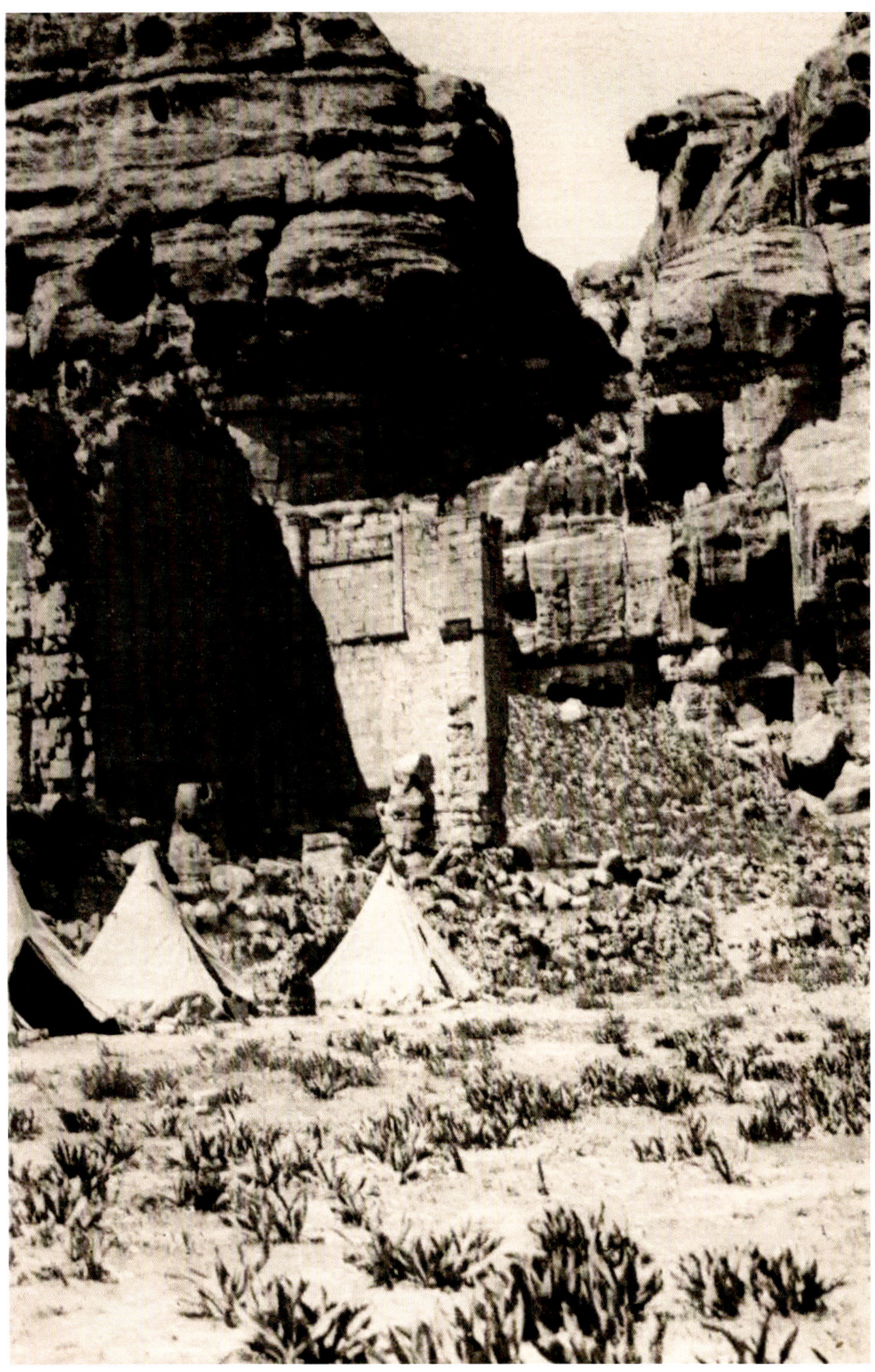

FRONT COURT OF QASR AL-BINT

"The pronaos [front court of Qasr al-Bint] is quite open, with four columns. In its back wall, which is virtually the front-wall of the Temple, is a huge arch of 20-feet span."
— SIR KENNEDY (1925, pg. 60)

Recapturing a different photograph of the arch itself was made impossible by the reconstruction of the back wall—from whose ruins the original photograph was taken. But the impressive span of stone and mortar is visible in the leftmost edge of these images. The four columns in the central vestibule mentioned by Sir Kennedy are made even more pronounced by the ongoing excavation of the entrance staircase, its brilliant white marble steps visible on the far right. Beyond the temple, the large tree shading the Nazal Camp building is a marked change from the debris-covered slope present during Sir Kennedy's visit.

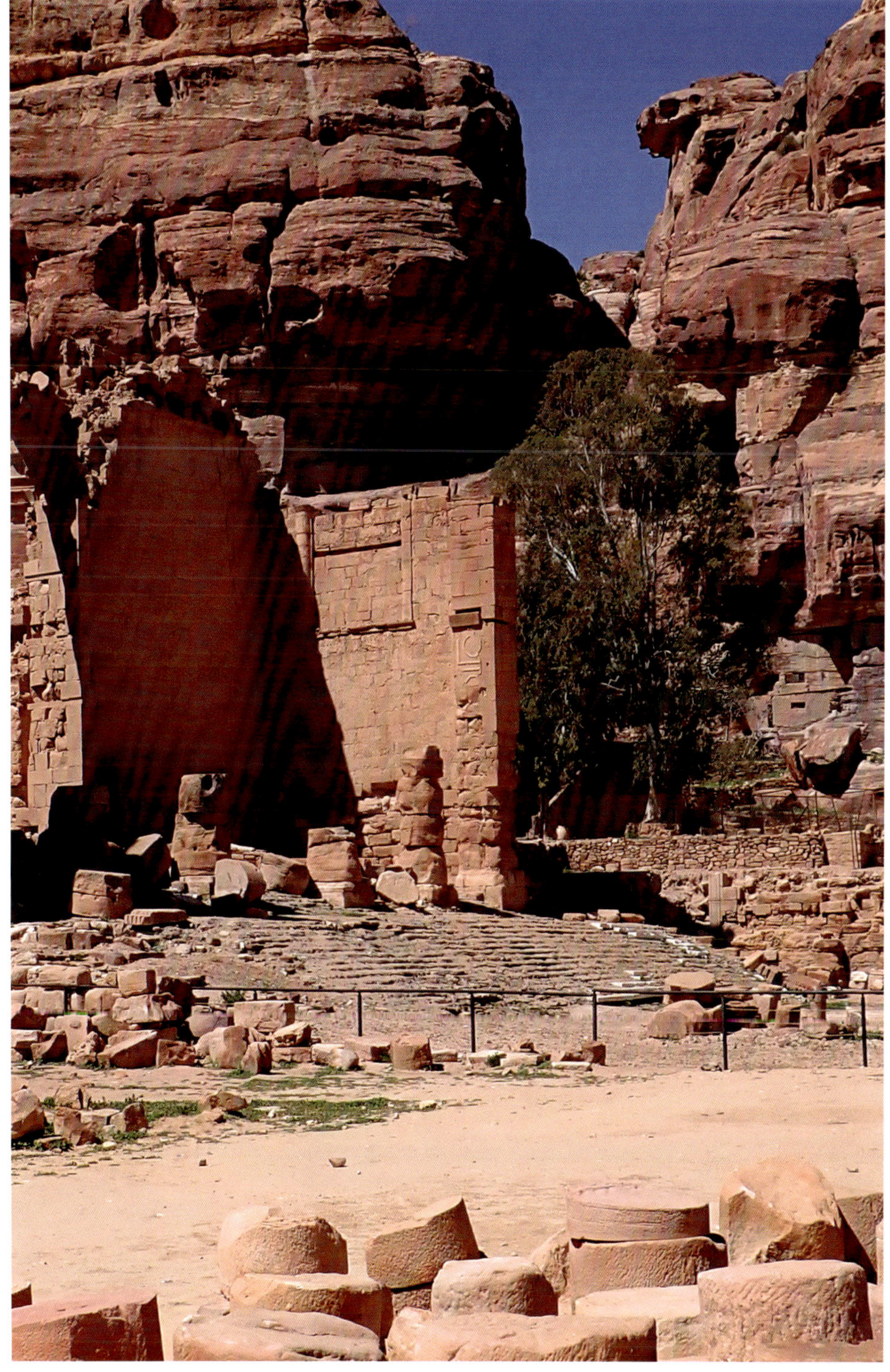

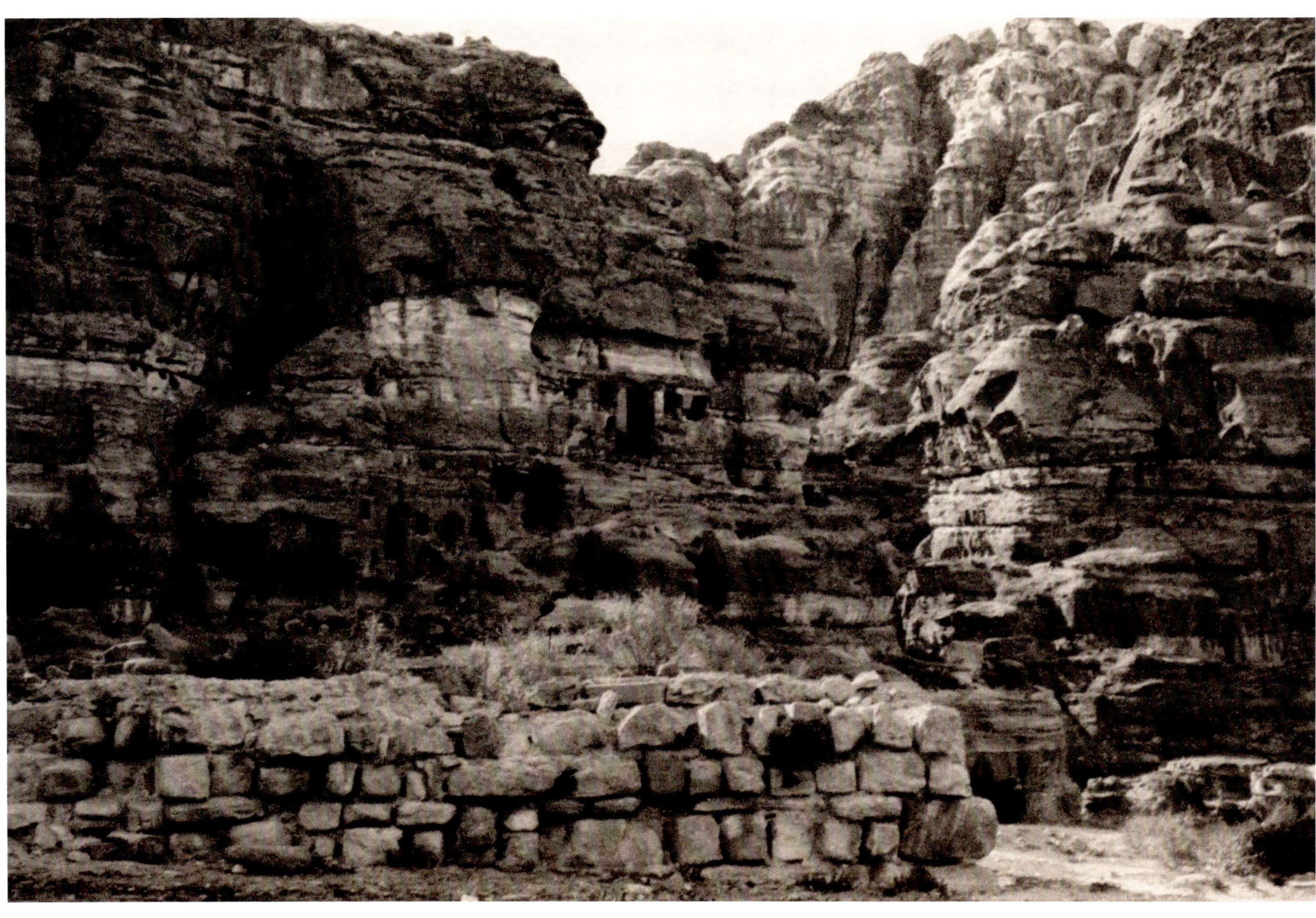

**BASE OF AL-HABIS
AND OLD PETRA MUSEUM**

"At a slightly lower level than the [Qasr al-Bint] Temple, and between it and the riverbed, stands the large masonry altar… Almost immediately beyond the temple there is visible somewhat high up on the east wall of al-Habis a large cave with a squared entrance, but without any façade… Below this cave there starts a long ramp running up the face of the wall northwards, a ledge partially natural and partially artificial… A little higher up, just before the ledge rounds the northern corner of the rock, it passes below the remarkable chamber or hall, with its doorway and four windows making it like the front of a house."
— SIR KENNEDY (1925, pg. 60, 62)

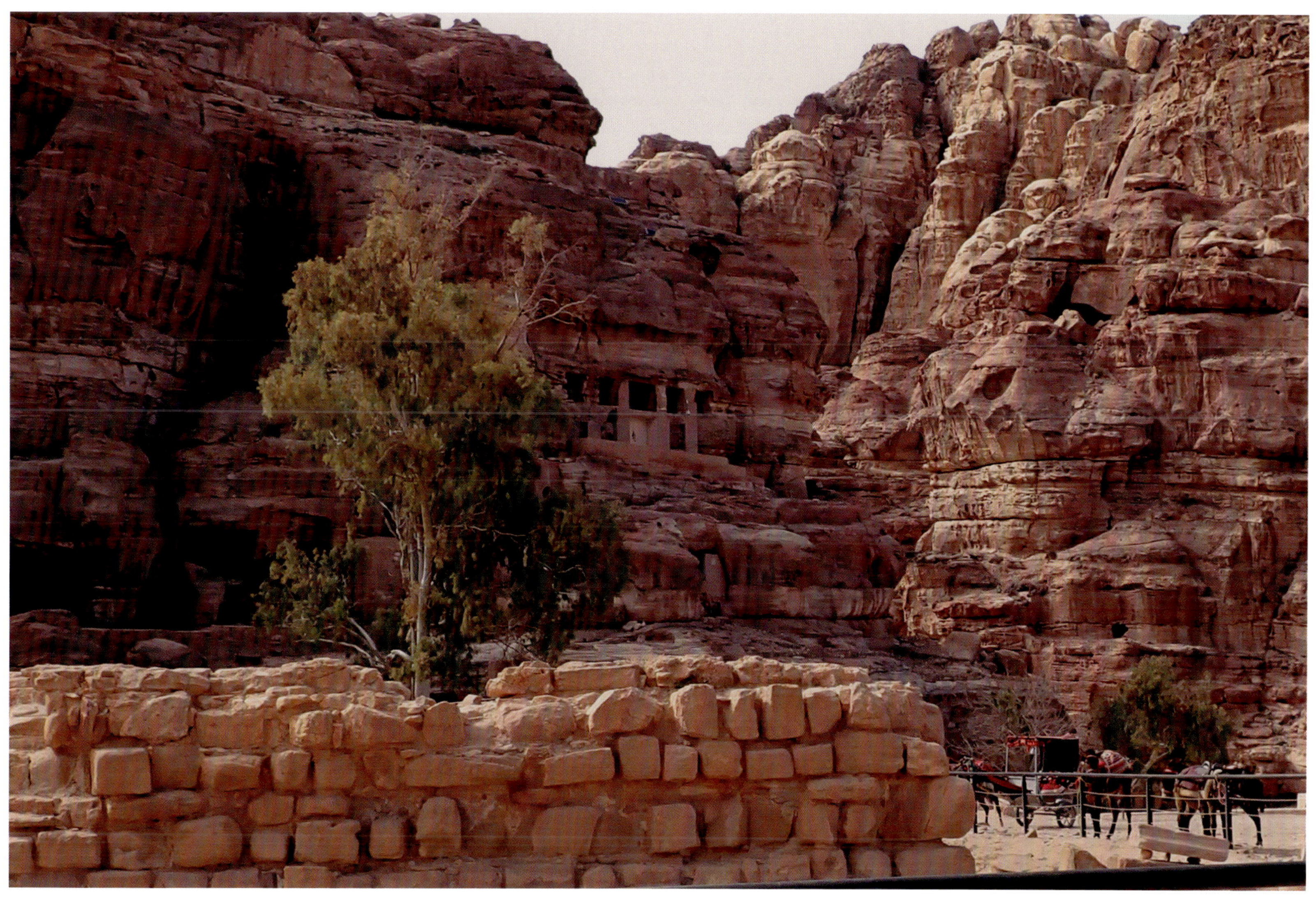

In 1963, the three small chambers within Sir Kennedy's "house" were enclosed and converted into an archeological museum to shelter and display artifacts from Petra's Edomite, Nabataean, Roman, and Byzantine eras. However, with the 2014 construction of the beautiful new Petra Nabataean Museum located outside Petra's front gate near the visitor center, the "Old Petra Museum" has been locked and remains closed to the public. In the foreground, the black metal fence erected to protect the curious stone platform protruding from the Qasr al-Bint has become a popular gathering place for donkeys and electric carts ready to escort visitors up the strenuous Deir trail or back to the Khazneh and entrance gate, respectively.

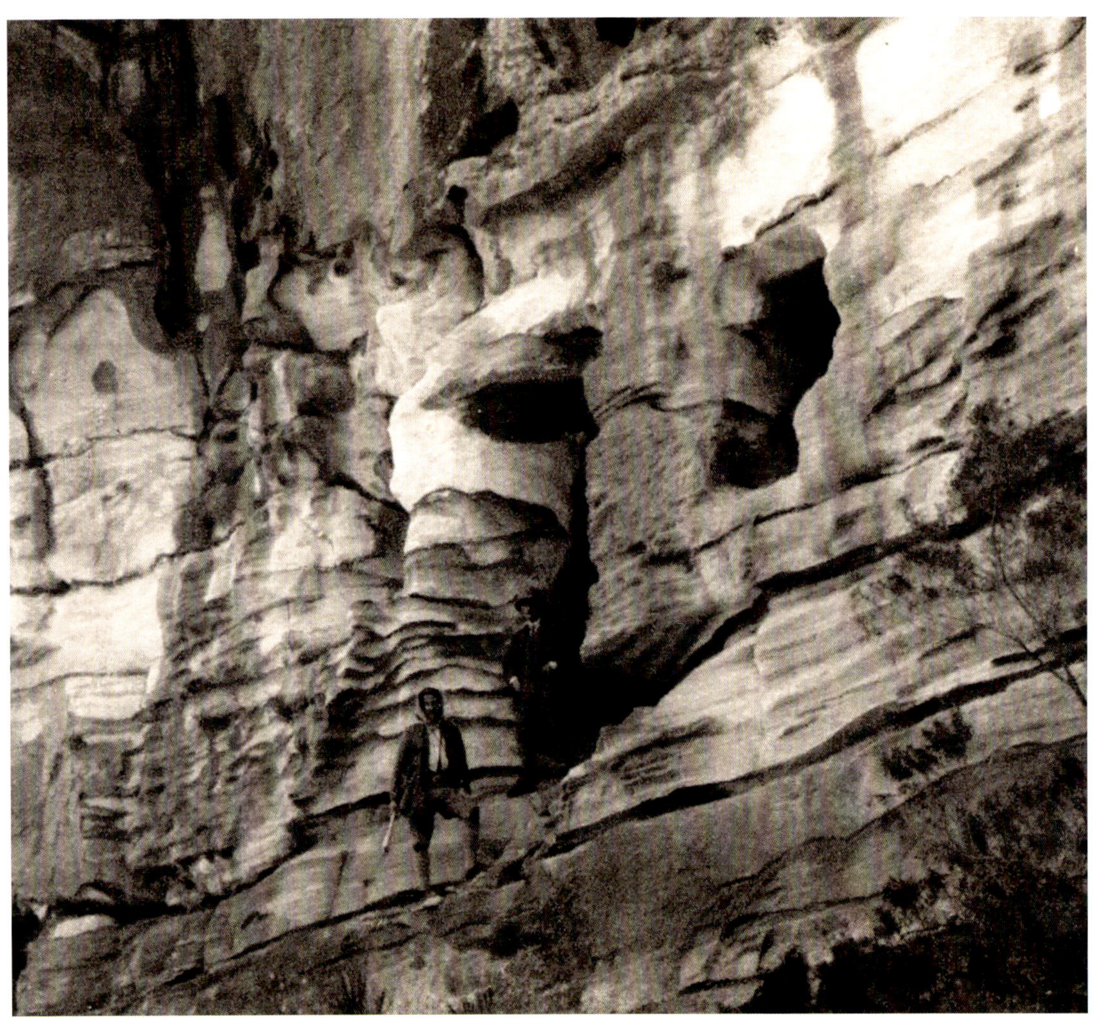

"On the same wall [of al-Habis], not much further round, is another 'house' with a window on each side of its doorway. [The photograph] shows that it is very rough in appearance and has obviously never had the trouble taken with its construction that must have been given to the other."
— SIR KENNEDY (1925, pg. 63)

With the harsh sun obscured by the massive al-Habis mount, the intricate dance of colors and minerals painting Petra's sandstone sing in the soft lighting of these images. The deep purples, vibrant reds and oranges, and the stark, sparkling whites highlight the natural beauty in even the simplest of façades. In this instance, it is the very decay and deterioration of the stone face that enhances its grandeur. My field assistant Dr. Casey Allen (left) and I (right) occupy the same places as Sir Kennedy's unnamed companions.

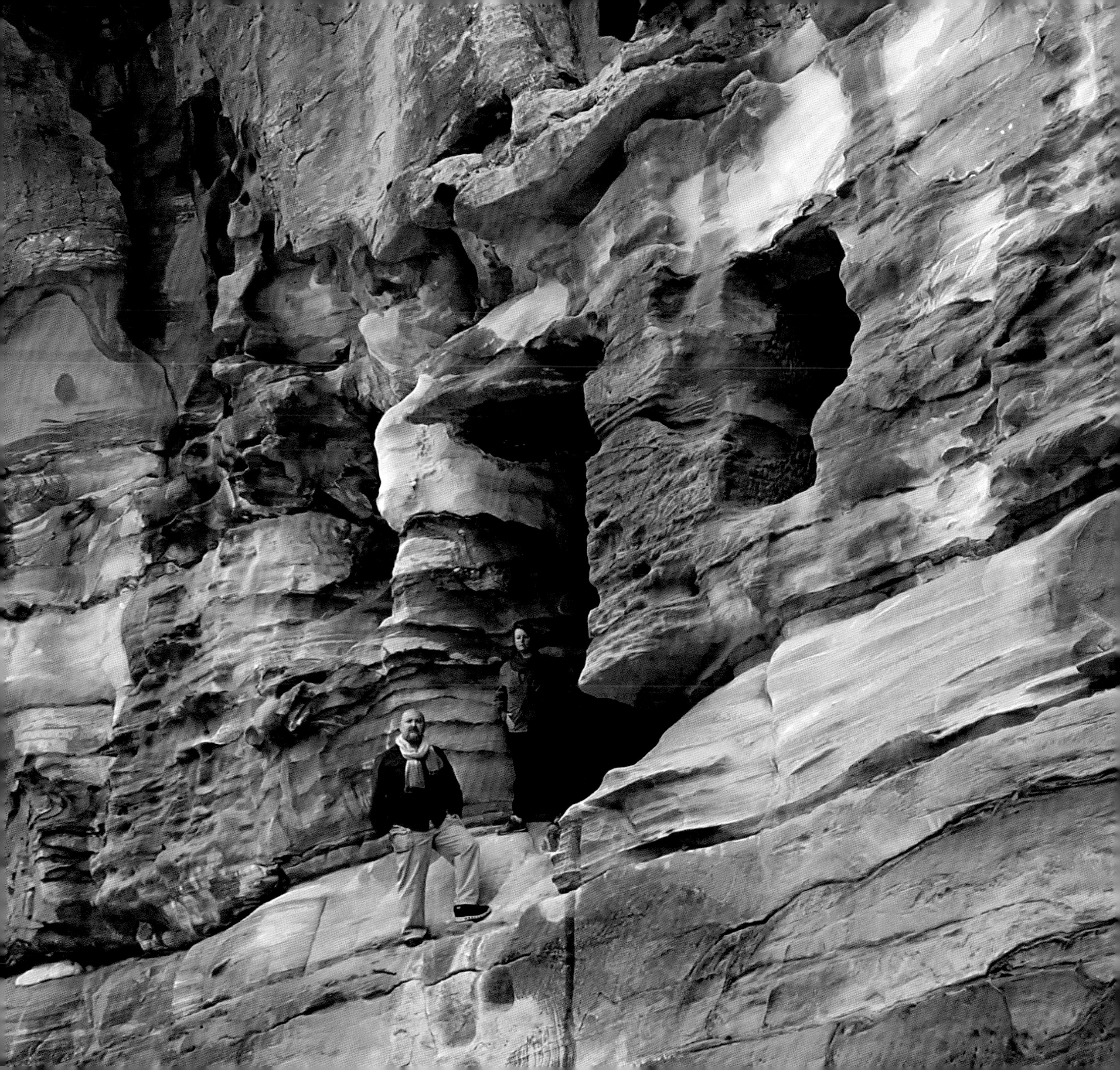

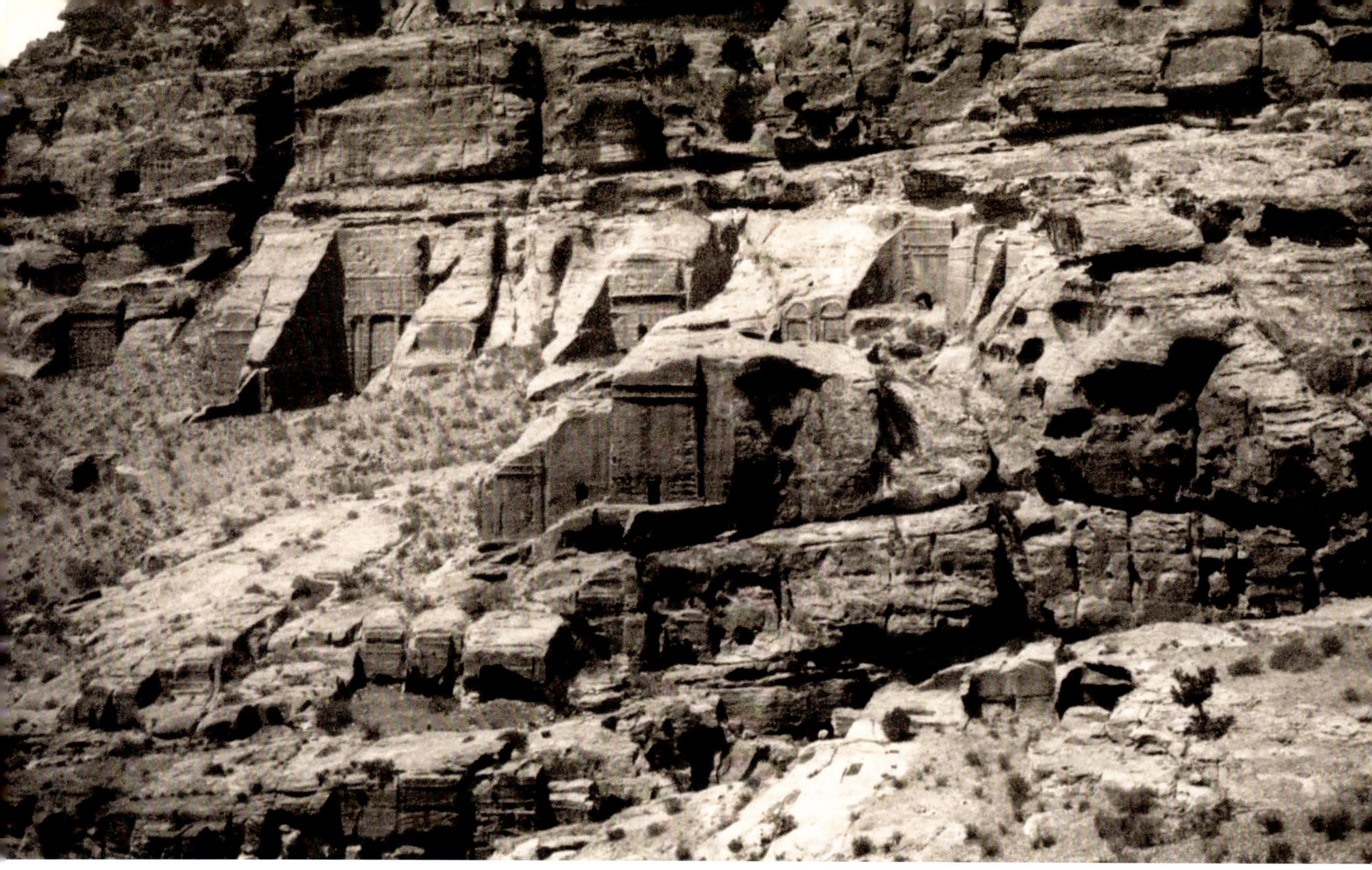

WADI SIYAGH

"A part of the east wall of al-Biyara, behind the rock of al-Habis, on the side of Petra opposite to the Siq, and shows also the condition of the lower and more ancient monuments which Brünnow [a famous early archaeologist in Petra] classified—only too accurately—as *zerstörte Gräber* (destroyed graves)." — SIR KENNEDY (1925, pg. 46)

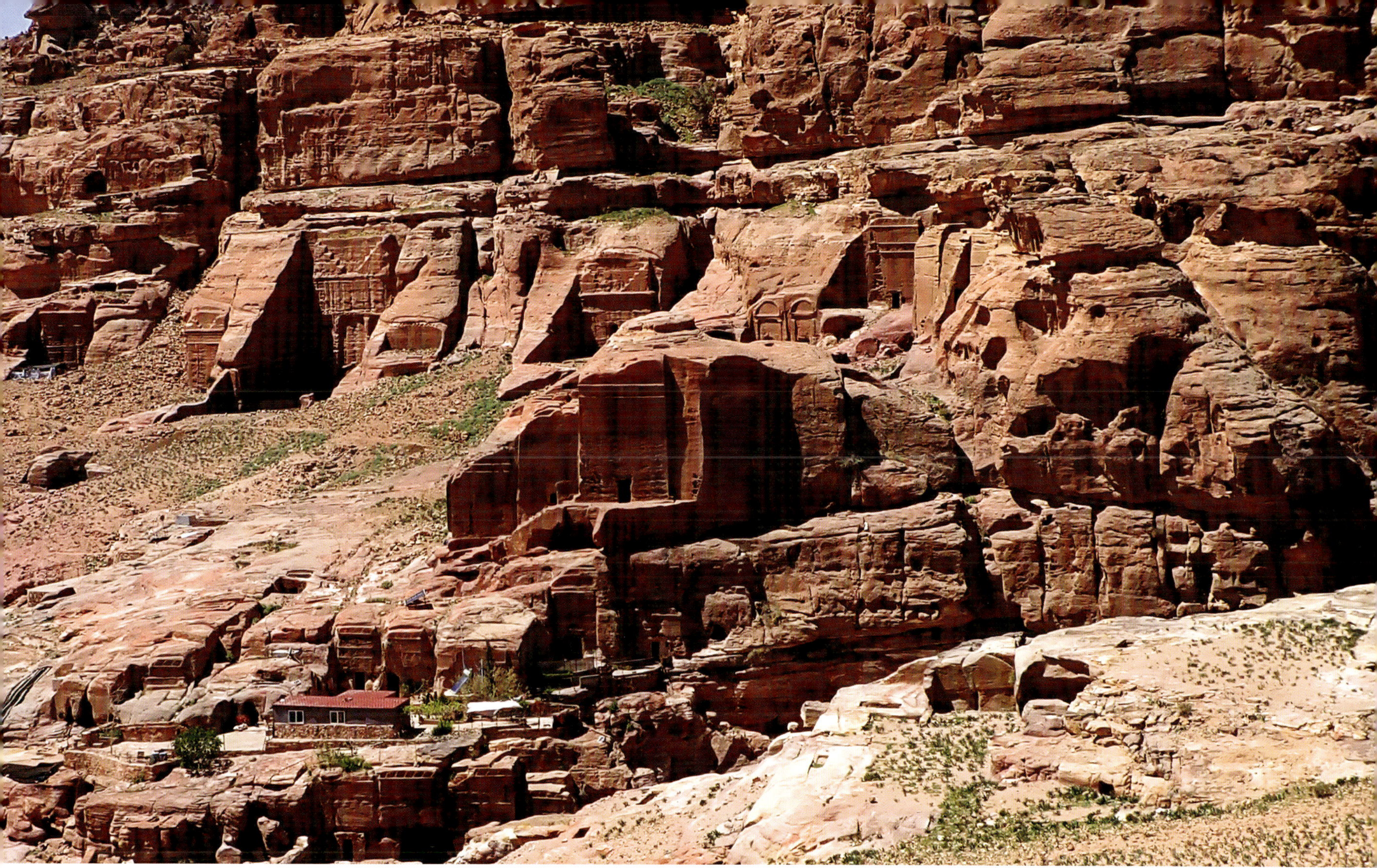

The Wadi Siyagh and the Road to Jabal al-Nabi Harun along the back side of al-Habis are not particularly common destinations for tourists, but the modern repeat highlights the generational Bedouin relationship with the place. The "destroyed" tombs have been resourcefully repurposed as storage space, livestock pens, homes, or whatever else is needed. The state-authorized addition of new buildings (bottom left) further establishes this area as a more residential part of historic Petra.

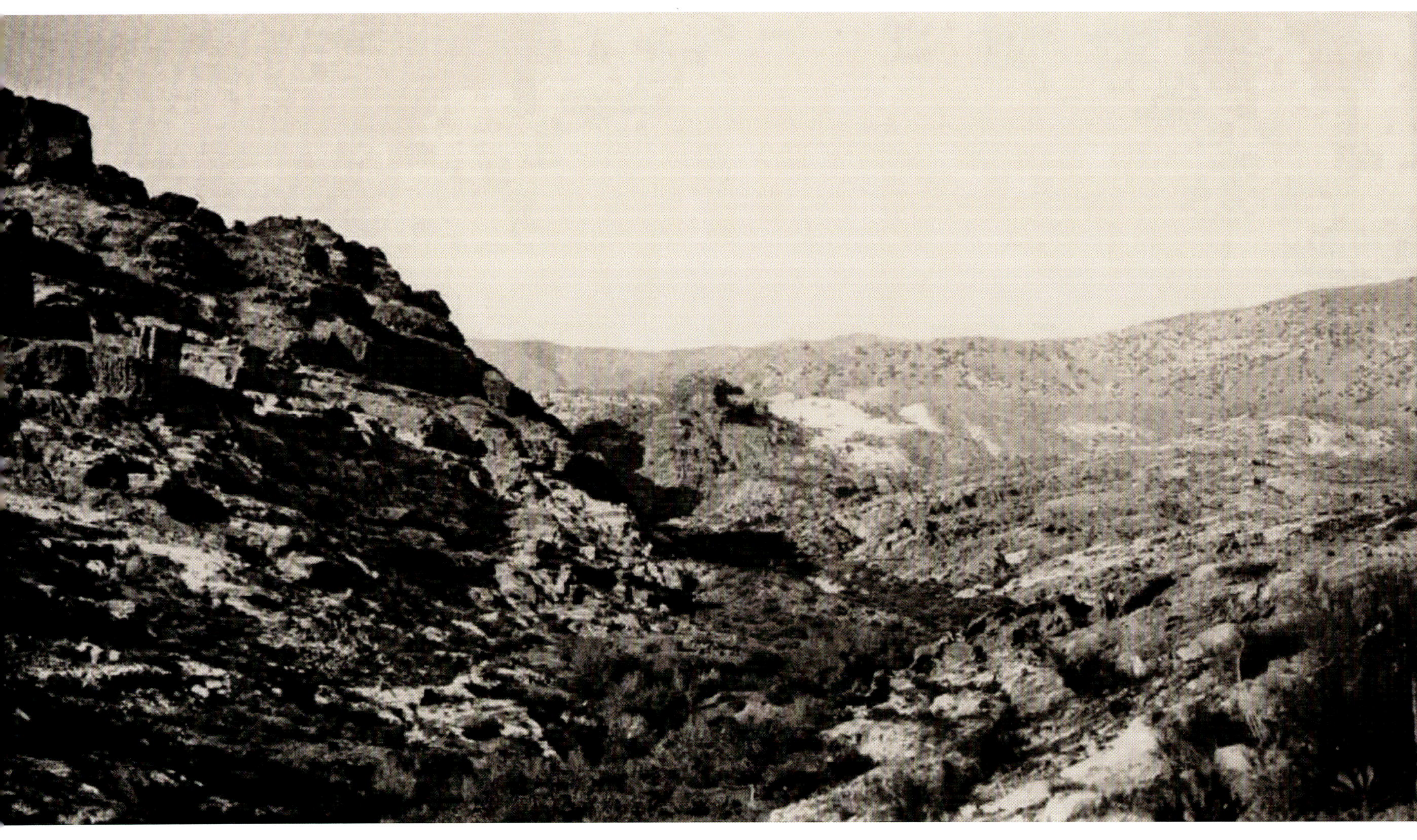

WADI TURKMANIYA
AND UMM SAYHOUN

"The normal approach from Petra is by
a route following the course of Wadi
Turkamaniya upwards to its watershed,
and thence descending with an easy
gradient through the scattered tumuli
of white sandstone to a wide open space,
which appears to have served as a camping
ground for caravans." — SIR KENNEDY
(1925, pg. 15)

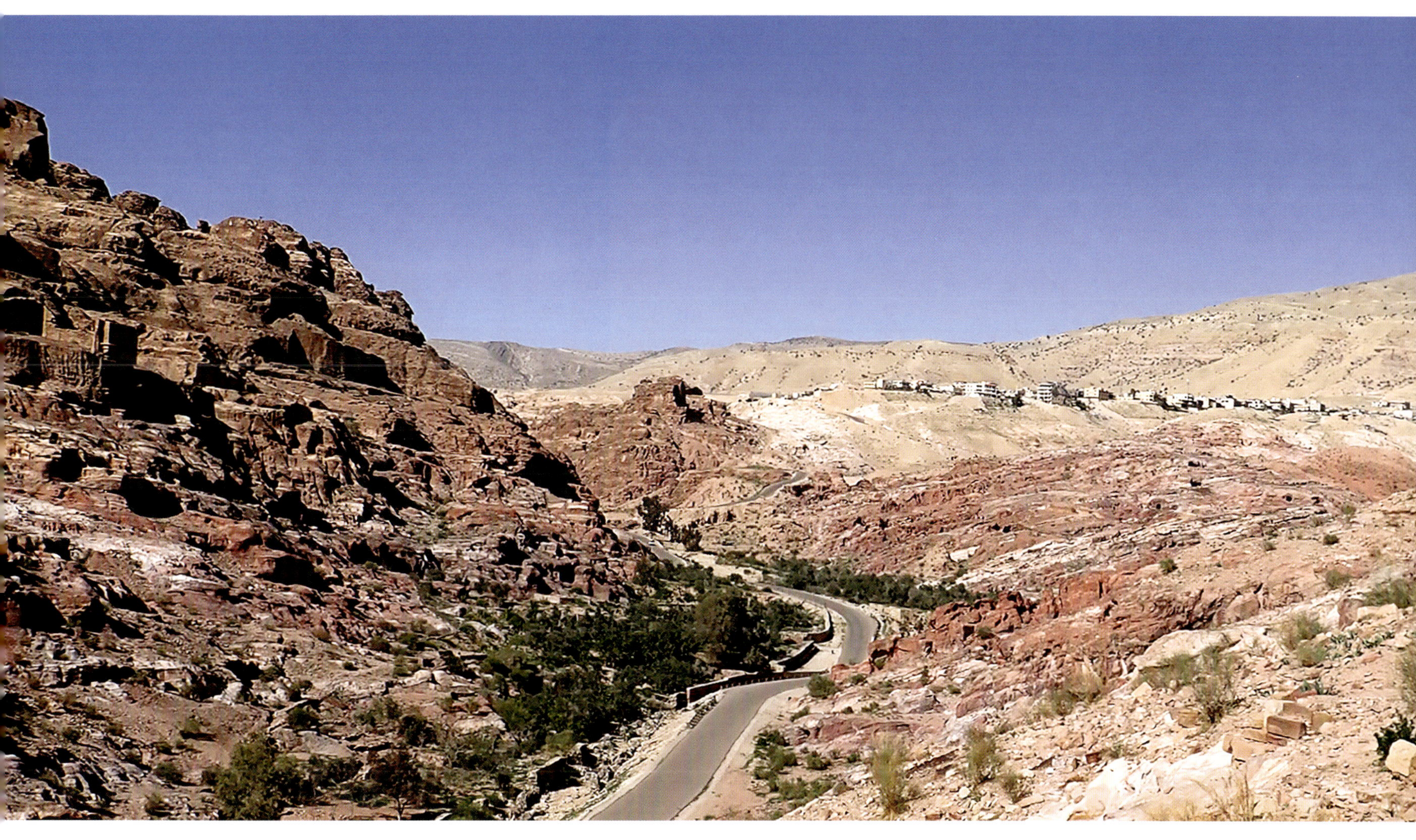

Taken from above the Abu Alaiqa Gate at the base of the valley, this view looks north across the recently paved service road weaving through the Wadi Turkmaniyah to the Bedouin village of Umm Sayhoun, whose modern buildings are seen perched atop what Sir Kennedy calls "the white ridge of Nasara." Taking advantage of the natural waterways navigating this valley, local lemon orchards line the road, giving the path a pleasant citrusy aroma.

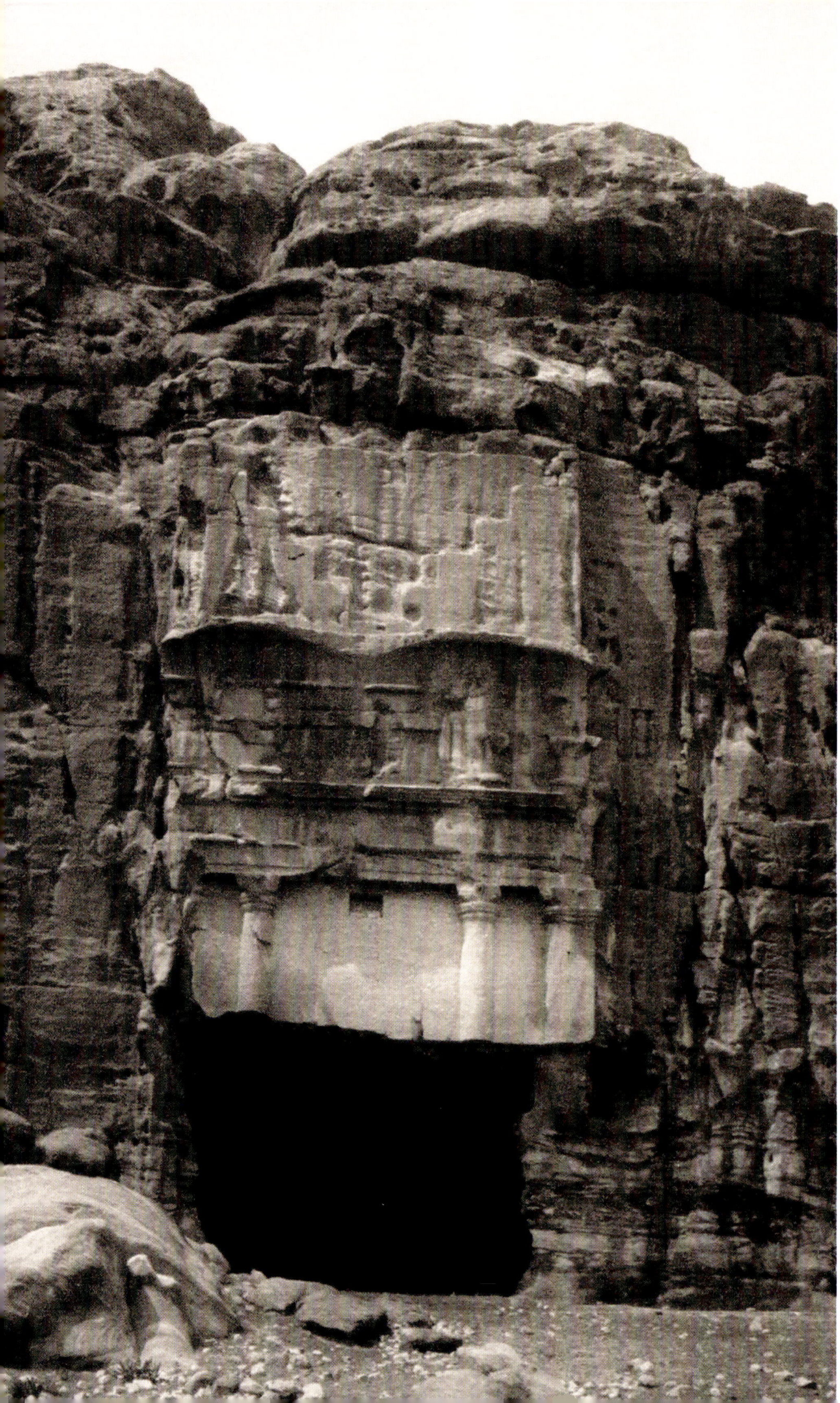

THE TURKMANIYA TOMB

"In the Turkamaniya tomb the attic is much elaborated, and is filled with a second order consisting of duplicated upper parts and capitals of the columns below... On the flat space between the two middle columns is a long Nabataean inscription, the only one of its kind." — SIR KENNEDY (1925, pg. 49)

A bit off the beaten track, this gaping
monument decorated with its impressively
preserved Nabataean inscription rests along
the western wall of the Wadi Turkmaniyah,
from which it gets its name. Aside from the
paved road that runs along the valley floor,
just beyond the view of the photograph and
deposition of materials in the foreground,
this yawning façade displays a surprising
resiliency, despite having the immediate
appearance of abject ruin.

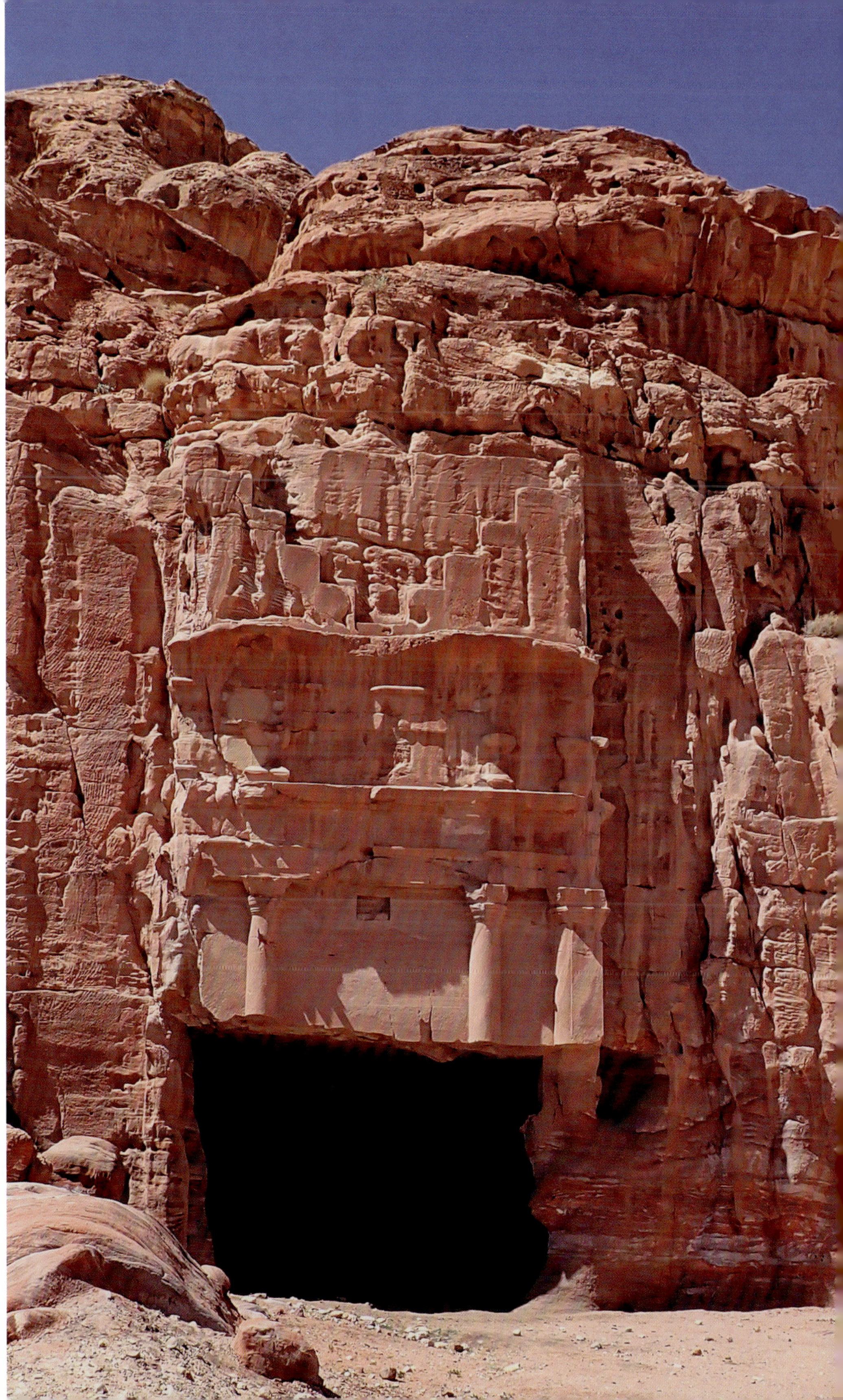

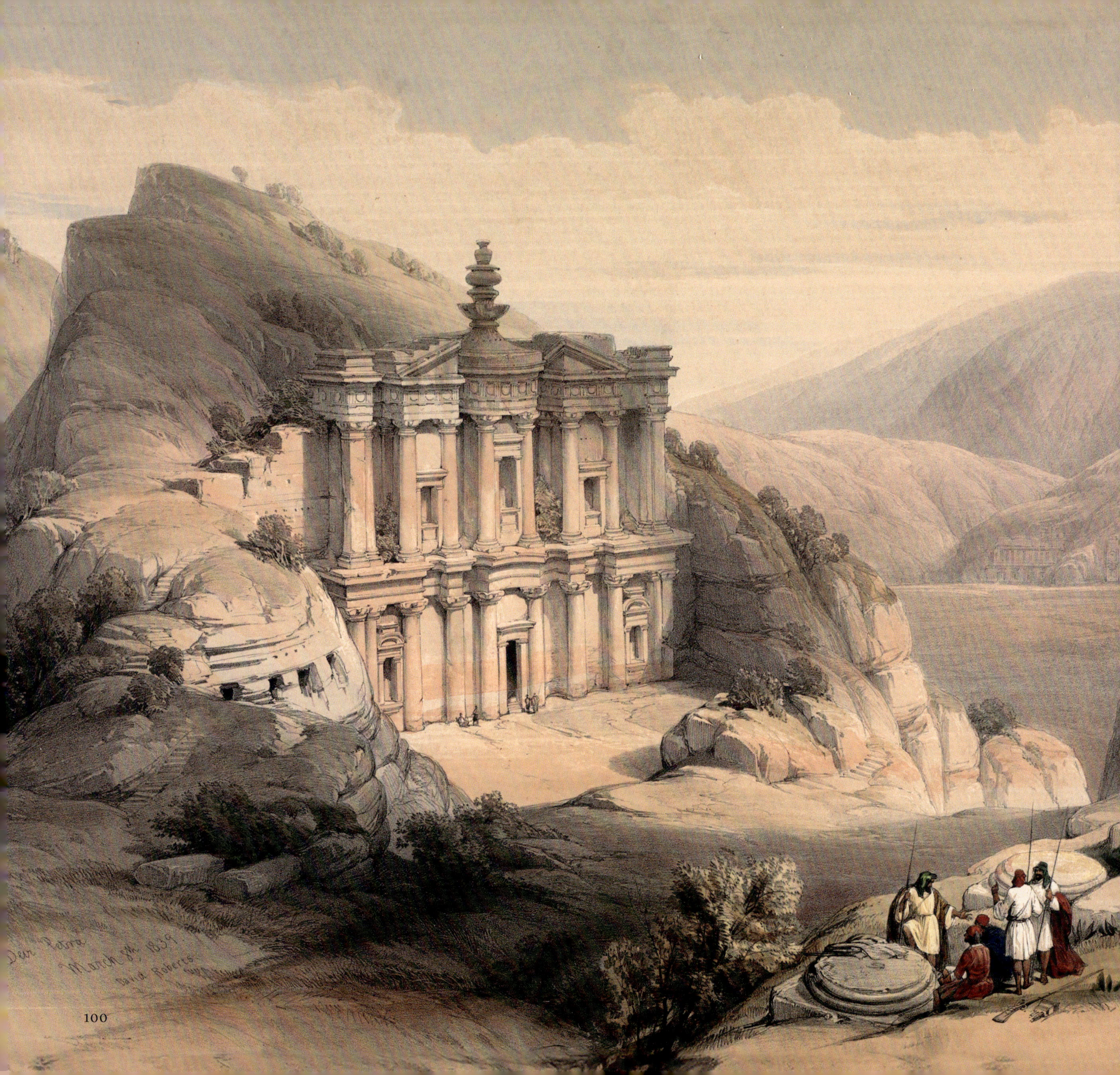
Der Petra
March 8th 1839
David Roberts

Top of the World:
Deir Plateau and the Northwest Ridges

Following the worn and weary carved steps up the northwestern mountains, this region goes off the beaten track to explore the lesser-known al-Muaisara monuments, takes side trips up secluded canyons, and ultimately arrives at the truly monolithic ad-Deir (the Monastery), the largest and most imposing monument in Petra.

> "As we reviewed the whole conception of that rocky stairway, mounting seven hundred feet from the brook, penetrating into the heart of the mountain, following the windings of the fantastic gorge, crossing every stratum of the many-hued sandstone; the steps, now yellow, now red, now banded, now white, now waving like a banner in the wind; the sides of the roadway adorned with seats and pools, and tablets and shrines; the smaller fissures filled with stairways leading into nooks unseen and unsuspected; the deep cuttings undertaken wherever the precipice left a space for a human foot; then this plaza surrounded by the wildest beauties of nature and the most wonderful structures; the views down the gorge into the city, over the whole Petra mass, over the chasms to Mount Hor and Aaron's tomb, and down the Arabah — it seemed to us that the combination is certainly one that no other city on earth can easily equal." — DR. WILLIAM LIBBEY AND DR. FRANKLIN HOSKINS[10]

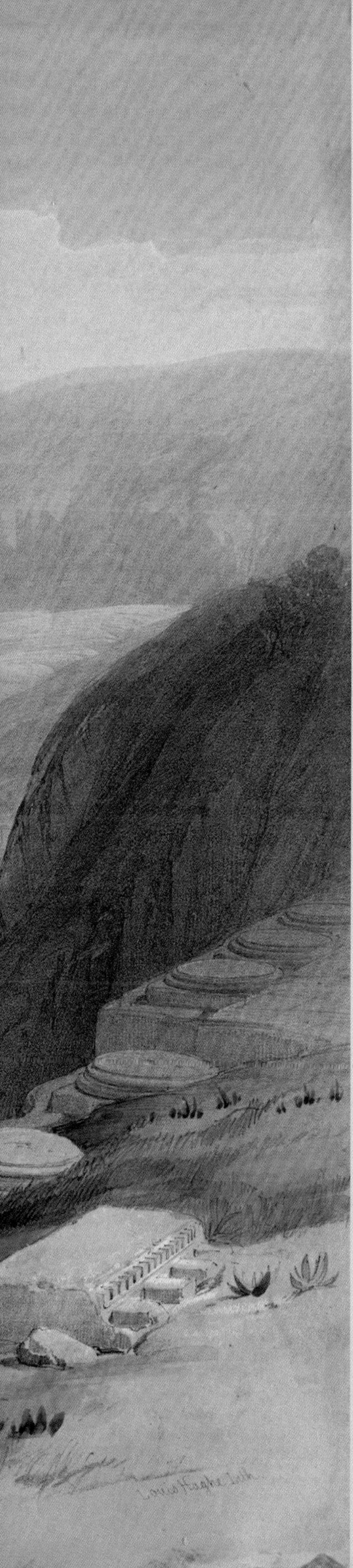

Lithograph by nineteenth-century artist David Roberts of monolithic Deir Monument

10 Libby and Hoskins, *The Jordan Valley and Petra*, 224.

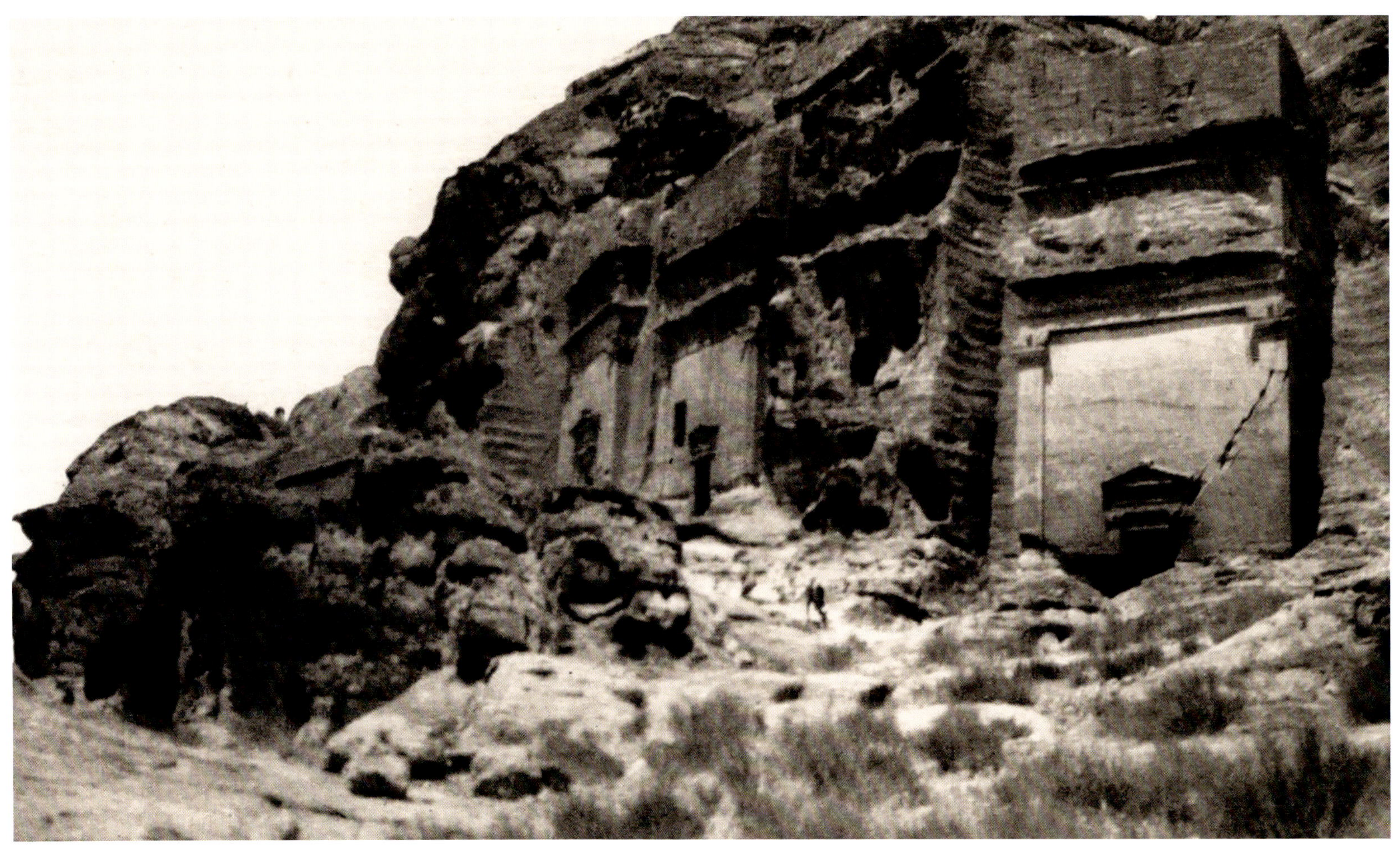

TOMBS IN WADI AL-MUAISARA

"For some unknown reason, but probably owing to unsoundness in the rock, the front of the second monument in the group, which apparently had an upper chamber, has fallen entirely away." — SIR KENNEDY (1925, pg. 50)

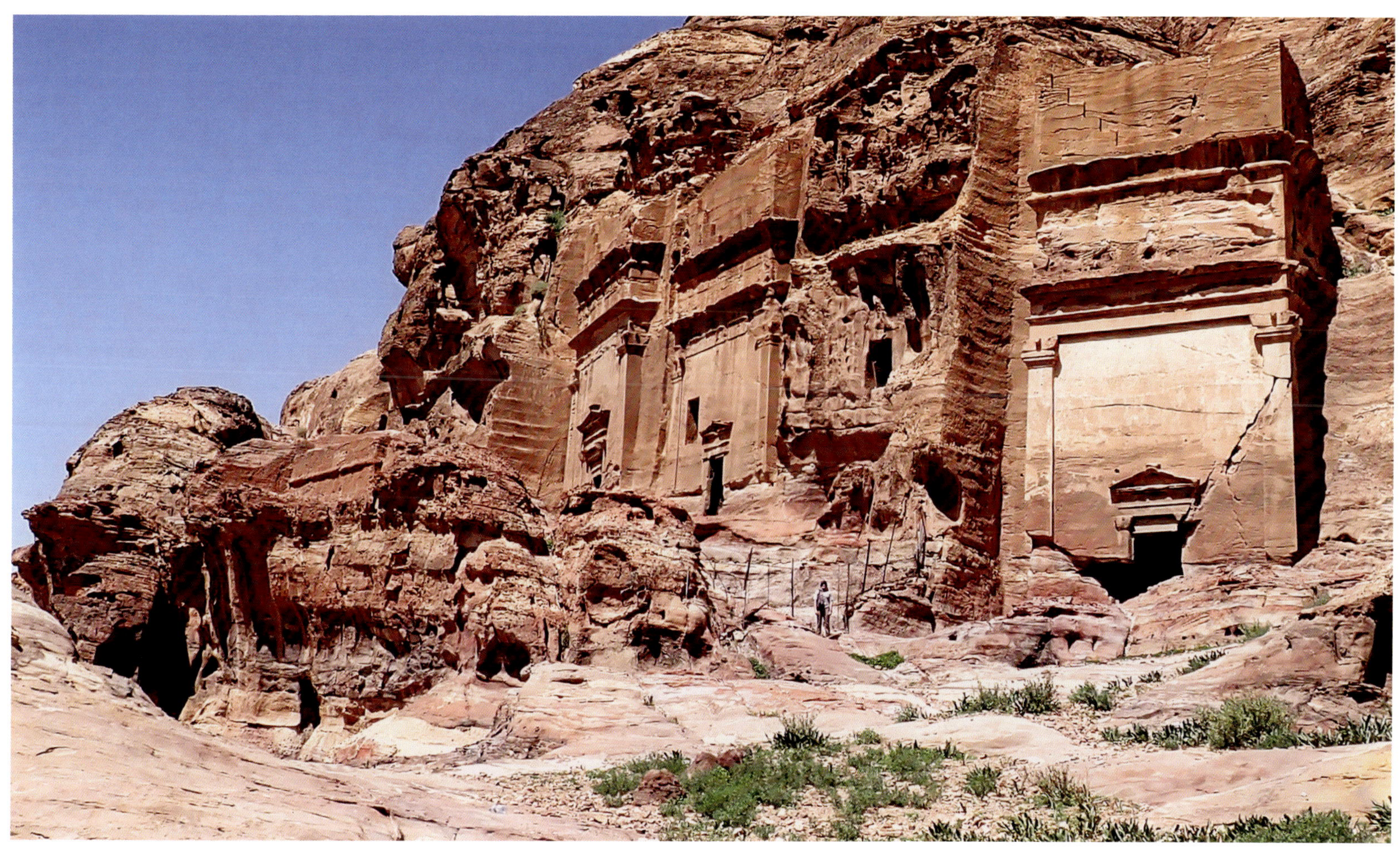

Tucked high within the Wadi al-Muaisara, these lofty monuments sit above the main Petra Valley. Local legend says the middle tomb was destroyed during the great earthquake in 363 AD, though the rounded appearance and characteristics of the decay are more congruent with Sir Kennedy's postulation of some kind of localized inherent weaknesses within the geology. The upper level has been fenced in to house goats and other livestock, with a rather large, and quite pungent, dung heap occupying the exact location where unflappable field assistant McKay Barker obligingly stood to replicate Sir Kennedy's companion. Many laughs and a good shoe cleaning took place immediately following the capture of this photograph.

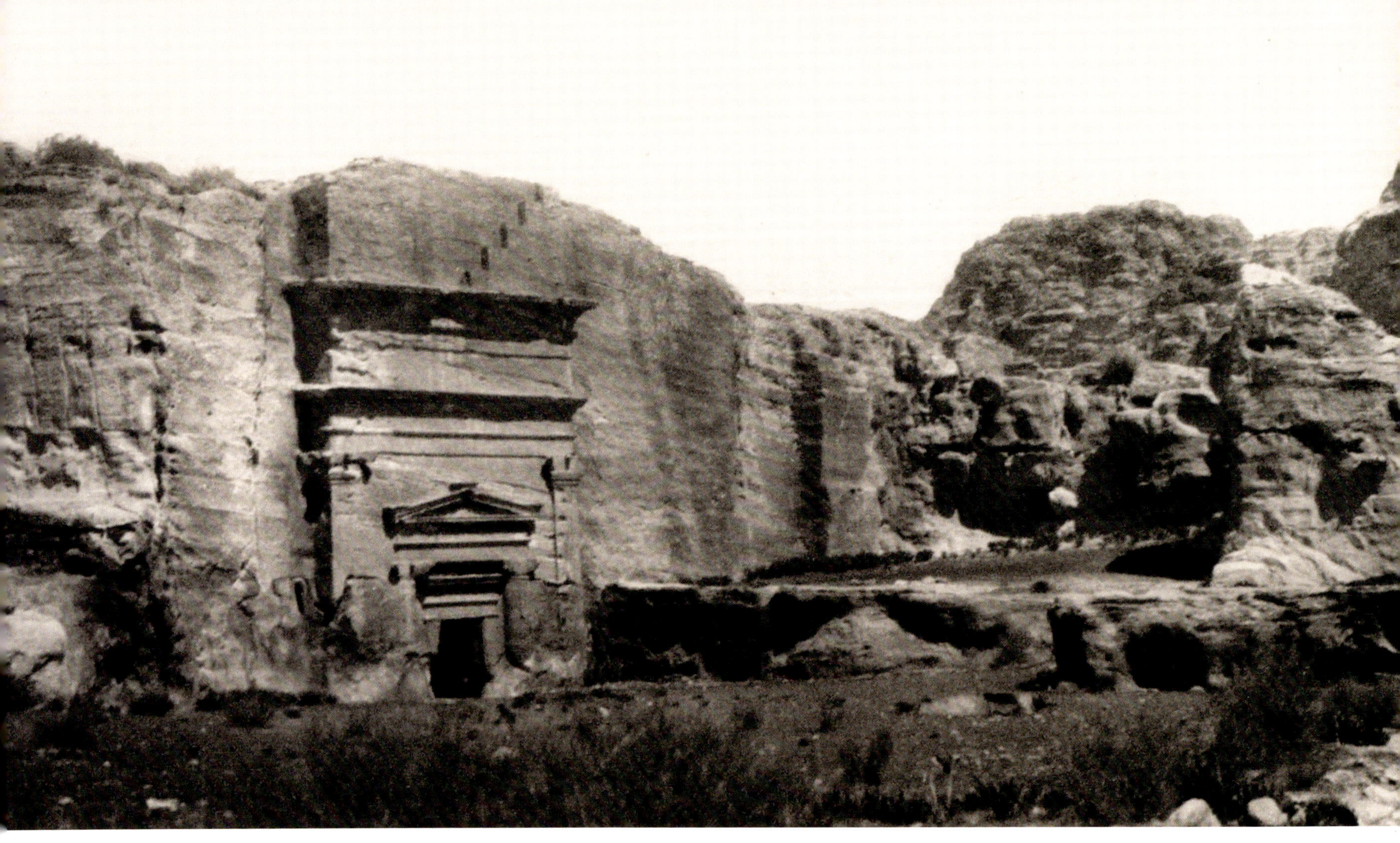

MONUMENT WITH COURT IN WADI AL-MUAISARA

"Beyond this [great court] there are various objects, and especially rather elaborate arrangements for water supply, which indicate that the whole region was of special importance for either religious or political ceremonials." — SIR KENNEDY (1925, pg. 66)

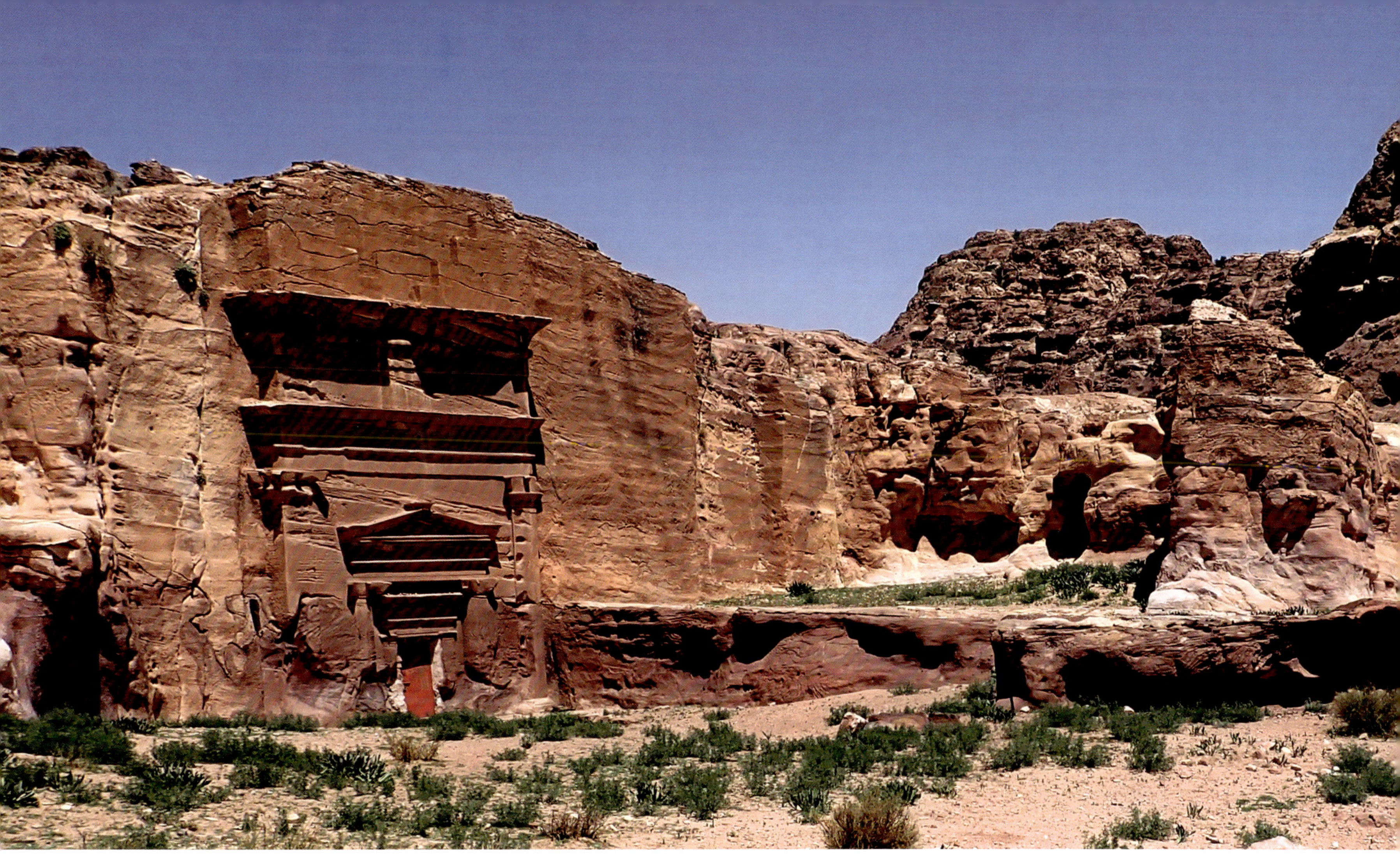

Even with the modern adaptation of the monument itself, the tranquility of this elevated platform—with its secluded courtyard and impressive façade—is a delightful surprise at the end of an undulating trail navigating several ridges and ravines. This hidden sanctuary is a welcome reprieve from the bustling city center below. Despite its peaceful setting, however, Bedouins warn against being in this region at night, as the Wadi al-Muaisara is a known home for jinn, devious spirits who prey on the weak of heart.

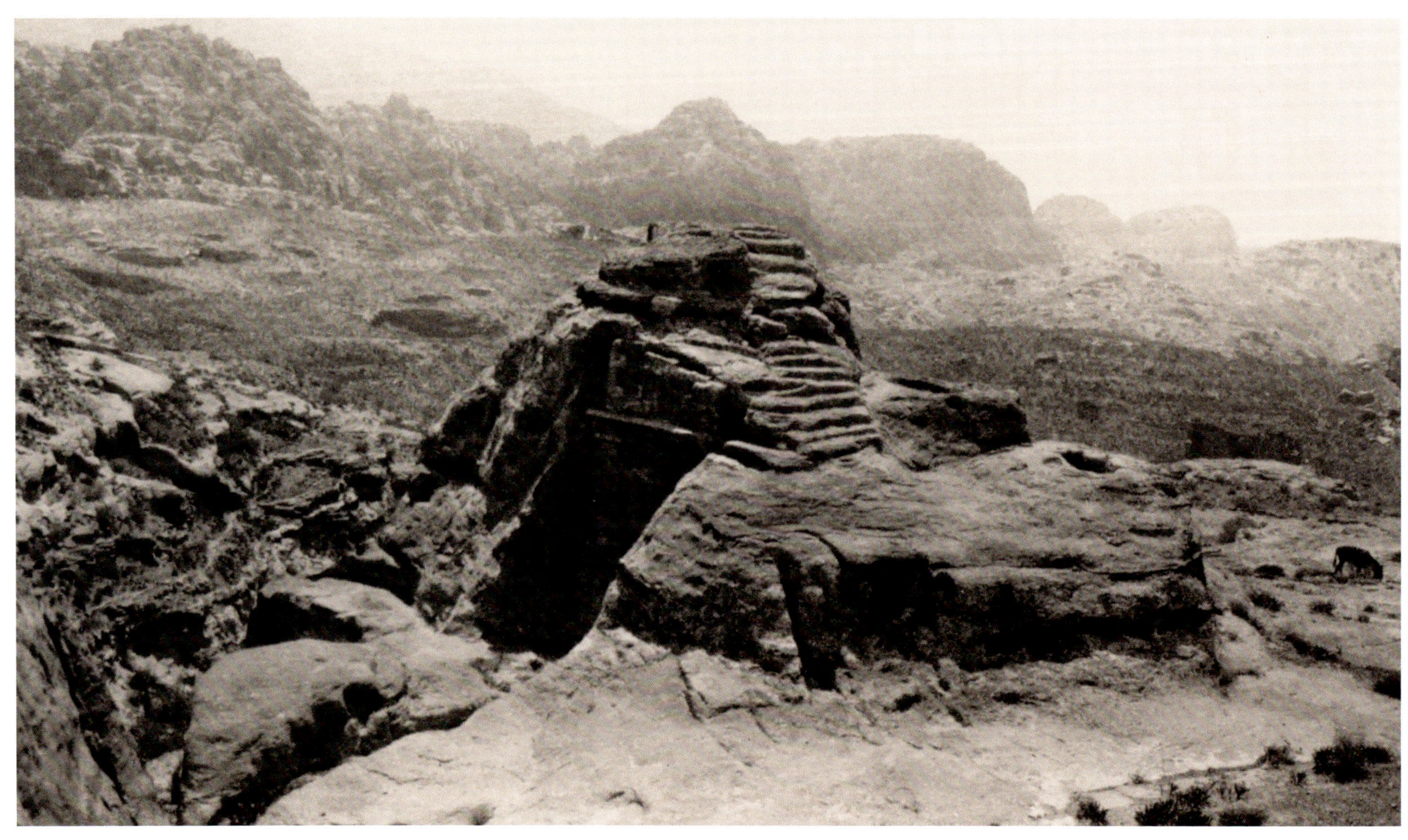

MONUMENT WITH HIGH PLACE ON AL-MUAISARA

"A comparatively clear part of al-Ma'aisara, directly overlooking the very literal "High Place", where the top of a somewhat isolated monument is used as an altar, approached by broad steps." — SIR KENNEDY (1925, pg. 67)

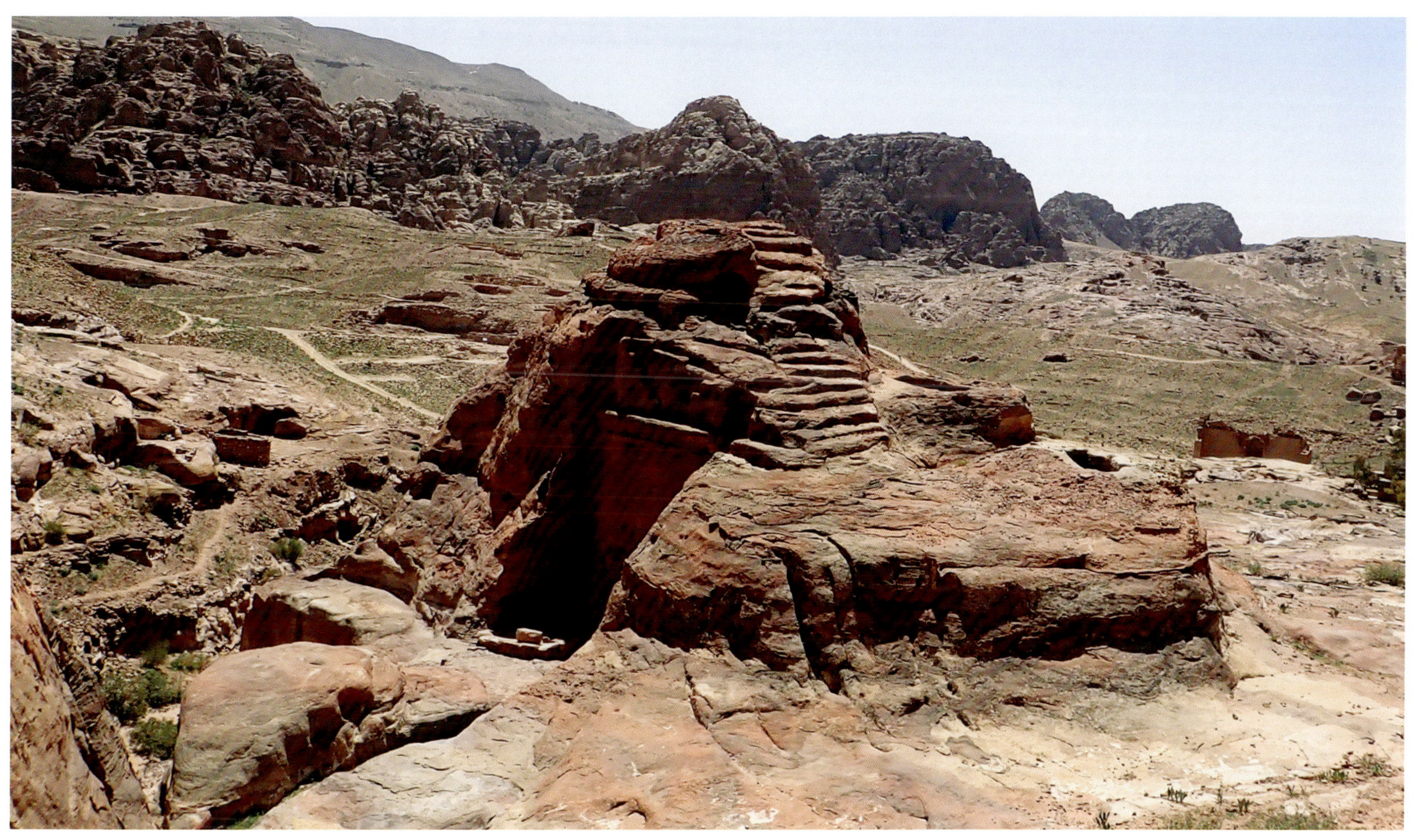

While Sir Kennedy was focused on the curious
monument in the foreground, the most
notable change is seen in the background.
New roads and broad walking trails transect
the valley where once it was a raw and
wild hillslope. The upper floors of the solitary
Qasr al-Bint can be seen just beyond the
elevated ridge (right).

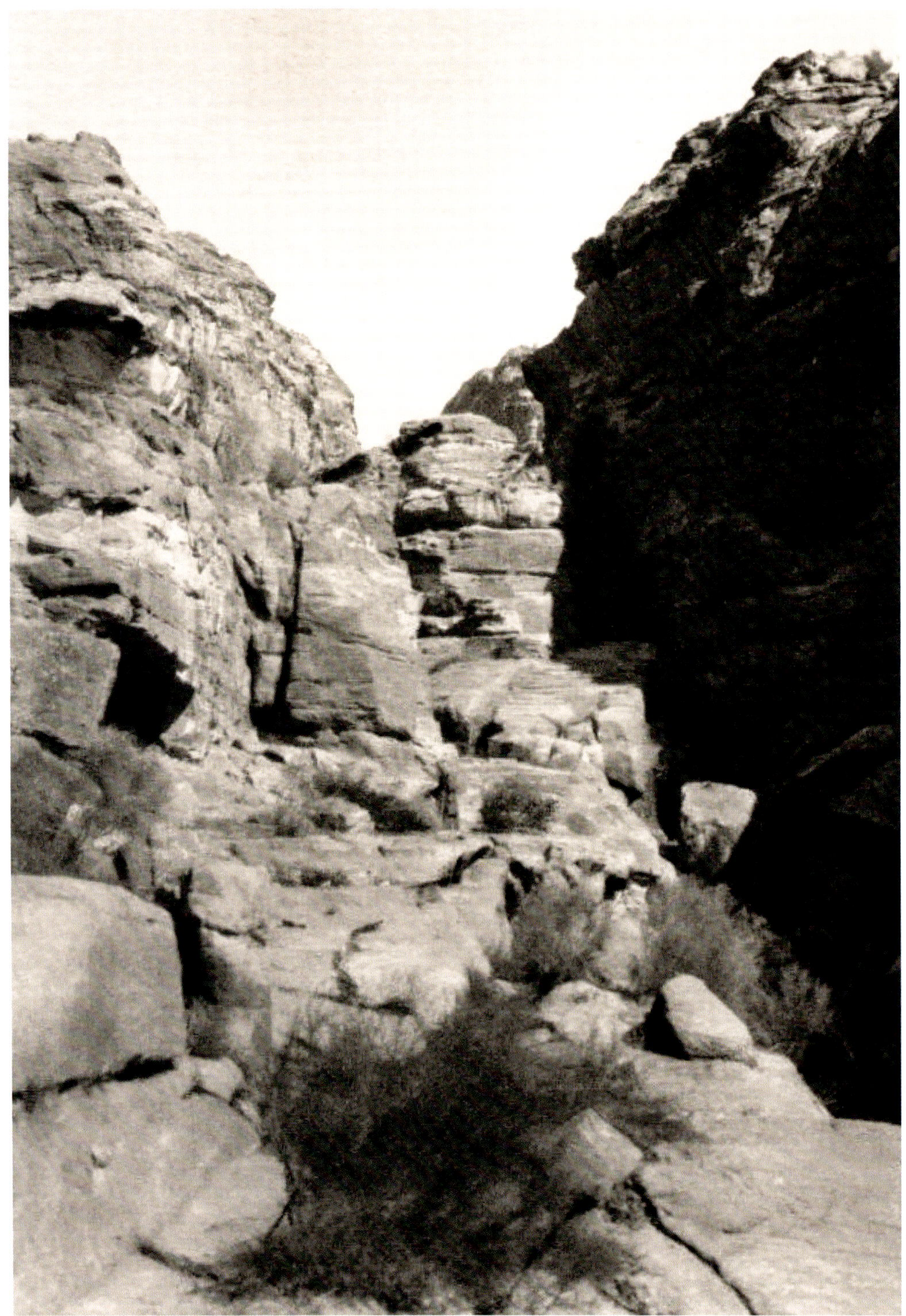

"[The Deir] stands on a rocky plateau... reached by a scramble up narrow and most picturesque gullies and in which the ascent is much facilitated by flights of steps not yet entirely worn away. This great massif of dark ruddy sandstone rises... above the town area in a galaxy of pinnacles and bosses, and is scored in every direction by steep valleys and abrupt ravines and gullies." — SIR KENNEDY (1925, pg. 11, 56)

The steep and harrowing trail up the Wadi
ad-Deir is an impressive and reward-
ing venture. Many visitors, historic and
contemporary, are awestruck by the trail's
sheer cliffs and narrow valleys through which
they climb, made possible in some places
by the restoration or replacement of the
original Nabataean steps. Strategically
located atop some of the more strenuous
stairways, small Bedouin stalls, such as those
shown here, offer visitors a short break
in their ascent to enjoy traditional desert tea
or peruse a multitude of trinkets, scarves,
and other keepsakes.

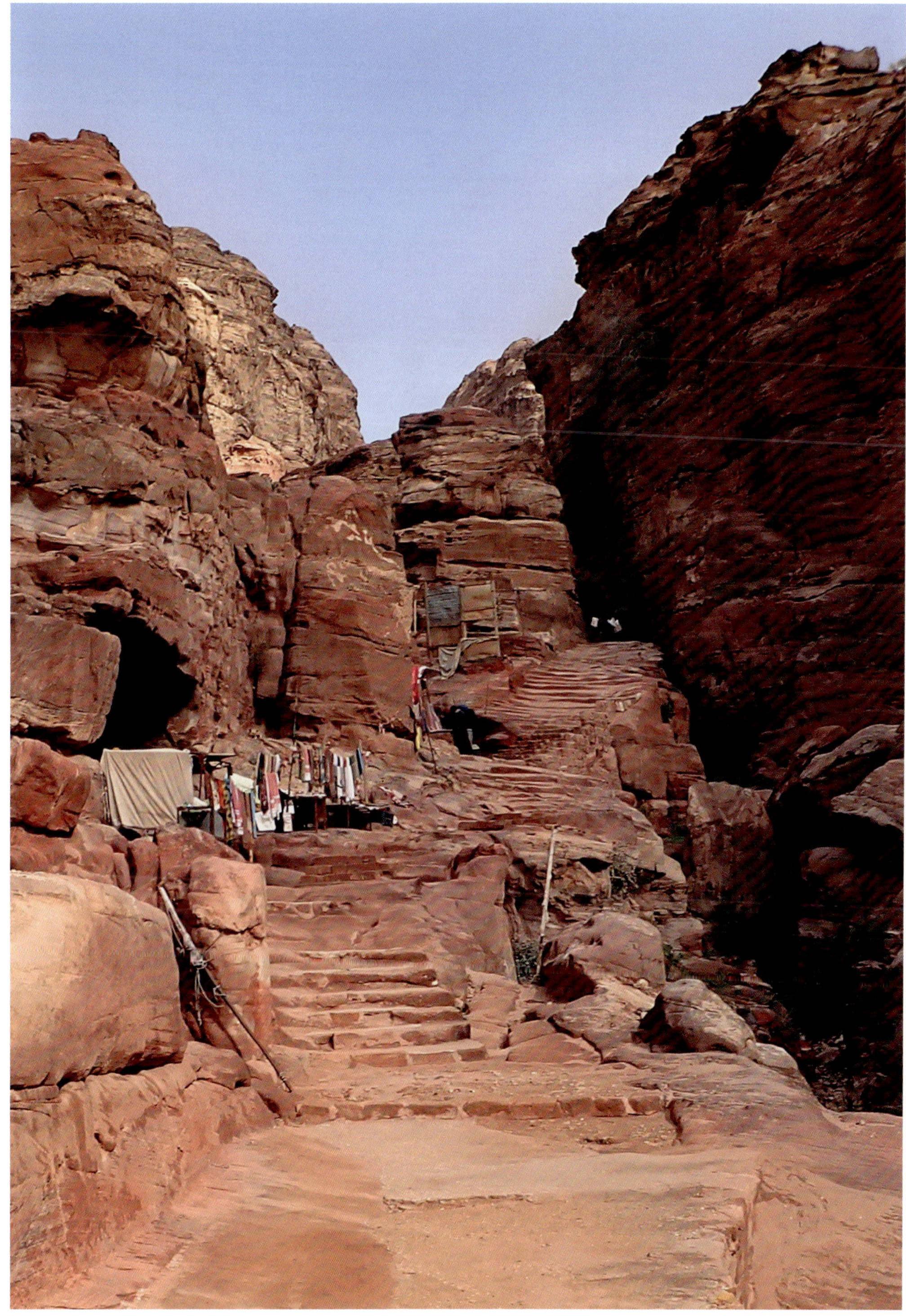

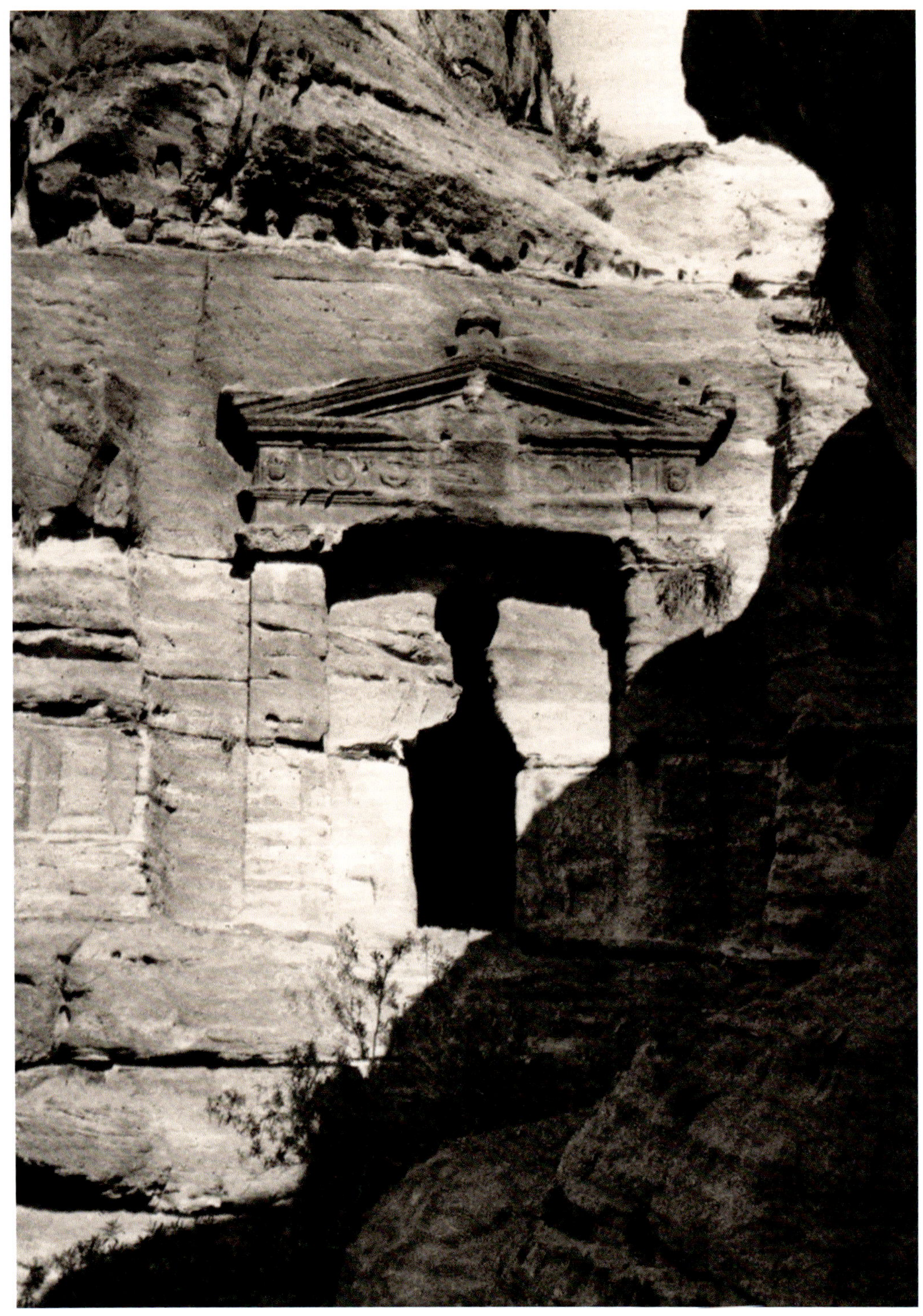

THE LION TRICLINIUM

"Near the foot of the Wadi al-Dair, at the head of a short ravine branching to the left, stands the monument which has been called the 'Lion Tomb', but which is in fact a triclinium, and not a grave. It owes its name to the fact that two small lions in low-relief are carved one on each side of the door."
— SIR KENNEDY (1925, pg. 57)

A hidden gem along the Wadi ad-Deir trail, the small Lion Triclinium monument is certainly worth the short detour. Nestled deep within a short, narrow side gorge, the feel of the place is cool, calm, and peaceful, despite the perpetual bustle of tourists trudging along the trail overhead. The ambiance is so comfortable here that we (almost) didn't mind having to wait several hours for the sun to penetrate the narrow ravine in just the right way to cast the distinctive stark shadows bifurcating the monument's façade. During this time, the only sounds interrupting the serenity were the lively yips and barks of stray puppies playing in a nearby cave.

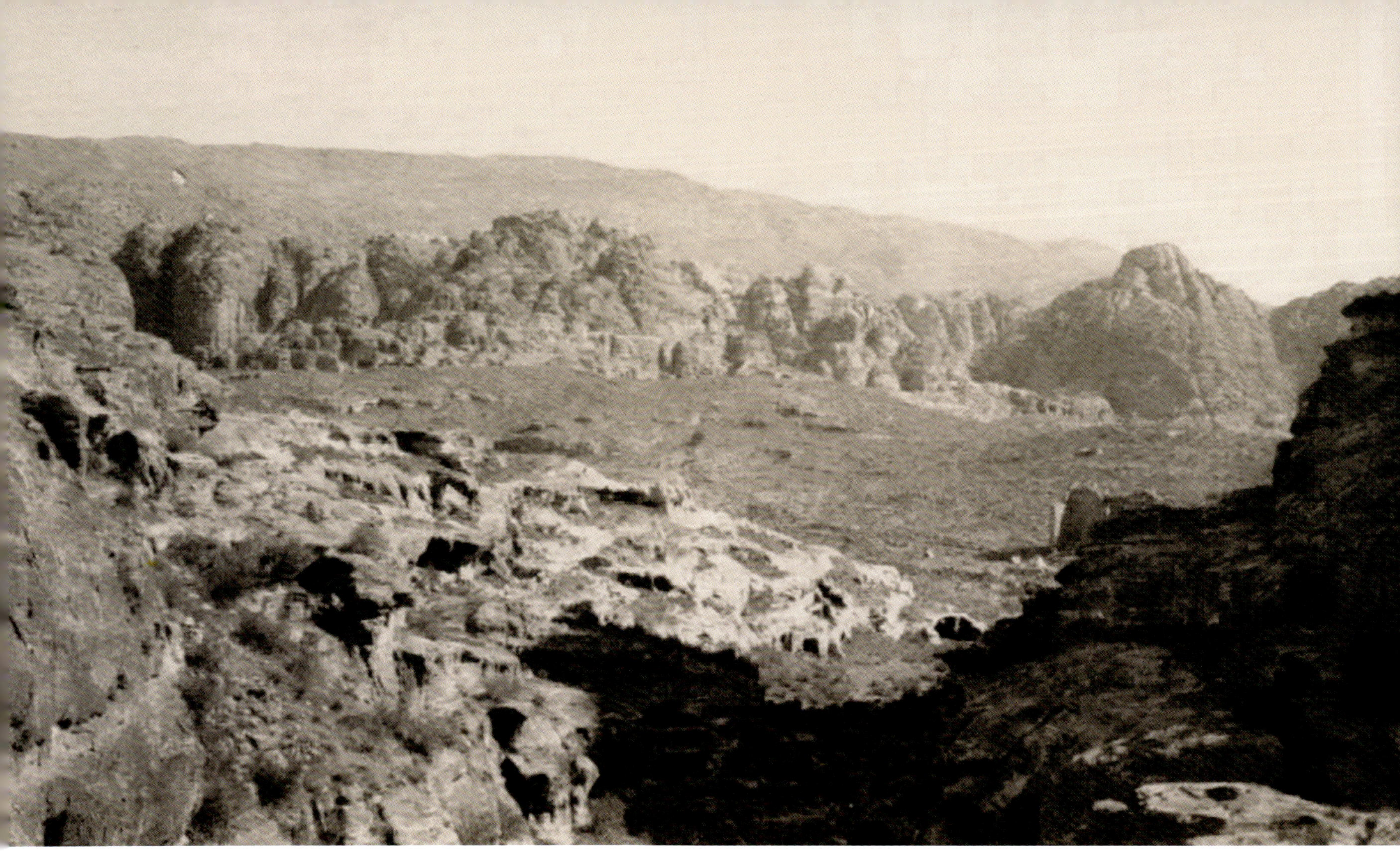

VIEW OF CENTRAL VALLEY FROM WADI AD-DEIR

"The city area [seen from Wadi ad-Deir above the Lion Triclinium] is roughly bisected from east to west by the channel of Wadi Musa itself, on either side of which the alluvial debris of the surrounding hill, brough down year after year by the seasonal torrents, is piled up in tumbled, undulating masses, whose natural eminences were used by the lords of Petra to form the *points d'appui* (points of support) of its circuit wall."
— SIR KENNEDY (1925, pg. 7)

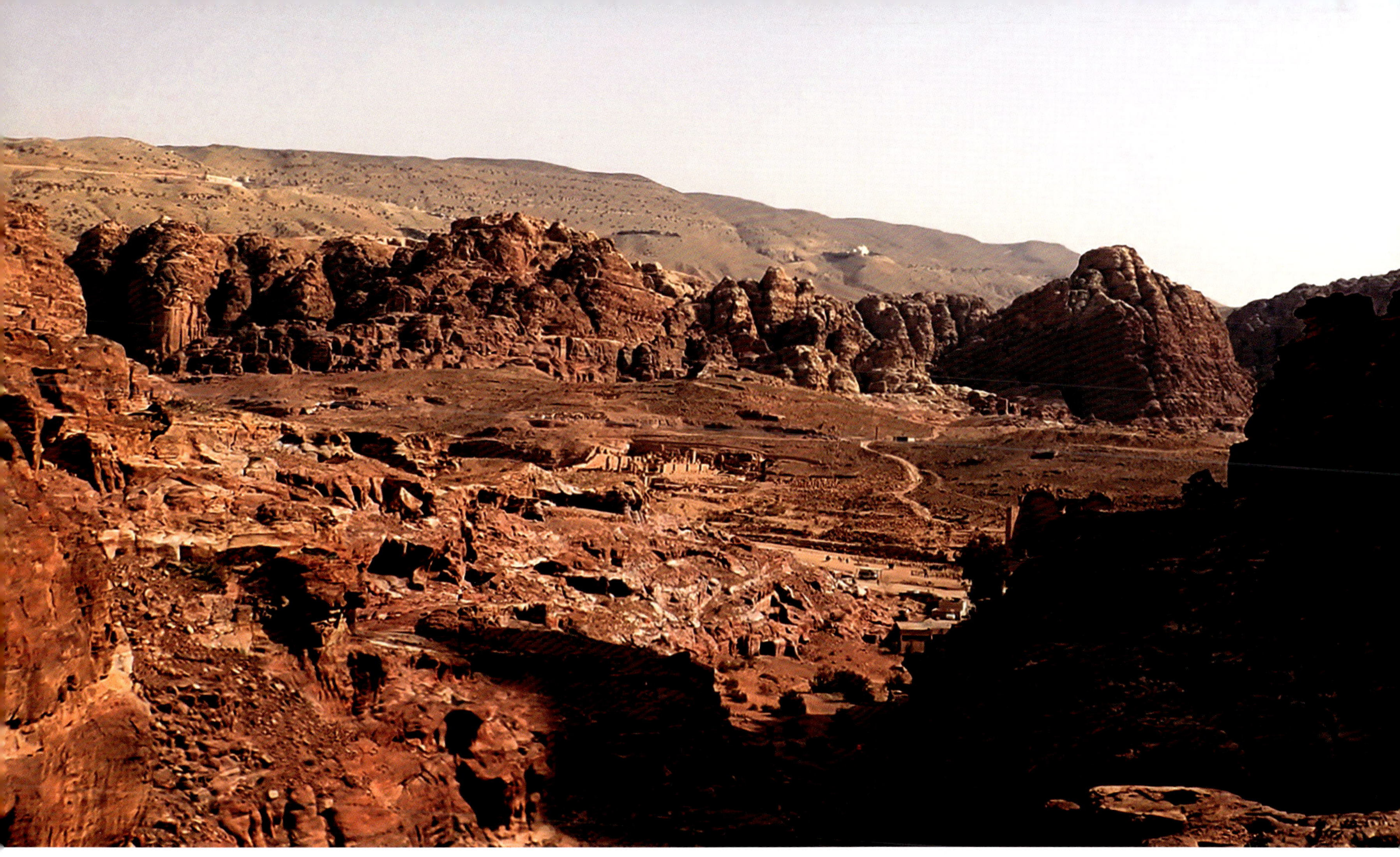

One of the only surviving photographs Sir Kennedy took of the entire central valley, this view looking back from the Wadi ad-Deir perfectly captures the grandeur of Petra's dramatic craggy setting, as well as showcases ways in which modern development has shaped the landscape. Large swaths of Sir Kennedy's "undulating masses" have been excavated to expose the Grand Temple and the adjacent Bath Complex (center), plus new trails and dirt roads now crisscross the hillside beyond, punctuated with the indominable Qasr al-Bint. The rear of the Basin Restaurant and modern toilet facilities are seen at the trailhead of Wadi ad-Deir. Farther in the foreground, the well-trod trail itself has been worn to a fine sandy path. Even with all this development, the overall view remains a wild chasm of sand and stone.

113

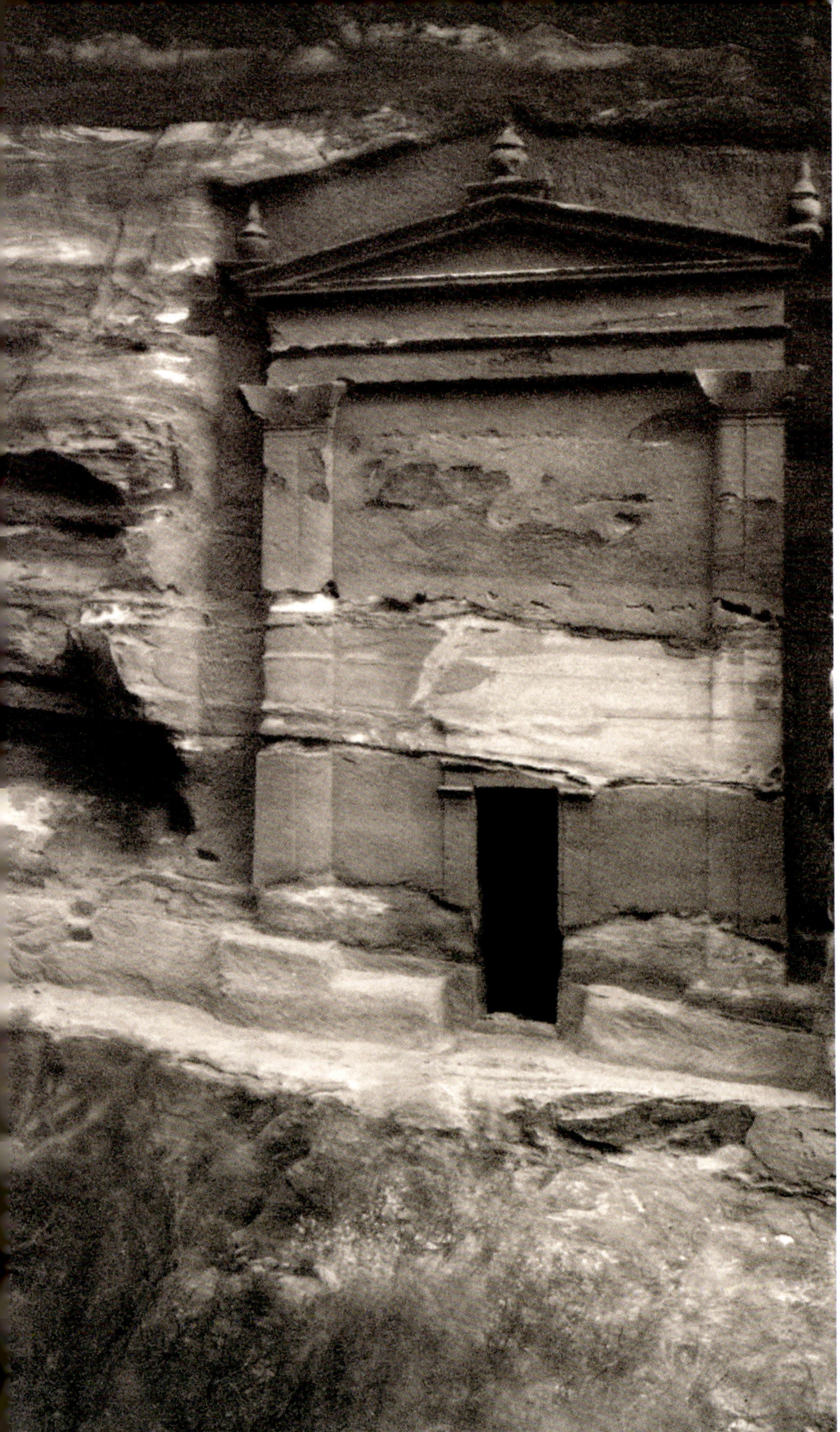

THE CAVE OF DAMAS

"Considerably higher up the ravine, beyond
the point where the Wadi al-Dair turns
westward, there stands on the east side
a severely classical façade. The photograph
shows more clearly than in most cases
the shape of the Nabataean capitals and the
compound section of the side pilasters.
The three urns are still standing on the
pediment." — SIR KENNEDY (1925, pg. 57)

Off the main trail and tucked away in an
adjoining canyon, the so-called Cave
of Damas is a pleasant surprise for anyone
willing to make the climb. The condition
of the façade is a conundrum: Its near perfect
conservation exhibiting exquisite fine-line
Nabataean stone dressings is transected by
large swaths of complete decay where the
colorful natural sandstone literally crumbles
at the slightest touch. The overlay of intricate
ancient carvings (petroglyphs) and complete
disintegration create a visual tension that
rivals the famous Silk Tomb in terms of raw
natural beauty.

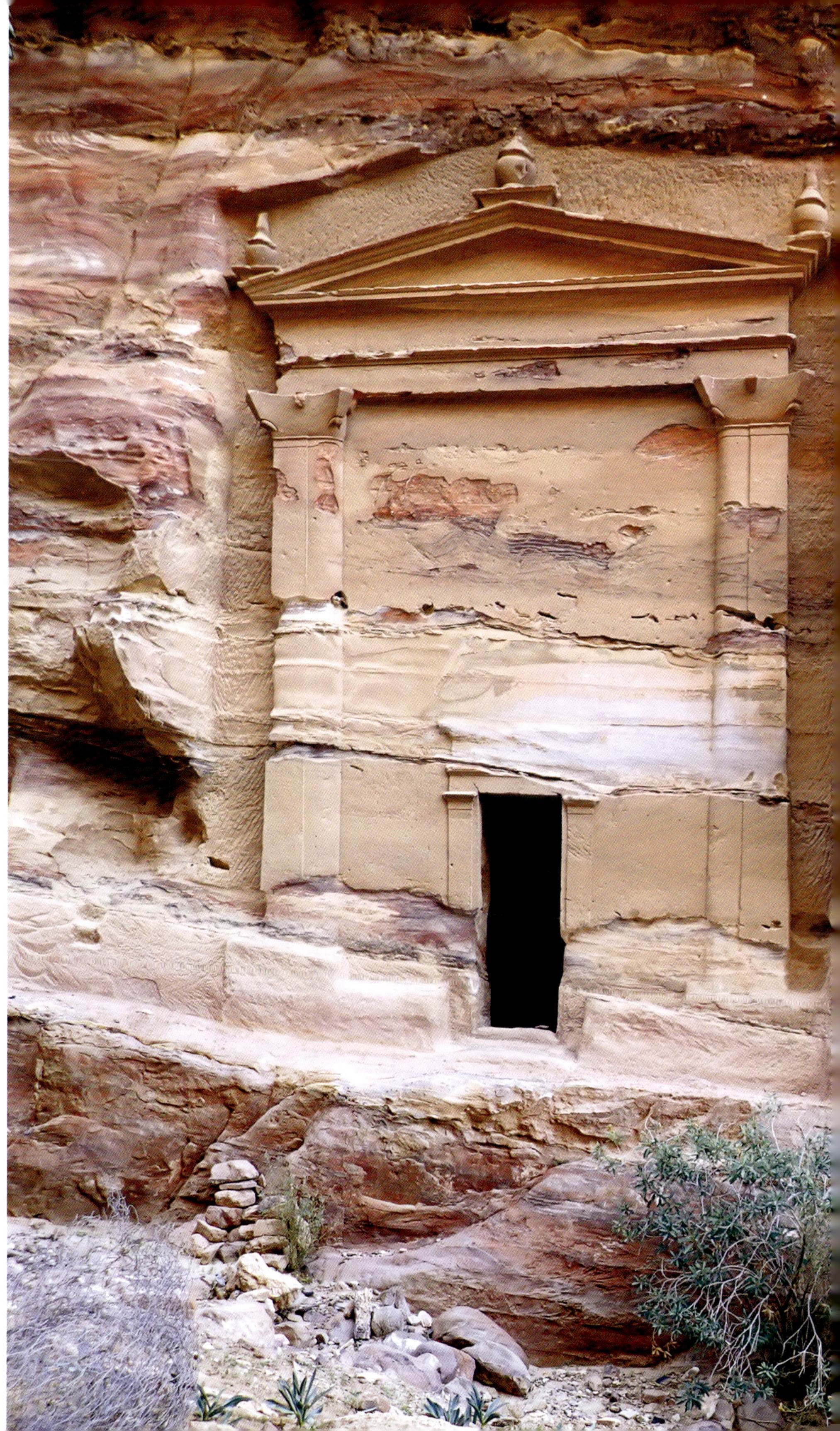

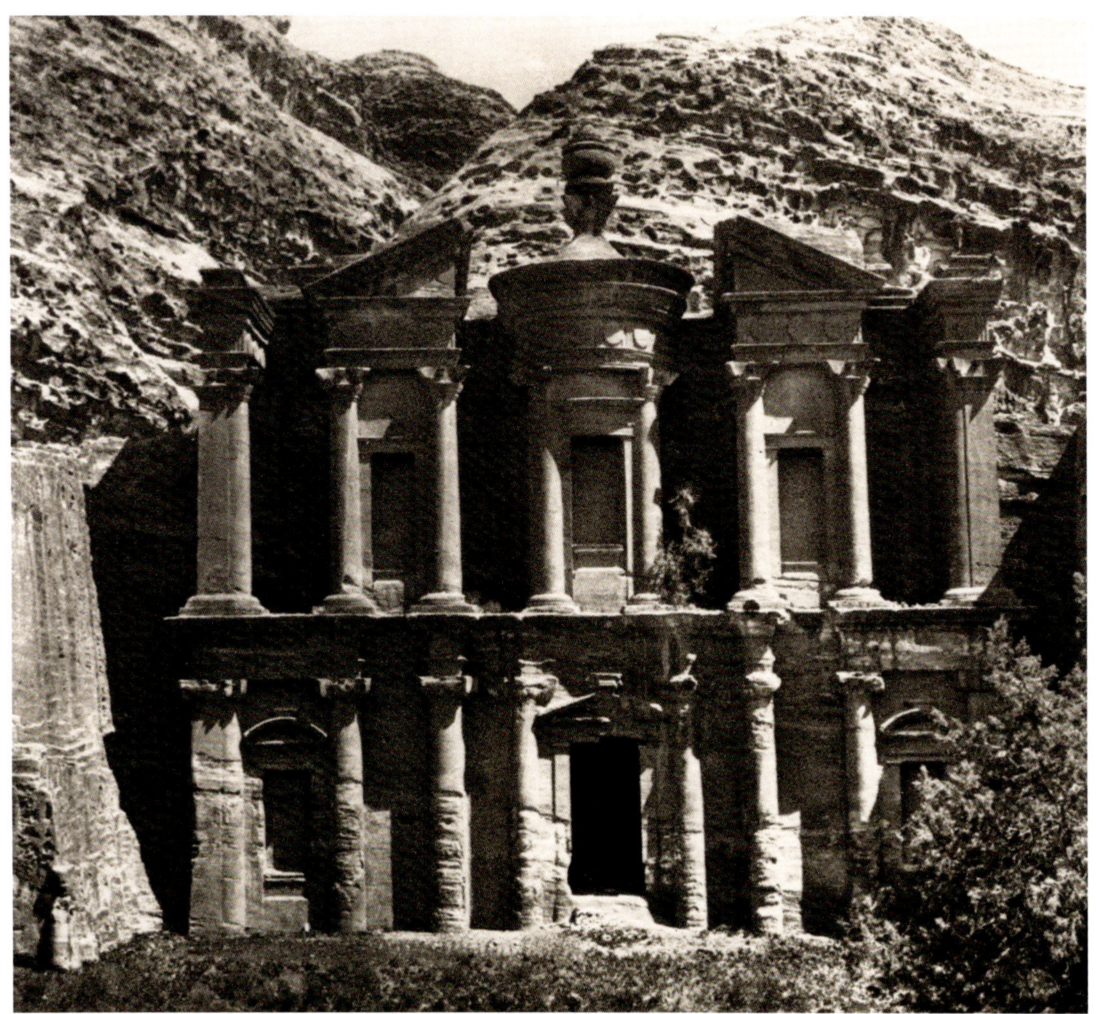

"The immense monument known as al-Dair (the 'Convent'). The great mass of rock out of which the Dair has been carved has been of such dimensions that the carved sides of the wings are carried up clear of the great recess, and from any distance appear actually as if they were side-walls of the main structure." — SIR KENNEDY (1925, pg. 56, 57)

It is difficult to convey the truly goliath scale of the Deir Monument, also called the Monastery, especially with trees in the way—an obstacle for both the historic and modern photographs, though positionings and leaf shape suggest they are two different trees. For reference, the "lip" from the ground to the base of the doorway is so high it is nearly impossible for anyone of average height to view the interior chamber without standing on a boulder or stool. The façade is best seen from a distance, perhaps from one of the many benches laid out near the Bedouin cafe, whose roof is seen at the base of the modern photograph. Visitors can sit and marvel at the magnitude of this giant while enjoying fresh juice, snacks, and the ubiquitous company of Petra dogs and cats wandering their way through the benches, seeking scraps, attention, or just a comfortable place to nap on the bright array of traditional Bedouin rugs.

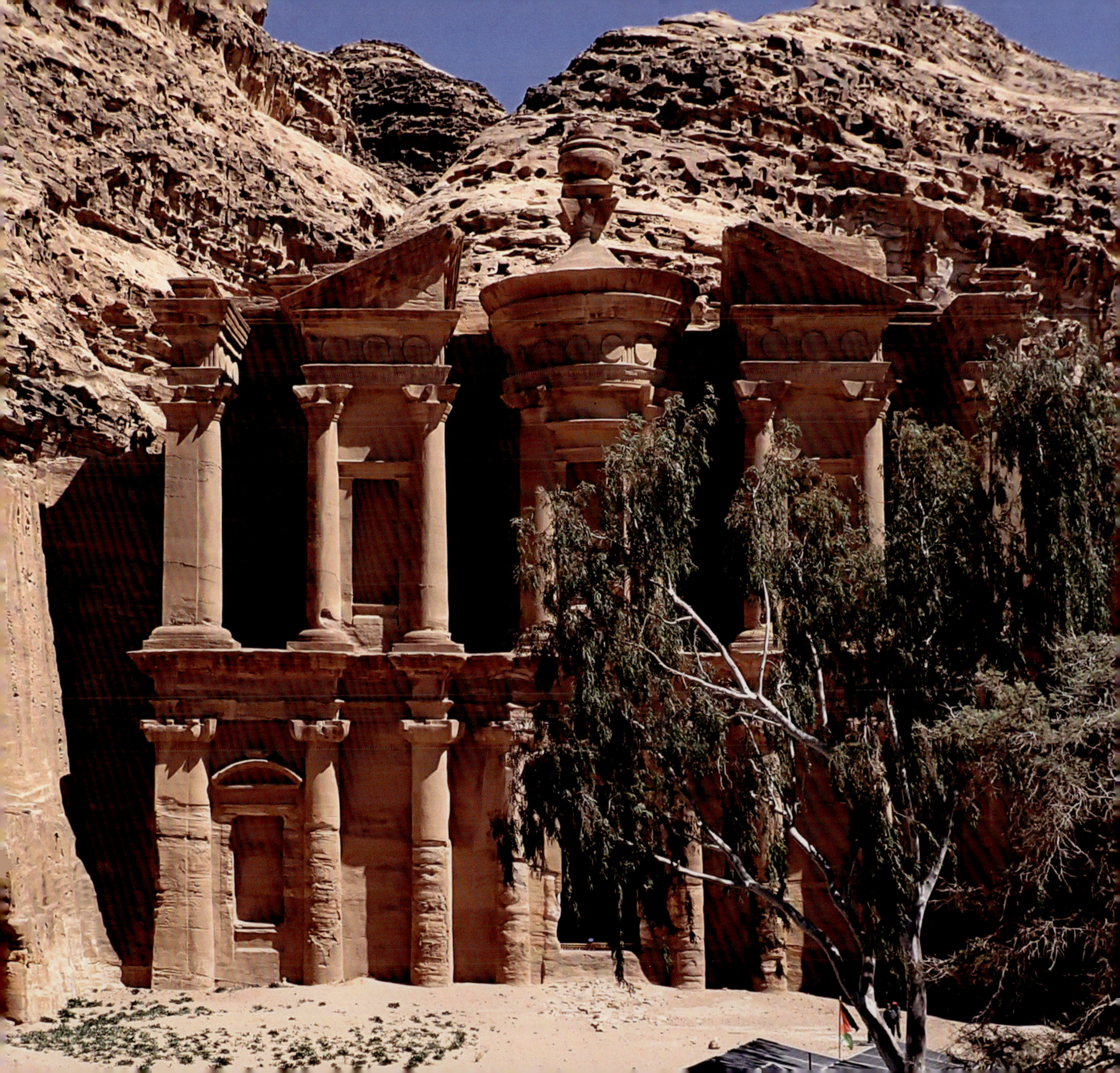

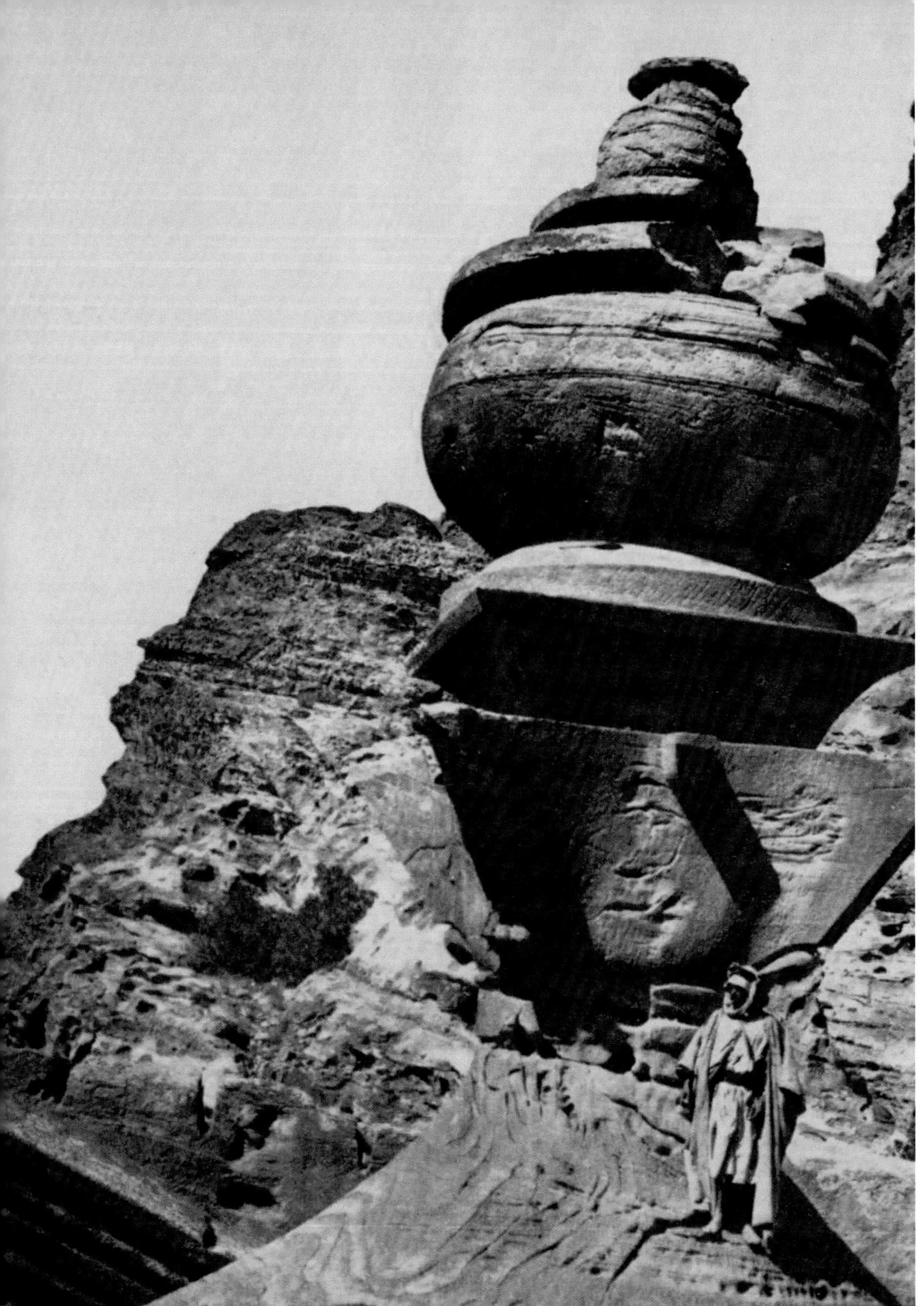

THE AD-DEIR URN

"It will be seen from the photograph that
this gigantic urn having a total height
of over 30 feet is supported by a gigantic
duplication of a Nabataean capital."
— SIR KENNEDY (1925, pg. 56)

The hazardous ascent to the Deir Urn is justifiably off limits to visitors and we had to make special arrangements to replicate Sir Kennedy's image. I am profoundly grateful to Ranger Yahya (featured in the modern repeat) for helping us skillfully navigate the perilous scramble up the massive temple. Without his guidance, the climb would have been impossible. His surefootedness is highlighted in the modern photograph, as the convenient broken ledge used as a step by Sir Kennedy's guide has since been filled with cement in efforts to stabilize the colossal urn, forcing Ranger Yahya to stand at an impressively steep angle and grip the base of the urn for support.

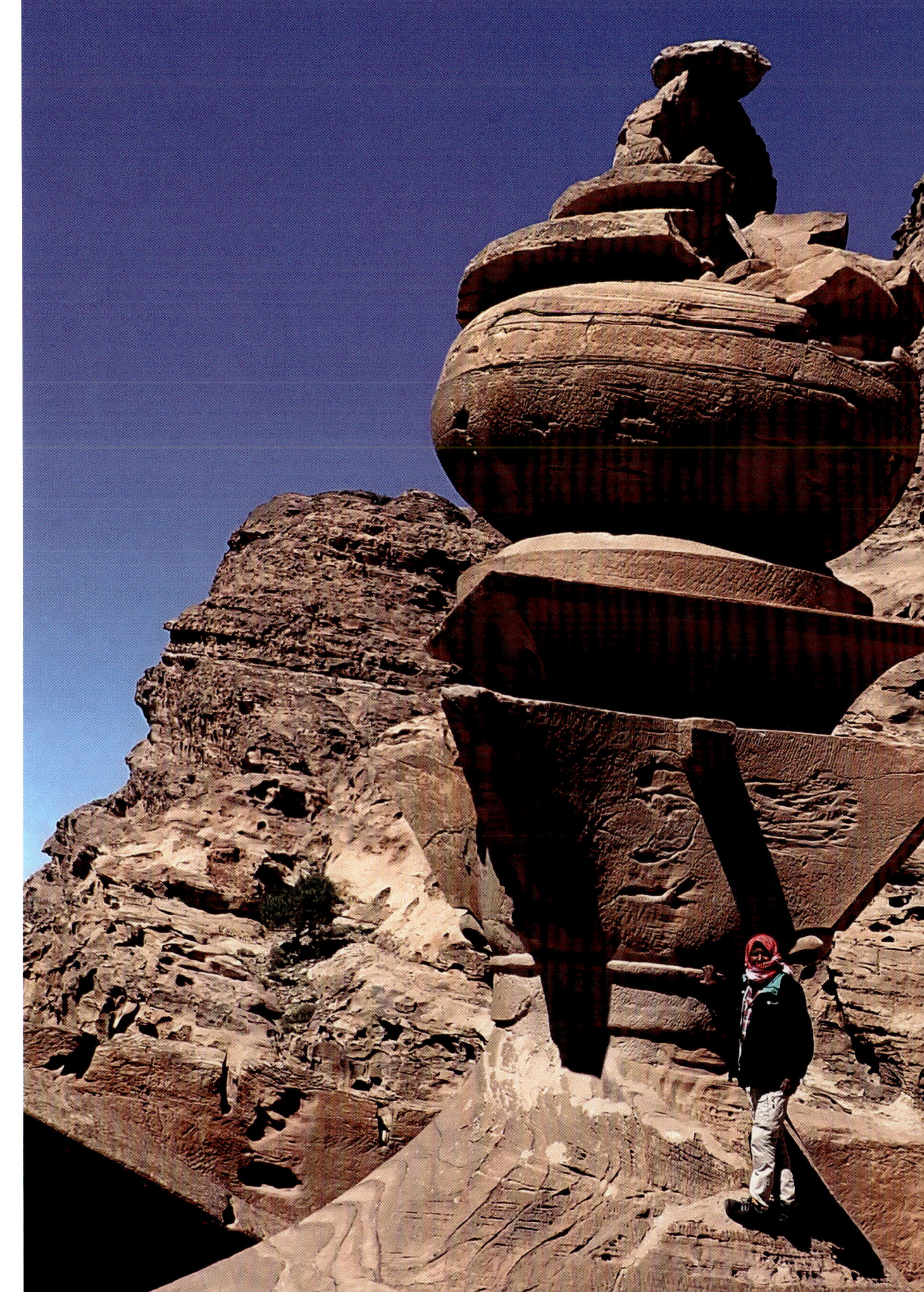

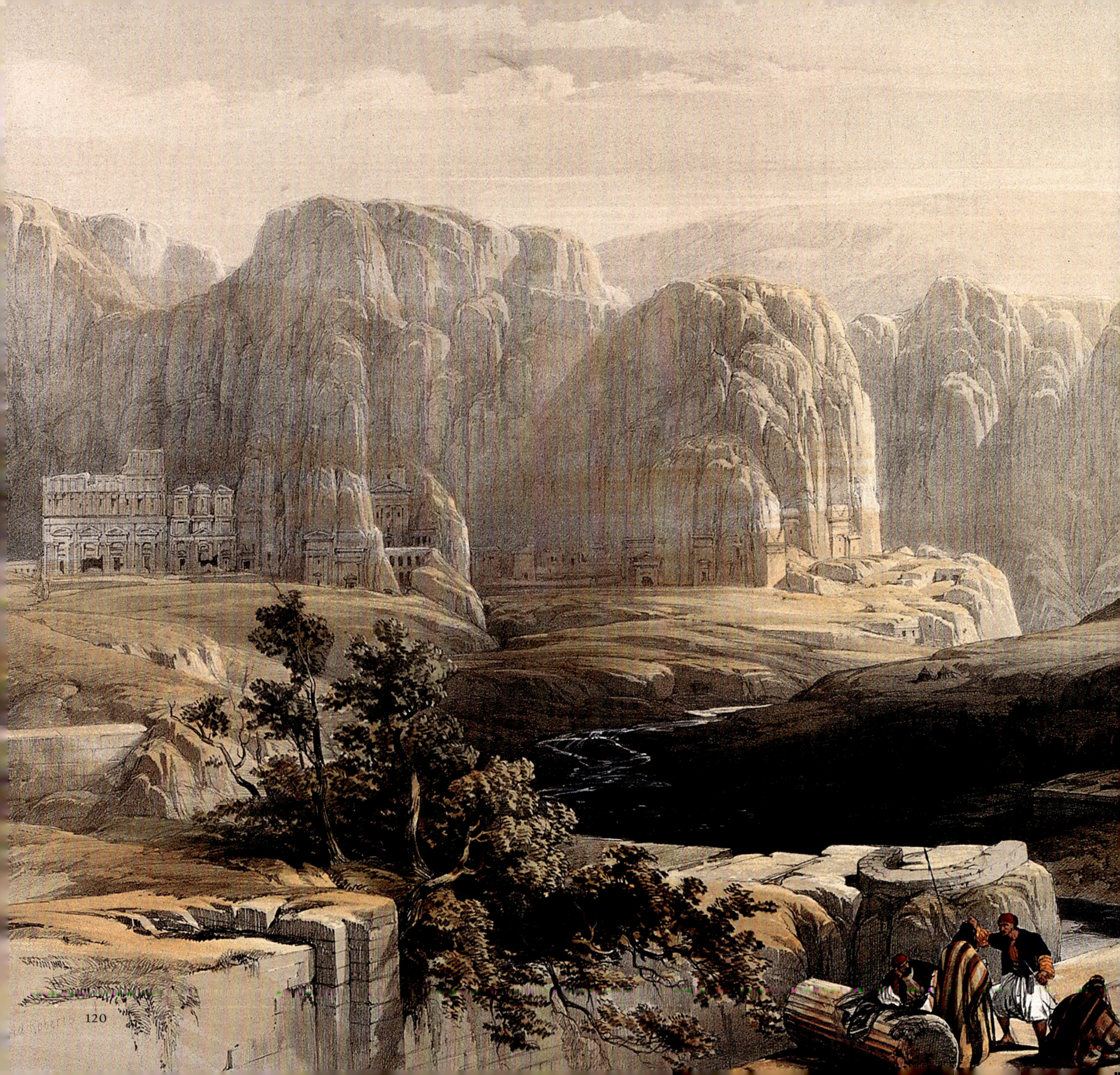

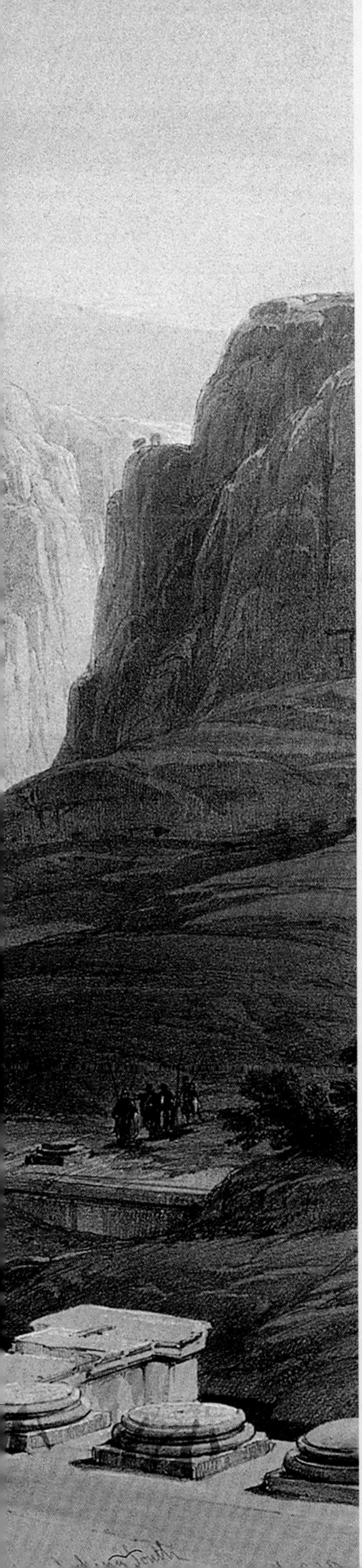

Trail to the Heavens:
Wadi Farasa, Obelisk Ridge, and the High Place of Sacrifice

For the more adventurous visitor, the region in the southeastern cliffs of Petra accommodates several hauntingly beautiful façades along the precarious trail leading to the infamous High Place of Sacrifice—where the Nabataean people conducted various religious ceremonies and offerings.

"Here on the mountain top, under the blue skies of heaven and the heat of the sun, the early inhabitants of Petra worshipped their gods; here sacrifices were offered on the well-preserved altars; whilst about them on all sides was nature's handiwork, and below them the valley with its hundreds of excavations in every shape and form." — MR. ARCHIBALD FORDER [11]

Lithograph by nineteenth-century artist David Roberts of the lofty Royal Tombs from across the valley along

11 A. Forder, *Petra, Perea, and Phoenicia* (London: Marshall Brothers, Ltd., 1923), 36.

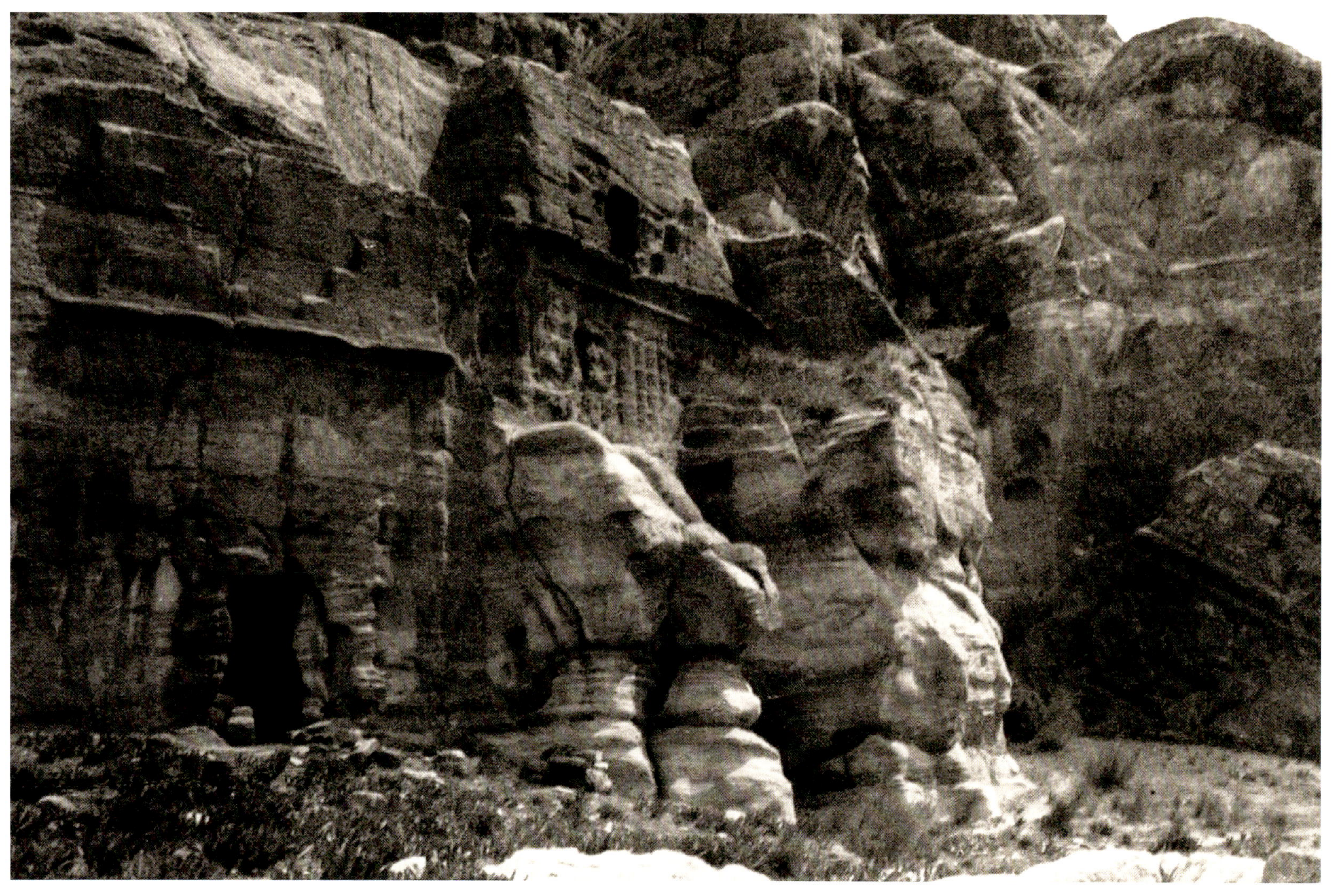

"A good illustration of the wonderful way in which the 'ravages of time' have added to the picturesqueness of the Petraean monuments. On the left is a corniced and decorated monument so worn that it is hardly possible to say whether it had originally two or four pilasters in front, or whether the doorway had any decoration. The two splendid buttresses which enclose the next monument do not appear to owe anything to the hands of man." — SIR KENNEDY (1925, pg. 50)

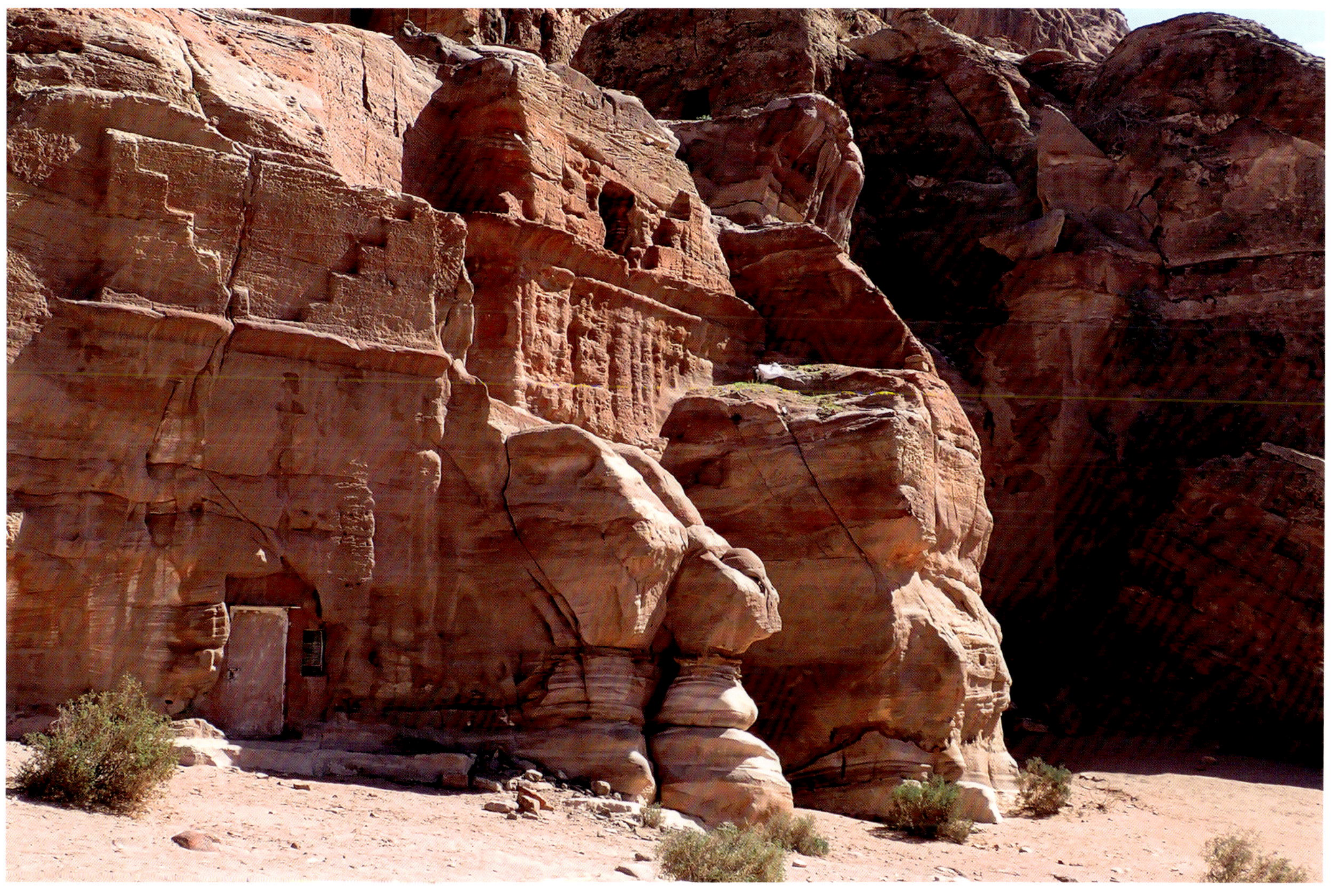

Welcoming visitors to the base of the Wadi Farasa trail, these impressively deteriorated tombs project a haunting hollow beauty. The modern addition of steel and cement makes the monument more utilitarian but does little to counter the eerie presence of the jagged façade. Interlacing cracks create the illusion that the mountain would crumble at the slightest touch.

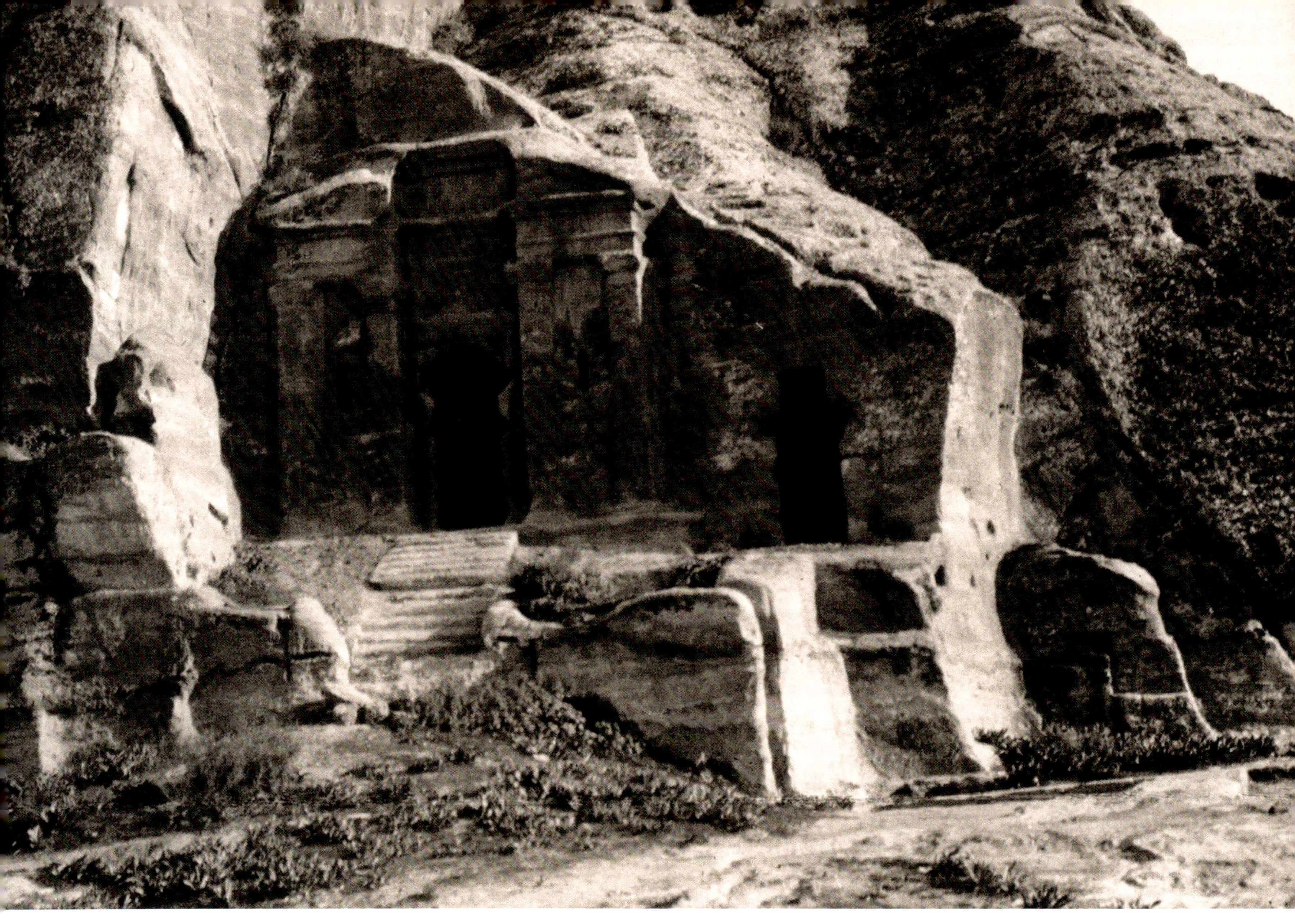

MONUMENTS IN WADI FARASA

"The striking monument is carved on a rock projecting at right angles from the Obelisk Ridge. . . . It is approached by the steps shown in the photograph from a platform which is itself reached by broad steps from the general level. . . . Some very serious cause would appear to be necessary to explain the abandonment of a chamber with such external pretensions to importance."
— SIR KENNEDY (1925, pg. 58)

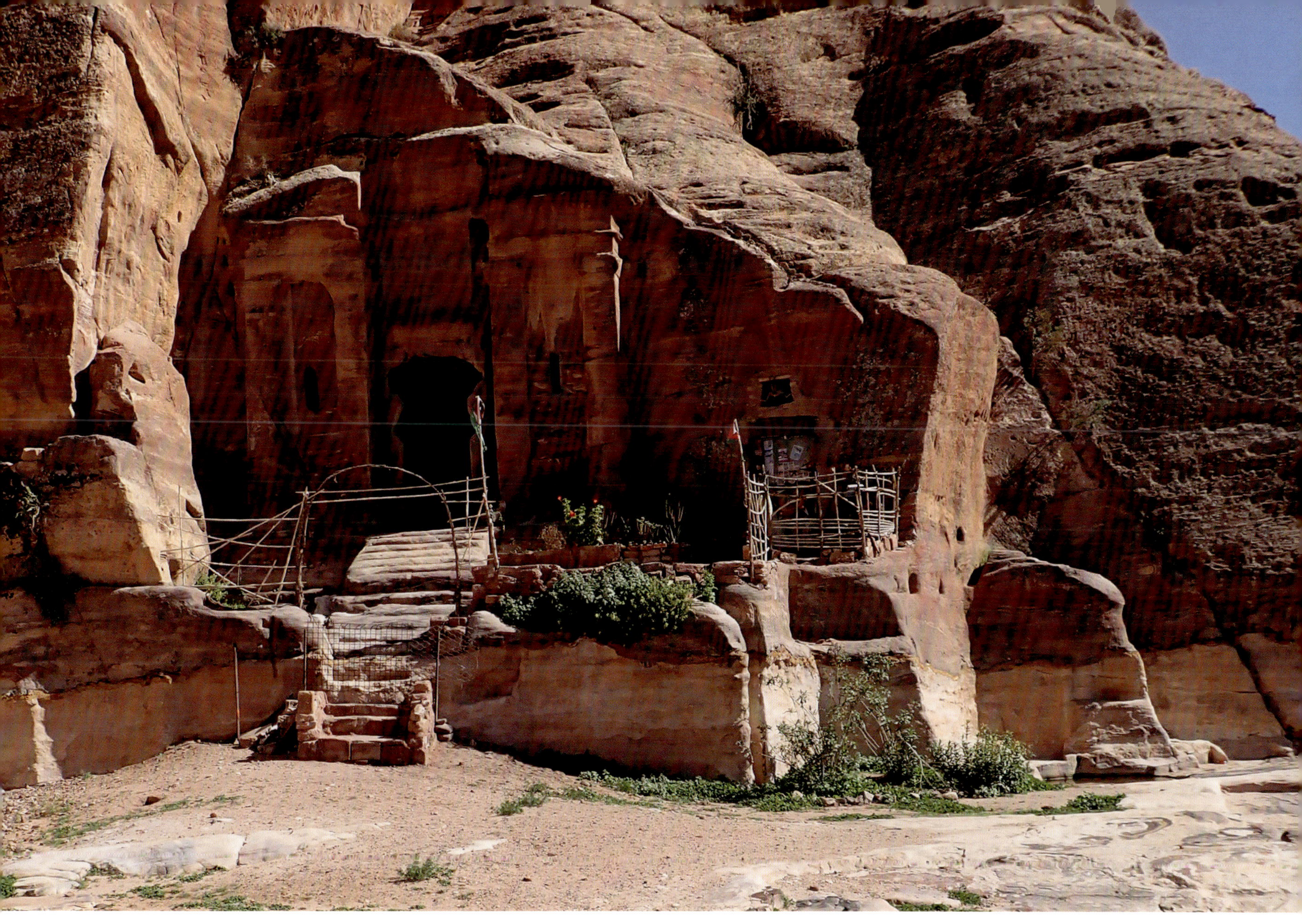

It seems the "abandonment" of this unique Wadi Farasa tomb was relatively short-lived. While permanent residency is no longer permitted in the valley, young enterprising Bedouin have reimagined the monument as a place to rest, drink tea, and show visitors what living in the hollowed façades was like. The extreme degradation of the soil in front of the platform has necessitated the addition of modern steps leading to the hewn stairway now decorated with a small wooden arch and cultivated vegetation.

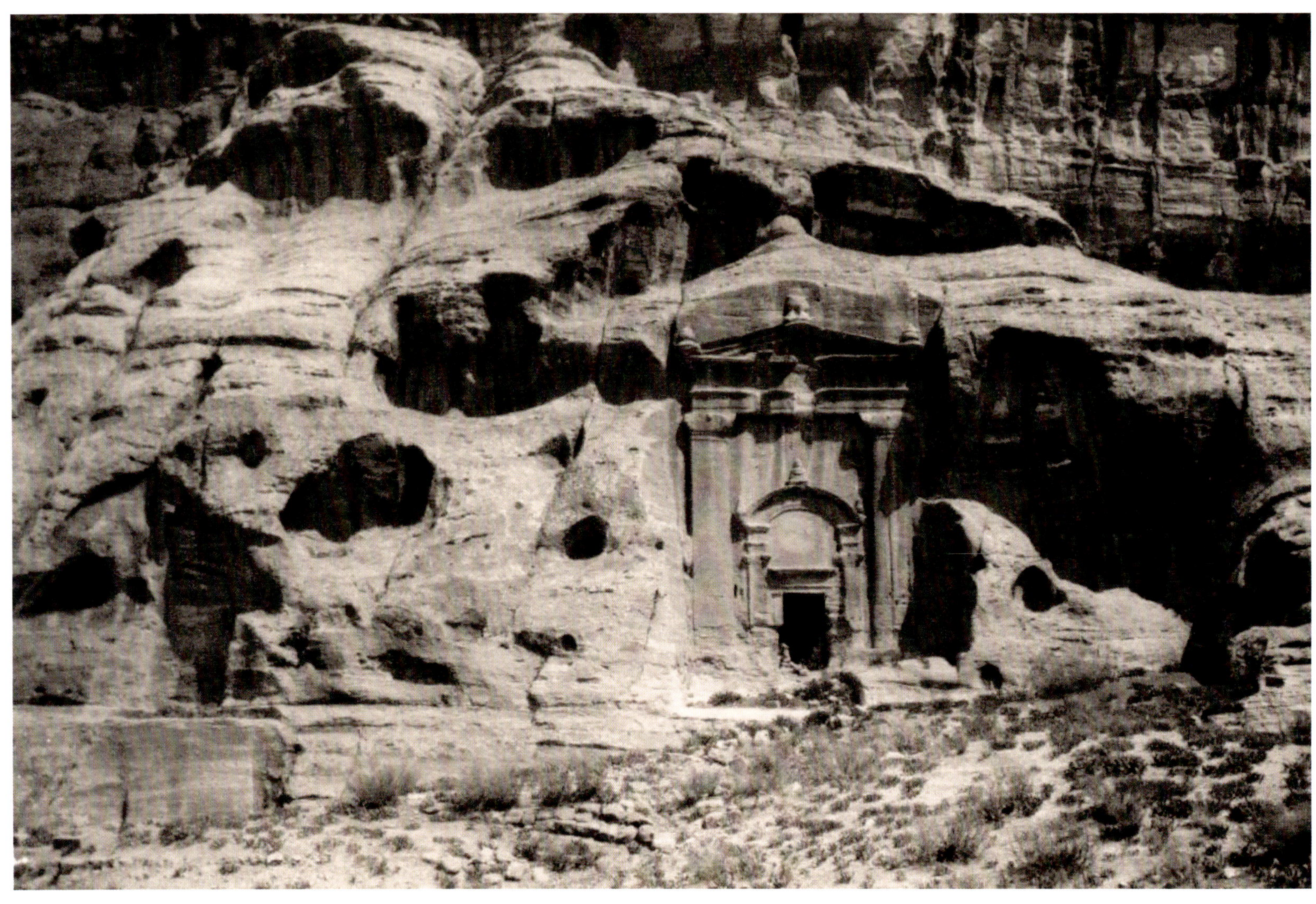

**CLASSICAL TOMB
IN WADI FARASA**

"[This tomb] on the Obelisk Ridge is one
of the most ornate and one of the best
preserved... Its special feature is the moulded
arch—with urns—as a mere decoration on
the front, carried over the architrave of the
door on two tall pilasters." —SIR KENNEDY
(1925, pg. 58)

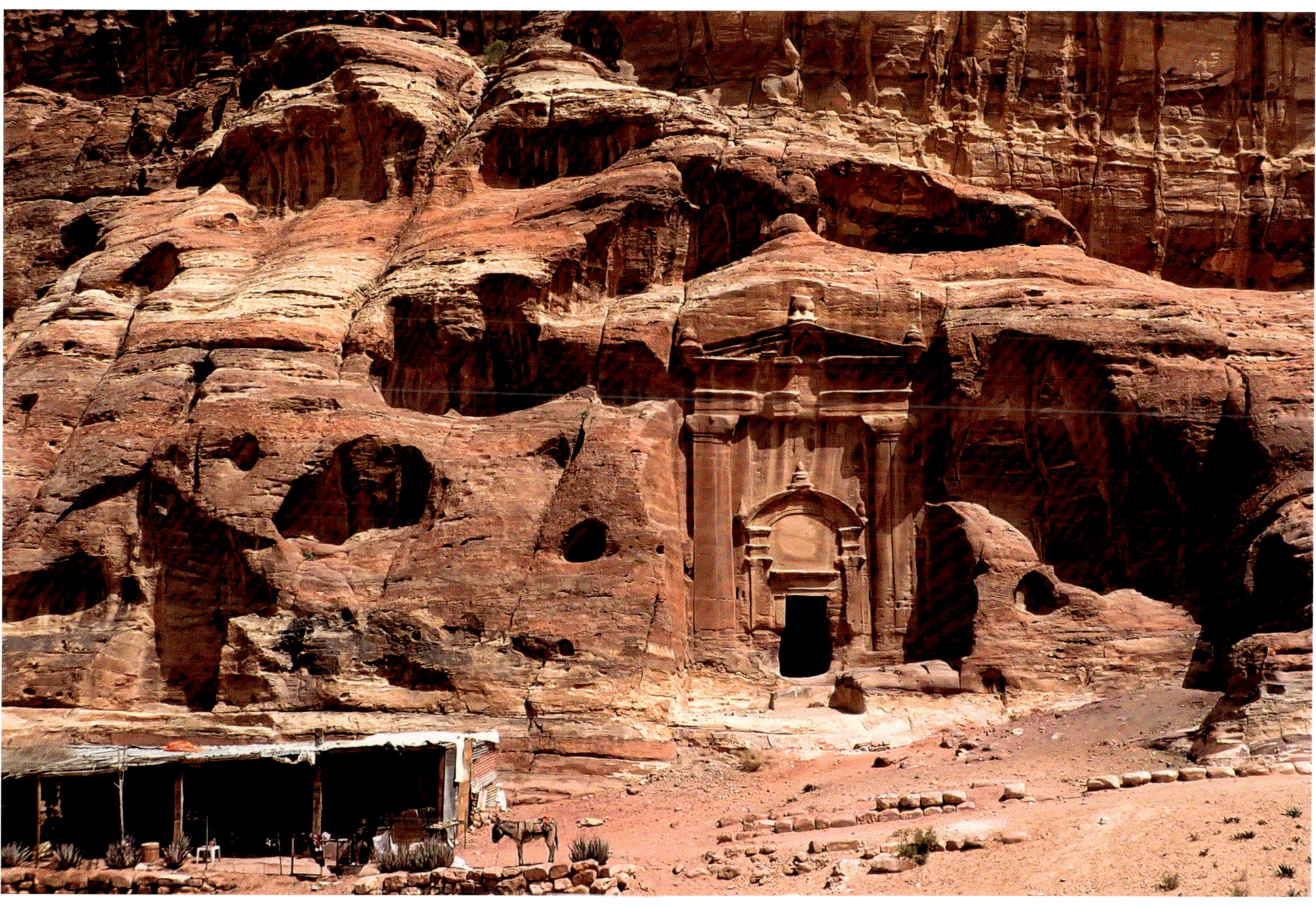

These images exemplify the otherworldly juxtaposition of delicately carved classical features—such as those celebrated on this isolated façade—and the raw, ragged, cavernous, wild cliffside into which Petra was hewn. The rich browns, reds, and golden hues of the cliffs seemingly drip down the stone face, almost as if the mountain itself is melting, and yet there, in the middle of this stoney ruin, stands a beautiful relic of ancient might. Over the past century, the only change is the addition of a small Bedouin stall (bottom left) and lines of excavated stones leading the way up the Wadi Farasa trail. It is little wonder why local Bedouin lore tells of jinn and spirits stalking this valley during the eerie calm of desert nights.

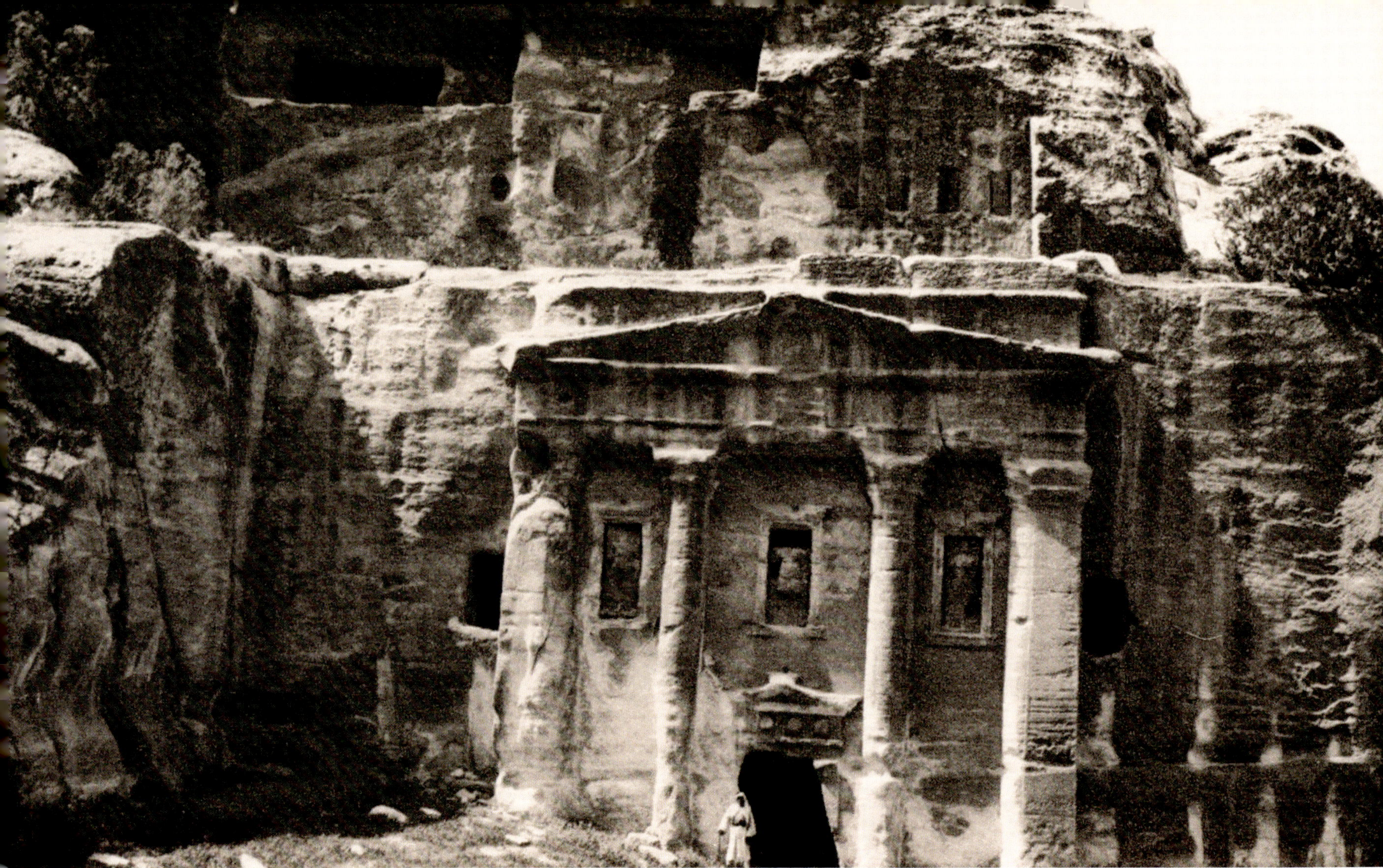

THE SOLDIER TOMB

"It is of quite straightforward classical design, with four pilasters and a plain frieze and pediment. In the three bays into with the columns divide the front are niches with statues, but the nature of the figures represented is not very certain... The monument contains two chambers, in one of which are four arch-topped niches, probably for burials." — SIR KENNEDY (1925, pg. 59)

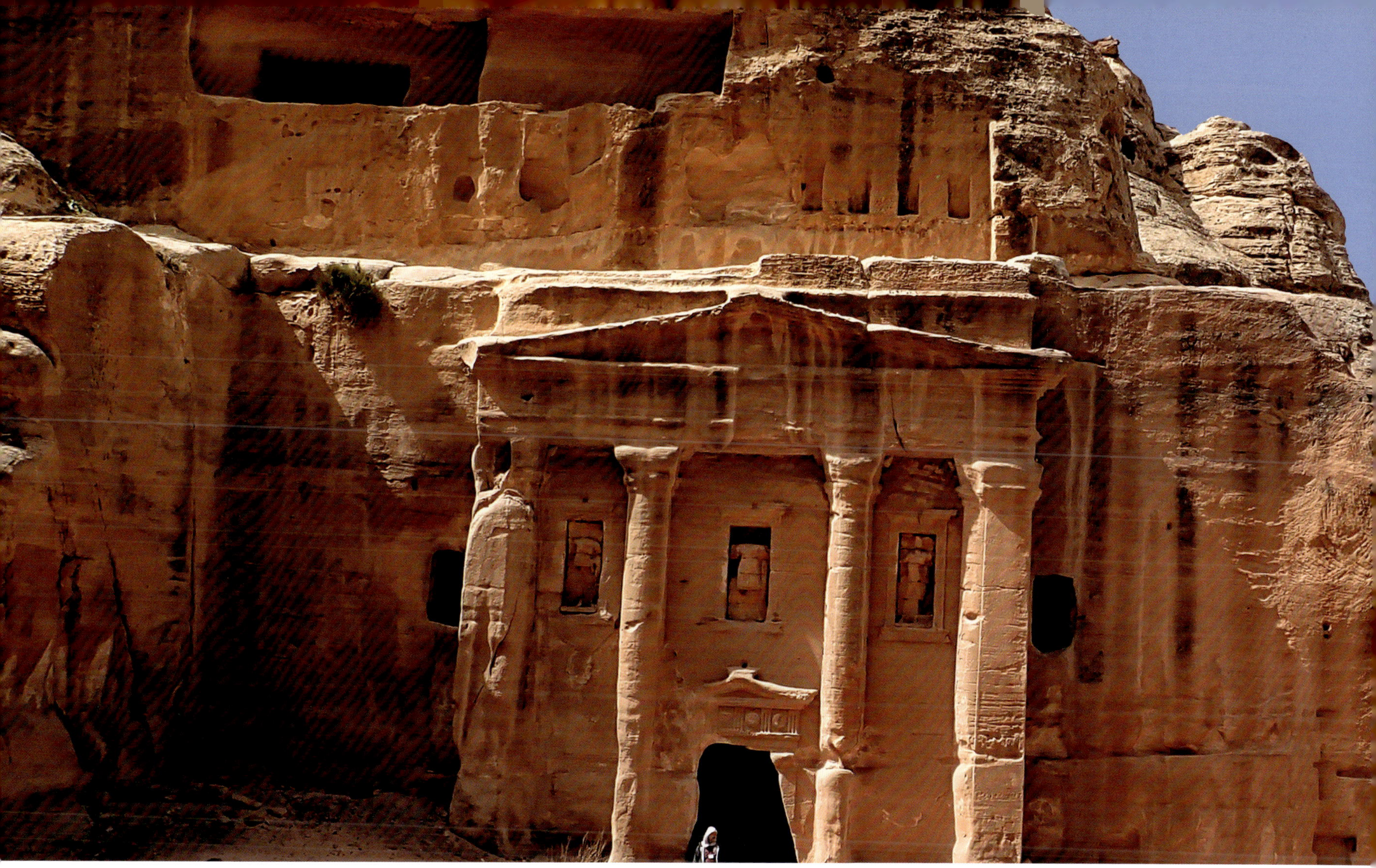

It is unfortunate Sir Kennedy's photograph is so spatially constricted, as some of the most dramatic changes at this location are in the courtyard just beyond the scope of the images. (A wider view of this monument is featured in the seasonal shadows example in the opening chapter.) Readers can get a semblance of how much the ground has receded—perhaps from either excavation or seasonal stormwaters, or a combination—by how much lower field assistant Dr. Casey Allen is standing in the monument's doorway compared to Sir Kennedy's companion. On the monument itself, trees and brush that once perched along the upper ledge have since died (or been removed) and a plucky new scrub has taken residence in the deep crag in the upper left, casting a new shadow across the resolute façade, which has since earned the name "Soldier Tomb."

129

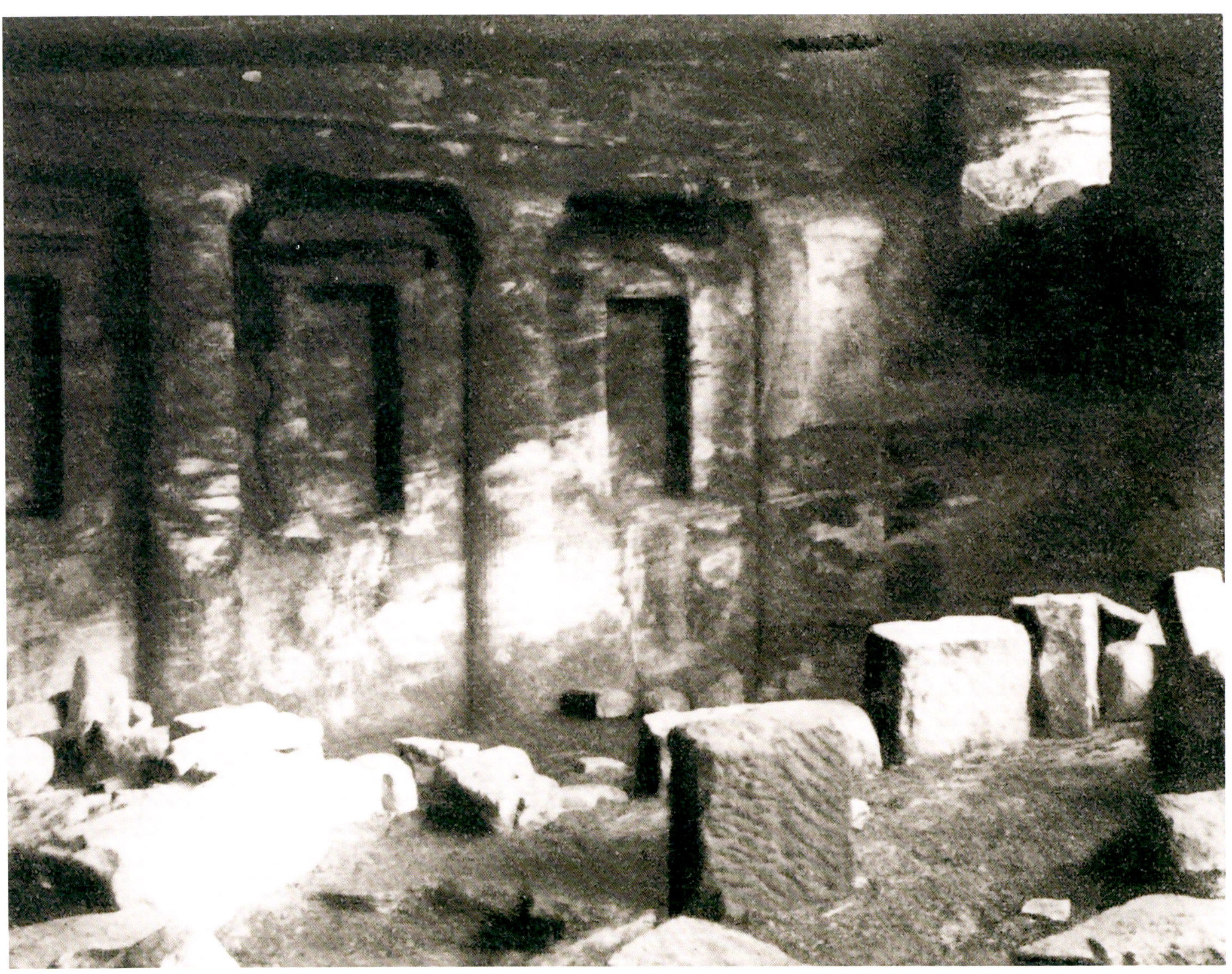

INSIDE THE FLUTED TOMB

"It is the only one of the Petraean rock chambers which has internal architectural decoration of this type... This monument, whatever its purpose may have been, has no architectural façade. We may, therefore, assume that it was never intended to have any... It is not possible to do any more than guess at the intention or function of this remarkable monument." — SIR KENNEDY (1925, pg. 58, 59)

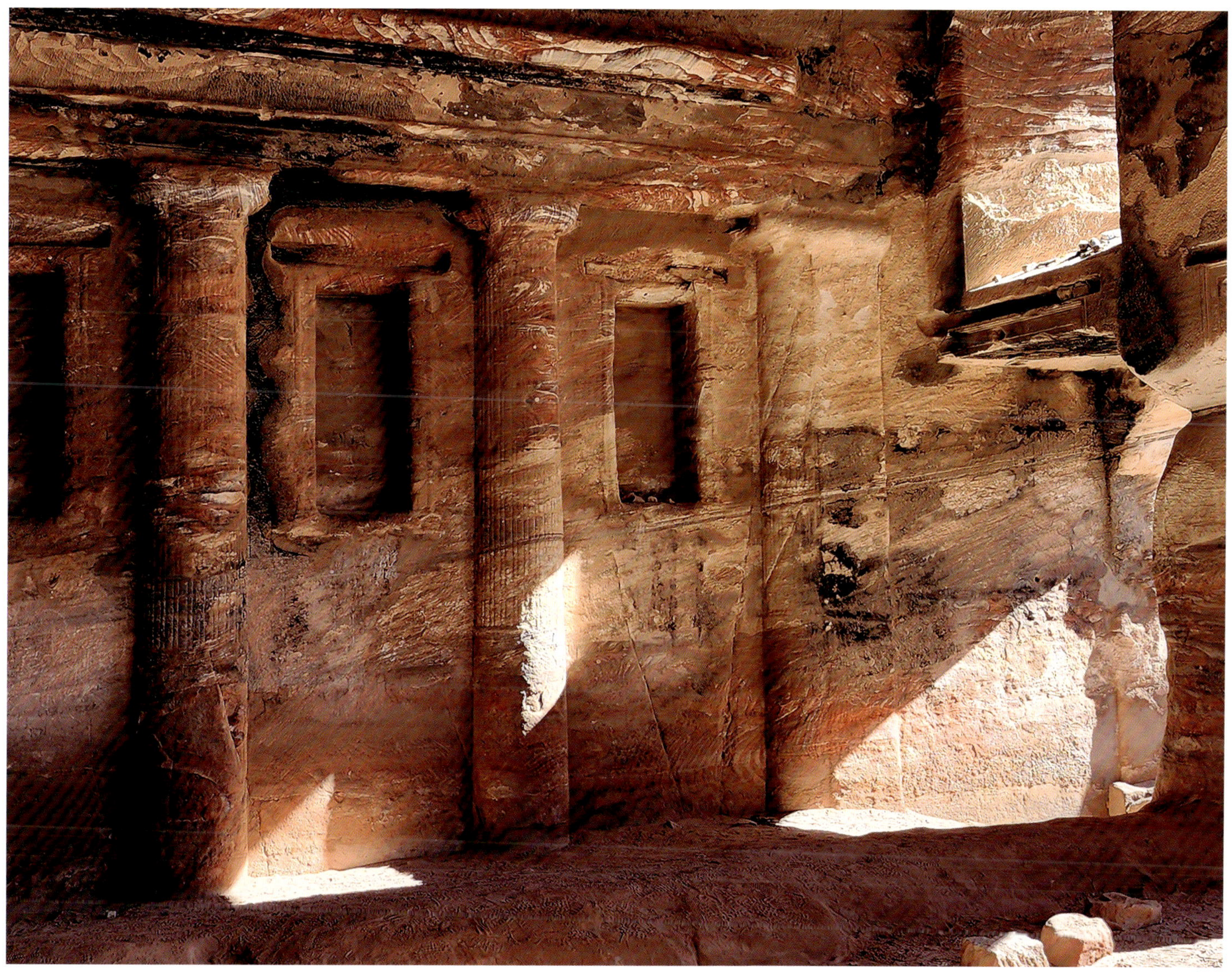

This monument is a curious contradiction, as expressed by Sir Kennedy. Most of the tombs in Petra feature heavily decorated exteriors with plain interiors, but this monument is the opposite. The intricate fluted columns—earning it the name Fluted Tomb—and multitude of carved alcoves in the naturally kaleidoscopic sandstone walls are hidden within an unadorned, unassuming exterior with nothing but a handful of roughly hewn doors and windows. Through the years, the remarkable monument has seen various forms of human intervention: the ceiling and walls blackened with soot from traditional Bedouin cooking fires, the clearing of the upper windows allowing new light to enter the chamber (explaining the different lighting shown in the two photographs), and the extensive excavations clearing the fallen columns and debris from the room's interior.

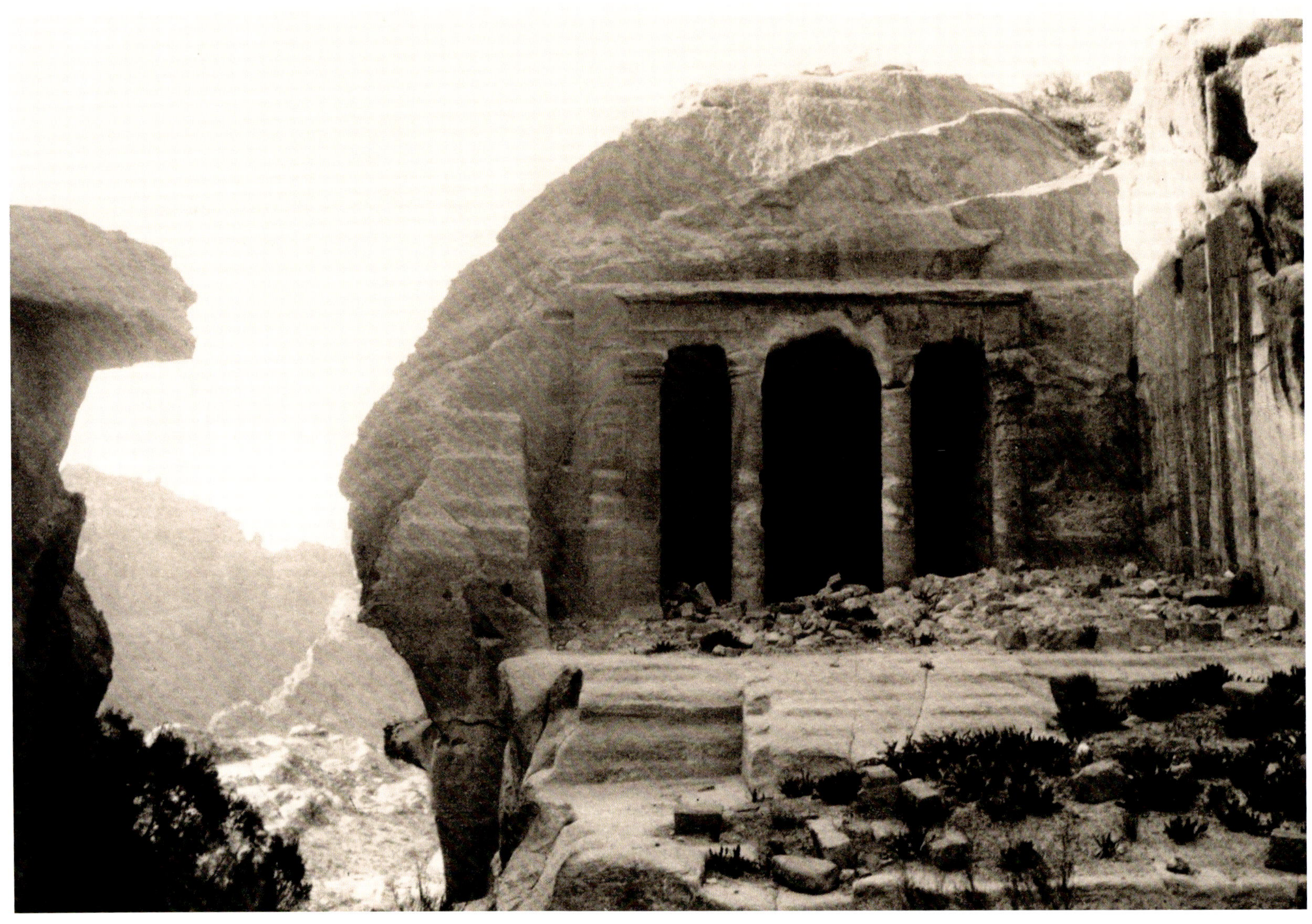

THE GARDEN TOMB

"The inner part of the northern Farasa Wadi is reached by a stairway up the very narrow passage on the left of [the photograph]. Immediately to the north of the opening stands the Temple, which is approached by steps, and which is fronted by a large cleared level space—once, no doubt, green with plants and trees." — SIR KENNEDY (1925, pg. 59)

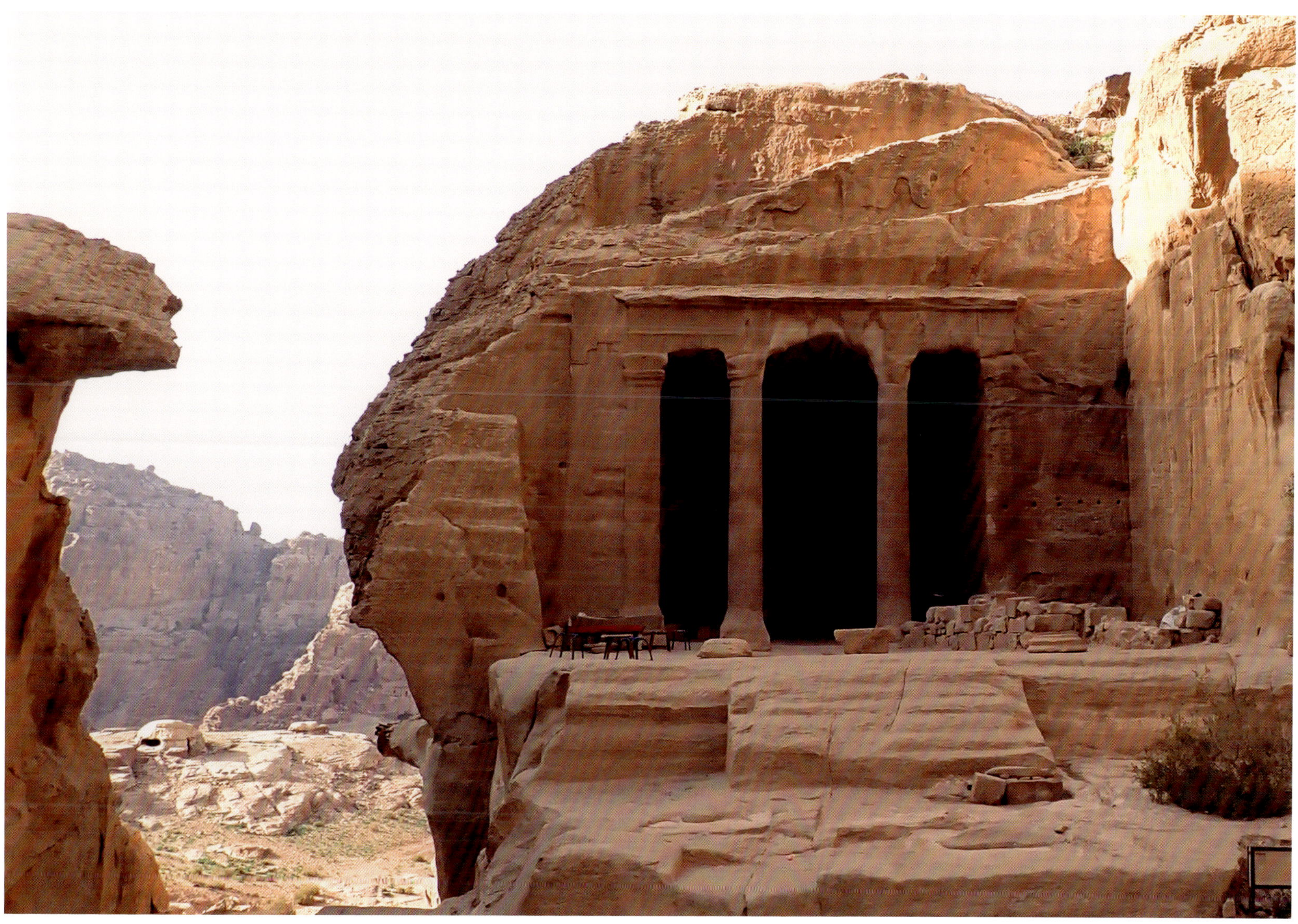

Now called the "Garden Tomb," this elevated monument and courtyard sits at the base of Jabal al-Madhbah's steep ascent to the High Place of Sacrifice. Cleared as part of the decade-long International Wadi Farasa Project in the early 2000s, the hollow columned façade now hosts a humble table and benches where Bedouins often host resting visitors navigating the trail up the mountain. While waiting for the setting sun to paint its harsh line across the courtyards inner wall, several Bedouin children delighted in showering my field assistant and me with their famous Bedouin hospitality: maintaining an endless supply of tea, writing their names in Arabic in the coarse desert sand, regaling with stories, and lending a hand up and down the stone steps (even when such 'help' was completely unnecessary). When I asked why they were so obliging, they replied "this is our way, and you are like my mother"—a testament to the kindness of Bedouin culture.

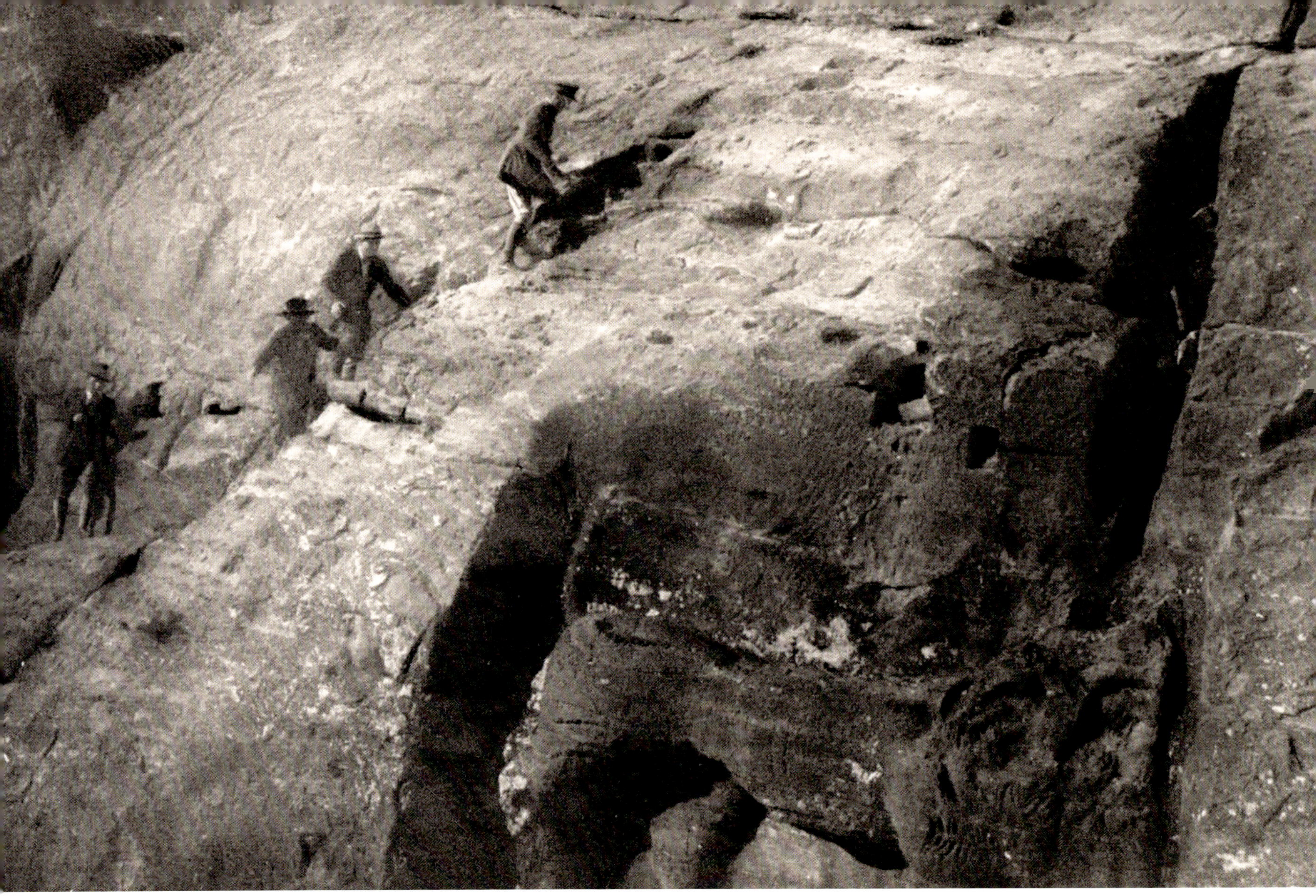

THE LION FOUNTAIN

"Not far from the [trail] is the remarkable relief of an animal supposed to be a lion. The photograph shows clearly the water channel which has been carefully shaped to direct its contents straight to the lion's head, with the results that the upper part of the head has been practically washed away."
— SIR KENNEDY (1925, pg. 69)

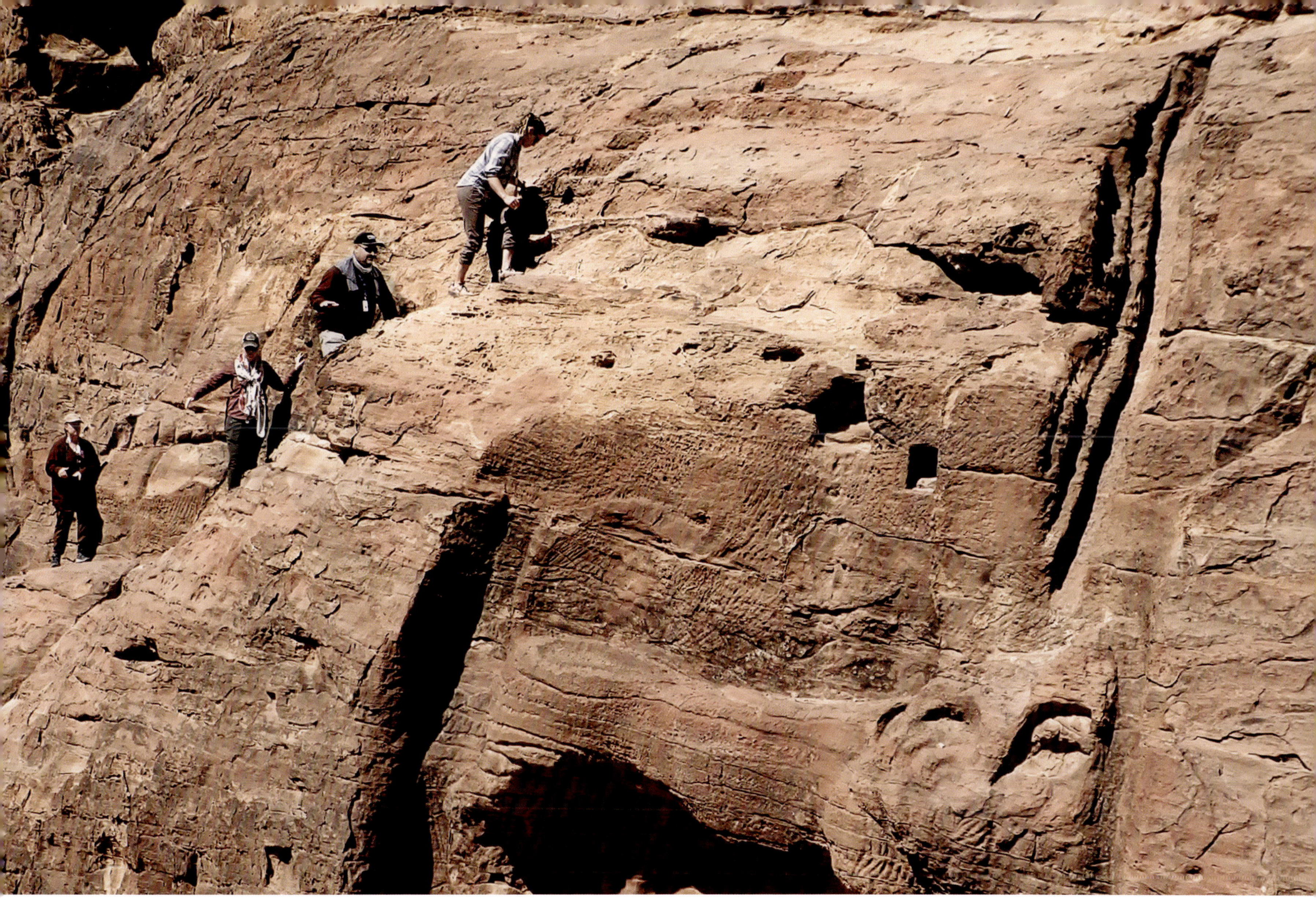

A particularly challenging photograph to replicate with the same lighting, the "Lion Fountain," as it is now called, remains an impressive feature carved into the al-Madhbah Mountain. The water channels leading to what is assumed to be the Lion's mouth (right) is more pronounced in the modern repeat, with its harsher lighting highlighting the subtle ridges.

The precarious climb along the narrow edge above the relief, replicated from left to right by myself and field assistants Molly Groom, Dr. Casey Allen, and McKay Barker, is (thankfully) no longer the primary means to ascend the mountain. Modern steps to the south facilitate a more pleasant path while also providing a breathtaking view of the valley below.

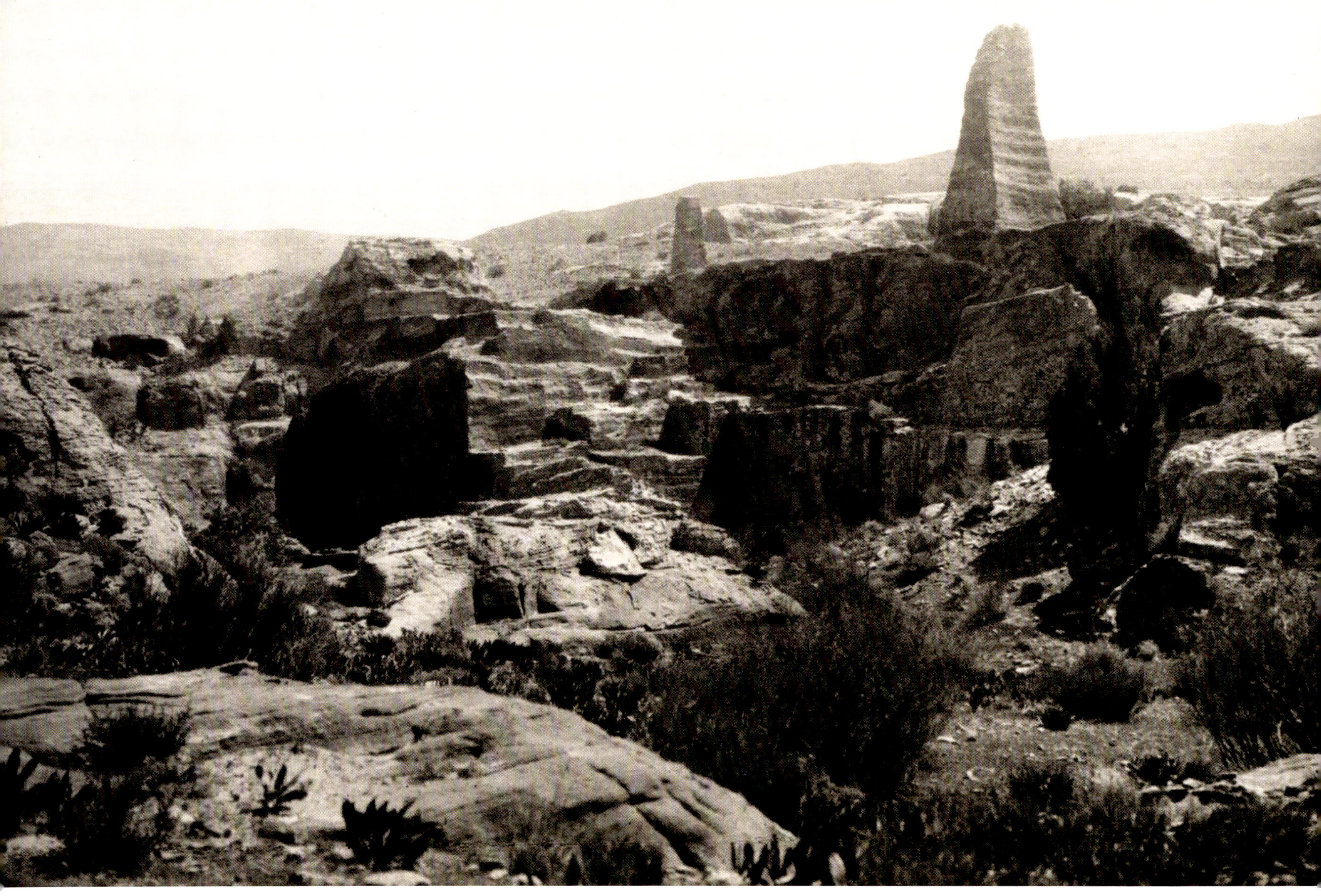

THE OBELISK RIDGE

"South of the Place of Sacrifice and separated from it by a great artificial corridor stand the two rough obelisks from which the ridge takes its name. . . . In general it must be said that there do not now remain any very definite indications that the obelisk plateau itself was a place of worship, but it is hardly possible to think that the sculptures who deliberately, and with so much trouble, left the two obelisks standing as they are by cutting away large masses of surrounding rock, do so without some definite cultural object." — SIR KENNEDY (1925, pg. 68)

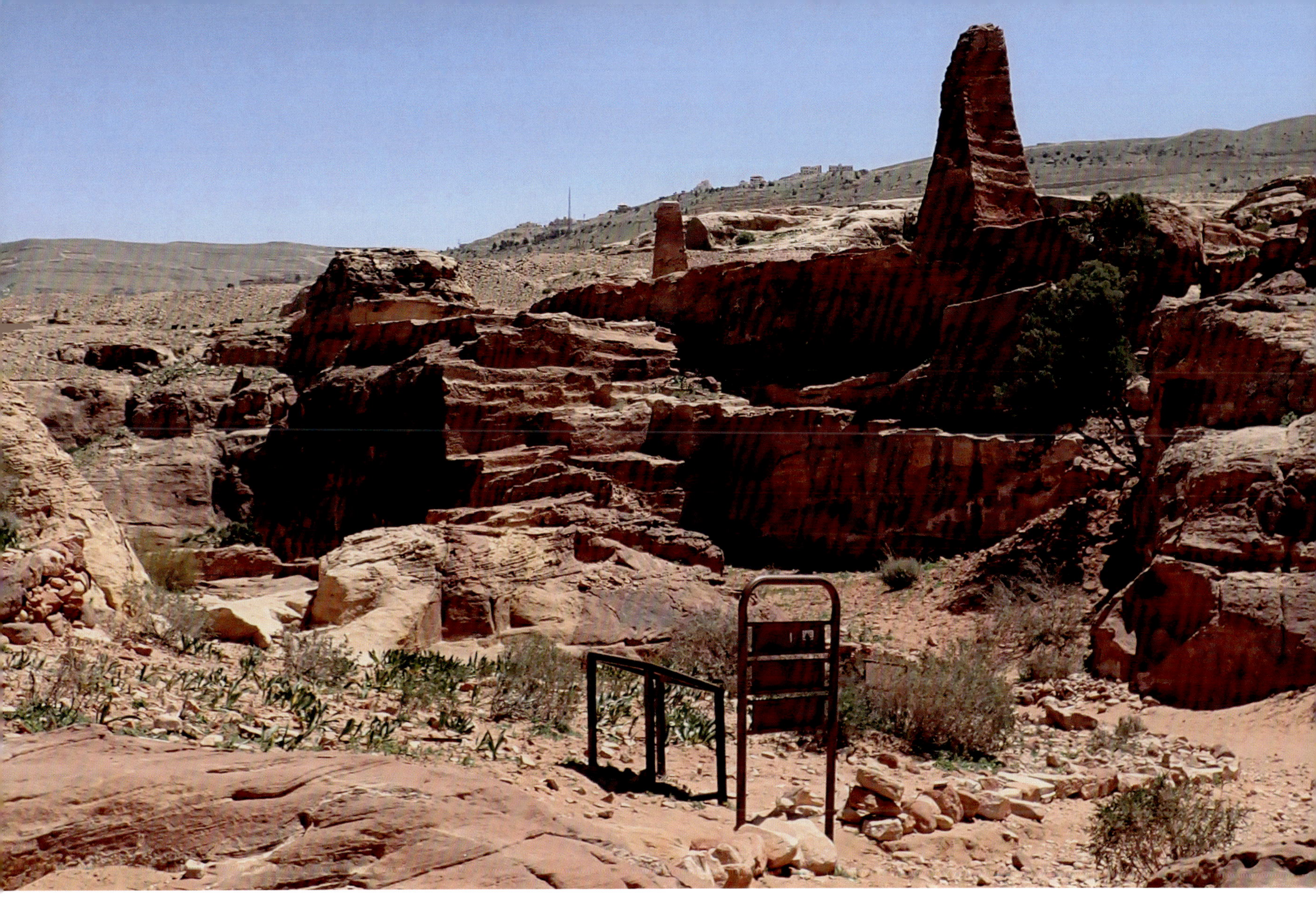

To echo Sir Kennedy, it boggles the mind that the two obelisks were not built up but rather the entire mountaintop was removed around them. The amount of work and dedication needed to complete this is nearly incomprehensible. Today, metal signposts lead the way to the various points of interest atop the Jabal al-Madhbah, and an informational sign tells visitors more about the Obelisk Ridge. While many repeat photographs only show the ghosts of vegetation, it is delightful to see the hardy desert tree of Sir Kennedy's photo still thriving in the nook of the quarry wall (right), although other bushes have since been removed to make way for the trail transecting the plateau. The silhouetted buildings along the upper reaches of Wadi Musa village pepper the ridge in the background, including the Petra Development and Tourism Regional Authority offices overlooking the massive landscape they are charged with protecting.

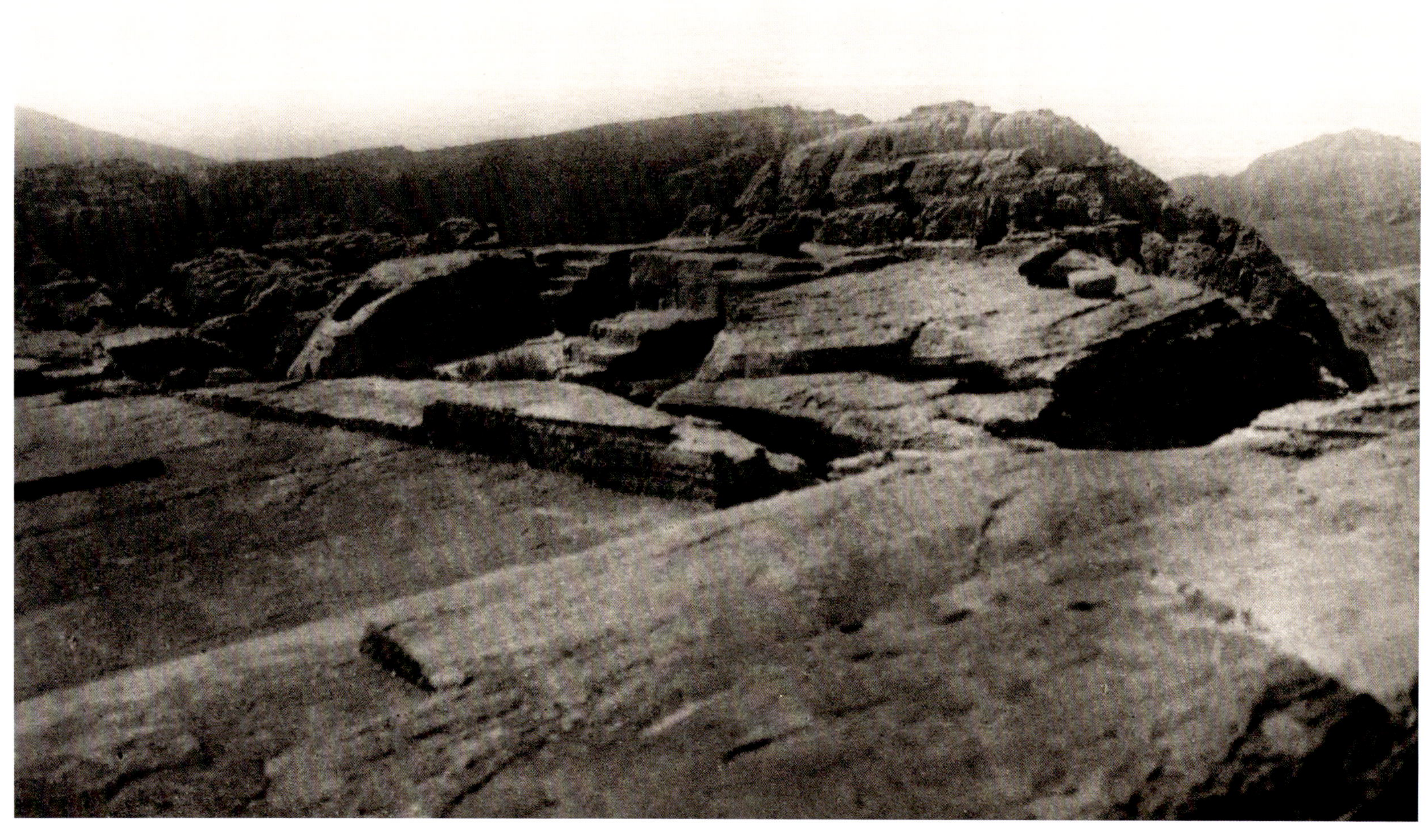

THE HIGH PLACE OF SACRIFICE

"The 'Place of Sacrifice' itself occupies a small and nearly level plateau close to the extremity of the Obelisk Ridge... Here it can only be noted that the nature and method of the sacrifices offered, as well as the details of ceremonial, still remain by no means certain. It is clear, however, that any animals sacrificed must have been small... witnessed by very few people, if any, besides the celebrants, for the simple reason that there is no room for others on the narrow ridge."
— SIR KENNEDY (1925, pg. 68)

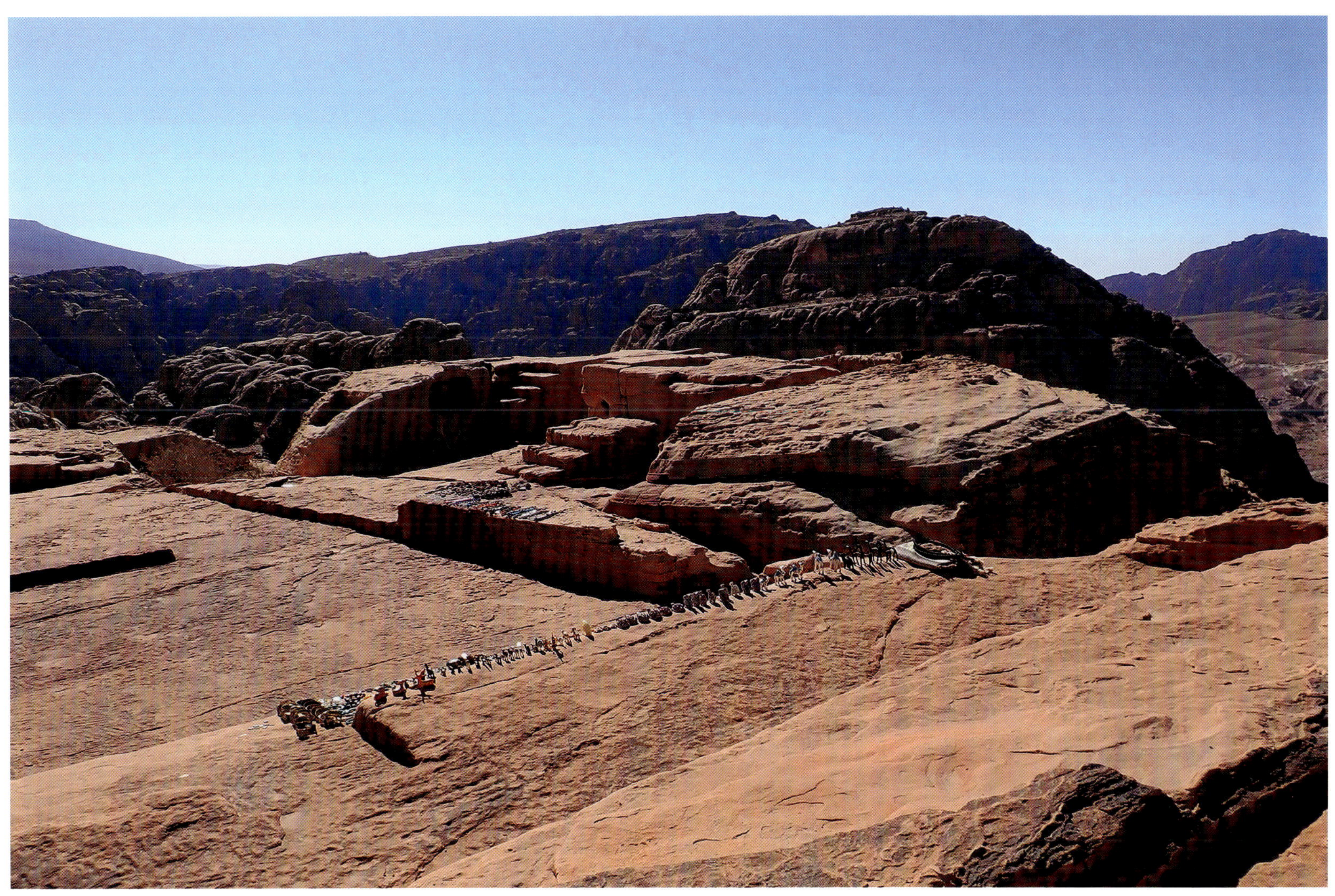

While imaginative archaeologists of old expound on how the circular basin atop the central altar is *obviously* meant to collect blood from human sacrifices, there is nothing to suggest the Nabataeans ever practiced such rituals. In truth, the fabled "High Place of Sacrifice" atop the Jabal al-Madhbah can be somewhat underwhelming, especially once weary travelers finally reach the small platform at the mountain's peak. However, after visitors move past the humble altar, often adorned with little trinkets and figurines as seen in the modern repeat, the unobstructed panoramic view across Petra is truly unparalleled, completely justifying the strenuous climb.

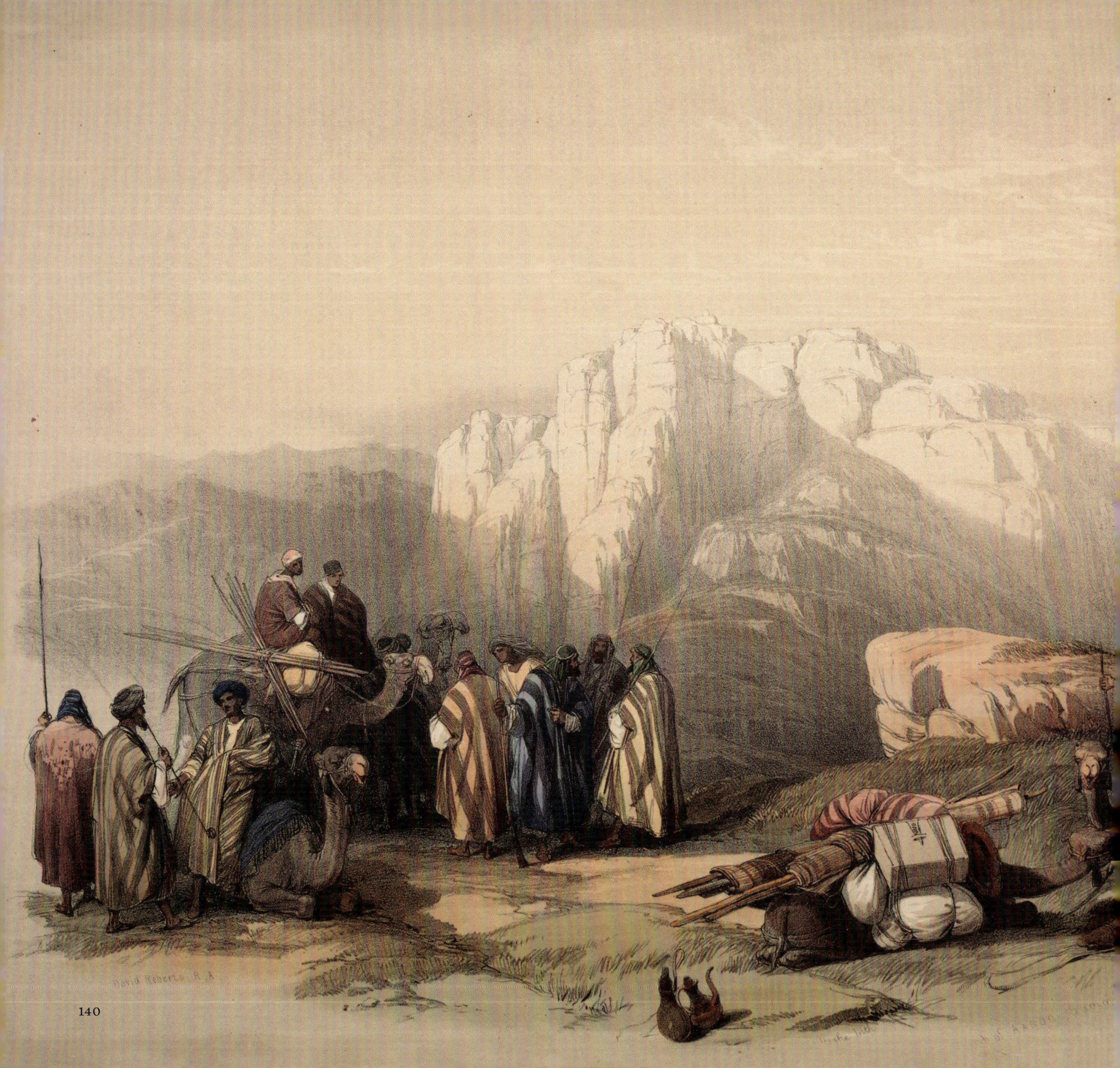
David Roberts. R.A.

Outer Fringes:
Jabal Harun, Bayda, Wadi Mousa, and the Southern Tombs

This section expands into the fringing areas still very much a part of Petra, but beyond the city center and primary tourism routes. These areas include the Sughra tombs in the south, the fabled tomb of Moses's brother Aaron at the highest point in Petra (Jabal Harun), various monuments scattered throughout the greater Bayda region to the north of the city, and an overarching view from the village of Wadi Musa.

> "It is true that in this wide landscape there is a 'scarcity of marked features,' compared with some other views in Syria and the Holy Land, but it also remains true that the outlook from Mount Hor [Jabal Harun] is one of the grandest conceivable over a waste of mountain solitude and the chasm of the Dead Sea."
> — DR. WILLIAM LIBBEY AND DR. FRANKLIN HOSKINS[12]

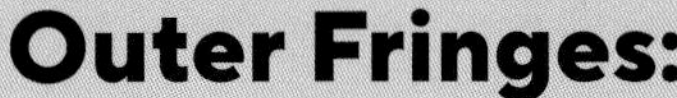

Lithograph by nineteenth-century artist David Roberts of a group of Arabs resting at the base of the Jabal Haroun (Mount Aaron).

12 Libby and Hoskins, *The Jordan Valley and Petra*, 248.

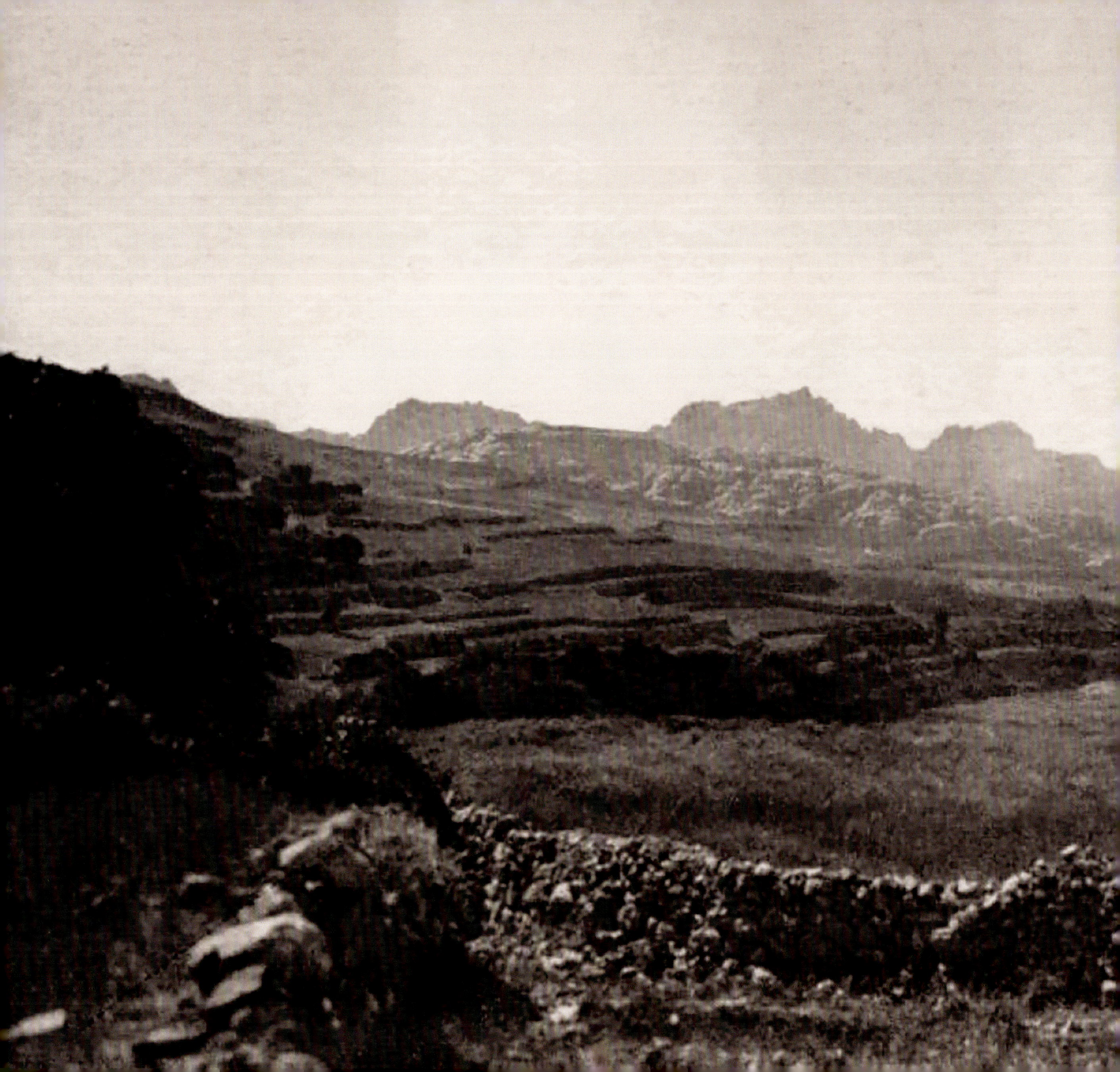

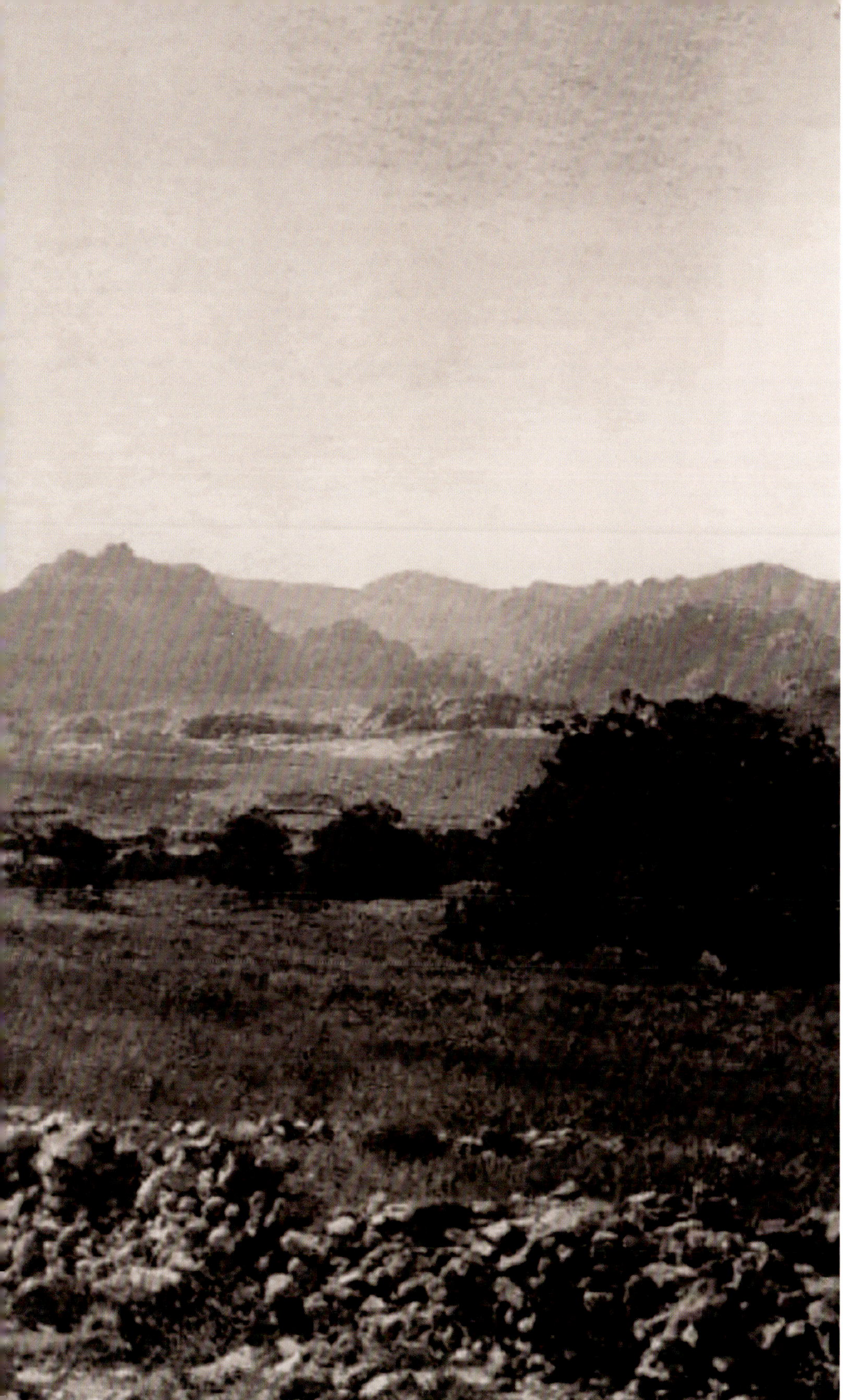

WADI MUSA

"The view of Petra from just above Ajli [now Wadi Musa] village, particularly at dawn before the rays of the rising sun have reached the pinnacled summits of the sandstone sierra, is one of infinite, ineffable charm. The soft hues of the rose-tinted rock barrier before one will later in the day harden into too crude outlines of light and shadow, but at that hour they float with an appearance of unreality like a veil before the mysteries one has dared to approach."
—SIR KENNEDY (1925, pg. 6)

Undeniably, some of the most profound landscape changes between Sir Kennedy's visit and today are seen along its fringes. The subtle agricultural terraces gently descending the hillside toward the valley in Sir Kennedy's photograph have vanished under the exponential growth of Wadi Musa—the gateway town to Petra. Where once there were trees and rubble now stand hotels, restaurants, and all manner of businesses geared towards servicing the immense tourism industry that dominates the region's economy. Incidentally, this photograph is positioned along a road just north of the cleverly named Cleopetra Hotel, which has served as my base of operations and second home while in Jordan for many years.

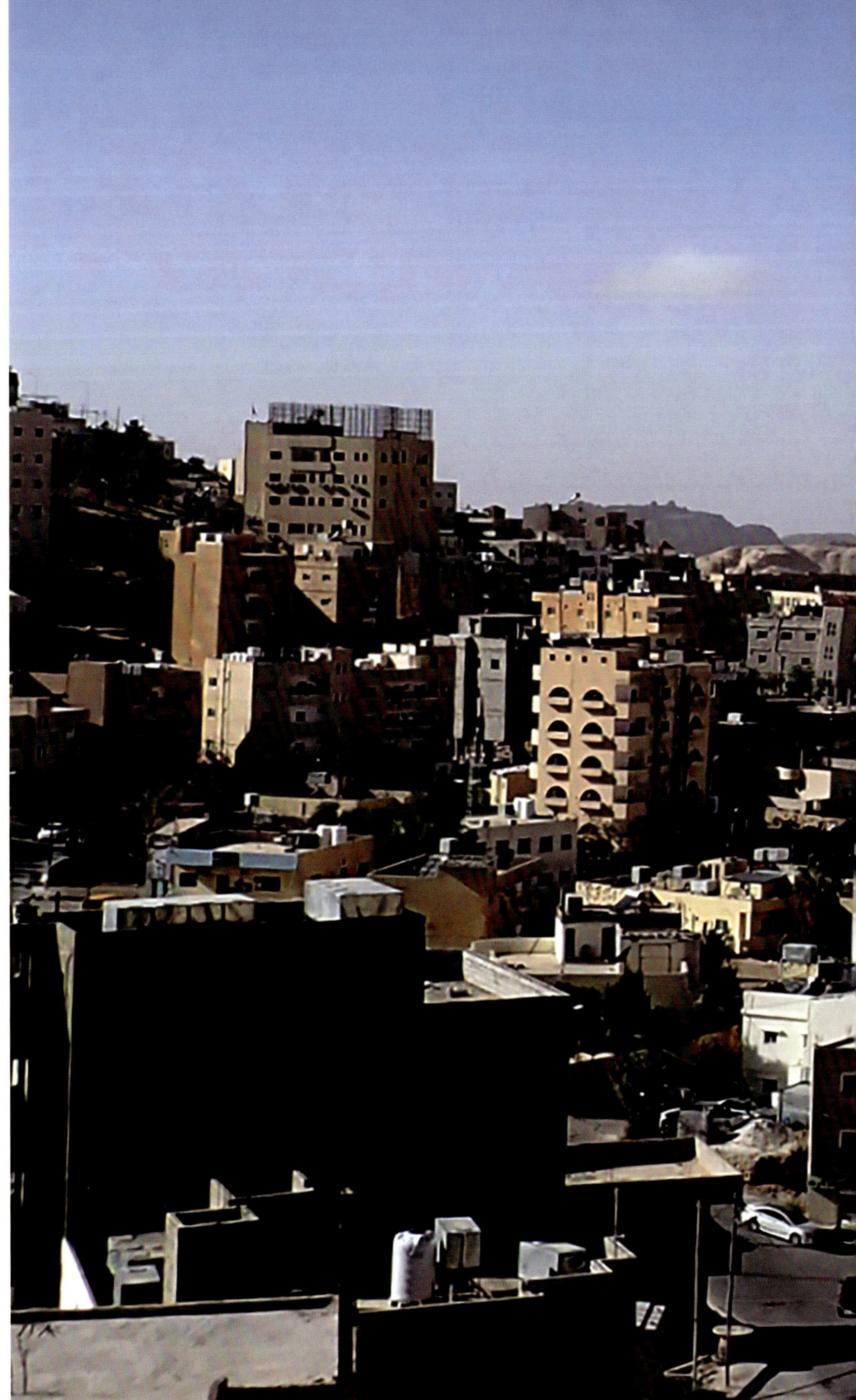

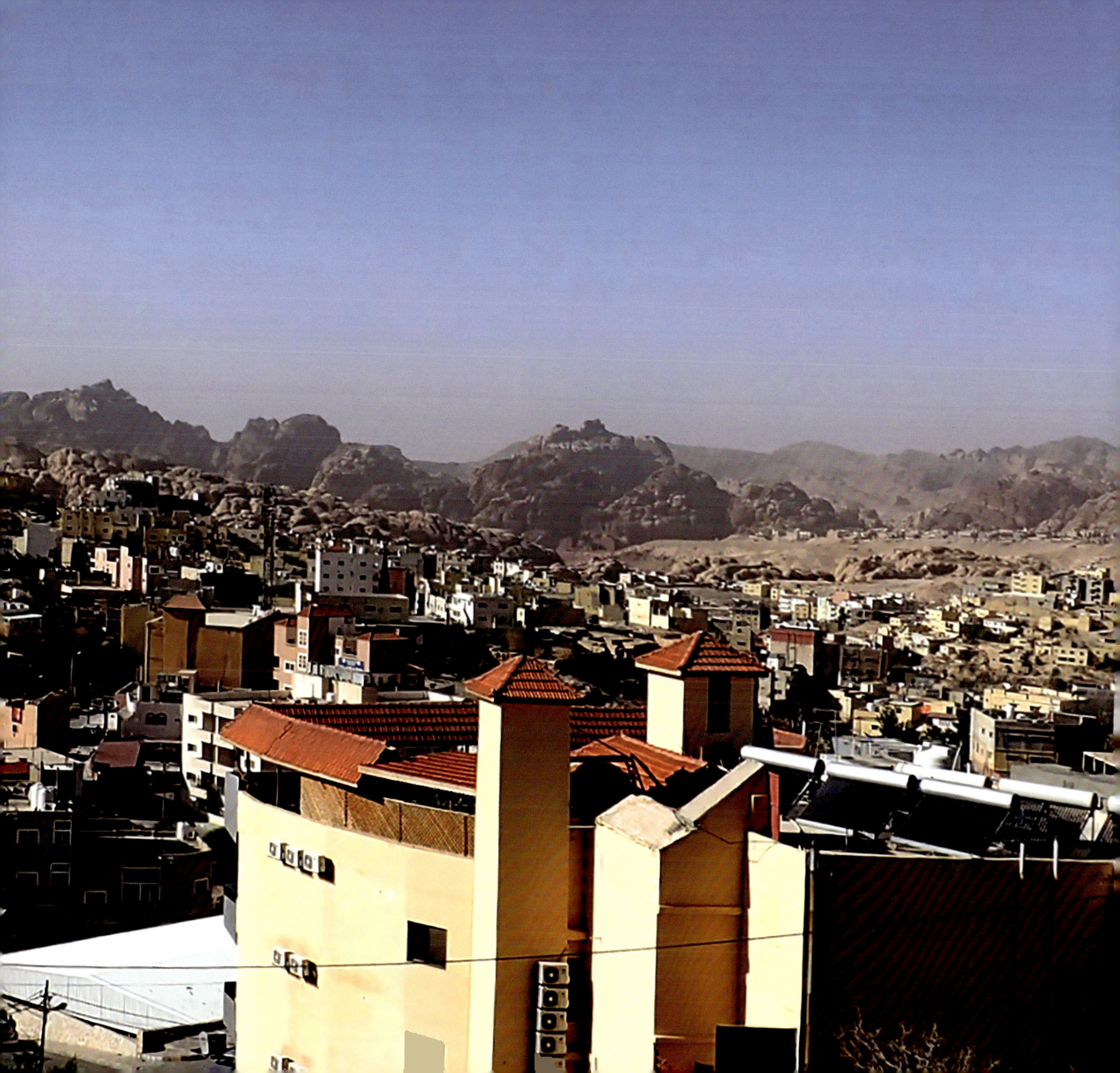

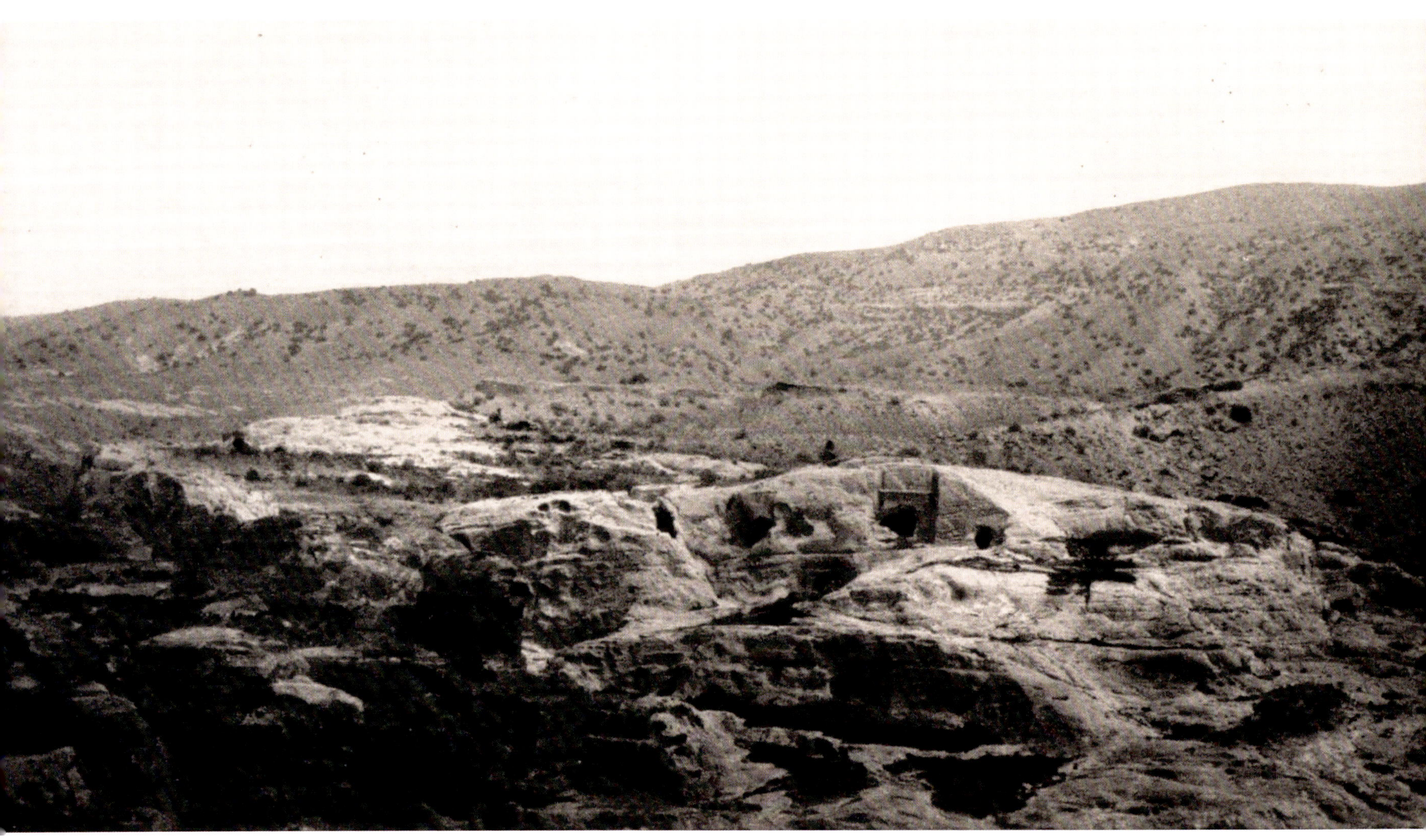

UMM SAYHOUN

"Still further north [of the main valley] the road runs through another group of cult monuments at the edge of the tributary of Wadi Turkmaniya called Umm Saihun [Sayhoun], a part of whose 'high place' is shown in the foreground of [the photograph], with the crags of the Turkmaniya watershed behind it." — SIR KENNEDY (1925, pg. 14)

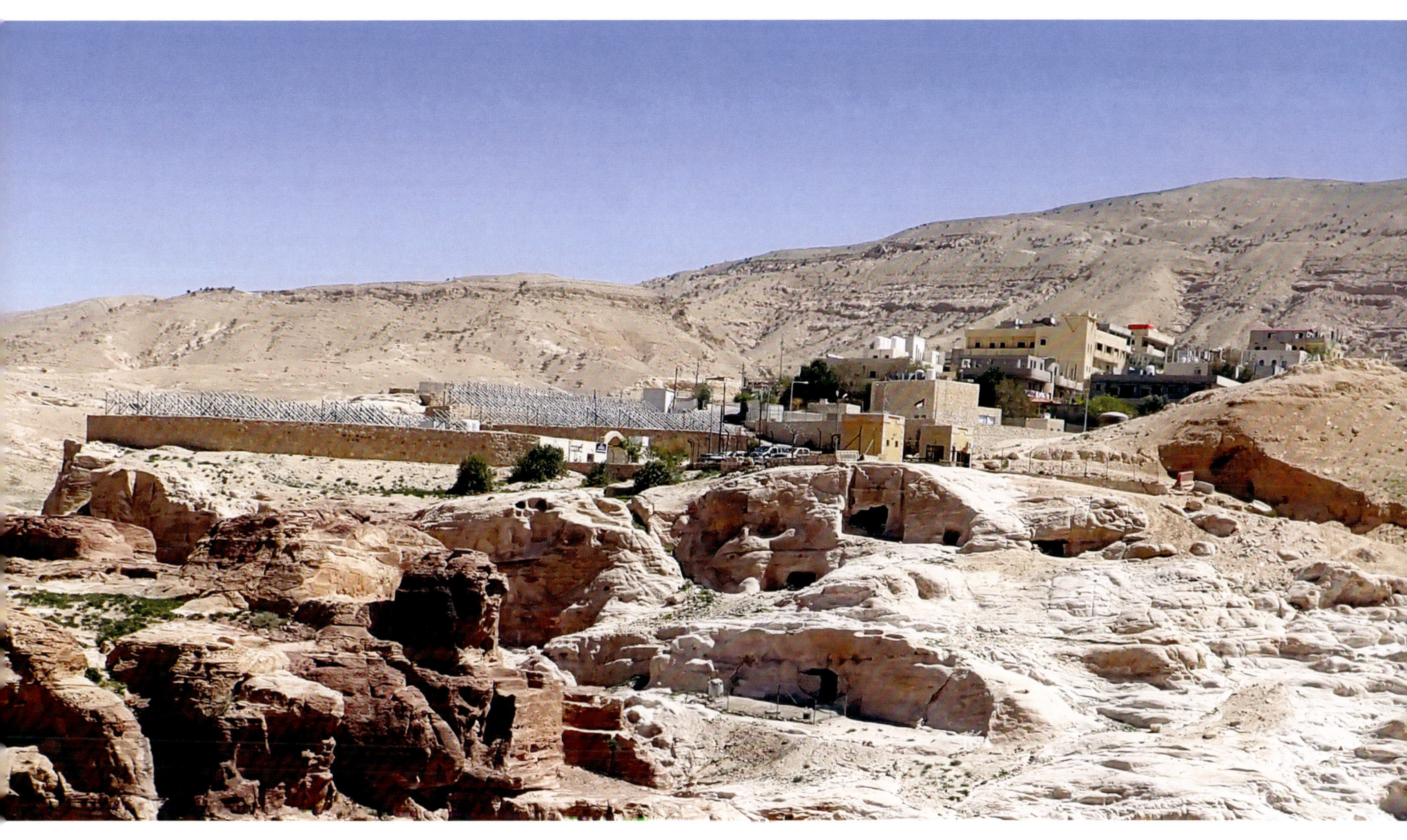

While there may be some residual trauma associated with the Bedouin relocation following UNESCO inscription, especially among the older generations, Umm Sayhoun is a gem of Petra and has a unique beauty all its own. As stated by a Bedouin friend: "The clans there are close-knit, with traditions, values and principles. They share joys and also share sorrows. It is a village that loves to help everyone in it." Indeed, throughout the years, I have been invited to share countless home-cooked *maqluba*, *galaya*, *mansaf*, and other traditional dinners with friends in the village. Lively conversations over savory Arabic coffee and post-dinner fruits are often punctuated by echos of playing children resonating through the walls of love-filled homes.

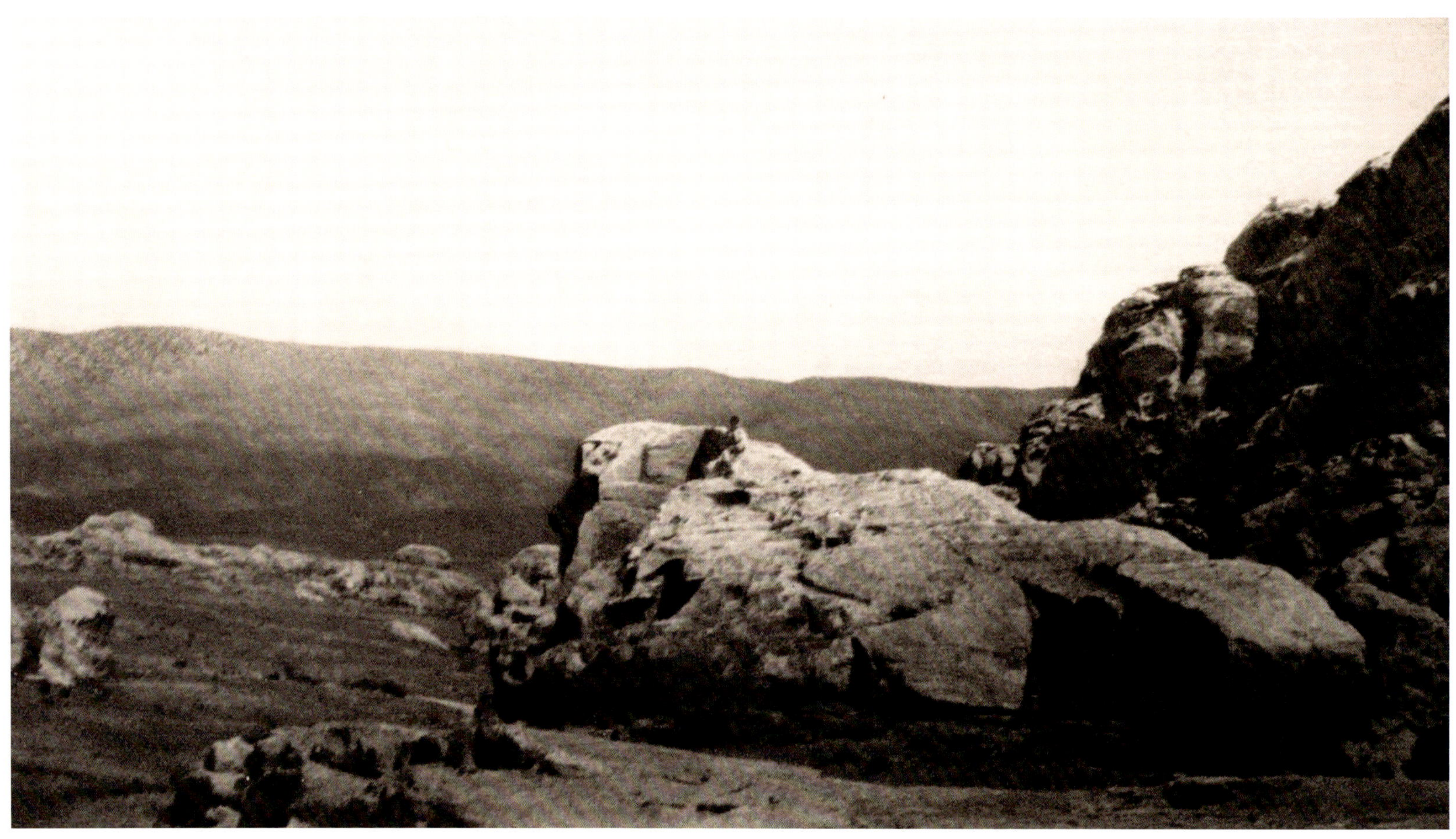

BAYDA VALLEY

"The valley now debouches into the Baidha [Bayda] area proper—a scattered mass of white tumuli and rock-masses, many of which contain burial chambers, courts, reservoirs, niches, etc., within a considerable plain." — SIR KENNEDY (1925, pg. 17)

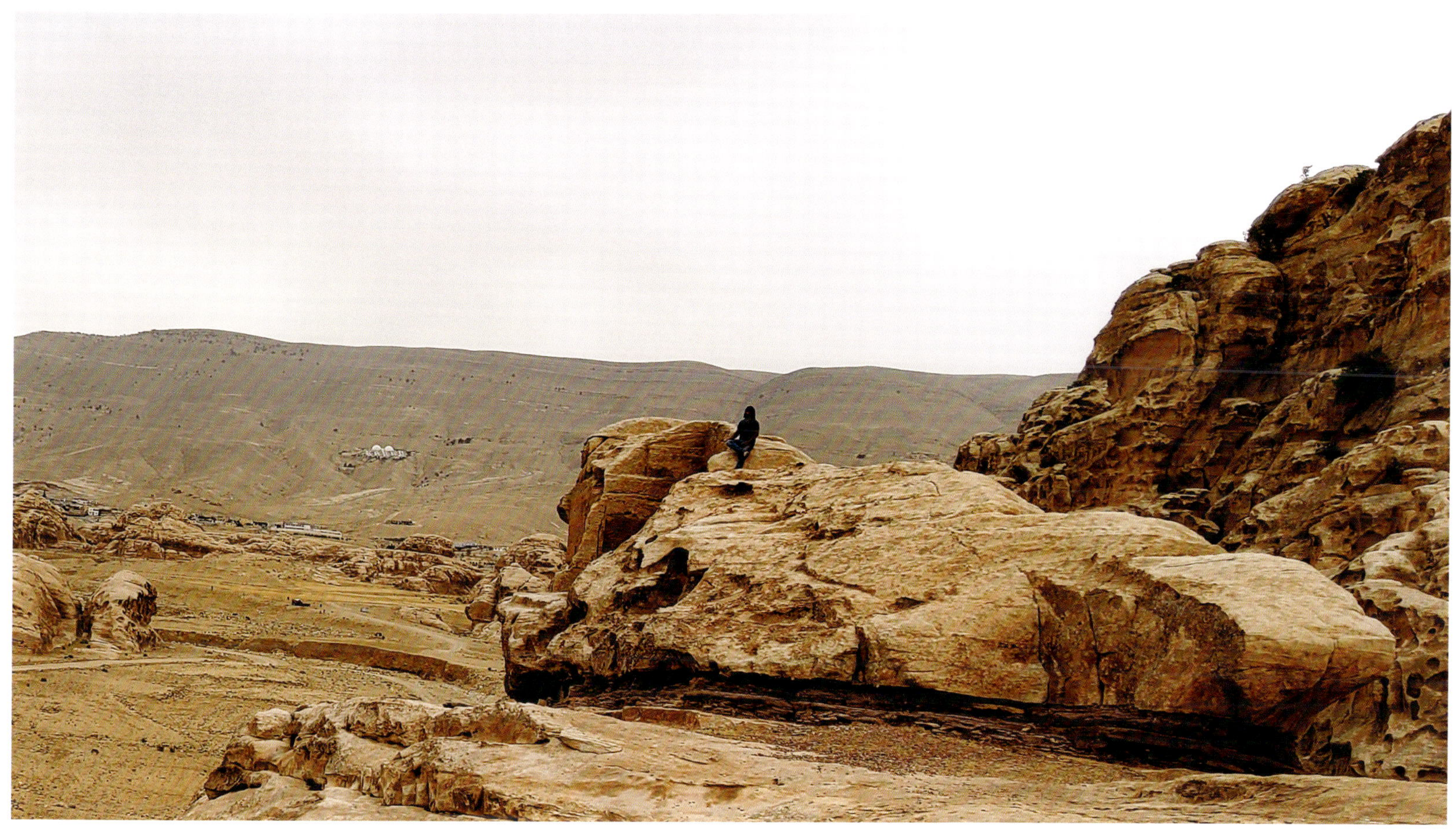

The sprawling Bayda Valley to the north is markedly softer than the harsh, ragged pinnacles of Petra proper. Composed mainly of the velvety white Disi Sandstone, monuments carved in these regions are rounder and brighter—a stark contrast from the iron-rich red cliffs to the south. The smooth stones are showcased here, with my Bedouin friend Habis al-Bdoul sitting atop the carved recess of an inset monument in place of Sir Kennedy's companion. The white domes of luxury "bubble camps" and new buildings occupy the mountainside in the background, manifestations of increasing tourism in the area.

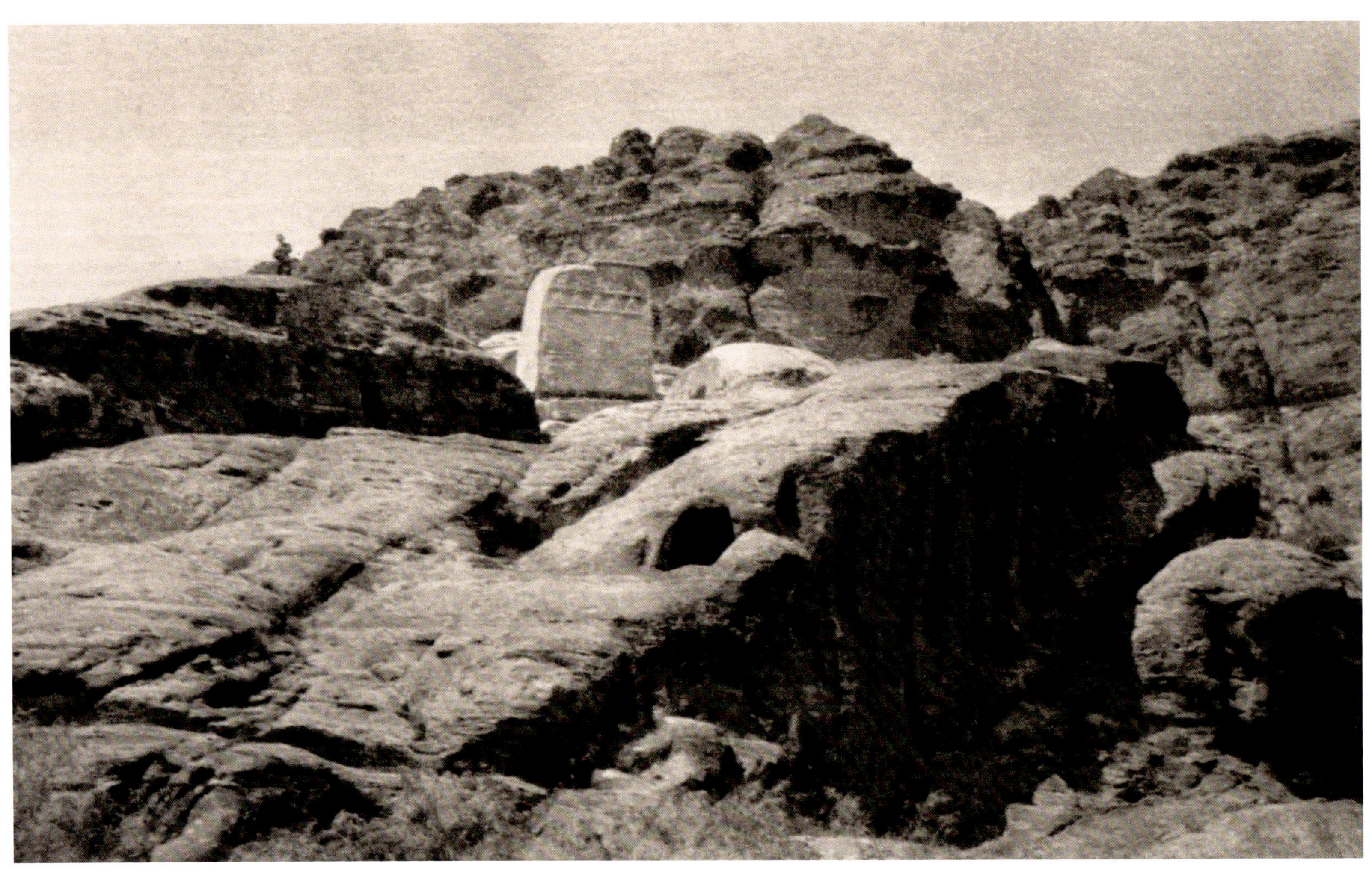

THE SUGHRA TOMBS

"One of the most notable of the block monuments—a Sahrij in the southern region... It has also an internal chamber, [but otherwise] in form it is nearly a duplicate of the Sahrij in the Bab al-Siq... The small chambers in these monuments, where they exist, were probably for burials as they appear too small for dwellings."
— SIR KENNEDY (1925, pg. 41)

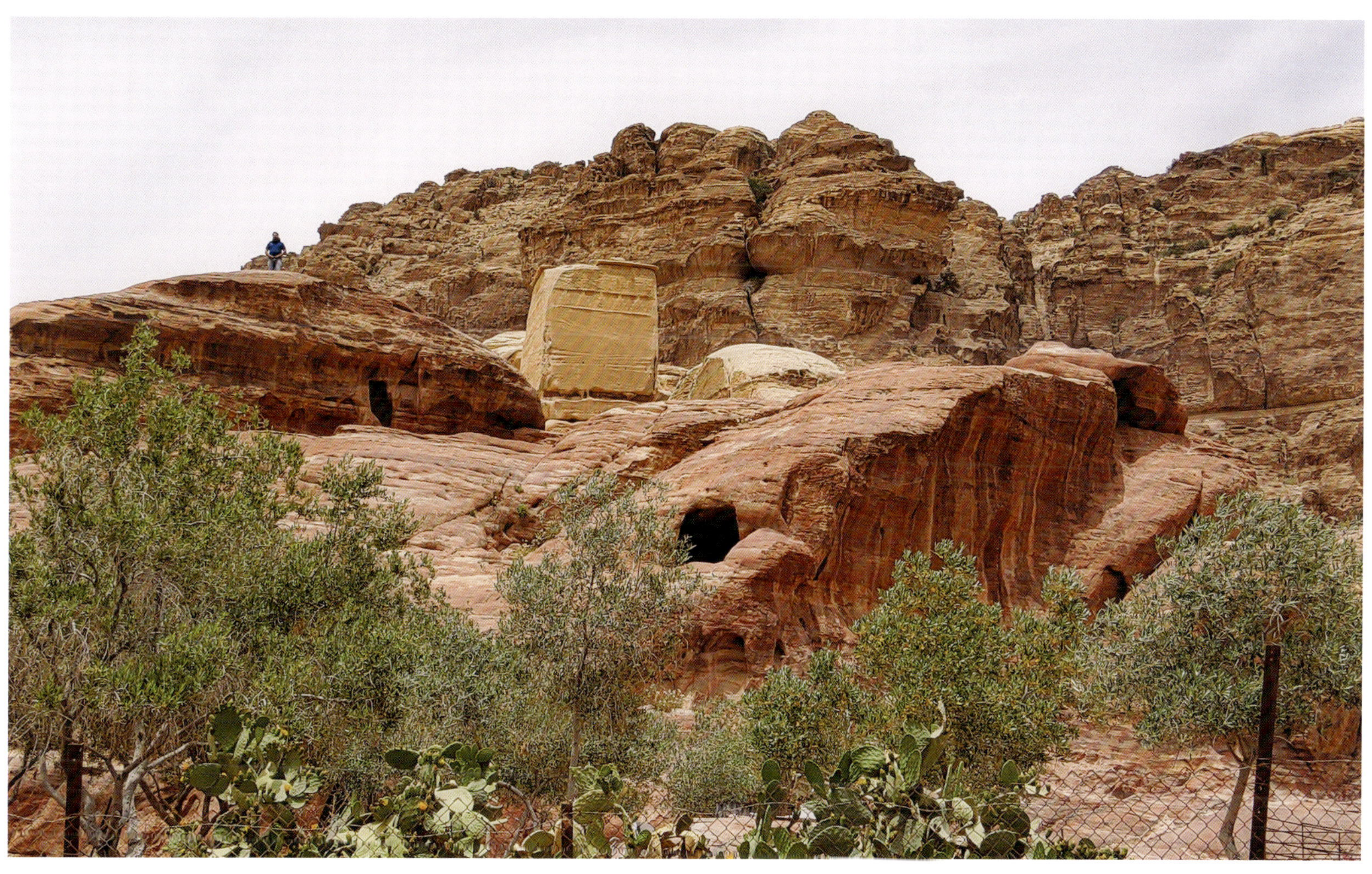

The decorated Djinn Block overlooks what is now a thriving little orchard planted by Bedouins who live in the region. The drought resistant olive and lemon trees are surrounded by prickly pear cactus and a small metal fence to stop wandering goats and sheep from munching on the foliage. In the upper right corner of the image, in place of Sir Kennedy's companion, Habis al-Bdoul provides scale for the impressive carved mass behind him and the valley below.

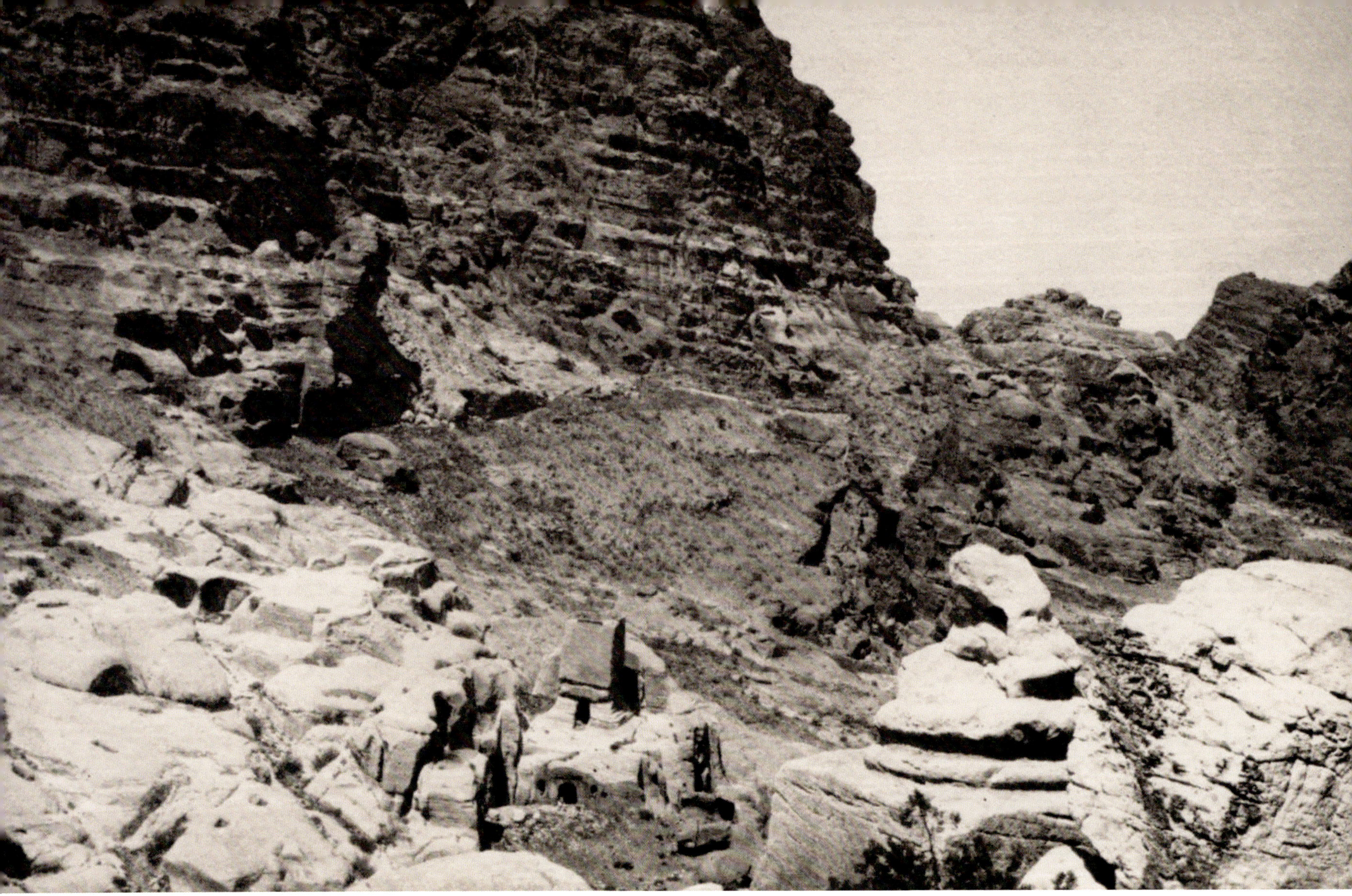

"The Snake Monument itself is unique
among Petraean carvings. The coils
of the serpent winds round a central block
on the top of a plain four-square block.
I know of nothing that can be said as
to its probable use or significance."
— SIR KENNEDY (1925, pg. 70)

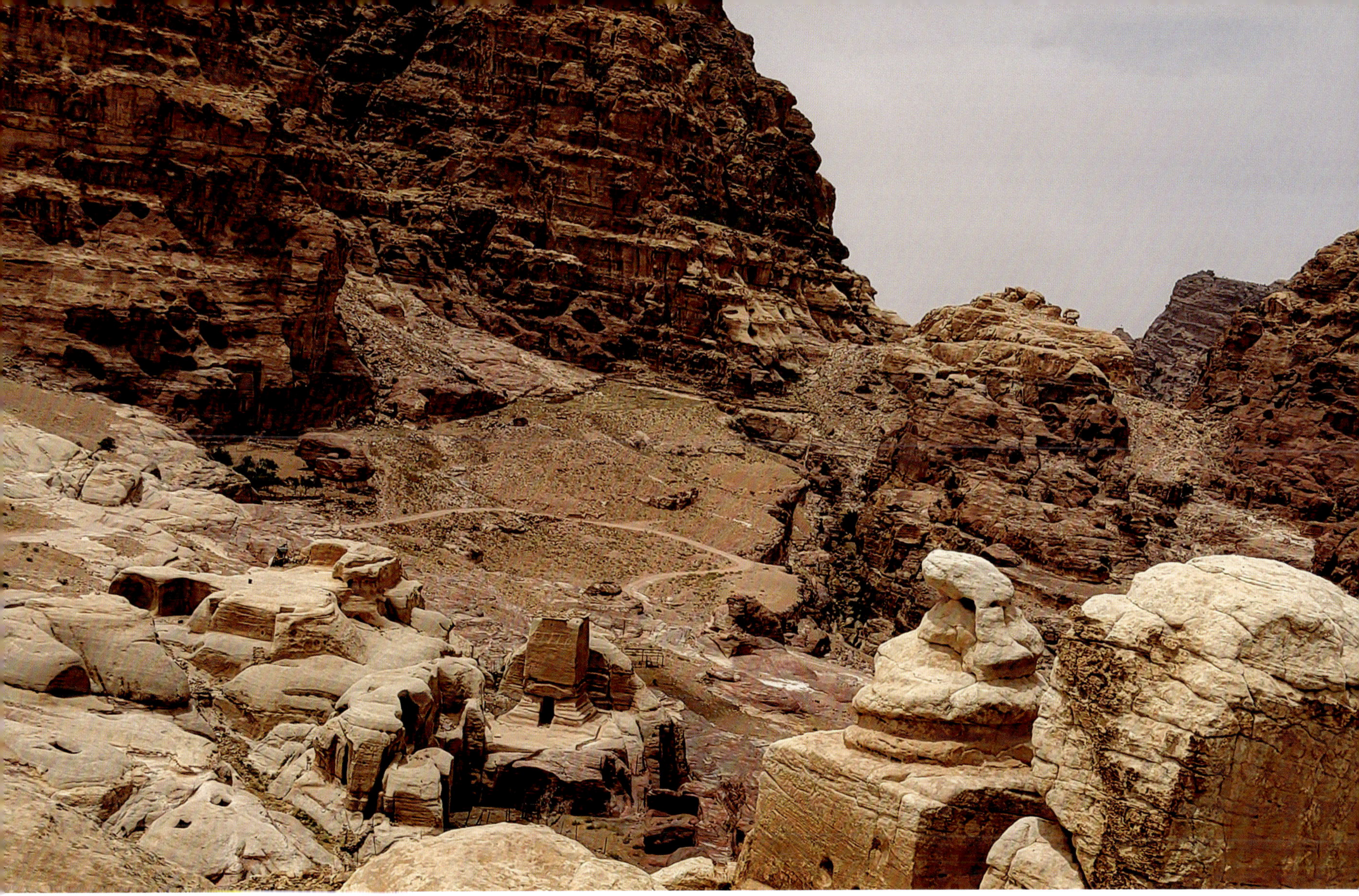

Taken from above looking across the southern tombs, the coiled "snake" is seen in the bottom right corner, though it takes a certain amount of imagination to see a serpent in the bulbous mass of carved stone. Landscape change appears to be relatively limited to differences in vegetation directly behind the stone serpent and in the courtyard of the block tomb below, as well as the addition of the winding gravel road in the background. Stalwart tourists can navigate this gravel road to Jabal Harun by foot, but a Bedouin escort by truck is much preferred, especially when nearing the end of the trail where the path steepens considerably.

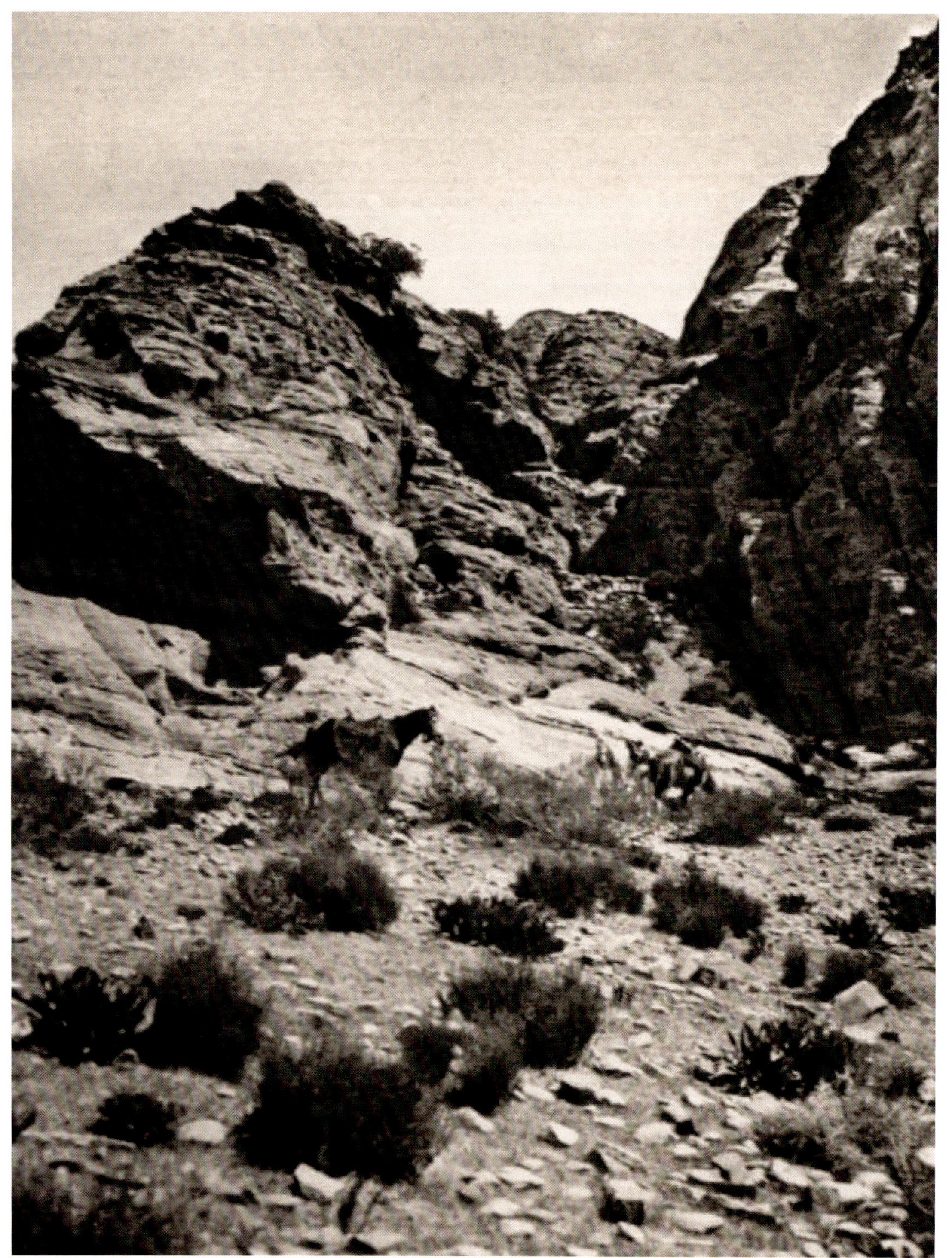

JABAL HARUN TRAIL

"The ascent over the rough stoney slope at first presents no difficulty, but as the summit is approached, the path becomes progressively steeper, narrower, and more difficult, while the most difficult parts have been made possible by steps cut into the rock. The whole of the ascent can be made on ponies up to a broad plateau immediately below the lofty knoll on whose summit the tomb [of Aaron] is perched. Here, amid some ruins of massive masonry, one dismounts to ascend a narrow and steep gully." — SIR KENNEDY (1925, pg. 9)

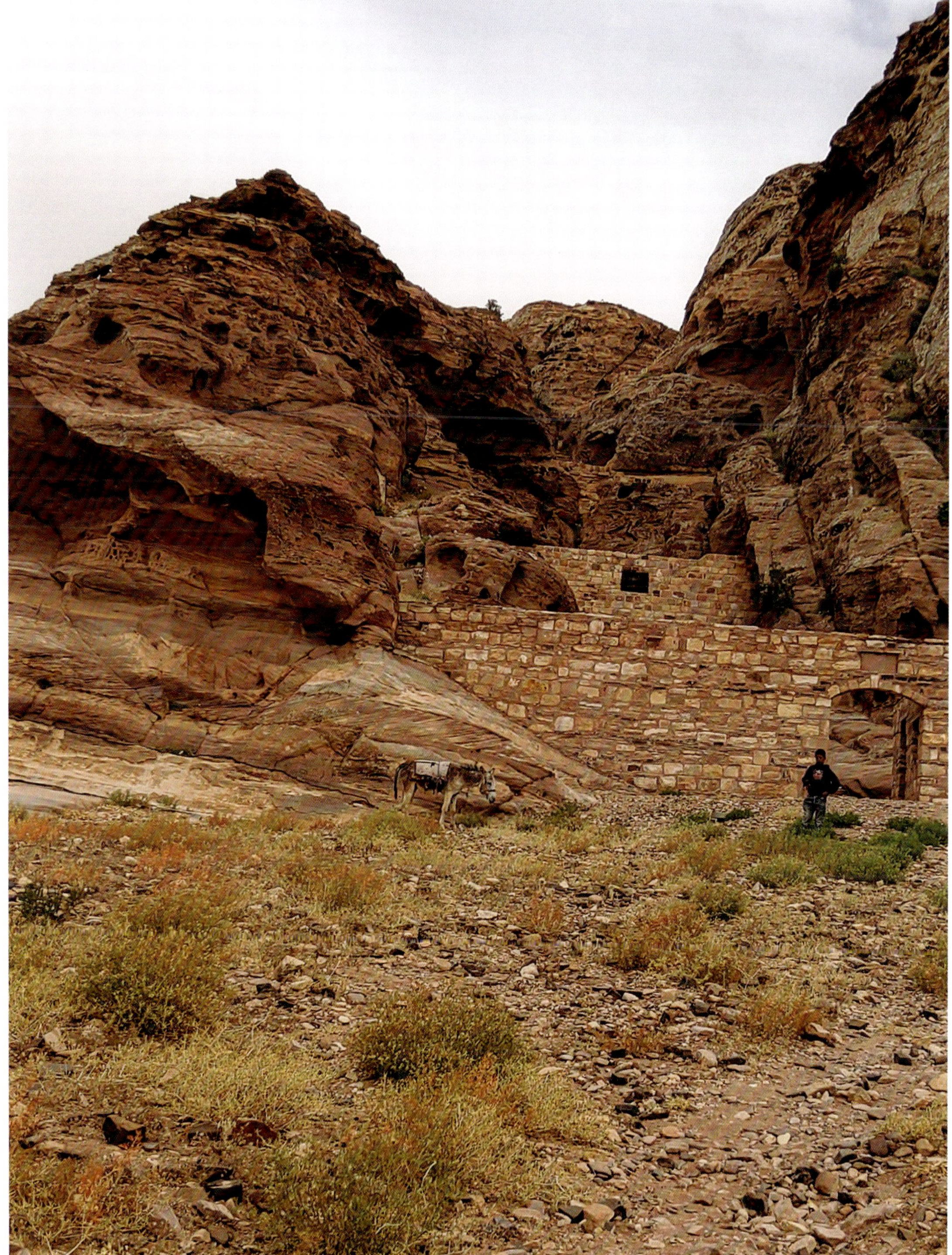

While Sir Kennedy arrived by pony, the trail today is typically shortened by approaching the plateau by vehicle, although many locals will still utilize mules and donkeys to transport goods and people up the rugged terrain—such as the young Bedouin boy and his donkey featured in the modern photograph. The ruined stairway leading the way to the summit has been fully restored and accentuated with a modern stone gateway built by the Petra Archaeological Park authorities in the late 2010s.

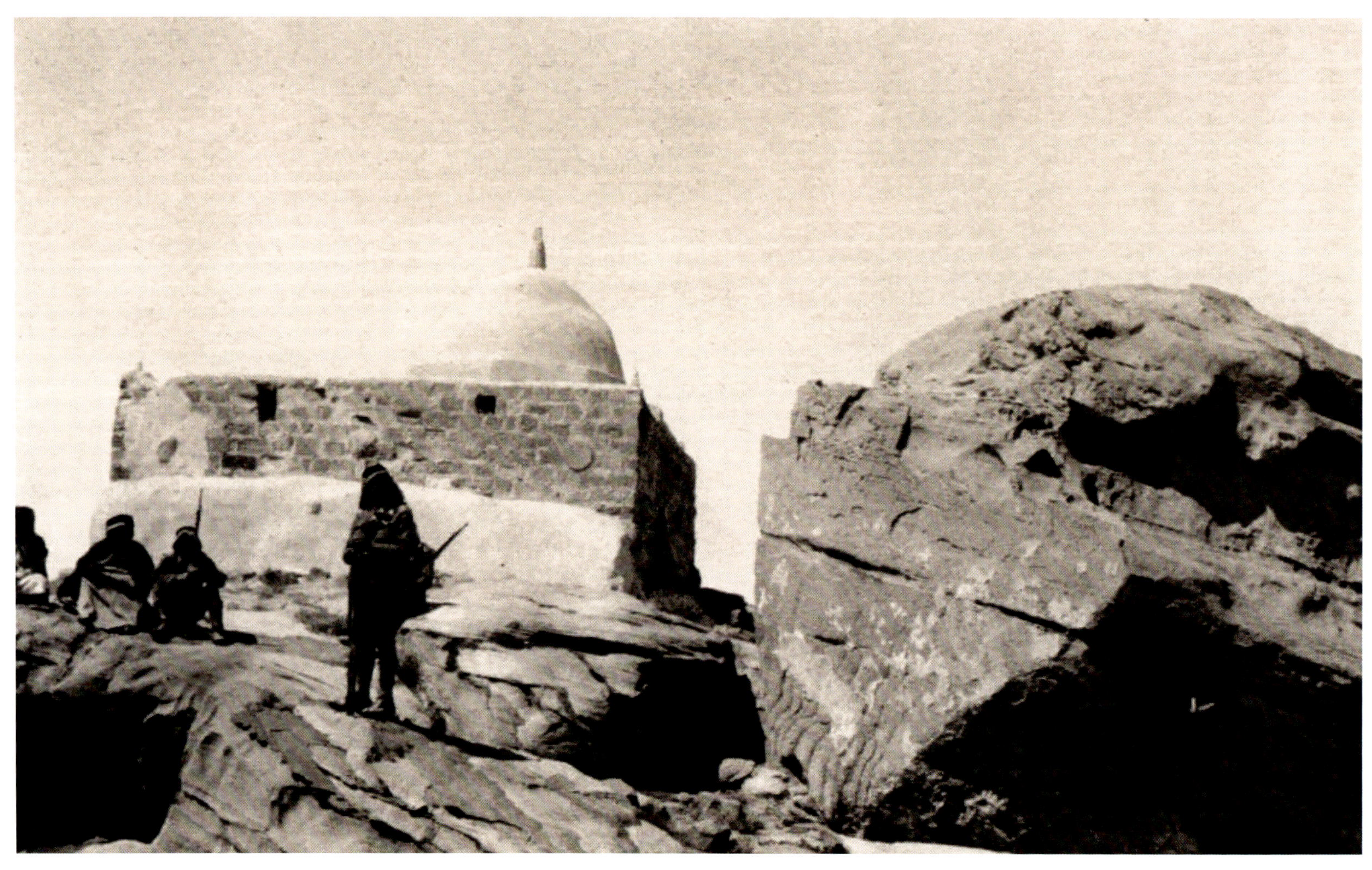

JABAL HARUN

"Jabal Harun, the highest of the Petra peaks, has been identified by some authorities as Mount Hor and, according to Muslim and local tradition, claims the honour of bearing on its summit the tomb of Aaron, from which it takes its Arabic name. The view from the summit [of Jabal Harun] is magnificent, especially towards the north, where the whole of Petra and the Wadi Araba lie before one, spread out as a map, with the line of Wadi Musa flowing in the latter far below, while the great temple of the Dair plateau stands out visibly from its setting of crags."
— SIR KENNEDY (1925, pg. 9)

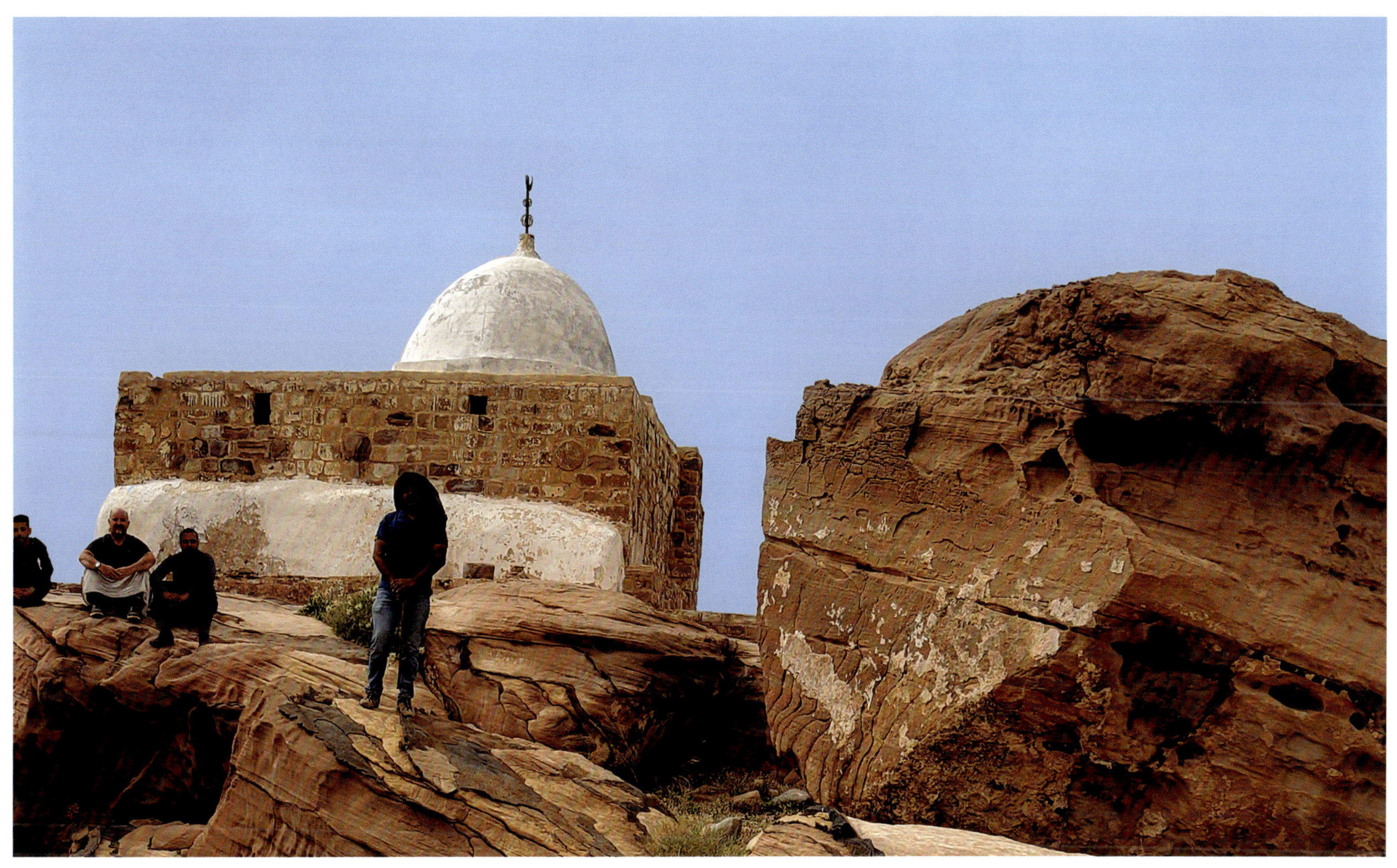

The small white dome of this humble shrine can be seen throughout Petra, marking the highest point of the region—the shining star atop a sea of rusty crags and sandy basins. The panoramic views offered at the peak are reward enough for making the climb, especially the uncanny visage of looking down at the lofty Deir Monument located just one peak away. The monument itself is a modest stone building, carefully maintained by locals and government entities, but it emanates a certain reverence that inspires tranquility and self-reflection. Replicating Sir Kennedy's companions, from right to left, are Habis al-Bdoul, Rami al-Bdoul, Dr. Casey Allen, and Ahmad al-Masry.

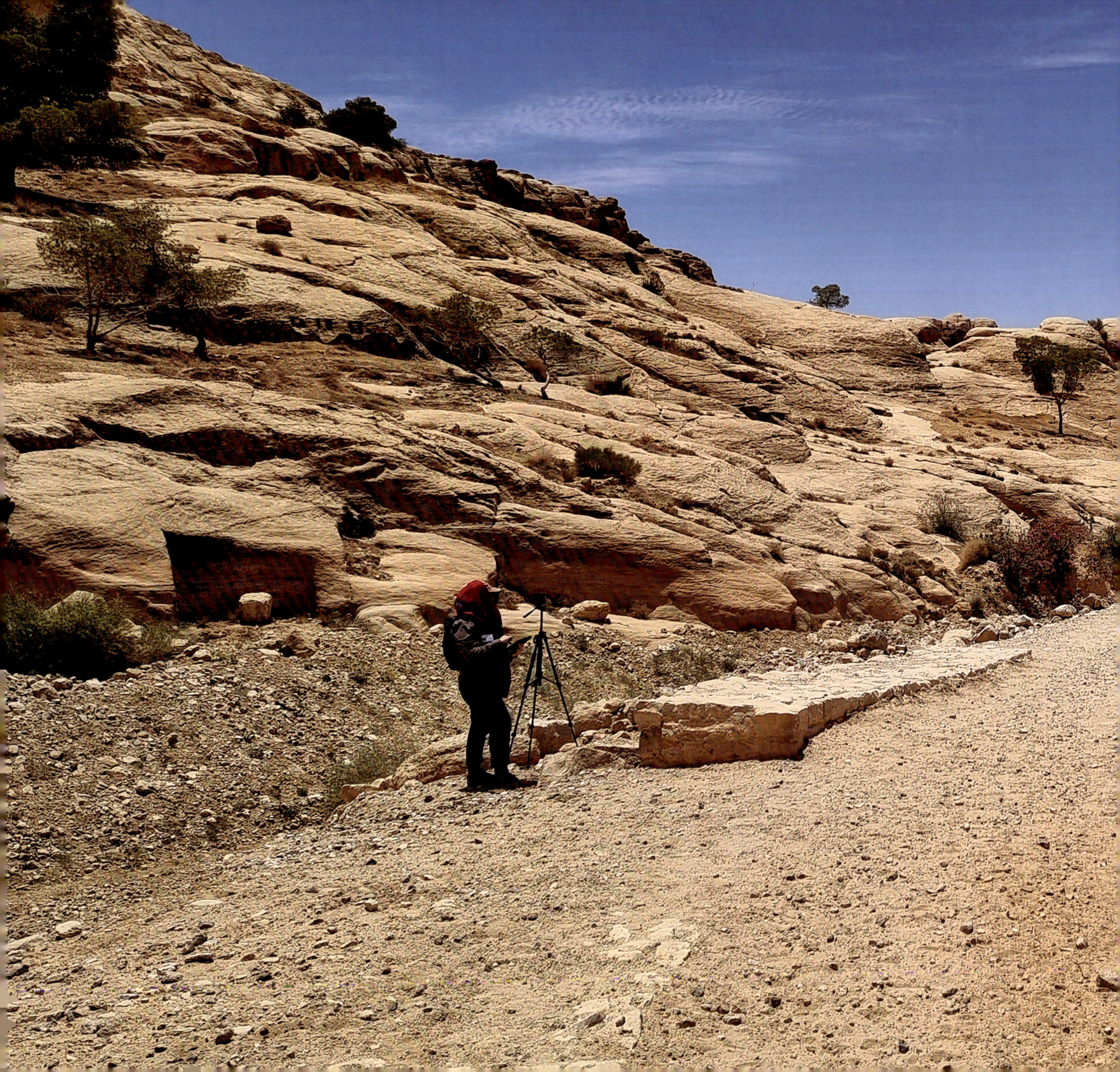

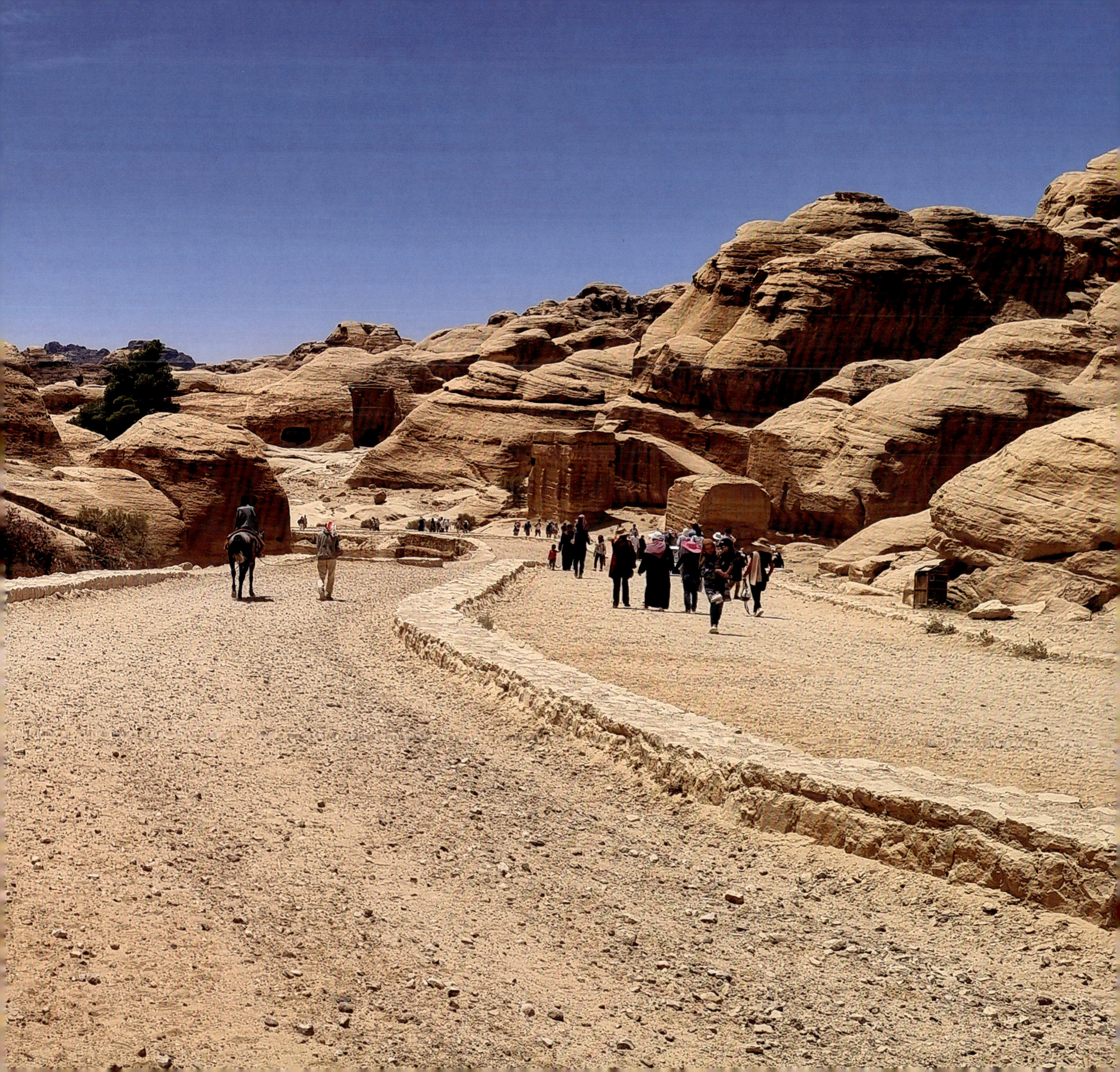

Petra's Enduring Legacy

Through Sir Kennedy's historic photographs, we are transported back in time to the early twentieth century and a very different Petra. Navigating the rugged terrain with what would have been a rather cumbersome camera entourage, the plucky elderly gentleman explored a wild expanse of ruined stone monuments, looming façades, and interweaving trails through the cliffsides. Beyond the semi-nomadic Bedouins inhabiting the valley, only the most intrepid—and privileged—traveler had access to this newly opened natural and cultural wonder. Sir Kennedy's mission was to bring the majesty and awe of Petra to the world, and to ask questions. Lots of questions. He recognized the limited view and interpretations of Petra's archaeological remains and wanted to encourage a more holistic and accurate understanding of the city's dynamic features:

The great series of rock-carved chambers and façades which have formed the chief interest of the place, and have been the object of so much curiosity and wonder and even admiration, have been very generally described by descriptively-minded visitors simply as 'tombs'. They are, in fact, of very varied nature and purpose.[13]

In other words, despite (or perhaps because of) Sir Kennedy's non-archaeological background, he saw Petra for what it is, rather than how it was being reported. In his opinion, the scientific reports did not adequately display the grandeur of Petra's complexity.

At his core, however, Sir Kennedy recognized the city's most fundamental feature: the unknown. In his own words, "Petra remains

13 Kennedy, Petra: *Its History and Monuments*, 38.

in reality, in spite of the work which has been done upon it, a riddle very largely unsolved."[14] Over the past century, countless amazing new marvels have been unearthed, such as the intricate mosaics of the Byzantine church, the impressive channels and underground plumbing of the Roman bathhouse, and unparalleled Nabataean hydrological engineering features throughout the city. Amidst these discoveries and the undaunted efforts by Jordanian and international agencies to safeguard and understand Petra's legacy, much of it still, indeed, remains "a riddle."

14 Ibid, 81.

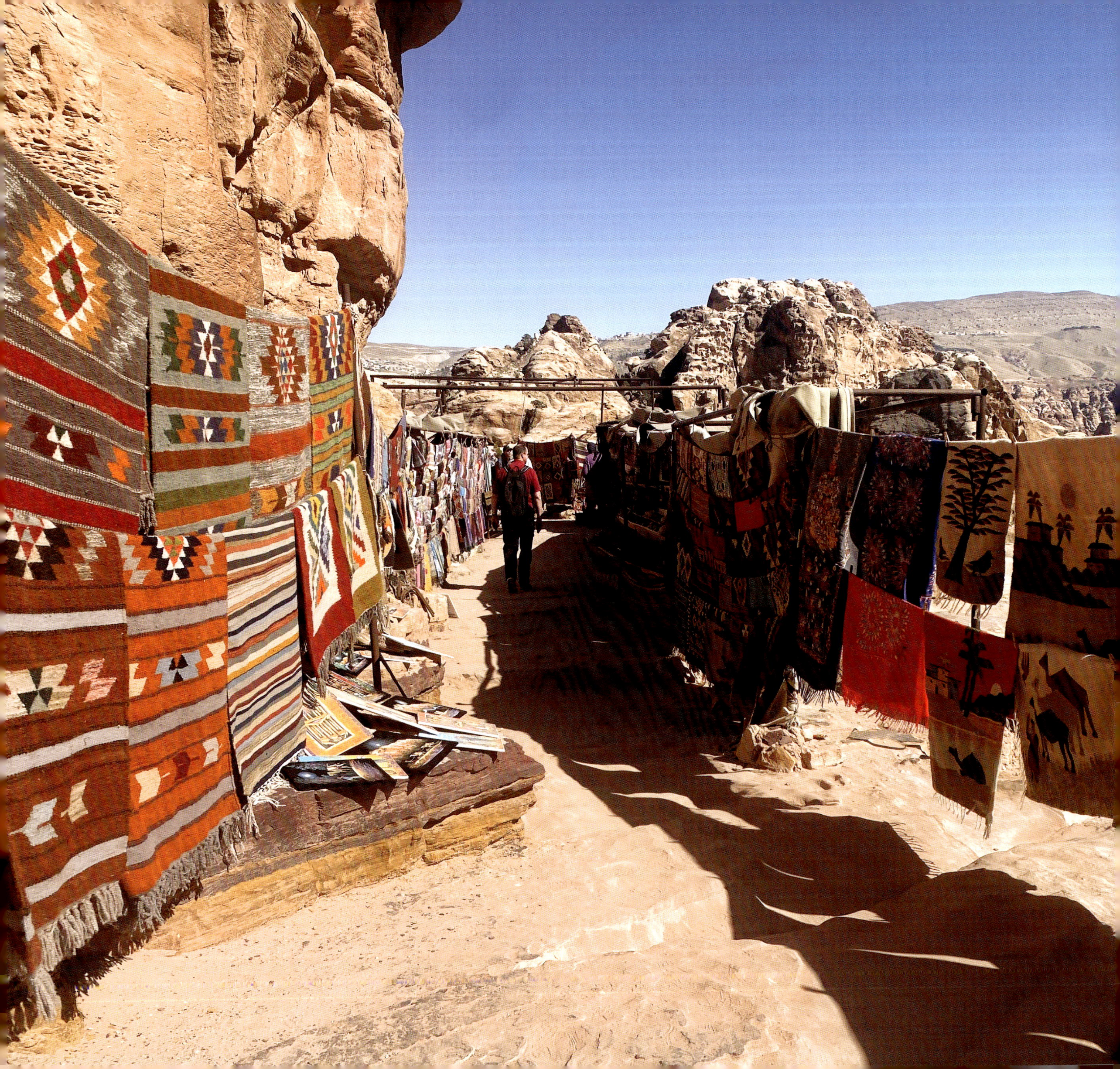

While Sir Kennedy's photographs give us a glimpse of the past, mine reveal changes that bring us to the present. What we see today is the continuation of Petra's extraordinary adaptability to its inhospitable environment. Where flash floods caused erosion, new plants have taken root, sometimes next to ruins freshly exposed by the rushing waters. Yet, through the centuries —regardless of nature's relentless onslaught and stone's natural decay—the carved monuments continue to stand steadfast as weather-worn sentinels guarding the resplendent city.

Part of what makes Petra such a fascinating place is its unique ability to incorporate change instead of resisting it. Even at the height of the city's Nabataean Era, Petra was never only Nabataean but a multicultural array of style and design, drawing inspiration from Roman, Hellenistic, Greek, and Egyptian motifs. It seems each phase of Petra's legacy has added new layers to the multifaceted landscape without negating or defacing those that came before. It is my hope that we can do the same by celebrating the past without degrading it.

In the modern repeated imagery, we see the new era in Petra's occupational history: tourism. Traditional tents and shops have been erected by local Bedouins to share their handicrafts as well as their culture and histories. And yes, always with tea, a ubiquitous ritual that symbolizes their friendly and inviting culture. The authorities have built museums, restaurants, and facilities to accommodate the valley's thousands of daily visitors. What better way to incorporate modern tourism into the rich historical record of Petra than as manifestations of hospitality, a cornerstone of Jordanian and Bedouin society? I frequently found myself to be the grateful recipient of extraordinary conviviality that is extended generously to Petra's guests. It is almost an odd sensation to be so warmly invited to join in traditional meals for absolutely no other reason than to enjoy your company. The people of Petra exemplify a genuine desire to connect. Taking a moment to rest in a dwindling spot of shade on a scorching summer day can easily turn into hours of chatting and laughing with a passing local on their way home—complete with a dinner invitation you are simply not allowed to refuse.

Colorful array of traditional and modern rugs, scarves, and trinkets at vender stalls along the Wadi Ad-Deir trail.

It is worth noting that while the Bedouins of Petra take pride in preserving their cultural heritage, they still face economic challenges in the modern era. Following Petra's 1985 induction in the World Heritage program and strict UNSECO regulations, Bedouins are no longer permitted to actively live within the city itself. The vast majority of the Badul Bedouins have been relocated to the government-built village of Umm Sayhoun outside of the archaeological park. This shift from a nomadic to a more settled existence wrought changes in their traditional lifestyle. Many Bedouin families have found alternative livelihoods by engaging in tourism-related activities, such as providing guided tours, selling handmade wares, or offering camel rides to visitors.

Where Sir Kennedy witnessed a sleepy desert refuge, today's Petra is a living, breathing entity, an internationally celebrated bucket list destination topping international travel wish lists. Beyond tourism, Petra continues to thrive as an endless place of learning, growing, and adaptation. Several international agencies, universities, and shareholders have conducted restoration efforts and educational programs to promote Petra's lasting legacy and secure its dynamic landscape and delicate features —diligent efforts for moving forward into the coming centuries.

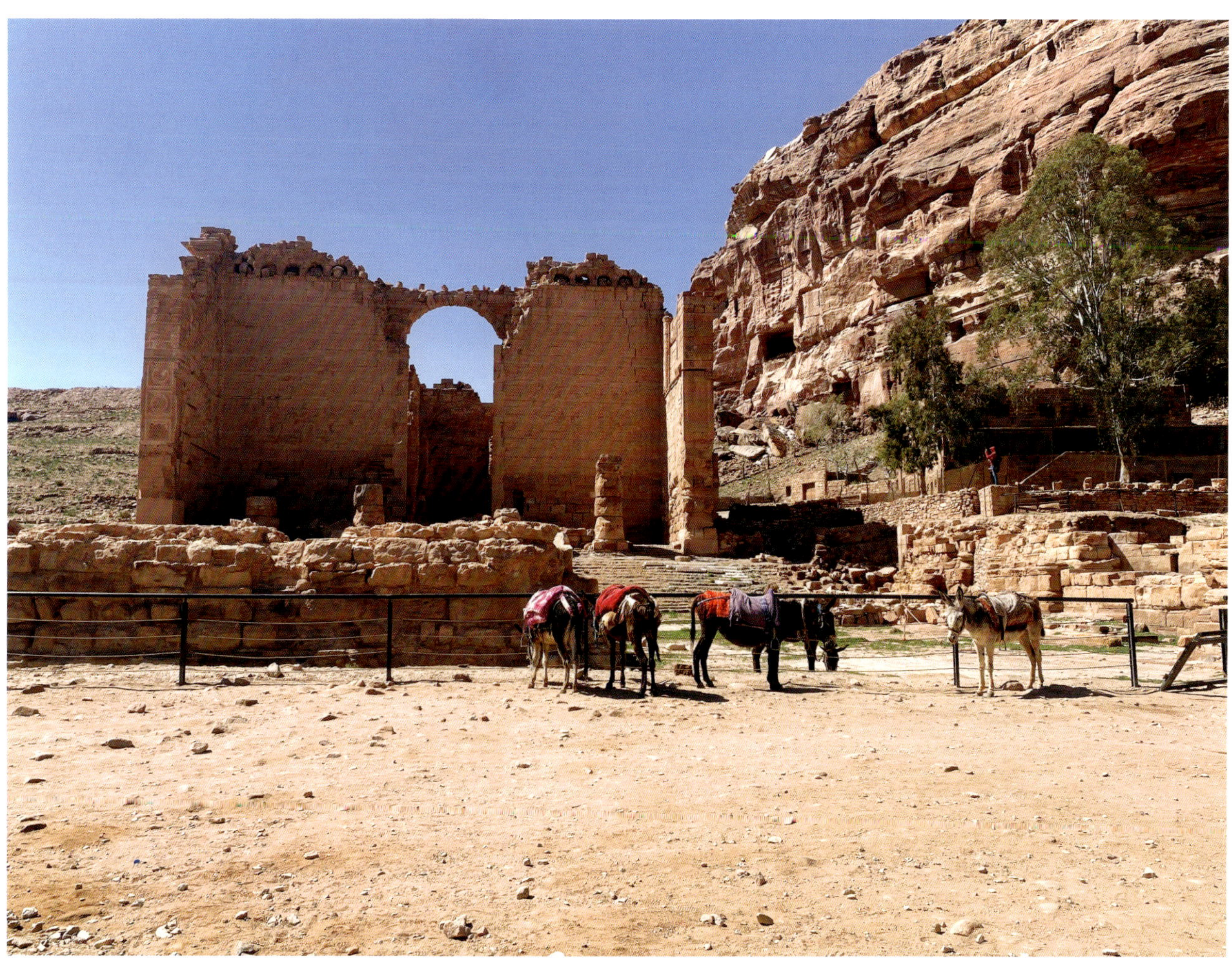

Donkeys resting at the base of the Qasr
al-Bint, tied to the fence erected to protect
the monument's marble stairway and
impressive arch.

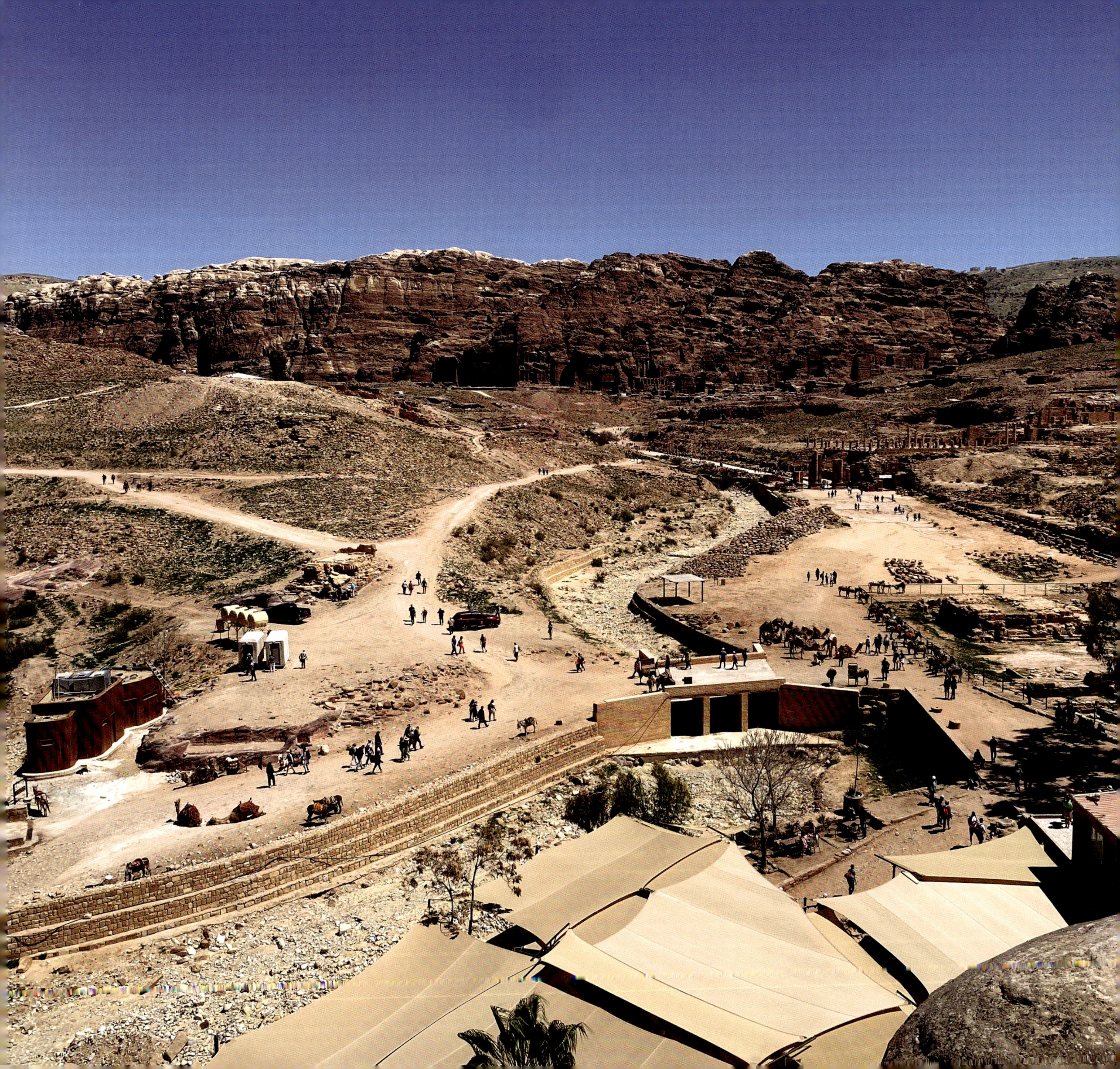

The massive influx of tourism represents perhaps the most significant changes witnessed between Sir Kennedy's photographs and my own, and tourism will no doubt continue to play a role in Petra's future. But what kind of role? Global tourism brings with it both opportunities and challenges. While some monuments have begun to deteriorate more intensely under the strain of continual tourist activity, others have experienced revitalization and restoration due to boosts in the local economy resulting from international recognition. The delicate balance between maintaining cultural authenticity and meeting the demands of a globalized world is a tightrope that both the Bedouin people and the Jordanian government continue to navigate daily.

The challenge of assuring Petra's legacy rests in finding sustainable ways to integrate economic development with the preservation of Jordan's cultural identity and the protection of the archaeological treasures around them. Echoing Sir Kennedy's astute observation a century ago, in many ways, the future of Petra remains "a riddle."

Thankfully, the Jordanian government and local communities alike are both committed to tackling Petra's multi-layered management demands. Considering its history of adaptability over thousands of years, the resilient city has proven itself capable of withstanding harsh elements of nature as well as various degrees of human habitation and influences.

Although, as people, we can do little to prevent or control environmental impacts on Petra's vibrant and multi-hued sandstone cliffs, we can take proactive steps to preserve and sustainably manage the site for generations to come. Earning UNESCO World Heritage status recognizes that Petra holds outstanding global importance for everyone, so visitors must share in its custodianship. Even the smallest efforts such as staying on the designated trails, refraining from touching or defacing the aging stone façades, and packing out whatever trash or rubbish you carried in, can help Petra continue captivating visitors for centuries to come. Being mindful travelers and respecting the landscape works in tandem with

View from al-Habis trail overlooking the Petra Valley. The modern additions of the canopied restaurant at the outcrop's base, the new wooden-clad toilet facilities to the left, and engineered bridge and canal controlling seasonal floods all exemplify the many physical manifestations of Petra's tourism industry and how we are altering the landscape.

the endless efforts of the Jordanian government,
nongovernmental agencies, and surrounding
communities to support Petra's resiliency and
continued survival.

With faith in Petra's legacy and the unwavering
draw of human curiosity, I predict others in the
future (perhaps in another hundred years) will
continue to pursue studies of landscape change
in the Rose Red City. While we have no idea what
the "field camera of the day" will look like in the
next century—although the possibilities are rather
exciting for those with a colorful imagination—
we can be quite certain the tenacity of Petra
and its people will continue to endure, one way
or another.

Whether this book finds you in the twenty-
first century or beyond, may the majesty of Petra
inspire you to wander through its hauntingly
beautiful ravines, marvel at the resolute
multicultural façades, stand agape at its sheer
size, and, if nothing else, be humbled by the
kindness of the people who bring it to life.

> Be awed,
> be enchanted,
> and say yes to the tea.

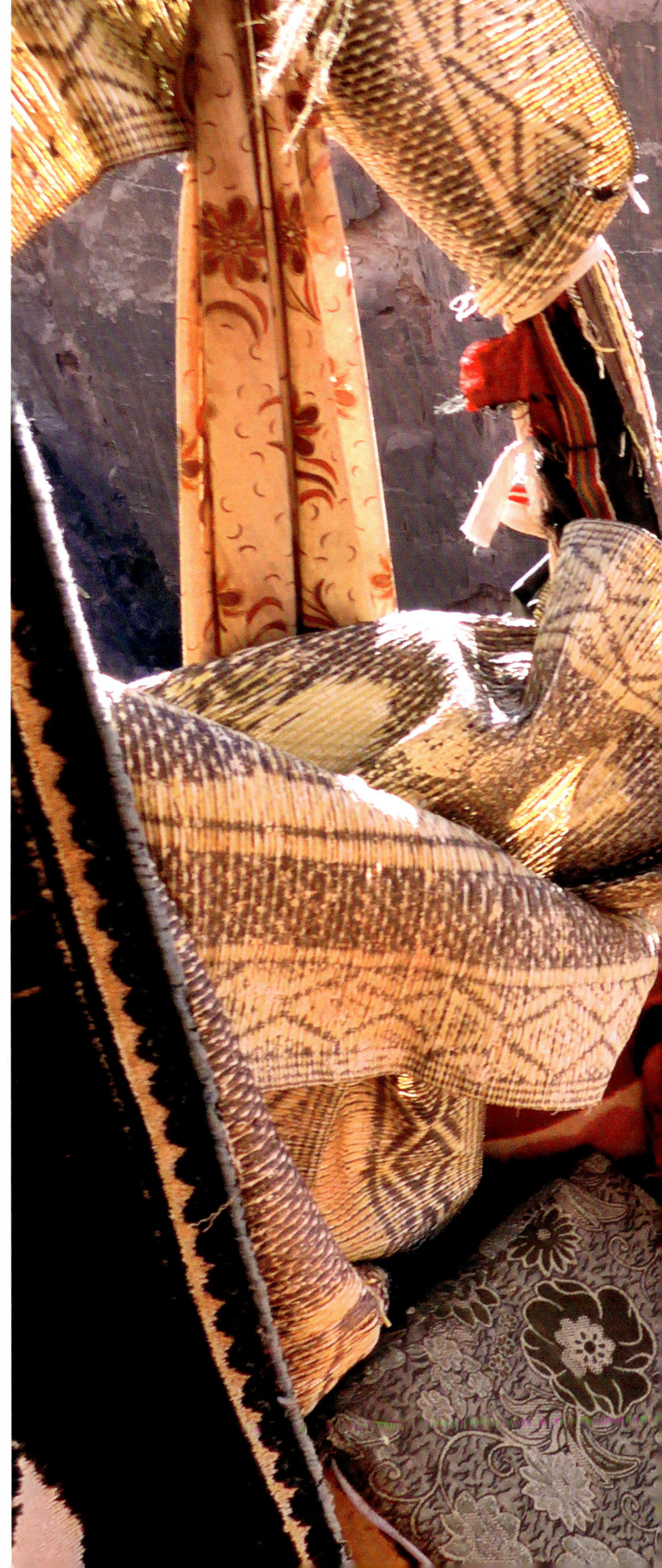

Toasting a full glass of traditional Bedouin tea
to the beauty and wonder of Petra from the
dramatic Jabal al-Khubtha overlook.

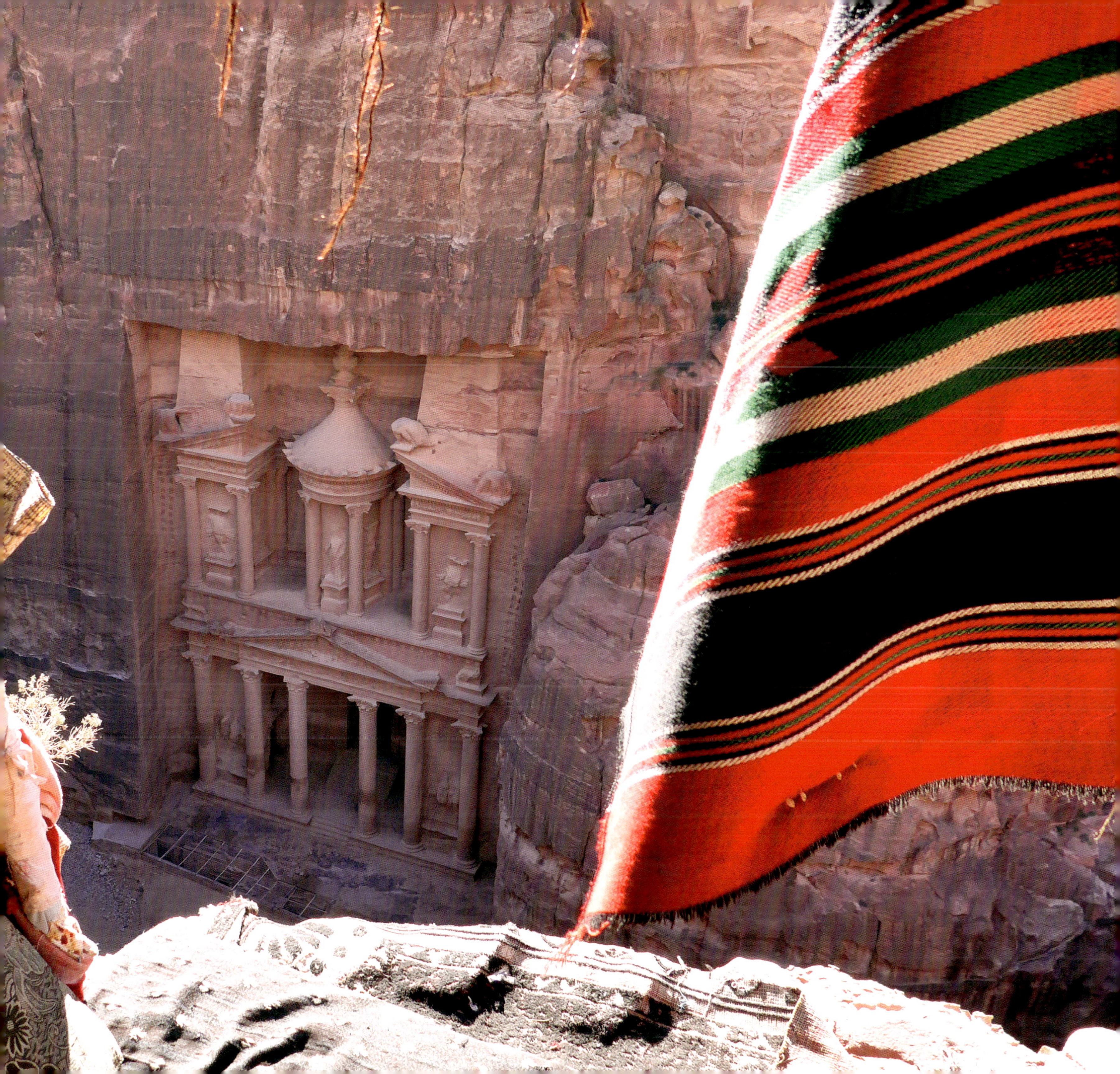

Acknowledgments

Special thanks are extended to several key people and agencies for their assistance in completing this volume. First and foremost, I must extend my sincere gratitude to the people and authorities of Petra, Jordan, for their unwavering cooperation throughout my research—even when it was so rudely interrupted by the COVID-19 pandemic. My work in this magnificent archaeological site would not have been possible without their hospitality, guidance, and assistance. Specifically, I am profoundly thankful to Ibrahim al-Farajat and his staff with the Petra Museum and the leadership of the Petra Development and Tourism Regional Authority for their invaluable contributions, expertise, and facilitation, enriching my research endeavors. Much appreciation is also extended to the Jordanian Department of Antiquities and the American Center of Research in Amman, Jordan, for graciously letting me peruse their extensive library collections and historic archives. And of course, my most gracious thanks to His Royal Highness Prince El Hassan bin Talal of the Jordanian royal family for his commitment to celebrating Jordan's cultural and archaeological treasures and his authorship of the foreword for this volume.

Additionally, I express my deepest appreciation to the local community members, scholars, and experts whose insights and perspectives have greatly enhanced my understanding of Petra's cultural heritage and historical significance. A personal thank you to my dear friends Ahmed al-Masry and Habis Abdullah al-Samahin al-Bdoul for their immense support, collaboration, and endless supply of tea (truly, a ridiculous amount of tea—and I loved every sip!). Thanks are also given to Mousla and Abdul al-Farajat at the Cleopetra Hotel for their warmest welcome, continued friendship, and for being my second home while conducting research in Petra.

Furthermore, I gratefully acknowledge the financial support provided by US State

Department's Fulbright Scholar program and the Jordanian-American Center for Educational Exchange, which enabled me to spend so much time in Jordan and complete this project. Support was particularly appreciated from former director Alain McNamara, Director Edward Prados, and program manager Lara Shadid for their indispensable assistance and encouragement.

Of course, I must also express my heartfelt gratitude to my field assistants McKay Barker and Molly Groom for accompanying me on my adventures, modeling in the modern repeats where necessary, and helping keep me on track when my ambitious goals would balloon beyond practicality. Beyond being a stellar field assistant and grip for nearly every field mission, I cannot thank Dr. Casey Allen enough for his indispensable knowledge, insights, and motivation throughout the entirety of this experience. Thank you for keeping me grounded and helping me bring this book to life.

In the preparation of this volume, I would also like to recognize the contributions of Kathleen Hauck Groom and Dr. Casey Allen for their invaluable expertise and guidance. Many thanks to Jake Anderson and Oro Editions for supporting the publication of this project and their passionate commitment to preserving the singular magic of books.

Finally, I must go all the way back to the beginning—to that starry-eyed graduate student overwhelmed by Petra's grandeur—and thank Dr. Thomas Paradise for inviting me into his world and introducing me to this magical place. Without his guidance, patience, and passion, my life would not be as colorful nor as exciting as it is today. Thank you for opening my eyes to Petra's magic and changing the trajectory of my life forever.

About Kaelin Groom

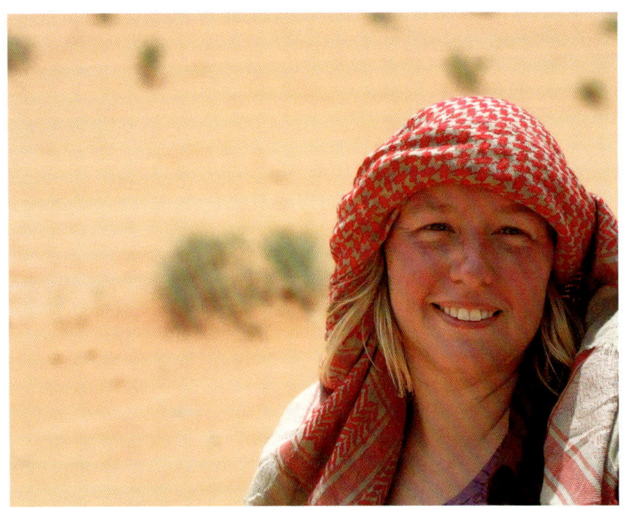

Dr. Kaelin Groom is fervently dedicated to fieldwork, discovery, and fusing art with science. Her life's mission, as a scholar and as a person, rests in understanding how our beautifully complex world all fits together--what makes it tick--to proactively conserve the past for the sake of the future through heritage science and cultural resource management. By maintaining an active and contributing role in each arena, her career is built upon bridging the rift between education, policy, and scientific research. For more information, visit kmgroom.com.

Map of Petra showing
the approximate location
of each repeat photograph
showcased in this book

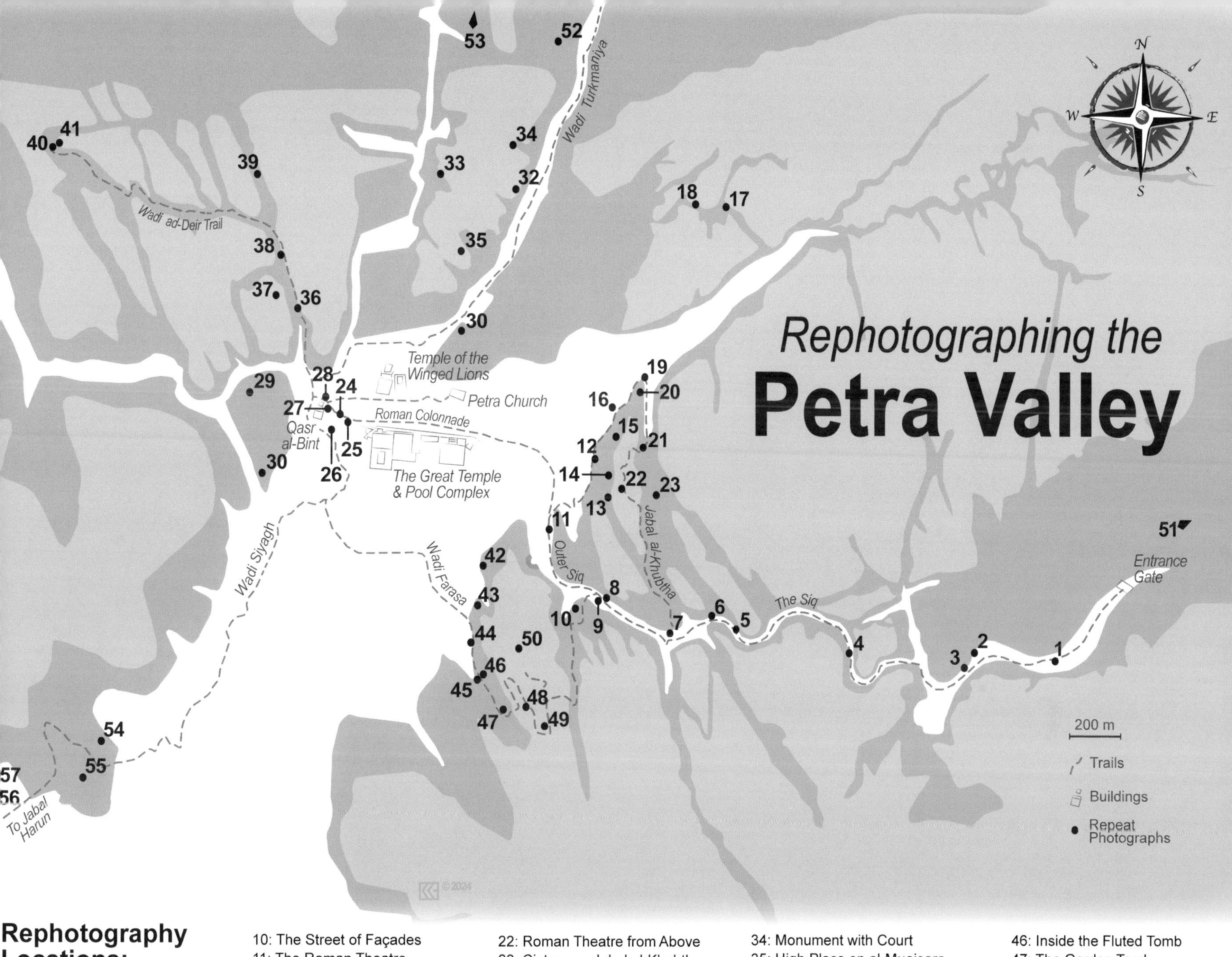

Rephotography Locations:

1: Trail from Entrance
2: Djinn Blocks at Bab as-Siq
3: Obelisk Tomb
4: The Siq
5: The Siq
6: Al-Khazneh Through the Siq
7: Al-Khazneh (The Treasury)
8: Tomb 825
9: Djinn Block in Outer Siq
10: The Street of Façades
11: The Roman Theatre
12: Eastern View of Outer Siq
13: The Urn Tomb
14: The Silk Tomb
15: The Royal Tombs
16: Nasara Ridge
17: Al-Nasara Monuments
18: The Armor Tomb
19: Sextius Florentinus Tomb
20: Jabal Al-Khubtha Trailhead
21: Al-Khubtha Trail Steps
22: Roman Theatre from Above
23: Cistern on Jabal al-Khubtha
24: City Center at Sunset
25: The Roman Temenos Gate
26: Qasr al-Bint
27: Front Court of Qasr al-Bint
28: Old Petra Museum
29: Chamber with Windows
30: Wadi Siyagh
31: Wadi Turkmaniya
32: The Turkmaniya Tomb
33: Tombs in Wadi al-Muaisara
34: Monument with Court
35: High Place on al-Muaisara
36: Wadi ad-Deir Trailhead
37: The Lion Triclinium
38: View of Valley from Wadi ad-Deir
39: The Cave of Damas
40: Ad-Deir (The Monastery)
41: The al-Deir Urn
42: Decaying Tombs in Wadi Farasa
43: Monuments in Wadi Farasa
44: Classical Tomb in Wadi Farasa
45: The Soldier Tomb
46: Inside the Fluted Tomb
47: The Garden Tomb
48: The Lion Fountain
49: The Obelisk Ridge
50: The High Place of Sacrifice
51: Wadi Musa
52: Umm Sayhoun
53: Bayda Valley
54: The Sughra Tombs
55: Above the Snake Monument
56: The Jabal Harun Trail
57: Jabal Harun

Select Bibliography and Further Readings

SIR KENNEDY AND HIS CONTEMPORARIES:

Brünnow, R.-E., von Domaszewski, A., & Euting, J. (1905). *Die Provincia Arabia* (Vol. 1). Strassburg, Germany: Karl J. Trübner.

Burckhardt, J. L. (1822). *Travels in Syria and the Holy Lands*. John Murray Publishing, London.

Doughty, C. M. (1923). *Travels in Arabia Deserta*. Boni & Liveright Inc., New York; J. Cape & The Medici Society Ltd., London.

Erskine, S. (1925). *The Vanishing Cites of Arabia*. E.P. Dutton & Co. New York.

Forder, A. (1923). *Petra, Perea, and Phoenicia*. Marshall Brothers, Ltd. London.

Kennedy, A. B. W. (1925). *Petra: Its History and Monuments*. Country life. London.

Libby, W. and F. E. Hoskins (1905) *The Jordan Valley and Petra*. Volume 2. G. P. Putman's Sons. New York London.

PETRA'S HISTORY AND ARCHAEOLOGY:

Bedal, L. (2000). *The Petra Pool-complex: A Hellenistic Paradeisos in the Nabataean Capital*: (results from the Petra "lower Market" Survey and Excavation, 1998). Gorgias Press LLC. Piscataway, NJ.

Browning, I. (1973). *Petra*. Park Ridge, NJ, Noyes Press.

Fiema, Z. T., Kanellopoulos, C., & Bikai, P.M. (2001). *The Petra Church*..American Center of Oriental Research. Amman, Jordan.

Harding, G. L. (1990). *The Antiquities of Jordan* (Rev. ed.). Great Britain: Redwood Press Limited.

Healey, J. F. (1993). *The Nabataean Tomb Inscriptions of Mada'in Salih*. Oxford: Oxford University Press.

Paolini, A., Vafadari, A., Cesaro, G., Quintero, M.S., Van Balen, K., and Pinilla, O.V. (2012). *Risk Management at Heritage Sites: A Case Study of the Petra World Heritage Site*. Amman, Jordan: UNESCO.

Paradise, T. R. (2005). "Petra revisited: An examination of sandstone weathering research in Petra, Jordan." *Geological Society of America Special Papers*, 390: 39–49.

Taylor, J. (2001). *Petra and the Lost Kingdom of the Nabateans*. London, UK: IB Tauris.

Tuttle, C. A. (2013). "Preserving Petra sustainably (one step at a time): The Temple of the Winged Lions Cultural Resource Management Initiative as a step forward." *Journal of Eastern Mediterranean Archaeology and Heritage Studies*, 1(1), 1–23.

TOURISM AND LANDSCAPE CHANGE:

Comer, D. (2012). "The Environmental and Cultural Heritage Impact of Tourism Development in Petra-Jordan." *Tourism and archaeological heritage management at Petra*, Springer: 131–44.

Di Giovine, M. A. (2008). *The heritage-scape: UNESCO, world heritage, and tourism.* Lexington Books.

Kalman, H. (2014). *Heritage planning: principles and process.* London and New York: Routledge.

Timothy, D. J., and S. W. Boyd (2006). "Heritage tourism in the 21st century: Valued traditions and new perspectives." *Journal of Heritage Tourism* 1(1), 1–16.

Williams, S., and A. A. Lew (2015). *Tourism Geography: Critical Understandings of Place, Space and Experience.* (3 ed.). London, UK: Routledge, Taylor & Francis Group.

MODERN JORDAN AND PETRA TODAY:

Bille, M. (2019). *Being Bedouin Around Petra: Life at a World Heritage Site in the Twenty-First Century.* New York, Oxford: Berghahn Books.

Kumaraswamy, P. R. (ed) (2019). *The Palgrave Handbook of the Hashemite Kingdom of Jordan.* Palgrave Macmillan, Singapore.

Maani, J. (2010). *Field Guide to Jordan* (2 ed.). The Hashemite Kingdom of Jordan. Maani Publishing. Amman, Jordan.

Ossorio, F. A. and Porter, B. A. (2010). *Petra: Splendors of the Nabataean Civilization.* White Star Publishers. Vercelli, Italy.

Ruben, I., and Taylor, J. (2010). *Beyond the Jordan (Baptism, Prophecy and Pilgrimage East of the River Jordan).* The Latin Vicariate/Fund for the Church of the Baptism of Jesus Christ. Amman, Jordan.

REPEAT PHOTOGRAPHY:

Groom, K. M. (2017). "Historic Repeat Photography as a Tool to Assess Touristic Landscapes: A Case Study in Petra, Jordan." *The First Conference on the Archaeology and Tourism of the Ma'an Governorate Official Report*, 56–78.

Kull, C. A. (2005). "Historical landscape repeat photography as a tool for land use change research." *Norsk Geografisk Tidsskrift* 59(4), 253–68.

Smith, T. (2007). "Repeat photography as a method in visual anthropology." *Visual Anthropology* 20(2-3), 179–200.

Webb, R. H., Boyer, D. E., & Turner, R. M. (2010). *Repeat Photography: Methods and Applications in the Natural Sciences.* Washington, DC: Island Press.

Image Credits

Page 8: Image © Kaelin Groom 2022

Page 17: Unknown Author – Engineering Heritage/Institution of Mechanical Engineers, free domain.

Page 12: Image © Casey Allen 2020

Page 20: Image © Casey Allen, 2022

Page 22: Image © Photo Arsenal Collector's Service 2024 (top) & Image © Kaelin Groom, 2024 (bottom)

Page 23: All images © Kaelin Groom, 2022

Page 25: Image © Casey Allen, 2024.

Page 27: Image © Casey Allen 2016

Page 30: Image © Casey Allen 2019

Page 32: David Roberts Image from Author's private collection

Page 56: David Roberts Image from Author's private collection

Page 80: David Roberts Image from Author's private collection

Page 100: David Roberts Image from Author's private collection

Page 120: David Roberts Image from Author's private collection

Page 140: David Roberts Image from Author's private collection

Page 158: Image © Casey Allen 2022

Page 162: Image © Molly Groom 2023

Page 165: Image © Molly Groom 2023

Page 166: Image © Molly Groom 2023

Page 169: Image © Casey Allen 2018

Page 173: Image © K. Groom Cartography, 2024.